Audio in Media:
The Recording Studio

Audio in Media:
The Recording Studio

Stanley R. Alten
Syracuse University

Wadsworth Publishing Company
An International Thomson Publishing Company

Belmont • Albany • Bonn • Boston • Cincinnati • Detroit • London • Madrid • Melbourne
Mexico City • New York • Paris • San Francisco • Singapore • Tokyo • Toronto • Washington

Associate Editor: Katherine Hartlove
Editorial Assistant: Jessica Monday
Production and Art Editor: Pat Waldo
Managing Designer: Stephen Rapley
Print Buyer: Barbara Britton
Permissions Editor: Robert Kauser
Copy Editor: Veronica Oliva
Proofreader: Meg Korones
Internal Design: Donna Davis
Cover Design: Ann Butler
Composition: Fog Press
Printer: Malloy Lithographing, Inc.
Cover Photograph: Courtesy of Walters-Storyk Design Group

Copyright © 1996 by Wadsworth Publishing Company
A Division of International Thomson Publishing Inc.
The ITP logo is a trademark under license.

Printed in the United States of America
1 2 3 4 5 6 7 8 9 10—01 00 99 98 97 96

Library of Congress Cataloging-in-Publication Data

Alten, Stanley R.
  Audio in media: the recording studio/Stanley R. Alten
    p.   cm
  Includes index.
  ISBN 0-534-26064-0
  1. Sound—Recording and reproducing—Equipment
and supplies. 2. Sound studios—Equipment and supplies.   I. Title
TK7881.4.A462   1996
621.389'3—dc20   95-34591
                                              CIP

For more information, contact Wadsworth Publishing Company:
Wadsworth Publishing Company
10 Davis Drive, Belmont, California 94002, USA

International Thomson Publishing Europe
Berkshire House 168-173, High Holborn
London, WC1V 7AA, England

Thomas Nelson Australia
102 Dodds Street
South Melbourne 3205, Victoria, Australia

Nelson Canada
1120 Birchmont Road
Scarborough, Ontario, Canada M1K 5G4

International Thomson Editorés
Campos Eliseos 385, Piso 7
Col. Polanco, 11560 México D.F. México

International Thomson Publishing GmbH
Königswinterer Strasse 418, 53227 Bonn, Germany

International Thomson Publishing Asia
221 Henderson Road, #05-10 Henderson Building
Singapore 0315

International Thomson Publishing Japan
Hirakawacho Kyowa Building, 3F
2-2-1 Hirakawacho, Chiyoda-ku
Tokyo 102, Japan

Respect technology, but revere talent.
Ham Brosious

BRIEF CONTENTS

DETAILED CONTENTS

PREFACE

Audio in Media: The Recording Studio is designed to serve both the aspiring and practicing music recordist, as well as the musician who wishes to learn about audio production. The focus of the book is studio-based music recording, with the emphasis on process—theory, operations, and techniques. The approach is non-technical. There is little question that technology is vital to music recording, but experience has shown that undue concentration on the technical aspects can have a tendency to distance the recordist from the music. The primary goals of the recordist should be to serve the vision of the musicians and the music.

Structure of the Book

Audio in Media: The Recording Studio is organized to be used in total or in parts, based on need and level of background, with no disruption in continuity. It assumes some knowledge of music.

In Part 1, *Principles,* Chapter 1, "Music Recording: A Perspective," provides an overview of what it takes to be a music recordist and the functions of the producer, engineer, and other production personnel. Chapter 2, "Sound and Hearing," introduces the physical behavior of sound and its relationship to human hearing. Chapter 3, "Acoustics and Psychoacoustics," develops the material in Chapter 2 as it applies to the objective behavior of received sound, its subjective effect on those who hear it, and how these factors affect studio and control room design and construction.

Part 2, *Equipment,* begins with Chapter 4, "Microphones," which discusses their principles, types, characteristics, and accessories. Chapter 5, "Consoles," covers the basic signal flow and design of multichannel production consoles, mainly the in-line console, with some attention given to the split-section design. Patching, console automation, and more recent console designs are also covered. Chapter 6, "Analog Recording," covers the characteristics of analog audiotape and tape recorders. Chapter 7, "Digital Recording," does the same thing with digital audiotape and tape recorders. It also covers basic digital theory and disk-based audio systems. Chapter 8, "Signal Processing," discusses the general principles of signal processing, the most common types of signal processors, and their effect on sound. Chapter 9, "Loudspeakers and Monitoring," deals with the relationship between loudspeaker selection and control room monitoring.

Although Part 3, *Preproduction,* consists of only one chapter, "Planning the Recording Session," it is an important section. Very often as preproduction goes, so goes the rest of the production.

Part 4, *Production,* deals with the techniques involved in miking and recording a studio session. The first two chapters are devoted to miking—Chapter 11 covering "Distant Miking: Ensembles," and Chapter 12, "Close Miking: Instruments." Chapter 12 also reviews the basic characteristics of selected families of instruments. Chapter 13 focuses on "The Recording Session" itself and a number of ways to navigate through it.

Part 5, *Postproduction,* begins with Chapter 14, "Editing," which describes techniques of editing audio on analog and digital audiotape and hard disk systems. It also addresses the aesthetic considerations that apply to editing music. Clearly this chapter could have also been placed after Chapter 15, "The Mixdown," as some recordings are not edited until the music tracks are combined and processed, which is what occurs in the mixdown. Chapter 16, "The Master," deals with preparation and labeling of the master tape before it is sent on to a mastering house for final CD mastering. Some attention is given to in-studio CD premastering, as well.

MIDI (Musical Instrument Digital Interface) is also an important part of today's recording scene for the recordist and the musician and certainly has a place in a book about music recording. However, the technology and techniques of MIDI have become so broad a topic that to treat MIDI adequately requires more space than this book permits. Indeed, many fine books about MIDI are available, a few of which are listed in the Bibliography.

Acknowledgments

Because *Audio in Media: The Recording Studio* is intended to serve the student and practitioner, it was important to seek counsel from the academic and professional worlds. To all those who have been so forthcoming in their help and guidance goes my heartfelt thank you! In particular:

I appreciate the guidance of the following reviewers:

Doug Mitchell, Middle Tennessee State University
John T. McDaniel, Michigan State University
Ricardo Schultz, Carnegie Mellon University
Michael G. Kaloyanides, University of New Haven
Howard M. Judkins, Orange Coast College
Alex Cima, Fullerton College
Dr. Marcus Engelmann, Allan Hancock College
Andres Edelstein, Berklee College of Music
John Monforte, University of Miami.

Special thanks go to producer, Keith Meyer, for his splendid research assistance.
Sincere gratitude also goes to Jim

Anderson, Producer; Malcolm Atkin, Air Studios, London; Bruce Bartlett, Crown International; Fred Betschen, Mark Studios, Buffalo; Craig Boyce, Studio Tech-nologies; Wade Bray, Sonic Perceptions; Jerry Bruck, Posthorn Recordings; Alison Burton, Air Studios, London; Peter D'Antonio, RPG Diffusor Systems; John Durant, Lexicon; James Goodman, Otari Corporation; David Gray, Sonic Solutions; Mead Killion, Etymotic Research; James Martin, Akai; Terry Pallata, Eventide; Skip Pizzi, *Broadcast Engineering Magazine;* David Pruski, Advanced Audio Productions, Buffalo; Ron Remschel, Sony; Camille Rizco, Doremi Labs; Bill Rowe, RSP Technologies; Ron Streicher, Pacific Audiovisual Enterprises; and Shelly Yakus, Producer.

Continued appreciation goes to the first-rate Wadsworth Publishing Company and their talented, creative, and easy to work with production staff. Particular thanks to Katherine Hartlove for her enlightened support.

PRINCIPLES

MUSIC RECORDING: A PERSPECTIVE

Music is fundamental to the cultural cravings of Mankind. Its sonic combinations and psychological rewards are infinite. Its aesthetic value fulfills basic human needs. Yet, musical taste is intensely personal: Two people listening to the same work may respond in two different ways, both valid. No one musical interpretation is definitive.

A single note on a single acoustic guitar string can generate a variety of sounds and responses, depending on whether the string is gut or steel, whether it is plucked with a finger or a pick, whether the pick is plastic or metal, the force with which the string is plucked, the type of wood and finish used to make the guitar, the acoustics of the room, and so on. Two recordings of the same music, say, Beethoven's Fifth Symphony, played in the same room, on the same audio system, in the same format, may have a variety of differences in, say, intonation, rubato, dynamics, and rendition. You may prefer one recording; someone else may prefer the other. That does not mean your choice is necessarily better; it means that, based on your perceptions, one is preferable to the other for certain reasons.

There are many ways to listen to music and many different elements to listen for. This is so for the general listener and the professional music recordist alike. But the professional recordist has added responsibilities: shaping the musician's sound and vision and passing critical judgment on a recording's aesthetic and technical qualities before it comes to market. To this end, individual taste and interpretation, although still important, are tempered by the professional's training, experience, and discriminating "ear."

Production Roles in Music Recording

In live studio music recording, production personnel perform three basic functions: producing, engineering, and providing technical support. Depending on the size of the facility and, if applicable, union regulations, these functions may be performed by one or a few persons in smaller operations, and by several persons in larger facilities. The additional personnel in larger facilities assist the producer, engineer, and chief technician.

Producer

Depending on their contractual relationship, a music **producer** may perform a number of business-related functions for a musician, group, or record label, outside the studio. But in a recording session, the producer is the most influential creative force next to the musicians. With developing talent, the producer is often the primary creative influence. Some producers work only in their own studio or with a particular musical group; others work for a record company and handle assigned sessions; still others freelance. Occasionally, producer and musician are one. Such an arrangement is not effected easily, however. Being one's own producer requires the extraordinary gift to be creator and critic at the same time. Few can do it successfully.

There are no rules for being an effective producer. But a good producer usually has a musical background and, in the parlance of audio, "ears"—not *perfect ears*, which do not exist, but *educated ears*. A good producer helps make the most of a musician's talent: provides a perspective the musician is often too close to the music to hear; shapes sound; improves performance; clarifies interpretation; focuses ideas; and believes in what the musician is trying to "say." In a recording session, which can be physically and psychologically demanding, a good producer is authoritative not authoritarian—tension and intimidation bridle the creative

process. Finally, a good producer is affable, respects the musicians and production staff, and creates an informal, comfortable working atmosphere.

Engineer

A good way to define the role of the engineer is to describe the relationship between the producer and the engineer: The producer knows how the music should sound, but it is up to the **engineer** to make sure that sound is realized. (Note, however, many producers are also engineers and vice versa, although they may not wear both hats at the same time.)

The engineer selects and directs microphone placement (this may be done by the recording group's engineer) and operates the control room equipment. In effect, the engineer ensures that the various types of gear used to route, record, and process audio give the sound the producer wants to create. But good engineers are more than equipment operators. They, too, must have "ears." They must know what sonic results can be obtained with a specific piece of equipment or by making a certain control adjustment. In many ways, the engineer is an extension of the producer. Theirs is a symbiotic relationship—two different "organisms" that combine their unique attributes for the common good of an artistically and technically successful recording. If it is up to the producer to make the music sound interesting, it is up to the engineer to make it sound good.

Technician

The terms *engineer* and *technician* are often used interchangeably. And, indeed, in many studios the same staff performs both functions. The primary job of the *technician* is to keep the equipment in top working order. This is no minor assignment given the complexity of today's technology. But more important, if the equipment is not operating up to specifications, the efforts of the producer and the engineer are of little consequence. Although the skill of the engineer can sometimes overcome equipment problems, poorly maintained equipment can ruin a recording, particularly today with the pristine clarity of digital sound. The technician's role is critical to successful sound recording; however, this book concentrates on the creative and operational aspects of music recording that relate to the producer and engineer.

Assistant Production Personnel

In addition to the principal production personnel, many recording sessions are involved enough to require assistants to help the producer and engineer. An **assistant producer** may counsel the producer, coordinate session logistics, keep session records, attend to the musicians' needs, and handle business matters.

An **assistant engineer** may set up the studio, arrange the mics, clean and prepare the equipment, set up the signal routing at the console and patch bay, help with console operation, load tape on the tape recorder, switch the tape recorder channels into the correct modes, and operate remote controls.

Another assistant present at many recording sessions is the gofer. The "gofer" is often someone aspiring to a career in music recording, who may or may not be a paid studio employee. The quid pro quo for being allowed to attend a session is that the gofer is the one to *go for* food, drink, or whatever the musicians and production staff

wish. It is worthwhile to remember that, regardless of the production role, the primary purpose of music recording is to serve the art.

The Educated Ear

Whichever your role in music recording, producer or engineer, to succeed there is one constant: You must have "ears." That means the ability to listen analytically and critically. "Analytical listening is the evaluation of the content and function of the music."* You must be able to listen with careful discrimination to the musical quality, style, interpretation, and nuance. "Critical listening is the evaluation of the characteristics of the sound itself and the integrity of... [its] technical quality."**

Training the ear takes time. An educated ear comes with years of perceptive listening and recording experience. What it does not come with is listening to music while talking, reading, bicycling with a Walkman, walking with a boom box, dozing on the beach with a portable radio, or riding in a car with the radio competing against motor, air conditioner, and highway sounds.

A good way to educate your ear is to learn music. If you are not a musician, learn to play a musical instrument. It makes little difference what level of proficiency you reach. Learning an instrument teaches you about the relationship between sound and music and gives you an understanding of the challenges a musician faces.

---

*William Moylan, *The Art of Recording* (New York: Van Nostrand Reinhold, 1992), p. 53.
**Moylan, p. 53.

This knowledge helps you, as producer or engineer, communicate with the musicians in their own language. The added benefit of knowing how to read music is a significant advantage in professional recording.

Analytical Listening

Study all kinds of music, regardless of the type(s) you prefer. Take courses in various musical genres. Listen to well-performed and well-produced CDs and LPs in rock, jazz, classical, country, and so on. If sheet music is available, follow it along with the music. Clearly, a wide range and a huge selection of recorded music is available; learning how to choose what to listen to is a matter of experience, background, and taste. A good way to begin is to choose award-winning recordings. Also, consult various professionals. Of course, if you ask a hundred different experts about their favorite recordings, you will probably get a hundred different opinions. But at least you broaden your listening base and have the context of their opinions as a basis for analysis. Reading reviews of CDs also gives you insight into why critics think a recording does or does not succeed. In fact, it is equally instructive to know why a recording does not "work" as it is to know why it does, perhaps even more so.

Critical Listening

Listen to recordings for different things: overall production values; technical quality; the sound (or performance) of the drums, flute, solo reed, keyboard, group vocal, string section, rhythm guitar fill, and so on; a vocalist rendering a lyric with meaning or just singing words; a vocalist entering a bit early or late to counterpoint the lyric against the accompaniment; polyrhythms playing off one another to create rhythmic excitement; the sonic differences between an acoustic and an electric bass or acoustic drums and a drum machine; the unique sound of a Zildjian™ cymbal or a Stratocaster™ electric guitar; violins that sound warm, thin, or rich; a concert grand piano with a percussive tonality or a tonality that "sings"; the slight changes in attacks and sustains affecting accents; the holding or releasing of notes for a fraction of a second more or less that alters rhythm; the musicians' technical proficiency; the spatial distribution of instruments in a stereo field; the spectral balance; the acoustics that enrich sound or dull it; the appropriateness of the mood or texture brought to a particular composition; stylistic and sonic differences among artists; the sonic difference between analog and digital sound or between 16-bit and 20-bit mastered CDs.

This is not to overwhelm you with detail or suggest that serious listening is clinical. *Feeling* the music and *sensing* what "works" are also critical to active analysis, as is being aware of the relationship between your taste and mood and your response.

Because response to music is personal, standards and guidelines for judging a recording are difficult to establish, and so listening is the key to improving aural discrimination. The ear is capable of constant improvement in its ability to analyze music. As your aural sensitivity improves, so will your level of auditory achievement. One way to speed realization of that goal is by understanding the elements of sound structure and their effects on response, which are discussed in Chapter 2.

2

Sound and Hearing

All sound—music, sounds, and speech—consists of basic components such as frequency, amplitude, timbre, velocity, phase, attack, duration, and decay. These terms are described differently in the associated fields of physics, acoustics, psychoacoustics, engineering, and electronics, whose correlations are the basis of the chapters in the rest of Part 1.

The Sound Wave

Sound begins with a vibrational disturbance of molecules. As the motion of the disturbed molecules transmits energy, it creates a **sound wave** that is conducted from one place to another. When an object is bowed, blown, struck, or plucked, or when the vocal cords are vibrated, air molecules closest to the source of the vibration are set into motion. A sound wave propagates as these molecules begin moving outward from the vibrating body. These molecules pass on their energy to adjacent molecules, starting a reaction much like the waves that result when a stone is dropped into a body of water. The transfer of momentum from one displaced molecule to the next propagates the original vibrations longitudinally from the vibrating object to the hearer. What makes this reaction possible is air or, more precisely, a molecular medium with the property of elasticity. **Elasticity** is the phenomenon in which a displaced molecule tends to pull back to its original position after its initial momentum has caused it to displace nearby molecules.

As a vibrating object moves outward, it compresses molecules closer together, increasing pressure. **Compression** continues away from the object as the momentum of the disturbed molecules displaces adjacent molecules and so produces a crest in the sound wave. When a vibrating object moves inward, it pulls the molecules farther apart and thins them, creating a **rarefaction**. This rarefaction also travels away from the object in a manner similar to compression, except that it decreases pressure, thereby producing a trough in the sound wave (see 2-1). As the

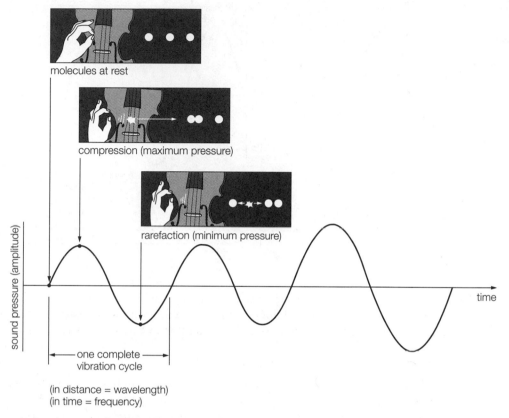

molecules at rest

compression (maximum pressure)

rarefaction (minimum pressure)

sound pressure (amplitude)

time

one complete vibration cycle

(in distance = wavelength)
(in time = frequency)

velocity = frequency times wavelength $V = F \times \lambda$

2-1 Components of a sound wave.   Compression and rarefaction in sound waves. The vibrating object causes compression when it moves outward (causing molecules to bump into each other). The vibrating object causes rarefaction when it moves inward (pulling the molecules away from each other).

sound wave moves away from the vibrating object, the individual molecules do not advance with the wave; they vibrate at what is termed their *average resting place* until their motion stills or until they are set in motion by another vibration. Inherent in each wave motion are the components that make up a sound wave: frequency, amplitude, velocity, wavelength, and phase (see 2-1, 2-2, and 2-13).

Frequency and Pitch

When a vibration passes through one complete up-and-down motion, from compression through rarefaction, it has completed one cycle. The number of cycles that a vibration completes in one second is expressed as its **frequency.** If a vibration completes 50 **cycles per second** (cps), its frequency is 50 hertz (Hz); if it completes

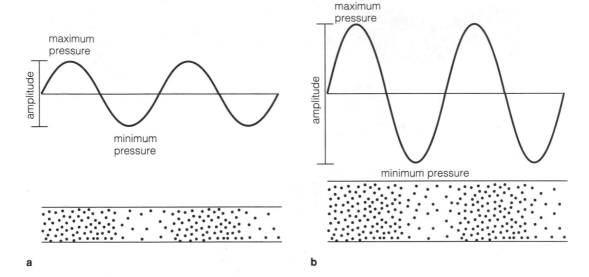

2-2 Amplitude of sound. The number of molecules displaced by a vibration creates the amplitude or loudness of a sound. Because the number of molecules in the sound wave in *b* is greater than the number in the sound wave in part *a*, the amplitude of the sound wave in *b* is greater.

10,000 cps, its frequency is 10,000 Hz, or 10 kilohertz (kHz).* Every vibration has a frequency, and generally humans are capable of hearing frequencies from 20 Hz to 20,000 Hz. Frequencies at the **high** and **low ends** of this range may be sensed more than heard, however.

Psychologically, we perceive frequency as **pitch**—the relative tonal highness or lowness of a sound. The more times per second a sound source vibrates, the higher its pitch. The G string of a guitar vibrates 196 times per second, so its fundamental frequency is

196 Hz. The A string has a frequency of 110 Hz, so the pitch of the G string is higher.

Pitch influences our perception of a sound's tonal characteristic—whether we hear it as bright, mellow, raspy, hissy, and so on. The range of audible frequencies, or the **sound frequency spectrum,** can be divided into sections, each having a unique and vital quality. The usual divisions in Western music are called octaves. An **octave** is the interval between any two frequencies that have a tonal ratio of 2 to 1. The range of human hearing covers about 10 octaves. Starting with 20 Hz, the first octave is 20 Hz to 40 Hz; the second, 40 Hz to 80 Hz; the third, 80 Hz to 160 Hz; and so on. The octaves, grouped into bass, midrange, and treble, are subdivided as follows:

■ **Low bass**—first and second octaves (20 Hz–80 Hz). These are the frequencies

---

*The term *cycles per second* was used to designate frequency until a few decades ago when the term *hertz* was adopted to honor Heinrich Hertz, who defined radio waves in 1886. The term *hertz* or the abbreviation *Hz* is used throughout this book.

associated with power, boom, and fullness. The lowest notes of the piano, organ, tuba, and bass are in this range. Sounds in these octaves need not occur often to maintain a sense of fullness. If they occur too often, or at too loud a level, the sound can become thick or muddy.

- **Upper bass**—third and fourth octaves (80 Hz–320 Hz). Most of the lower tones generated by rhythm and other support instruments such as drums, piano, bass, cello, trombone, and French horn are in this range. They establish a balance in musical structure. Too many frequencies from this range make sound boomy; too few make it thin. When properly proportioned, pitches in the second, third, and fourth octaves are very satisfying to the ear because we perceive them as giving sound an anchor—that is, fullness or bottom. Frequencies in the upper bass range serve aural structure the way the horizontal line serves visual structure, by providing a foundation.

- **Midrange**—fifth, sixth, and seventh octaves (320 Hz–2,560 Hz). The midrange gives sound its intensity. It contains the fundamental and the rich lower harmonics and overtones of most sound sources.* The midrange does not necessarily generate pleasant sounds, however. Too much emphasis of sixth octave frequencies is heard as a hornlike quality; too much emphasis of seventh octave frequencies is heard as a tinny quality; extended listening to midrange sounds can be annoying and fatiguing.

- **Upper midrange**—eighth octave (2,560 Hz–5,120 Hz). We are most sensitive to frequencies in the eighth octave, a rather curious range. The lower part of the eighth octave (2,560 Hz–3,500 Hz) contains frequencies that, if properly emphasized, improve the intelligibility of lyrics. These frequencies are roughly 3,000 Hz to 3,500 Hz. If these frequencies are unduly emphasized, however, sound becomes abrasive and unpleasant; and vocals, in particular, become harsh and lispy, making some consonants difficult to understand.

  The upper part of the eighth octave (above 3,500 Hz), on the other hand, contains rich and satisfying pitches that give sound definition, clarity, and realism. Listeners perceive a sound source frequency in this range (and also in the lower part of the ninth octave, up to about 6,000 Hz) as being nearby, and for this reason it is also known as the **presence range**.

- **Treble**—ninth and tenth octaves (5,120 Hz–20,000 Hz). Although the ninth and tenth octaves generate only 2 percent of the total power output of the sound frequency spectrum, and most humans do not hear much beyond 16,000 Hz, they give sound the vital, lifelike qualities of brilliance and sparkle, particularly in the upper ninth and lower tenth octaves. Increasing loudness at 5,000 Hz, the heart of the presence range, gives the

---

*A **fundamental**, also called the first harmonic, is the lowest or basic pitch of a musical instrument, its **harmonics** are exact multiples of the fundamental, and its **overtones**, also known as **inharmonic overtones**, are pitches that are not exact multiples of the fundamental. If a trumpet sounds a low G, the fundamental is 392 Hz, its harmonics are 784 Hz, 1,568 Hz, 3,136 Hz, and so on, and its overtones are the frequencies in between (see the section on timbre). Sometimes in usage, harmonics also assume overtones. Another term for harmonics and overtones is *partials*. A harmonics-related term that is sometimes confused with inharmonic is **enharmonic**. Enharmonic notes are two different notes that sound the same—for example, C# and Db, D# and Eb, G# and Ab.

impression that there has been an overall increase in loudness throughout the midrange. Reducing loudness at 5,000 Hz makes a sound seem farther away and transparent. Too much emphasis above 6,000 Hz makes sound hissy and brings out electronic noise. Too little emphasis above 6,000 Hz dulls sound.

Amplitude and Loudness

We have noted that vibrations in objects stimulate molecules to move in pressure waves at certain rates of alternation (compression–rarefaction) and that rate determines frequency. Vibrations not only affect the molecules' rate of up-and-down movement but also determine the number of displaced molecules that are set in motion from equilibrium to a wave's maximum height (*crest*) and depth (*trough*). This number depends on the intensity of a vibration; the more intense it is, the more molecules are displaced. The greater the number of molecules displaced, the greater the height and depth of the sound wave. The number of molecules in motion, and therefore the size of a sound wave, is called **amplitude** (see 2-2). Our subjective impression of amplitude is a sound's loudness or softness. Amplitude is measured in decibels.

The Decibel

The **decibel** (dB) is a dimensionless unit used to compare the ratio of two quantities usually in relation to acoustic energy, such as sound pressure, and electrical energy, such as power and voltage. It is abbreviated small *d* capital *B* because it stands for one-tenth (deci) of a Bel (from Alexander Graham Bell). The decibel was adopted because the Bel is too large a quantity to work with practically.

Sound Pressure Level

Acoustic sound pressure is measured in terms of **sound pressure level** (dB-SPL) because there are periodic variations in atmospheric pressure in a sound wave. Humans have the potential to hear an extremely wide range of these periodic variations, from 0 dB-SPL, the threshold of hearing, to 120 dB-SPL, the threshold of pain, and beyond (see 2-3). The range of the difference in decibels between the loudest and quietest sound a vibrating object makes is called **dynamic range.** Because this range is so wide, a logarithmic scale is used to compress loudness measurement into more manageable figures. (On a linear scale a unit of 1 adds an increment of 1. On a logarithmic scale a unit of 1 multiplies by a factor of 10.)

Humans have the capability to hear loudness at a ratio of 1 to 10,000,000 and greater. Sound at 60 dB-SPL is 1,000 times louder than sound at 0 dB-SPL; at 80 dB-SPL it is 10 times louder than at 60 dB-SPL. If the amplitude of two similar sounds is 100 dB-SPL each, their amplitude, when added, would be 103 dB-SPL. Nevertheless, most people do not perceive a sound level as doubled until it has increased about 10 dB-SPL. The approximate range of amplitude and frequency heard by the music listener compared to the total range of human hearing is displayed in 2-4.

There are other acoustic measurements of human hearing based on the interactive relationship between frequency and amplitude. These measurements are discussed in "Frequency and Loudness" later in this chapter.

Signal Level

In order for acoustic energy to be processed through electrical equipment it must be **transduced,** or converted, into electric energy. Electric energy is measured in decibels in

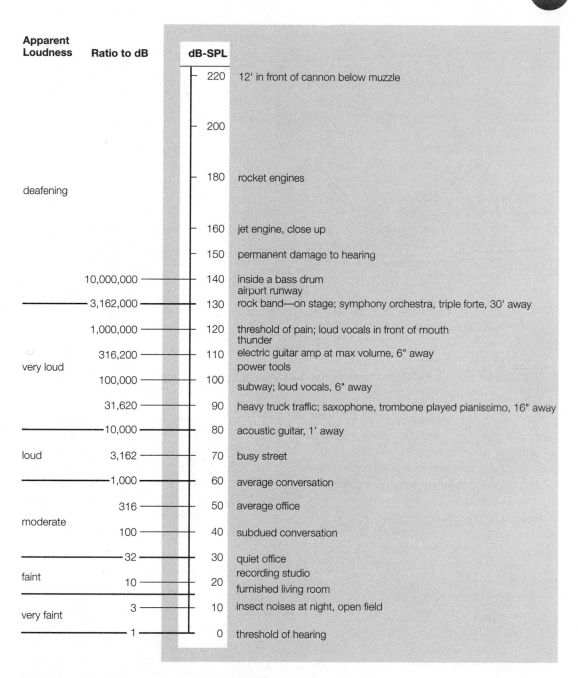

Apparent Loudness	Ratio to dB	dB-SPL	
		220	12' in front of cannon below muzzle
		200	
deafening		180	rocket engines
		160	jet engine, close up
		150	permanent damage to hearing
	10,000,000	140	inside a bass drum
			airport runway
	3,162,000	130	rock band—on stage; symphony orchestra, triple forte, 30' away
	1,000,000	120	threshold of pain; loud vocals in front of mouth
			thunder
very loud	316,200	110	electric guitar amp at max volume, 6" away
			power tools
	100,000	100	subway; loud vocals, 6" away
	31,620	90	heavy truck traffic; saxophone, trombone played pianissimo, 16" away
	10,000	80	acoustic guitar, 1' away
loud	3,162	70	busy street
	1,000	60	average conversation
	316	50	average office
moderate	100	40	subdued conversation
	32	30	quiet office
faint	10	20	recording studio
			furnished living room
very faint	3	10	insect noises at night, open field
	1	0	threshold of hearing

2-3 Sound pressure levels of various sound sources

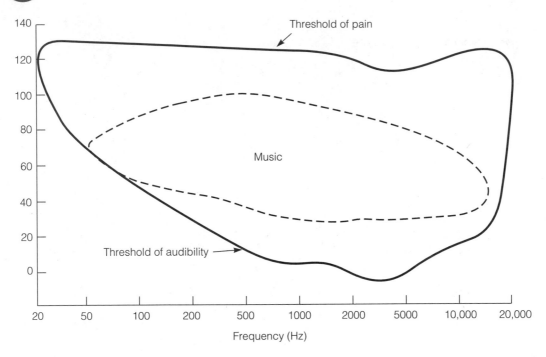

2-4 Range of human hearing compared to the range of frequency and sound level of music

relation to power (dBm) and voltage (dBv, dBu, and dBV). It is difficult to discuss these measurements here fully because they involve mathematical formulas and technical terminology that are beyond the scope of this book (see Table 2-1).

In measuring an electric circuit, a foremost concern is **impedance**—that property of a circuit, or an element, which restricts the flow of alternating current (AC). Impedance is measured in **ohms** (Ω), a unit of resistance to current flow. The less resistance in a circuit the better.

Frequency and Loudness

Based on our discussion of frequency and amplitude, you might assume that just as pitch gets higher when frequency increases,

so does loudness become greater as amplitude increases. Frequency and amplitude, however, are interdependent, and the assumption is not valid. Varying a sound's frequency also affects perception of its loudness, and varying a sound's amplitude affects perception of its pitch.

Equal Loudness Principle

The response of the human ear is not equally sensitive to all audible frequencies (see 2-5). Depending on loudness, we do not hear low and high frequencies as well as we hear middle frequencies. In fact, the ear is relatively insensitive to low frequencies at low levels. Oddly enough, this is called the **equal loudness principle** rather than that of unequal loudness (see 2-6).

Table 2-1 Power and voltage measurements in dB

dBm is an electrical measurement of power. It is referenced to 1 milliwatt. The voltage drop across a 600-ohm resistor through which 1 milliwatt of power is being dissipated is the standard studio zero reference level. (A resistor is a device that opposes the flow of current.) Any voltage that results in 1 milliwatt is 0 dBm, which is the same as 0.775 volts across a 600-ohm impedance. +30 dBm is 1 watt; +50 dBm is 100 watts.

dBv and **dBu** are units of measurement for expressing the relationship of decibels to voltage—0.775 volt to be exact. This figure comes from 0 dBm, which equals 0.775 volt. The difference between dBv and dBu is that dBv is measured only across a 600-ohm line. dBu (the *u* stands for units) is a more flexible reference because it permits use of the decibel scale to obtain a relative level without regard to a standard impedance, that is, 600 ohms.

dBV is also a measure of voltage but with decibels referenced to 1 volt. This measurement is used where the dBm—600 ohm/1 milliwatt—value is impractical, as it is with the measurement of microphone sensitivity where the zero reference is 1 volt. +10 dBV is equal to 20 volts.

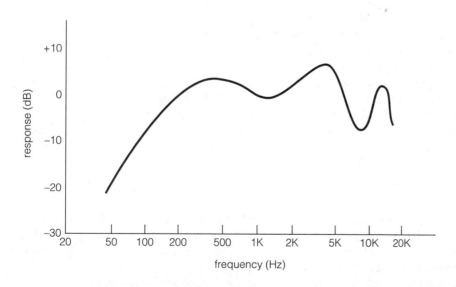

2-5 Responses to various frequencies by the human ear. This curve shows that the response is not flat and that we hear midrange frequencies better than low and high frequencies.

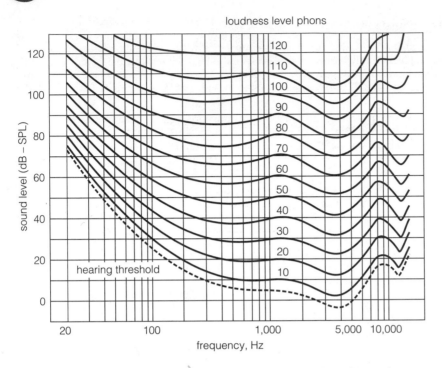

2-6 Equal loudness curves. These curves illustrate the relationships in 2-5 and our relative lack of sensitivity to low and high frequencies as compared with middle frequencies. A 50-Hz sound would have to be 50 dB louder to seem as loud as a 1,000-Hz sound at 0dB. To put it another way, at an intensity, for instance, of 40 dB, the level of a 100-Hz sound would have to be 10 times the SPL of a 1,000-Hz sound for the two sounds to be perceived as equal in loudness. (This graph represents frequencies on a logarithmic scale. The distance from 20 to 200 Hz is the same as from 200 Hz to 2,000 Hz or from 2,000 Hz to 20,000 Hz.) (Based on Robinson-Dadson.)

The equal loudness principle has important implications for the music recordist. You have to be aware of the levels at which you record and play back sound. If you have the loudness of a sound at a high level during recording and at a low level during playback, both bass and treble frequencies will be reduced considerably in volume and may seem to disappear. The converse is also true: If sound level is low when recording and

high when playing back, the bass and treble frequencies will be too loud relative to the other frequencies and may even overwhelm them.

If a guitarist plucks all six strings equally hard, you do not hear each string at the same loudness level. The high E string (328 Hz) sounds louder than the low E string (82 Hz). To make the low string sound as loud, the guitarist would have to pluck it harder. This

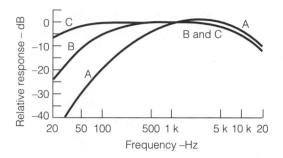

2-7 Frequency responses of the A, B, and C weighting networks

Table 2-2 Sound level ranges of the A, B, and C weighting networks

Weighting Network	dB
A	20–55
B	55–85
C	85–140

suggests that the high E string may sound louder because of its higher frequency. If you sound three tones—50 Hz, 1,000 Hz, and 15,000 Hz—at a fixed loudness level, however, the 1,000-Hz tone sounds louder than either the 50-Hz or the 15,000-Hz tone.

In a live concert, sound levels are usually louder than they are on a home stereo system. Live music often reaches levels of 100 dB-SPL and higher. At home, levels may go as high as 70–75 dB-SPL. Sound at 70 dB-SPL requires more bass and treble boost than does sound at 100 dB-SPL to obtain equal loudness. Therefore, the frequency balances you hear at 100 dB-SPL will be different when you hear the same sound at 70 dB-SPL.

Because sensitivity of the ear varies with frequency and loudness, meters that measure sound pressure level are designed to correspond to these variations by incorporating one or more **weighting networks.** A weighting network is a filter used for weighting a frequency response before measurement. Generally, three weighting networks are used, A, B, and C. The A and B networks bear close resemblances to the response of the human ear at 40 and 70 phons, respectively. (A **phon** is a dimensionless unit of loudness level related to the ear's

subjective impression of signal strength. For a tone of 1,000 Hz, the loudness level in phons equals the sound pressure level in decibels.) The C network corresponds to the ear's sensitivity at 100 phons and has an almost flat frequency response (see 2-7). Decibel values for the three networks are written as dBA, dBB, or dBC. The level may be quoted in dBm, with the notation "A Weighting."

The A weighting curve is preferred for measuring lower-level sounds. The B weighting curve is usually used for measuring medium-level sounds. The C weighting, which is essentially flat, is used for very loud sounds (see Table 2-2).

Masking

Another perceptual response dependent on the relationship between frequency and loudness is **masking**—obscuring of one sound by another when each is a different frequency and both vibrate simultaneously or within a split second of each other. High-frequency sounds are easier to mask than low-frequency sounds, and loudness is relative to other sounds present at the same time. The effect of masking is greatest when frequencies are close to each other, diminishing as frequencies become farther apart.

If a 100-Hz tone and 1,000-Hz tone are sounded together at the same level, both tones will be audible, but the 1,000-Hz tone will be perceived as louder. Gradually increasing the level of the 100-Hz tone and keeping the amplitude of the 1,000-Hz tone constant will make the 1,000-Hz tone more and more difficult to hear. If a 900-Hz tone is somewhat softer than a 1,000-Hz tone, the 900-Hz will be masked. If an LP record has scratches (high-frequency information), they will probably be masked during loud passages and audible during quiet ones. A symphony orchestra playing full blast may have all its instruments involved at once; however, flutes and clarinets will probably not be heard over trumpets and trombones because woodwinds are generally higher in frequency and weaker in sound level than are the brass.

To summarize from the examples noted above and from other masking experiments that have been performed:

- Pure tones close together in frequency mask each other more than tones widely separated in frequency. (A **pure tone** is a single frequency devoid of harmonics and overtones.)

- A pure tone masks tones of higher frequency more effectively than tones of lower frequency.

- The greater the loudness of the masking tone, the broader the range of frequencies it can mask.

- Masking by a narrow band of noise shows many of the same features as masking by a pure tone; again tones of higher frequency are masked more effectively than tones of lower frequency than the masking noise.

- *Forward masking* refers to the masking of a tone by a sound that ends a short time (up to about 20 or 30 milliseconds) before the tone begins.

- *Backward masking* refers to the masking of a tone by a sound that begins a few

milliseconds after the tone begins.

- *Central masking* is masking a tone in one ear by noise in the other ear.*

Awareness of masking is important in recording and mixing sound. A sound source that is audible and defined by itself may be altered in tonal quality or masked when combined with other sound sources. Hence, compensating for altered tone quality through equalization and placement in the aural imaging are necessary to overcome masking.

The Ear, Hearing Loss, and Behavior

A sound wave is a physical force; hearing loss and adverse nonaural effects result if the ear is exposed to loud levels for too long. Unfortunately, hearing loss from exposure to loud sound is not regenerative (self-corrective). The ear is durable and capable of hearing sounds over a wide dynamic range, but it is also a delicately integrated mechanism. It is divided into three parts: (1) the **outer ear**, (2) the **middle ear**, and (3) the **inner ear** (see 2-8).

The Ear

Sound waves first reach and are collected by the *pinna* (or *auricle*), the visible part of the outer ear. The pinna helps us to determine the direction of high-frequency sounds. It also provides initial frequency conditioning; it has a resonant frequency of about 4,500 Hz to 5,000 Hz. (A **resonant frequency** is the exact, or almost the exact, fundamental frequency at which an object vibrates.) The

---

*List from Thomas D. Rossing, *The Science of Sound*, 2nd ed., (Reading, MA: Addison-Wesley, 1990), p. 101.

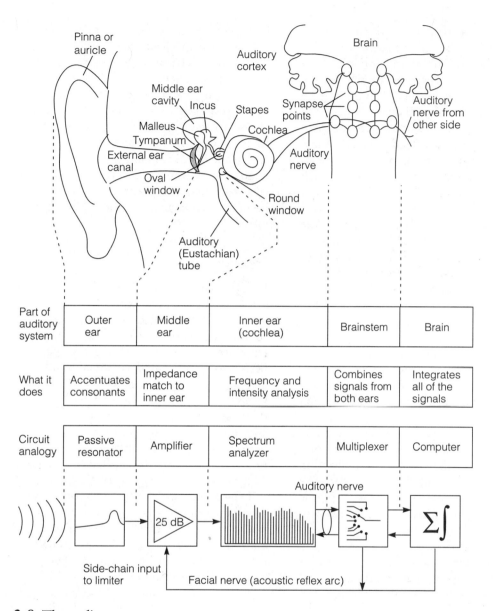

2-8 The auditory system

sound waves are then focused through the *ear canal,* or *meatus,* to the *ear drum (tympanum)* at the beginning of the middle ear.

The tympanic membrane of the *middle ear* is attached to another membrane, the *oval window,* by three small bones—the *malleus, incus,* and *stapes.* These three bones are called *ossicles* and are shaped like a hammer, anvil, and stirrup. The ossicles act as a mechanical lever changing the small pressure of the sound wave on the ear drum into a much greater pressure. The gain is almost 25 dB. The combined action of the ossicles and the area of the tympanum allow the middle ear system to act as a sort of impedance-matching amplifier between the low impedance of the air in the ear canal and the high impedance of the inner-ear fluids. The ossicles also help protect the inner ear from pressure changes and loud sounds. The middle ear system takes about one-tenth of a second to react and, therefore, provides little protection from sudden loud sounds. The ear drum makes the portion between the outer and middle parts of the ear airtight. The *eustachian (auditory) tube,* which connects the middle ear to the oral cavity, provides the pressure equalization between the outer and the middle ear. The oval window passes the vibrations of the middle ear to the inner ear, specifically to the cochlea. All middle-ear action takes place in an area the size of a small cube.

The *inner ear* contains the *semicircular canals,* which are necessary for balance, and a snail-shaped structure called the *cochlea.* The cochlea is filled with fluid whose total capacity is a fraction of a drop. It is here that sound becomes electricity in the human head. Running through the center of the cochlea is the *basilar membrane,* resting upon which are hair cells comprising the *organ of Corti,* the "seat of hearing." The organ of Corti is actually composed of frequency-specific nerve endings—about 30,000—which feed the auditory nerve where the electrical impulses are passed on to the brain. Each hair cell has many hairs or *cilia* that bend when the basilar membrane responds to a sound. The hair cells closest to the oval window respond to high frequencies, and those closest to the other end of the spiral respond to low frequencies. High sound-pressure levels can cause the cilia to break or shear off. As the cilia become damaged, hearing impairment increases (see 2-9).

Hearing Loss

Hearing damage caused by exposure to loud sound varies with the exposure time and the individual. Prolonged exposure to loud sound decreases the ear's sensitivity. Decreased sensitivity (1) creates the false perception that sound is not as loud as it actually is and (2) necessitates increasing levels to compensate for the hearing loss, thus making a bad situation worse.

After exposure to loud sound for a few hours, you may have experienced the sensation that your ears are stuffed with cotton. This is known as *temporary threshold shift* (TTS)—a reversible desensitization in hearing that disappears in anywhere from a few hours to several days. TTS is also called *auditory fatigue.* With TTS, the ears have, in effect, shut down to protect themselves against very loud sounds.

Prolonged exposure to loud sounds can bring on *tinnitus,* a ringing, whistling, or buzzing in the ears, even though no loud sounds are present. Tinnitus is a danger signal that the ears may already have or soon will suffer *permanent threshold shift* with continued exposure to loud sound.

One audiologist's good advice is: If it's loud, turn it down. If you can't turn it

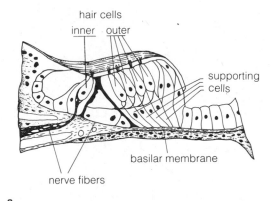

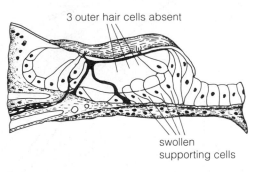

a   **b**

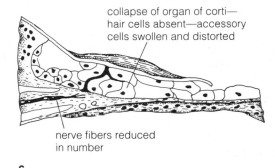

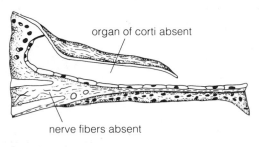

c   **d**

2-9 Increasing degrees of noise-induced permanent damage to the organ of Corti. (*a*) Normal organ of Corti, (*b*) partial injury, (*c*) severe injury, (*d*) total degeneration.

down, keep your distance (or wear ear plugs). If your ears are ringing, answer them!*

Behavior

Deterioration of the auditory nerve endings occurs through the natural aging process and usually results in a gradual loss of hearing first in the higher frequencies and then in the lower frequencies (see 2-10). Prolonged listening to loud sounds adversely affects the auditory nerve endings and hastens their deterioration. It is not uncommon for young people who are constantly exposed to loud sound levels to have the hearing acuity of a 70-year-old person. To avoid premature deterioration of your auditory nerves, do not expose them to excessively loud sound levels for extended times (see 2-11 and Table 2-3). If you are in the presence of loud sound, particularly music, wear special earplugs designed to reduce loudness without seriously degrading frequency response.

*Richie Moore, Ph.D., "Tips from the Doctor," *EQ*, February 1993, p. 44.

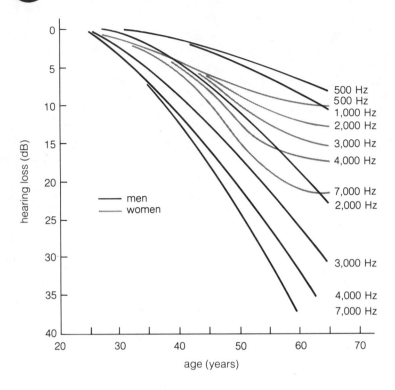

2-10 Typical hearing loss for various age groups of men and women

Table 2-3 Hours of exposure to high sound levels permitted by the U.S. government and the British Occupational Hygiene Society

U.S. Government—Occupational Safety and Health Act		British Occupational Hygiene Society	
Sound Level (dB-SPL)	*Daily Permissible Hours of Exposure*	*Sound Level (dB-SPL)*	*Daily Permissible Hours of Exposure*
90	8	90	8
92	6	91	6
95	4	93	4
97	3	94	3
100	2	96	2
105	1	99	1
110	½	102	½
115	¼	105	¼

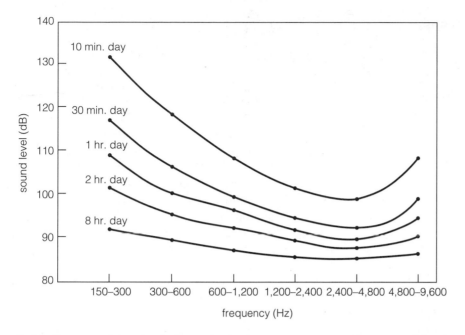

2-11 Damage risk criteria for a single-day exposure to various sound levels

Some options among available earplugs are custom-fit earmolds, disposable foam plugs, reusable silicon insert plugs, and industrial headsets. The custom-fit earmold is best to use for listening to loud music. It provides 15 dB to 20 dB of balanced sound-level reduction and attenuates all frequencies evenly. The disposable foam plug is intended for one-time use. It provides noise reduction from 12 dB to 20 dB, mainly in the high frequencies. The reusable silicon insert plug is a rubberized insert cushion that covers a tiny metal filtering diaphragm. It reduces sound levels by approximately 17 dB. The silicon insert plug is often used at construction sites and firing ranges. The industrial headset has a cushioned headpad and tight-fitting earseals. It provides maximum sound-level attenuation, often up to 30 dB, and is particularly effective at low frequencies. This is the headset commonly used by personnel around airport runways

and in the cabs of heavy construction equipment (see 2-12).

Loud sound levels also produce adverse physiological effects. Sounds transmitted to the brain follow two paths. One path carries sound to the auditory center, where it is perceived and interpreted. The other goes to the brain centers that affect the nervous system. Loud sound taking the latter path can increase heart rate and blood pressure; constrict small blood vessels in the hands and feet; contract muscles; release stress-related hormones from adrenal glands; disrupt certain stomach and intestinal functions; and create dry mouth, dilated pupils, tension, anxiety, fatigue, and crankiness. These stress reactions are believed to be an evolutionary holdover from the days when loud sound could mean trouble or danger for our prehistoric ancestors.

The human ear is a very sophisticated electro-mechanical device. And as with any

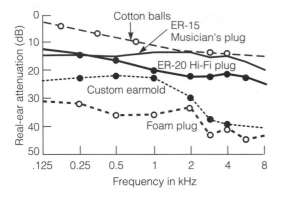

2-12 Attenuation effects of selected hearing protection devices. Notice that compared to a variety of commonly used hearing protectors the Musician's and Hi-Fi plugs have relatively even attenuation across the frequency spectrum. (The ER-15 and ER-20 are products of Etymotic Research™.)

device, regular maintenance is wise, especially for the audio professional. Make at least two visits a year to a qualified ENT (Ear, Nose, and Throat) specialist to have your ears inspected and cleaned. The human ear secretes wax to protect the ear drum and cochlea from loud sound pressure levels. Let the doctor clean out the wax. Do not use a cotton swab. You risk the chance of infection and jamming the wax against the ear drum, which obviously exacerbates the situation. If you must clean your ears between visits, ask the ENT doctor the safest way to do it.

The implications of all this should be obvious, especially to someone working in audio. Not only are one's hearing in particular and one's overall physiological well-being in general at risk, but so is one's livelihood.

Velocity

Although frequency and amplitude are the most important physical components of a sound wave, another component—**velocity,** or the speed of a sound wave—should be mentioned. Velocity usually has little impact on pitch or loudness and is relatively constant in a controlled environment; sound travels 1,130 feet per second at sea level when the temperature is 70 degrees Fahrenheit. (In water it travels 4,800 feet per second, and in solid materials such as wood and steel it travels 11,700 and 18,000 feet, respectively, due to the greater conductivity of the relatively denser molecular structures.) Velocity changes significantly, however, in very high or low temperatures, increasing as air warms and decreasing as air cools. For every change of 1 degree Fahrenheit, the speed of sound changes 1.1 feet per second.

It is worth noting, although it is too complex to discuss in detail here, that humidity also affects velocity. Sound is absorbed more and therefore travels faster in wetter air than in drier air. For example, if you live or work near railroad tracks, you might be able to tell whether rain is on the way by how much closer a passing train sounds on a humid day compared to on a dry day.

Wavelength

As noted previously, each frequency has a **wavelength,** determined by the distance a sound wave travels to complete one cycle of compression and rarefaction. That is, the physical measurement of the length of one cycle is equal to the velocity of sound divided by the frequency of sound ($\lambda = v/f$) (see 2-1). Therefore, frequency and wavelength change inversely with respect to each other. The lower a sound's frequency, the longer its

Table 2-4 Selected frequencies and their wavelengths

Frequency (Hz)	Wavelength	Frequency (Hz)	Wavelength
20	56.5 feet	1,000	1.1 feet
31.5	35.8	2,000	6.7 inches
63	17.9	4,000	3.3
125	9.0	6,000	2.2
250	4.5	8,000	1.6
440	2.5	10,000	1.3
500	2.2	12,000	1.1
880	1.2	16,000	0.07

wavelength; the higher a sound's frequency, the shorter its wavelength (see Table 2-4).

Understanding the concept of wavelength will be important later when we consider binaural hearing, acoustics, and studio design.

Acoustical Phase

Acoustical phase refers to the time relationship between two or more sound waves at a given point in their cycles. Because sound waves are repetitive, they can be divided into regularly occurring intervals. These intervals are measured in degrees (see 2-13).

If two identical waves begin their excursions at the same time, their degree intervals will coincide and the waves will be *in phase*. If two identical waves begin their excursions at different times, their degree intervals will not coincide and the waves will be *out of phase*.

Waves that are in phase reinforce each other, increasing amplitude. Conversely, waves that are out of phase weaken each other, decreasing amplitude When two sound waves that are exactly in phase (0-degree phase difference) and have the same frequency, shape, and peak amplitude

are added, the resulting waveform will be twice the original peak amplitude (see 2-14a). Two waves that are exactly out of phase (180-degree phase difference) and have the same frequency, shape, and amplitude cancel each other (see 2-14b). These two conditions rarely occur in the studio, however.

It is more likely that sound waves will begin their excursions at different times. If the waves are partially out of phase, there would be **constructive interference**, increasing amplitude, where compression and rarefaction occur at the same time, and **destructive interference**, decreasing amplitude, where compression and rarefaction occur at different times (see 2-15). The implications of acoustical phase are critical to an understanding of acoustics, creation of time-related effects, and microphone placement, discussed in Chapters 3, 8, 11, and 12.

Timbre

For the purpose of illustration, sound is often depicted as a single, wavy line (see 2-1). Actually, a wave that generates such a sound (known as a **sine wave**) is a **pure tone**.

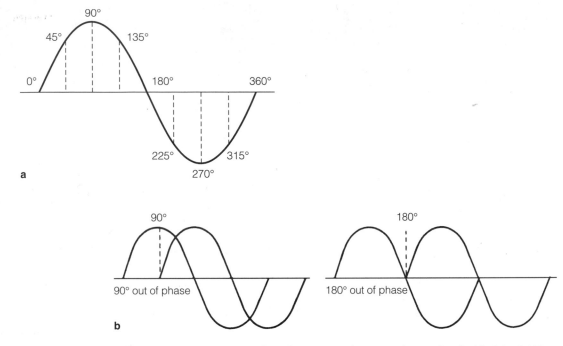

2-13 Sound waves. (*a*) Phase is measured in degrees, and one cycle can be divided in 360°. It begins at 0° with 0 amplitude, then increases to a positive maximum at 90°, decreases to 0 at 180°, increases to negative maximum at 270°, and returns to 0 at 360°. (*b*) Selected phase relationships of sound waves.

Most sound, however, consists of several different frequencies that produce a complex **waveform**—a graphic representation of a sound's characteristic shape, usually displayed on test equipment (see 2-16). Each sound has a unique harmonic structure that distinguishes it from all other sound (see 2-17). This difference between sounds is what defines their **timbre**—tone quality or tone color. Timbre has been defined as that attribute of auditory sensation whereby a listener can judge that two sounds are dissimilar regardless of similar pitch, loudness, or duration.*

Unlike pitch and loudness, which may be considered as unidimensional, timbre is multidimensional. The sound frequency spectrum is an objective scale of relative pitches; the table of sound pressure levels is an objective scale of relative loudnesses. But there is no objective scale that orders or compares the relative timbres of different sounds. The best we can do is try to articulate our subjective response to a particular distribution of sonic energy or to know how harmonics affect timbre. For example, sound consisting mainly of lower harmonics and played by cellos may be perceived as mellow, mournful, or quieting; these same lower frequencies played by a bassoon may be perceived as raspy, comical, or hornlike.

Each harmonic or set of harmonics adds a characteristic tonal color to sound,

*Definition based on R. L. Pratt and P. E. Doak, "A Subjective Rating Scale for Timbre," *Journal of Sound and Vibration,* 45 (1976): 317.

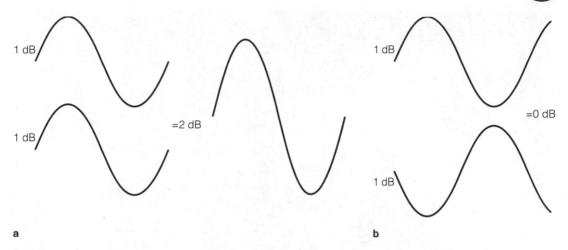

a   b

2-14 Sound waves in and out of phase.   (a) In phase: Their amplitude is additive. Here the sound waves are exactly in phase—a condition that rarely occurs. It should be noted that dB do not add linearly. These values have been assigned only to make a point. The actual additive amplitude here would be 6 dB. (b) Out of phase: Their amplitude is subtractive. Sound waves of equal amplitude 180 degrees out of phase cancel each other. This situation also rarely occurs.

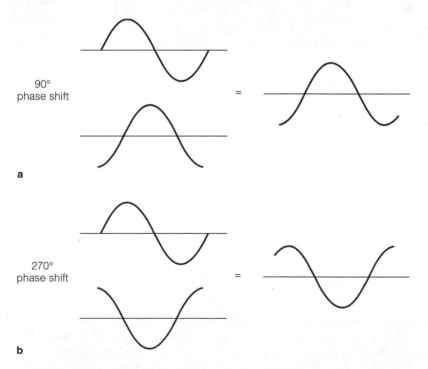

2-15 Waves partially out of phase (*a*) increase amplitude at some points and (*b*) decrease it at others

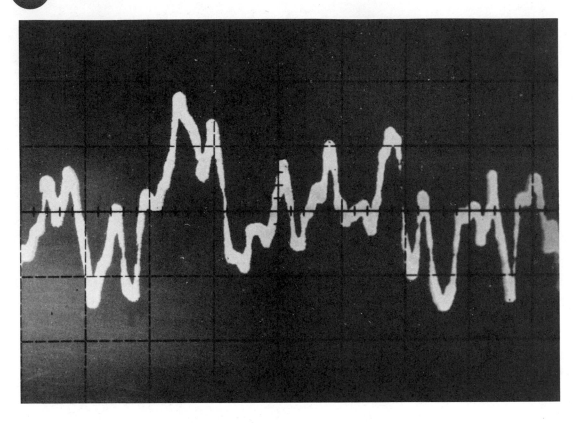

2-16 A complex waveform displayed on an oscilloscope

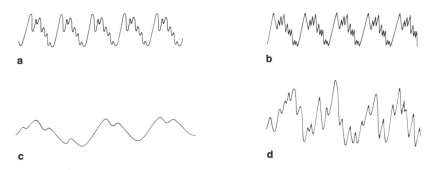

2-17 Waveforms showing differences between musical sounds and noise. (*a*) The pitch C from a piano. (*b*) The pitch C from a clarinet. (*c*) The waveform of an oboe. (*d*) The waveform of a noise. Notice its irregular pattern compared to the regular pattern of musical sounds.

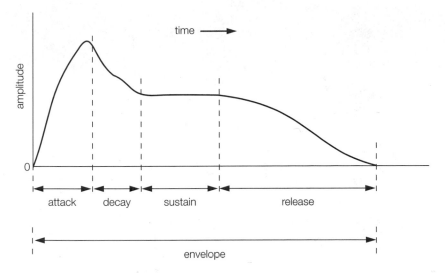

2-18 Sound envelope

although harmonics have less effect on changes in timbre as they rise in pitch above the fundamental. In general, even-numbered harmonics—second, fourth, and sixth—create an open, warm, filled-out sound. Odd-numbered harmonics—third and fifth—produce a closed, harsh, stopped-down sound.

The second harmonic, an octave above the fundamental, can be barely audible, yet it adds fullness to sound. The third harmonic (called *musical twelfth* or *quint*) softens sound. Harmonics above the seventh harmonic give sound edge, bite, and definition.

Sound Envelope

Another factor that influences the timbre of a sound is its shape, or envelope, which refers to changes in loudness over time. A **sound envelope** has three stages: (1) **attack**—how a sound starts up after a sound source has been vibrated, (2) **internal dynamics**—variations in loudness and sustain after the attack, and (3) **decay**—the

time and manner in which a sound diminishes to inaudibility. The sound envelope may also be divided into four stages: (1) attack, (2) initial decay, (3) sustain, and (4) release (ADSR) (see 2-18).

Two notes with the same frequency and loudness can produce different sounds within different envelopes. A bowed violin string, for example, has a more dynamic sound overall than does a plucked violin string. If you take a piano recording and edit out the attacks of the notes, the piano will start to sound like an organ. Do the same with a French horn and it sounds similar to a saxophone. Edit out the attacks of a trumpet and it creates an oboelike sound.

To this point we have examined the components of a sound wave and how they are heard without taking into consideration that we hear most sound in built-up or enclosed spaces. Behavior of sound waves in such spaces, and our perception of them, is the province of acoustics and psychoacoustics, which we will discuss in the next chapter.

Acoustics and Psychoacoustics

At concerts in St. Mark's Square in Venice, Italy, musicians are situated in certain parts of the plaza, depending on the music they are playing. For example, if it is Wagner, they sit in one place; if it is Mozart, they sit in another. They do this to take advantage of the sound quality peculiar to different locations in the square. One location generates more sound reflections, enriching sound and thereby enhancing Wagner's robust, full-bodied music. Another location generates fewer reflections, thinning sound and thereby enhancing Mozart's more subtle, delicate music.

In the final taping of a recent studio recording session, the producer noticed that the ensemble's overall sound was duller and more lifeless than it had been during rehearsals the day before. The musicians retuned their instruments; the producer rehoned the performance; the engineer rechecked microphone operation and placement and retested control room equipment—all to no avail. Then, one of the production crew noticed a few of the studio's reversible wall panels had been reversed. Their absorptive sides, instead of their reflective sides, were facing outward, thereby soaking up more sound waves.

The principles at work in these examples are based on **acoustics**—the objective study of the physical behavior of sound—and **psychoacoustics**—the perception of physical sound stimuli. Although both subjects are quite complex, at least a rudimentary knowledge of each is important to understanding their critical influences on hearing, sound dispersion, sound shaping, and studio and control room design.

Controlling the behavior of sound waves in an enclosed space for perceptual and artistic ends is a never-ending challenge in the performance and recording of acoustically generated audio. An insight into the difficulty begins with an understanding of how we discern sound waves reaching our ears.

Binaural Hearing

Both human ears are anatomically and functionally similar. By itself, each provides sufficient information for perception of pitch, loudness, and timbre. The use of only one ear, however, impairs perception of two elements essential to the fullest enjoyment of sound: location and dimension.

Sound Localization

If you are at a party where people are talking, music is playing, and plates are clattering, hearing with both ears—**binaural hearing**—makes it possible to focus your attention on a particular conversation or sound and push all other sounds into the background. This is difficult to do with one ear. Two factors produce this focusing ability, the so-called cocktail party effect: (1) the difference in a sound's intensity and (2) the difference in its arrival time as it reaches your two ears.

Intensity of Sound

A sound from a single source usually reaches one ear before it reaches the other. A sound emitted toward the left side of the head reaches the left ear first; a sound emitted toward the right side of the head reaches the right ear first.

When sound waves encounter an obstacle, frequencies with wavelengths shorter than the obstacle bounce off it, while frequencies with wavelengths longer than the obstacle bend or diffract around it. The average adult head is roughly 7 inches wide. Therefore, once the higher frequencies—with wavelengths about 7 inches or less—reach, say, the left ear, they reflect off the head, casting a "sound shadow" on the opposite side of the head. The result is a more intense sound in the left ear than in the right ear. Lower frequencies—with wavelengths about 7 inches or more—diffract around the head, causing the sound to reach the right ear slightly later than it reaches the left ear. In this case the result is that the sound waves reaching the left and right ears are slightly out of phase.

From this we may conclude that higher frequencies (that is, shorter wavelengths) are more directional and easier to localize than are lower frequencies (longer wavelengths). Somewhere between 1,000 Hz and 5,000 Hz, however, wavelengths may partially bounce off and partially diffract around the head; at these frequencies it is difficult to tell from where a sound is coming.

Time of Arrival

There is an important addition to this principle known as the **precedence effect** or **Haas effect** (after one of its originators). When a sound is emitted in a sound-reflective space, **direct sound** reaches our ears first, before it interacts with any other surface. **Indirect** or **reflected sound,** on the other hand, reaches our ears only after bouncing off one or a few surfaces. If similar sounds reach the ear within about 20 milliseconds of one another, the reflected sounds and the direct sound are usually perceived as coming from the same direction. As the time between the direct and indirect sound reaching the ears increases beyond 20 milliseconds, localization becomes increasingly difficult.

Another aspect of the precedence effect is that direct and reflected sounds reaching the ear approximately 10 to 20 milliseconds after the original waves are perceived as a single sound; the ear does not distinguish them. This is called **temporal fusion.** This effect gradually disappears as the time interval between direct and reflected sound increases from roughly 30 to 50 milliseconds. Once the time interval becomes greater than 50 milliseconds, however, repetitions of the sound are heard as echo.

Dimension

The relationship between the arrival time and intensity of a sound reaching your ears also affects the depth and breadth of a perceived sound. Listen to a compact disc on a good audio system. Switch the system back and forth from stereophonic (two-channel) to monophonic (one-channel). Notice that the sound is fuller, richer, and more spacious in the stereo mode. What creates this perceived sonic depth and breadth is the combined effect of intensity and time differences between the direct and reflected waves.

Direct Sound, Early Reflections, Reverberation, and Echo

The acoustic "life cycle" of a sound wave can be divided into three components: **direct sound** (or direct waves), early reflections, and reverberation (see 3-1).

Direct waves reach the listener without bouncing off any surface (see 3-2). They provide information about a sound's origin, its size, and its tonal quality.

Early reflections hit at least one surface before reaching the listener roughly 10 to 30 milliseconds after the direct sound (see 3-2). Although they are perceived as part of the direct sound, the time between their arrival and arrival of the direct sound adds loudness and fullness to the initial sound and helps to create our subjective impression of the room's size.

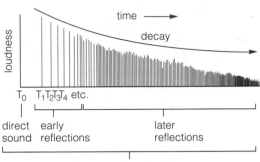

3-1 Anatomy of reverberation in an enclosed apace. At $time_0$ (T_0) the direct sound is heard. Between T_0 and T_1 is the initial time delay gap—the time between the arrival of the direct sound and the first reflection. At T_2 and T_3 more early reflections of the direct sound arrive as they reflect from nearby surfaces. These early reflections are sensed rather than distinctly heard. At T_4 repetitions of the direct sound spread through the room, reflecting from several surfaces and arriving at the listener so close together that their repetitions are indistinguishable.

Reverberation (reverb for short) usually results when sound reflects from many surfaces, reaching the listener more than 10 milliseconds after the direct sound (see 3-2). Reverberation is densely spaced reflections created by random, multiple, blended repetitions of a sound. Reverb fills out the loudness and body of a sound and contains most of a sound's total energy. And depending on the **decay,** or reverberation, **time** (the time it

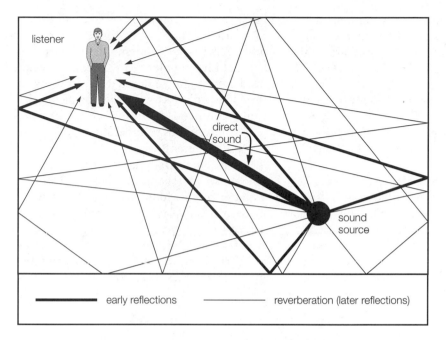

listener

direct
sound

sound
source

early reflections   reverberation (later reflections)

3-2 Acoustical behavior of sound in an enclosed room

takes a sound to decrease 60 dB-SPL after its steady-state sound level has stopped), reverb also provides information about the absorption and reflectivity of a room's surfaces, as well as about a listener's distance from the sound source. The longer it takes a sound to decay, the larger and more hard-surfaced the room is perceived to be, and the farther from the sound source the listener is or feels him- or herself to be.

If the path of the reflections is long— 50 milliseconds or greater—the reflections are perceived more and more as a distinct repetition of the direct sound, often inhibiting sonic clarity. This perceptible sound repetition is called **echo.** In large rooms discrete single echoes are sometimes perceived. In small rooms these repetitions, called **flutter echoes,** are short and come in rapid succession. They usually result from reflections

between two parallel surfaces that are highly reflective. Because echoes usually inhibit sonic clarity, studios and concert halls are designed to eliminate them.

Matching Acoustics to Program Material

Although the science of acoustics is highly developed, there is no such thing as a sound room with perfect acoustics. The sonic requirements, for example, of rock, jazz, and classical music recording all differ markedly.

A reverberant studio might be suitable for a symphony orchestra because the reflections add needed richness to the music, as they do in a concert hall. The extremely loud music a rock-and-roll group generates, however, would swim amid too many sound reflections, becoming virtually unintelligible. At the same time, a studio with relatively few reflections, and therefore suitable for rock-and-roll, may render the sound of a jazz ensemble lifeless.

Rooms with reverberation times of 1 second or more are considered to be "live"; rooms with reverberation times of 1/2 second or less are considered to be "dead" (see 3-3).

Live rooms reinforce sound, making it relatively louder and more powerful, especially, although not always, in the lower frequencies. They also tend to diffuse detail, smoothing inconsistencies in pitch, tonal quality, and performance. In dead rooms sound is reinforced little or not at all, caus-

ing it to be concentrated, weak, and lifeless. Inconsistencies in pitch, tonal quality, and other aspects of undesirable performance are readily apparent. In instances where dead rooms are required for recording, as they are with rock-and-roll, artificial electronic and acoustic means are used to provide appropriate reverberation effects (see 3-4 and Chapter 8).

In the final analysis, preference for the amount of reverberation and reverb time is a matter of individual taste, as all judgments in sound should be. Generally, however, acousticians have calculated optimum reverb times for various types of sonic material that have proved suitable for emulation in the production room (see 3-5).

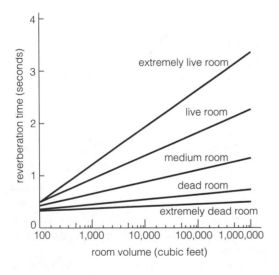

3-3 Room liveness in relation to reverberation time and room size

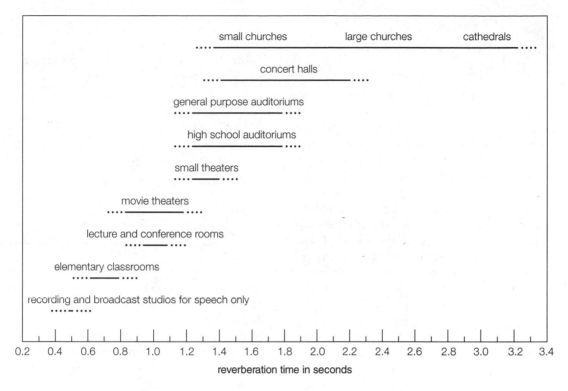

3-4 Typical reverberation times for various performance spaces

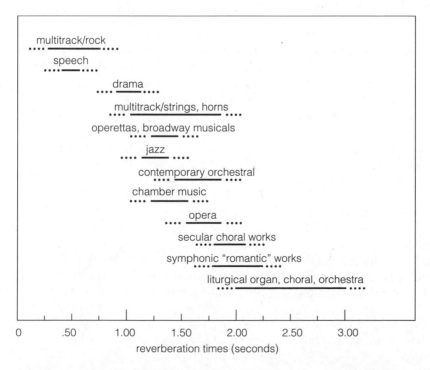

3-5 Optimum reverberation times for various types of music and speech produced indoors

Studio Design

Now that you have some idea of how sound waves behave in an acoustic environment and how that behavior affects aural perception, it is logical to consider the factors that influence this behavior: (1) the isolating of sound outside and inside a room, (2) the dimensions of the room, (3) the shape of the room, (4) absorption, reflection, diffraction, and diffusion in the room, and (5) the variable acoustic features of the room. These five factors are directly related to one overriding concern: noise.

Noise

Noise—unwanted sound—is enemy number one in audio production. Noise is everywhere. Outside a room noise comes from traffic, airplanes, jackhammers, thunder, rain, trees rustling, people shouting, stereos playing, and so on. Inside a room noise can be generated by fluorescent lights, ventilating and heating systems, air conditioning, and appliances. And these are only the more obvious examples. A few not so obvious examples include the "noise" made by the random motion of molecules, by our nervous and circulatory systems, and by our ears. In short, noise is part of our existence and can never be completely eliminated. (Audio equipment also generates **system noise,** and recording tape generates tape noise.)

Even though unwanted sound is always present, in producing audio it must be brought within tolerable levels so that it does not interfere with the desired sound. Among other things, noise can mask sounds, make lyrics unintelligible, create distraction, and cause annoyance.

To this end, acousticians have developed **Noise Criteria (NC)** that identify, by means

Table 3-1 Recommended Noise Criteria (NC) levels for selected rooms

Type of Room	Recommended NC Curve	dB
Broadcast and recording studios	NC 15–25	25–35
Concert halls	NC 20	30
Drama theaters	NC 20–25	30–35
Motion picture theaters	NC 30	40
Sports coliseums	NC 50	60

of a rating system, background noise—also called *ambient noise*—levels (see 3-6). From this rating system, NC levels for various types of rooms can be derived (see Table 3-1). This raises the question: Once NC levels for a particular sound room are known, how is noise control accomplished?

Isolation

Sound studios must be isolated to prevent outside noise from leaking into the room and to keep loud sound levels generated inside the room from disturbing neighbors. This is accomplished in two ways: (1) by determining the loudest outside sound level against the minimum acceptable NC level inside the studio, which is usually between NC 15 and 25 (approximately 25–35 dBA), depending on what type of sound the studio is used for; and (2) by determining the loudest sound level inside the studio against a maximum acceptable noise floor outside the studio.

For example, assume the maximum measured noise outside a studio is 90 dB-SPL and the maximum acceptable noise level inside a studio is 30 dB-SPL, at, say, 500 Hz. (These values are always frequency-dependent but are usually based on 500 Hz.)

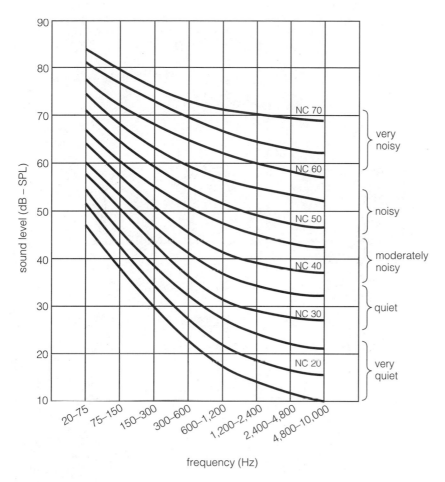

3-6 Noise Criteria (NC) curves

That means the construction of the studio must reduce the loudness of the outside sound level by 60 dB. If the loudest sound inside a studio is 110 dB-SPL and the maximum acceptable noise outside the studio is 45 dB-SPL, then the studio's construction must reduce the loudness level by 65 dB.

The amount of sound reduction provided by a barrier—wall, floor, or ceiling—is referred to as **transmission loss (TL)**. Because TL works both ways, determining barrier requirements is equally applicable to sound traveling from inside to outside the studio and vice versa. Therefore, the barriers constructed to isolate the studio in our example would have to reduce the loudness level by at least 65 dB (500 Hz).

Just as it is convenient to define a noise spectrum by a single NC number, so it is useful to measure a barrier on the basis of its transmission loss. Such a measurement is called **sound transmission class (STC)**. Sound transmission classes vary with the type and mass of materials in a barrier. A

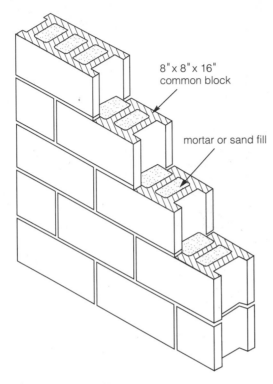

3-7 Studio wall construction with an STC of 50–55

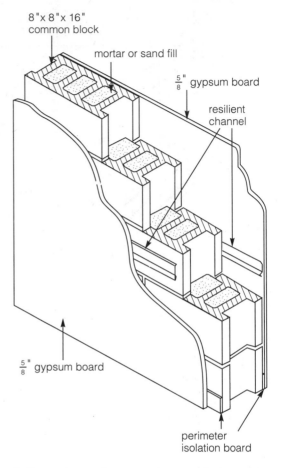

3-8 Studio wall construction with an STC of 65–70

4-inch concrete block has an STC of 48, indicating that sound passing through it will be attenuated by 48 dB. An 8-inch concrete block has an STC of 52, which means it attenuates 4 dB more sound than the 4-inch block.

This may appear relatively straightforward—making mathematical calculations and physically implementing them. It is anything but. It also involves judgment and ears. Meeting the various acoustic noise reduction requirements of a studio involves coordinating the construction of various barriers and systems, such as walls, ceiling, floor, windows, corridors, doors, and the heating, ventilation, and air conditioning. Because an in-depth discussion of these factors are beyond the scope of this book, Figures 3-7 to 3-9 are intended to provide some idea of the considerations involved.

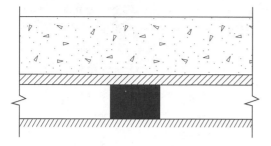

a

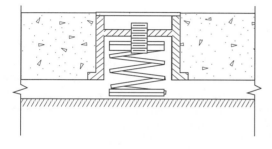

b

3-9 Floating floor: (*a*) isolation mount system, (*b*) spring system

Dimensions

Sometimes, a room's dimensions accentuate noise by reinforcing certain frequencies, thereby altering, or "coloring," the natural sound. This may also increase reverb time. Such coloration also affects perception of tonal balance, clarity, and imaging. Recordings mixed in a control room with these problems will sound markedly different when played in another room. Other factors, related to the shape of and construction materials used in a studio (discussed in the following two sections), may also affect coloration.

Rooms have particular resonances at which sound will be naturally sustained. These are related to the room's dimensions. **Resonance** results when a vibrating body with the same natural frequencies as another body causes it to vibrate sympathetically and increases the amplitude of both of them at those frequencies if the vibrations are in acoustic phase.

The story is told of soldiers on horseback galloping across a wooden bridge. The sound created by the hoofbeats on the wood generated the resonant frequency of the bridge, causing it to collapse. In another incident, wind excited the resonant frequency of a modern steel-and-concrete bridge, increasing amplitude until it was torn apart.* By generating resonant frequencies, you can break glass—whether the sound you use is live or on tape. These are interesting examples, but they are extreme for our purpose.

In a room, resonances occur at frequencies whose wavelengths are the same as or a multiple of one of the room's dimensions. These resonances are called **room modes**—increases in loudness at resonant frequencies that are a function of a room's dimensions. When these dimensions are the same as or multiples of a common value, the resonance amplitude is increased. This creates unequal representation of the frequencies generated by a sound source. In other words, certain frequencies will be reinforced while others will not be (see Table 3-2). To avoid additive resonances, room dimensions should not be the same, nor be integer multiples of one another (see Tables 3-3, 3-4, and 3-5).

Resonance is not always bad, however. The tubing in wind and brass instruments, the pipes in an organ, and the human

---

*Tacoma Narrows Suspension Bridge at Puget Sound, Washington, in 1940.

Table 3-2   Simplified table of reinforced frequencies in a room 10 by 20 by 30 feet. If this table were continued, each frequency that occurs in the height dimension would recur in the other two dimensions.

	Height—10 Feet	*Width—20 Feet*	*Length—30 Feet*
Fundamental	150 Hz	75 Hz	50 Hz
2nd harmonic	300 Hz	150 Hz	100 Hz
3rd harmonic	450 Hz	225 Hz	150 Hz
4th harmonic	600 Hz	300 Hz	200 Hz
5th harmonic	750 Hz	375 Hz	250 Hz
6th harmonic	900 Hz	450 Hz	300 Hz
7th harmonic	1,050 Hz	525 Hz	350 Hz
8th harmonic	1,200 Hz	600 Hz	400 Hz

Table 3-3   Selected preferred studio ratios

	Height	*Width*	*Length*
a	1.0	1.14	1.39
b	1.0	1.28	1.54
c	1.0	1.50	2.40
d	1.0	1.80	2.10

Table 3-4   Preferred studio dimensions using the ratios in Table 3-3

	Height	*Width*	*Length*
a	9 feet	10.1 feet	12.5 feet
b	9 feet	11.5 feet	13.8 feet
c	9 feet	13.5 feet	21.6 feet
d	9 feet	16.2 feet	18.9 feet
a	10 feet	11.4 feet	13.9 feet
b	10 feet	12.8 feet	15.4 feet
c	10 feet	15.0 feet	24.0 feet
d	10 feet	18.0 feet	21.0 feet
a	15 feet	17.1 feet	20.8 feet
b	15 feet	19.2 feet	23.1 feet
c	15 feet	22.5 feet	36.0 feet
d	15 feet	27.0 feet	31.5 feet

mouth, nose, chest, and throat are resonators. Air columns passing through them excite resonant frequencies, creating sound. Without resonators such as the "box" of a guitar or violin, weak sound sources would generate little sound. Some studios use this principle to construct resonators that help amplify certain frequencies to enhance the type of sound being produced. As we shall see in the section headed "Absorption, Reflection, Diffraction, and Diffusion," resonators are also used to absorb sound.

Shape

Acoustics is a science of interacting relationships. Although studio walls, floors, windows, and so on may have been properly constructed and the dimensions conform to a set of preferred standards, studio shape is also important to good noise reduction and sound dispersion.

Except for bass frequencies, sound behaves like light; its angle of incidence is equal to its angle of reflectance (see 3-10, which shows equal angles of incidence and reflectance). If a studio has reflective parallel

Table 3-5 Simplified table of frequencies in a studio with preferred dimensions. Using the preferred dimension of 9 feet by 10.1 feet by 12.5 feet, from Table 3-4, for example, only one frequency, 300 Hz, recurs in another dimension. Compare to Table 3-2.

	Height—9 Feet	*Width—10.1 Feet*	*Length—12.5 Feet*
Fundamental	150 Hz	136 Hz	60 Hz
2nd harmonic	300 Hz	272 Hz	85 Hz
3rd harmonic	450 Hz	409 Hz	128 Hz
4th harmonic	600 Hz	545 Hz	171 Hz
5th harmonic	750 Hz	681 Hz	214 Hz
6th harmonic	900 Hz	818 Hz	257 Hz
7th harmonic	1,050 Hz	954 Hz	300 Hz
8th harmonic	1,200 Hz	1,090 Hz	342 Hz

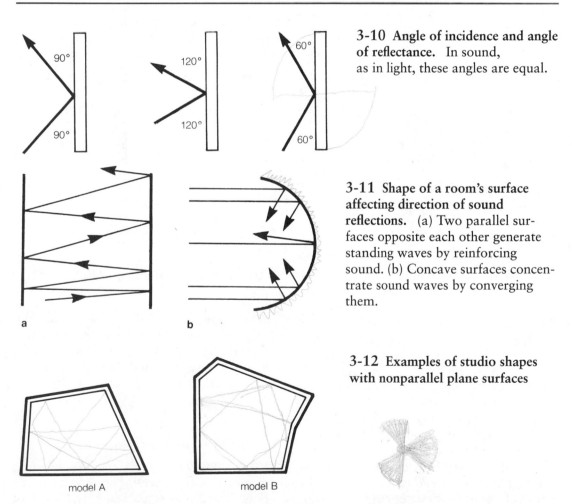

3-10 Angle of incidence and angle of reflectance. In sound, as in light, these angles are equal.

3-11 Shape of a room's surface affecting direction of sound reflections. (a) Two parallel surfaces opposite each other generate standing waves by reinforcing sound. (b) Concave surfaces concentrate sound waves by converging them.

3-12 Examples of studio shapes with nonparallel plane surfaces

a

b

model A

model B

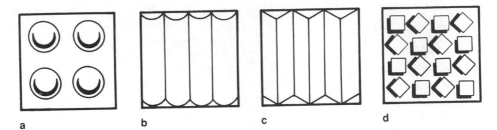

3-13 Examples of studio walls with different surface shapes: (*a*) spherical, (*b*) cylindrical, (*c*) serrated, and (*d*) a combination of square and diamond

3-14 Glass between the control room and the studio. Note that glass is angled down toward the floor for sound dispersal and to avoid studio light reflections.

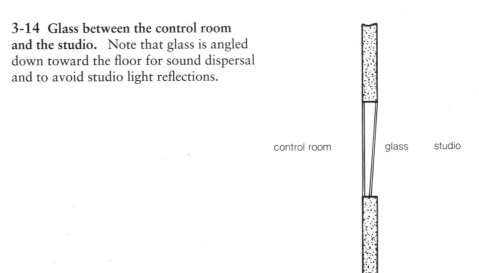

control room   glass   studio

walls, sound waves reinforce themselves as they continuously reflect between opposing surfaces (see 3-11a, which shows parallel surface reflection). If there are concave surfaces, they serve as collecting points, generating unwanted concentrations of sound (3-11b, which shows concave surface reflection). A studio should be designed to break up the paths of sound waves.

Typical studio designs have adjacent walls at angles other than 90 degrees (see 3-12) and different shaped wall surfaces (see 3-13 and 3-14) to help disperse the sound waves. But it is not enough to break up the paths of sound waves; they must be controlled once they hit a surface.

Absorption, Reflection, Diffraction, and Diffusion

When sound hits a surface, one, or a combination, of five things happens, depending on the surface's material, mass, and design. Sound is absorbed, reflected, partially absorbed and reflected, diffracted, or diffused.

Absorption and Reflection

When sound hits a surface and is absorbed, it is soaked up. There is little or no reflection, hence, the sonic result is lifeless or dead. When sound hits a surface and is

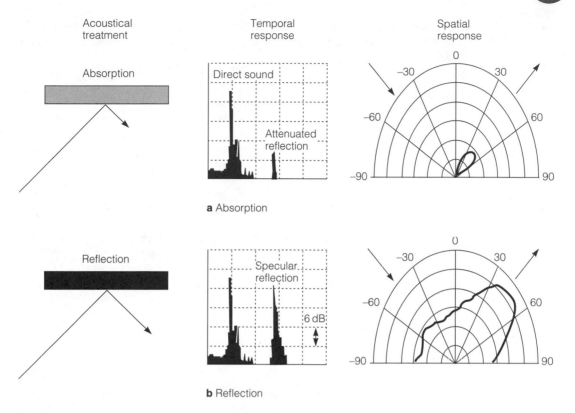

a Absorption

b Reflection

3-15 Absorption and reflection in relation to temporal and spatial response

reflected, it bounces off the surface and is perceived as echo or reverberation, depending on its interaction with other live surfaces in the vicinity. Conditions in which sound is completely absorbed or reflected are rare. Most materials absorb and reflect sound to some degree (see 3-15).

The amount of indirect sound energy absorbed is given an acoustical rating called a **sound absorption coefficient.** Theoretically, on a scale from 1.0 to 0.0, material with a sound absorption coefficient of 1.0 completely absorbs sound, while material with a sound absorption coefficient of 0.0 is completely sound reflectant. Soft, porous materials absorb more sound than do hard, nonporous materials. Drapes, for example, have

a higher absorption coefficient than does glass. However, sound absorption ratings for the same material vary with frequency (see Table 3-6).

Three classifications of acoustic absorbers are porous absorbers, diaphragmatic absorbers, and Helmholtz resonators. Examples of **porous absorbers** are acoustical tiles, carpets, fiberglass, and urethane foams (see 3-16a, b). Porous absorbers are most effective with high frequencies. Because the wavelengths of high frequencies are short, they tend to get trapped in the tiny air spaces of the porous materials. The range and degree of high-frequency absorption depends on the density and thickness of the porous materials.

Table 3-6   Sound absorption coefficients of commonly used materials (figures for people—adult, youth, and child—are determined by adding their absorption units to other absorbers in a room)

Materials	125 Hz	250 Hz	500 Hz	1,000 Hz	2,000 Hz	4,000 Hz
¾-in. mineral fiber acoustical tile						
hard backing	0.03	0.27	0.83	0.99	0.82	0.71
suspended	0.68	0.67	0.65	0.84	0.87	0.74
1-in. fiberglass tile						
hard backing	0.06	0.25	0.68	0.97	0.99	0.91
suspended	0.69	0.95	0.74	0.98	0.99	0.99
Brick						
unglazed	0.03	0.03	0.03	0.04	0.05	0.07
painted	0.01	0.01	0.02	0.02	0.02	0.03
Carpet, heavy						
on concrete	0.02	0.06	0.14	0.37	0.60	0.65
on foam pad	0.08	0.24	0.57	0.69	0.71	0.73
Concrete block						
coarse, unpainted	0.36	0.44	0.31	0.29	0.39	0.25
painted, sealed	0.10	0.05	0.06	0.07	0.09	0.08
Fabric						
10 oz. medium velour hung flat						
to wall	0.03	0.04	0.11	0.17	0.24	0.35
14 oz. medium velour draped						
to half area	0.07	0.31	0.49	0.75	0.70	0.60
18 oz. heavy velour draped						
to half area	0.14	0.35	0.55	0.72	0.70	0.65
Floor materials						
concrete or terrazzo	0.01	0.01	0.01	0.02	0.02	0.02
tile on concrete	0.02	0.03	0.03	0.03	0.03	0.02
wood parquet on concrete	0.04	0.04	0.07	0.06	0.06	0.07
wood on wood joists	0.15	0.11	0.10	0.07	0.06	0.07
Glass						
std. window glass	0.35	0.25	0.18	0.12	0.07	0.04
heavy plate glass	0.18	0.06	0.04	0.03	0.02	0.02
Gypsum wall board						
nailed to 2 × 4 studs	0.29	0.10	0.05	0.04	0.07	0.09
Plaster						
smooth, on brick	0.01	0.02	0.02	0.03	0.04	0.05
rough, on lath	0.14	0.10	0.06	0.05	0.04	0.03
¾-in. plywood paneling	0.28	0.22	0.17	0.09	0.10	0.11
Water surface, as in a swimming pool	0.008	0.008	0.013	0.015	0.020	0.025
Audience, seated in upholstered seats	0.60	0.74	0.88	0.96	0.93	0.85
unoccupied cloth-covered seats	0.49	0.66	0.80	0.88	0.82	0.70
unoccupied leather-covered seats	0.44	0.54	0.60	0.62	0.58	0.50
Chairs, metal or wood, occupied	0.15	0.19	0.22	0.39	0.38	0.30
People						
adult				4.2		
youth				3.8		
child				2.8		

a

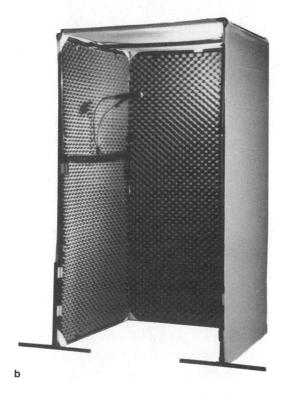

b

3-16 (*a*) Polyurethane-foam sound absorber and (*b*) polyurethane-foam sound absorber lining a portable sound booth

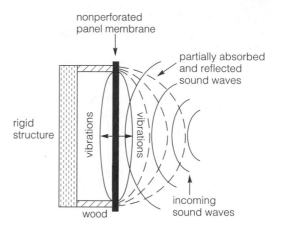

nonperforated panel membrane

partially absorbed and reflected sound waves

rigid structure

vibrations

vibrations

incoming sound waves

wood

3-17 Diaphragmatic absorber. The approaching sound wave strikes the cover panel or diaphragm, setting it into motion and canceling resonant frequencies and reflecting nonresonant frequencies.

Diaphragmatic absorbers are generally flexible panels of wood or pressed wood mounted over an air space (see 3-17). When a sound wave hits the panel, it resonates at a frequency (or frequencies) determined by the stiffness of the panel and the size of the air space. Other sound waves of the same frequency (or frequencies) approaching the panel, therefore, are dampened. Diaphragmatic absorbers are used mainly to absorb low frequencies. For this reason they are also called *bass traps*. This principle can also be applied to absorbing high frequencies. Because it is difficult to completely dissipate standing waves, especially in small rooms, even with optimal acoustics, bass traps are usually designed to introduce significant absorption for frequencies between 30 and 100 Hz.

A **Helmholtz resonator** functions, in principle, not unlike the action created by someone blowing into the mouth of a soda bottle. The tone created at the frequency of the bottle's resonance is related to the air mass in the bottle. If the bottle is filled with water,

3-18 Helmholtz resonator. As a sound wave at or close to the natural frequency of the absorber strikes the opening, the air in the neck vibrates. These vibrations are sent out toward the approaching sound wave. Phase cancellation occurs, and the approaching wave is absorbed.

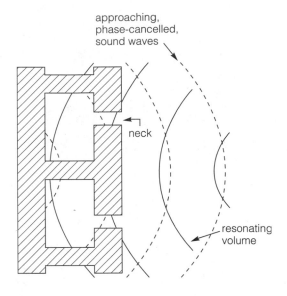

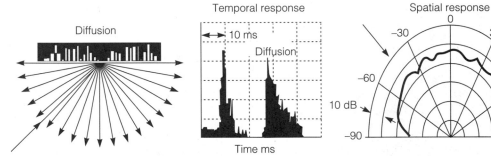

3-19 Diffusion in relation to temporal and spatial response

the air mass is reduced, so the pitch of the tone gets higher. Helmholtz resonators are often designed to absorb sound at specific frequencies or within specific frequency ranges, usually the lower-middle frequencies (see 3-18).

Diffraction

When sound reaches a surface, in addition to being partially absorbed and reflected, it diffracts—spreads or bends around the surface. The amount of **diffraction** depends on the relation between wavelength and the distances involved. You will recall that each frequency has a wavelength; bass waves are longer, treble waves shorter. Hence, the diffraction of bass waves is more difficult to control acoustically than the diffraction of treble waves.

Diffusion

The overriding challenge for the acoustician is to control the physical behavior of sound waves in a studio. The goal is the uniform distribution of sound energy in a room so that its intensity throughout the room is approximately equal (see 3-19). This is called **diffusion.** No matter how weak or

3-20 Abffusor.™ Provides reflection control by simultaneously using absorption and diffusion down to 100 Hz for all angles of incidence.

strong the sound, regardless of its wavelength, the diffused energy is reduced in amplitude and spread out in time, falling off more or less exponentially. Figures 3-20, 3-21, and 3-22 display various forms of diffusors to meet specific needs.

Variable Acoustics

Basic principles of acoustics apply to any room in which sound is generated. As noted earlier, however, a room's purpose has a great deal to do with how those principles are applied. If a studio is used for popular music and speech, the acoustics must absorb

more individual sound than they diffuse so there is minimal interference from other sounds or from reverberation, or from both. On the other hand, studios used for classical music and some types of jazz should diffuse more sound than they absorb to maintain a balanced, blended, open sound imaging.

Theoretically, this means that a studio designed to fulfill one sonic purpose is inappropriate for another. In fact, to be more functional, many studios are designed with variable acoustics. They have movable panels, louvers, walls, or gobos to alter diffusion, absorption, and reverb time (see 3-23 to 3-25).

3-21 Omniffusor.™ Sound diffusor that scatters sound into a hemisphere, useful when omnidirectional coverage and high sound attenuation are desired.

3-22 B.A.S.S. Trap.™ Bass absorbing soffit system to control low-frequency reverberation in small rooms.

a

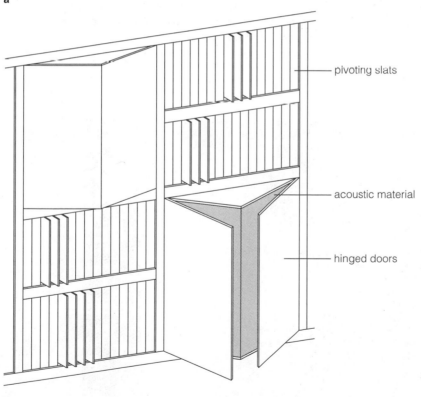

pivoting slats

acoustic material

hinged doors

b

3-23 Example of acoustic treatment along walls. (*a*) Scoring stage with alternating doors and slats that can be opened or closed to vary acoustics. (*b*) Detail of doors and slats shown in *a*.

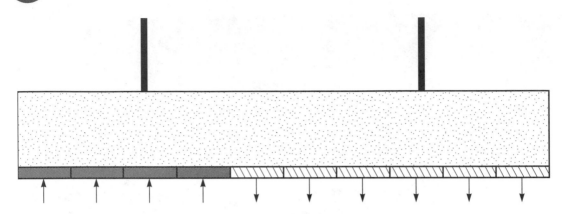

3-24 Sketch of a variable, adjustable, acoustic partition used in one recording studio. This partition is connected to the ceiling and can be raised or lowered to vary studio reverberation time between 2 and 4 seconds. Reverb times can be further refined by turning the bottom panels to their reflective or absorbent surfaces. For example, in recording an orchestra the panels over the strings and woodwinds could be turned to their reflective side to enhance these weaker-sounding instruments, and the panels over the brass and tympany could be turned to their absorptive side to help control these stronger-sounding instruments.

3-25 Movable baffles or gobos showing absorbent and reflective surfaces

Control Room Design

Sonic purpose also affects design differences between studios and control rooms. Studios are designed for sound that is appropriate for microphone pickup, whereas control rooms are designed for listening to loudspeakers. Therefore, to accurately assess the reproduced sound in a control room the main challenge is to reduce the number of unwanted reflections at the monitoring location(s) (see Chapter 9). There are a number of different approaches to the problem.

One is the *Live-End–Dead-End* (*LEDE*) concept (LEDE is the trademark of Synergetic Audio Concepts), in which the front of the control room is sound absorbent, while the rear of the control room reflects sound, directing it toward the operator's position. This design helps maintain a diffuse sound field. As the reflected sound continues past the operator toward the front of the room, it is absorbed by the dead end of the room. This absorption helps to minimize unwanted buildup of room reflections that would otherwise color the sound (see 3-26). Another concept is displayed in 3-27.

Ergonomics

Sound control is obviously the most important factor in studio and control room design, but human needs should not be ignored. Recording sessions are stressful enough without production personnel having to endure poor lighting, hard-to-reach equipment, uncomfortable chairs, and so on. Designing an engineering system with the human element in mind is called **ergonomics.** Here are a few of the more important ergonomic considerations:

- *Lighting.* Studio and control room atmospheres are important in a recording session, and lighting goes a long way in enhancing the environment, adjustable lighting in particular. One producer may like a lot of light in the control room, while another producer may prefer it dim. Musicians may like low-key light, assorted colored lights, or flashing lights, depending on the music and the emotional bolstering they may need. Clearly, if music has to be read, notes taken, and so on, there must be sufficient light to comfortably do so.

- *Size.* Ample room for personnel and equipment should prevent a cramped, claustrophobic feeling.

- *Position of equipment.* Equipment and remote controls should be situated within arm's reach, and easy access should be provided to equipment that cannot be so positioned. The operator should be located at the point where hearing and seeing are optimal.

- *Furniture.* Furniture should be functional, rather than just decorative, and reflect as little sound as possible. Chairs should be comfortable and move around easily on wheels without squeaking. A chair should have a five-star base so it does not tip, slould be flexible for sliding or leaning, and should be adjustable. Most people prefer arm rests and even flexible headrests. A chair should provide back support, particularly in the lower back, and should not cut off blood circulation in the legs. Cushions should be firm and shaped to support the body. If different contoured chairs are needed to accommodate the regular control room personnel, it is worth the investment.

- *Floor covering.* Rugs should be static-free and permit anything on wheels to move about easily.

In production, make it as easy on yourself as possible.

a

b

3-26 Live-End–Dead-End control room. (*a*) Live-End part of the
control room. (*b*) Dead-End part of the control room.

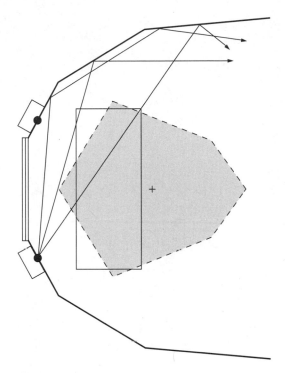

3-27 The shaded area in this control room design is a reflection-free zone

PART

2

Equipment

Microphones

The analogy can be made that microphones are to the music recordist what colors are to a painter. The more colors and hues available to a painter, the greater the possibilities for coloration in a visual canvas. For the music recordist, the more models of microphones there are, the greater the variety of tones in the sonic "palette," and hence, the greater the possibilities for coloration in designing an aural canvas.

When choosing a microphone, there are a number of attributes to consider about its particular "color" and "hue." They fall into three major categories: transducer type, directional characteristics, and sound response.

Transducer Type

The microphone is a **transducer** that converts acoustic energy into electric energy. The device that actually does the transducing is mounted in the mic head and is called the *element*. Each type of microphone gets its name from the element it uses. There are five types: three normally used by professionals—(1) moving-coil,[*] (2) ribbon, (3) capacitor (or condenser)—which we will discuss in detail; and two used by nonprofessionals—(4) *ceramic* and (5) *crystal*. The difference between a professional and a nonprofessional microphone is in the sound quality produced.

After a microphone changes acoustic energy into electric energy, the electric energy

---

[*]The term *dynamic* is often used to describe moving-coil microphones. Actually, dynamic microphones constitute a class of mics that transduce energy electromagnetically by means of a conductor moving in a magnetic field. This classification also includes ribbon types, sometimes called *velocity* microphones. To avoid confusion, we will designate a microphone's type by its element, not its classification, although in actual use it probably would be more convenient to use the term *dynamic* synonymously with *moving coil*. Capacitor mics, classified as electrostatic, used to be called condenser mics because of their element, and the name has remained in popular usage. However, enough time has passed since their element has been a capacitor to make continued use of *condenser* misleading, unless, of course, the mic has a condenser element.

flows through a circuit as voltage. You will recall that the resistance the flow of voltage encounters in the circuit is called *impedance*. Less resistance means lower impedance. Microphones used for professional recording are usually in the low-impedance range of 150 to 600 ohms.

Low-impedance microphones have two advantages over high-impedance mics: (1) They are much less susceptible to hum and electric noise, such as static from motors and fluorescent lights; and (2) they can be connected to long cables without increasing the noise. For these reasons professionals use low-impedance mics (and equipment).

Types of Low-Impedance Microphones

Three types of low-impedance microphone are in professional use: The moving-coil, ribbon, and capacitor (or condenser).

Moving-Coil Microphones

In a **moving-coil microphone** the transducing element consists of a coil of wire attached to a Mylar diaphragm suspended in a magnetic field (see 4-1). When sound waves move the diaphragm, they move the coil, which gives the element its name. As the coil moves in the magnetic field, voltage is induced within the coil; the voltage is the electric-energy analog of the acoustic energy that first caused the diaphragm to vibrate.

Ribbon Microphones

In **ribbon microphones** the diaphragm and moving coil are replaced with a thin, corrugated metal ribbon suspended in a strong magnetic field (see 4-2). As the ribbon vibrates from the pressure of the sound waves, voltage is induced in the ribbon.

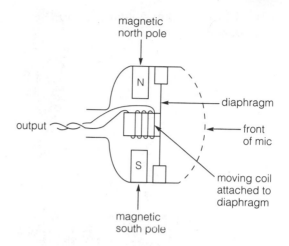

4-1 The element of a moving-coil microphone

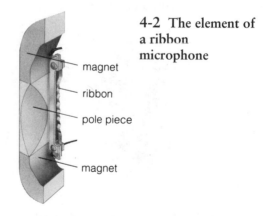

4-2 The element of a ribbon microphone

The long, vertical ribbon design found in older ribbon mics makes the element quite fragile (see 4-3). Strongly blown sounds or sudden, loud changes in sound pressure can damage the ribbon.

A newer design places a smaller ribbon longitudinally between the pole pieces. This, and other design features (such as a less fragile element and stronger casing), makes this type of ribbon mic more durable and

4-3 Older model of ribbon microphone

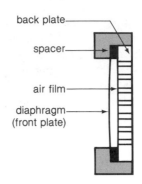

back plate
spacer
air film
diaphragm (front plate)

4-6 Cross-section of the element in a capacitor microphone

4-4 Newer model of ribbon microphone with smaller, longitudinal ribbon

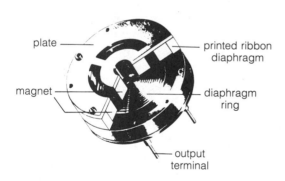

plate
magnet
printed ribbon diaphragm
diaphragm ring
output terminal

4-5 Printed-ribbon microphone element

able to take louder sound-pressure levels than its predecessors (see 4-4).

Ribbon microphones are sometimes called *velocity* or *pressure-gradient* microphones. Both sides of the ribbon are exposed to the velocity of the air molecules and are activated by the difference in pressure between the front and back of the ribbon.

The most recent addition to ribbon design is the **printed-ribbon microphone**, sometimes also called the *regulated-phase* microphone (see 4-5). In principle, it operates like the conventional ribbon pickup, but in a considerably more rugged design. In other words, it has the durability of a moving-coil mic with the compliance—ease of diaphragm movement—of a ribbon microphone.

A spiral aluminum ribbon is printed on a diaphragm made of polyester film. Two ring magnets in front of the diaphragm and two in the back produce the magnetic structure. Sound waves arrive at the diaphragm through the inner and outer ring openings and also through the center hole of the inner magnet.

Capacitor Microphones

Capacitor microphones operate on a principle different from that of the moving-coil and ribbon types. They transduce energy using voltage (electrostatic) variations instead of magnetic (electromagnetic) variations. The capacitor design consists of two parallel plates separated by a small space (see 4-6). The front plate is a thin, metalized plastic diaphragm, the only moving part in the mic head, and the back plate is fixed.

4-7 External power supply for an older, tube-type condenser microphone

a   b

4-8 Power supplies in capacitor microphones. (*a*) Battery location in one model and (*b*) smaller-size battery in electret model.

Together these plates or electrodes form a **capacitor**—a device that is capable of holding an electric charge. As acoustic energy moves the diaphragm back and forth in relation to the fixed back plate, the capacitance change causes a voltage change, varying the signal. The signal output, however, has a very high impedance and requires a preamplifier (mounted near the mic capsule) to make it usable.

Because the capacitor requires polarizing voltage and the preamplifier requires power voltage to operate, capacitor microphones must have a separate power supply. The older, tube-type condensers came with a bulky, external power supply for condensers and preamp (see 4-7). Today, capacitor mics are powered by batteries contained inside the microphone (see 4-8) or by a phantom power supply that eliminates the need for batteries altogether. Phantom power supplies may be at the console, installed in the studio microphone input circuits, or portable, thereby providing voltage the instant a mic is plugged in. Some capacitor microphones have an *electret* diaphragm. An electret is a material (high-polymer plastic film) that can hold a charge permanently, thus eliminating the need for external polarizing voltage. Because a small battery is all that is required to power the preamp, **electret microphones** can be made more compact (see 4-8b).

General Transducer Performance Characteristics

Each microphone has its unique sound quality. It is not a matter of one microphone being better than another, but that one microphone may be more suitable for a particular application than another.

Moving-coil microphones are well suited for high sound-pressure-level applications. They are quite rugged and generate low self-noise. They tend to be less susceptible to humidity and wide temperature variations. They are usually less expensive than the other professional types and come in a wide variety of makes and models.

Generally (there are a number of exceptions), the frequency response of moving-coil mics is transparent; they tend not to color sound. They are slower to respond to **transients**—sounds that begin with a quick attack, such as a drum hit or breaking glass, and then quickly decay.

The more mass to the parts inside a microphone that must be moved by sound pressure, the less accurate the reproduction, especially in relation to transients. The element in a moving coil mic has considerably more mass than the element in a capacitor microphone, which has the lowest mass of the three types of professional mics. This makes the capacitor mic best suited to handling transient sounds. The ribbon has relatively low mass; its transient response is between the moving-coil and capacitor mics.

Ribbon microphones are not widely used today, except in music recording and live concerts and for the speaking voice. They are more expensive than many moving-coil mics and even the newer, more rugged models have to be handled with care, particularly when it comes to loud sound levels.

Older-type ribbon mics have mediocre high-frequency response, which can be turned into an advantage because it gives sound a warm, mellow quality. The longitudinal ribbon mics have a more extended high-frequency response. The *printed-ribbon microphone* also has good high-frequency response, but it is somewhat limited at low frequencies. Generally, ribbon mics have low self-noise but have the lowest output level of the three major types. This means a poorer signal-to-noise ratio if the mic is too far from the sound source or if the cable run is too long.

Capacitor microphones are high-performance instruments. They reproduce clear, detailed sound and are the choice among professional-quality microphones when it is necessary to record sounds rich in harmonics and overtones. Capacitor mics have high sensitivity, which makes them the preferred microphone for distant miking. They also have the highest output level, which gives them a wide signal-to-noise ratio. These advantages come at a cost, for capacitors are generally the most expensive type of microphone.

Directional Characteristics

A fundamental rule of good microphone technique is that a sound source should be **on-mic**—at an optimal distance from the microphone and directly in its pickup pattern. **Pickup pattern** refers to the direction(s) from which a mic hears sound. Depending on the design, a microphone is sensitive to sound from (1) all around—**omnidirectional,** (2) its front and rear—**bidirectional,** or (3) its front only—**unidirectional** (see 4-9). Omnidirectional mics are also called **nondirectional,** and unidirectional mics are also

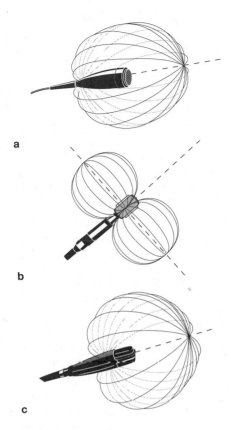

4-9 Pickup patterns:
(*a*) omnidirectional, (*b*) bidirectional,
and (*c*) unidirectional or cardioid

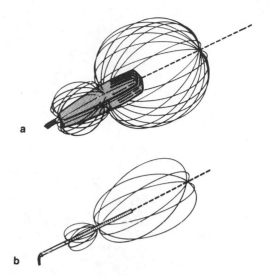

4-10 Pickup patterns:
(*a*) supercardioid and (*b*) hypercardioid

called **directional. Cardioid** is still another commonly used name for a unidirectional microphone because its pickup pattern is heart-shaped. Three unidirectional patterns used in music recording are cardioid, super-cardioid, and hypercardioid (see 4-10).

Figures 4-9 and 4-10 show basic microphone directionalities. The precise pattern varies from mic to mic. To get a better idea of a microphone's pickup pattern, its polar response diagram should be studied (see the next section).

A microphone's unidirectionality is facilitated by ports at the side and/or rear of the mic that cancel sound coming from unwanted directions. (For this reason you should not cover the ports with a hand or with tape.) In relation to ports, directional microphones are referred to as **single-entry**, or **single-D™** —having ports in the capsule, or **multiple-entry**, also called **variable-D™** —having ports in the capsule and along the handle. In a single-entry directional mic the rear-entrance ports handle all frequencies (see 4-11). A multiple-entry directional mic has several ports, each tuned to a different band of frequencies (see 4-12). The ports closer to the diaphragm process the higher frequencies; the ports farther from the diaphragm process the lower frequencies. Ports also influence a microphone's proximity effect, which is discussed later in this chapter.

ports

4-11 Microphone with single-entry ports. (Note: This figure and Figure 4-12 indicate the position of the ports on these microphones. The actual ports are concealed by the mic grille.)

ports

4-12 Microphone with multiple-entry ports

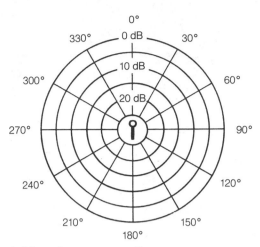

4-13 Polar response diagram

Polar Response Diagrams

A microphone's directional sensitivity, or **polar response pattern,** can be displayed on a graph (see 4-13). The graph consists of concentric circles, usually divided into segments of 30 degrees, to depict directionality. Reading inward or outward, the circles represent sound levels; the interval between each circle is usually 5 dB.

The omnidirectional polar pattern shows that sound is picked up almost uniformly from all directions (see 4-14). The bidirectional polar pattern indicates maximum sensitivity to sound coming from the front and rear, from 0 and 180 degrees (see 4-15). Sensitivity decreases toward the sides. Sound that reaches the mic at roughly 50, 130, 230, and 310 degrees is reduced by 5 dB; sound at 60, 120, 240, and 300 degrees is reduced by 10 dB; and for sound at 90 and 270 degrees, there is minimal response.

The cardioid polar pattern illustrates response from, in effect, one direction, with maximum sound rejection at 180 degrees

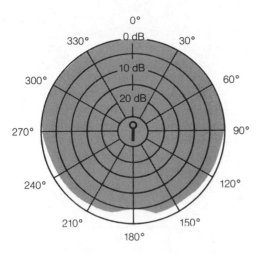

4-14 Omnidirectional polar diagram

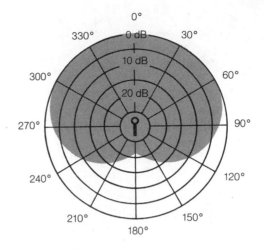

4-16 Unidirectional or cardioid polar diagram

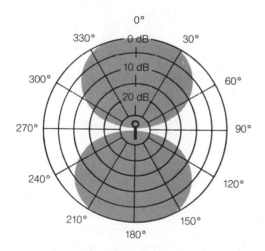

4-15 Bidirectional polar diagram

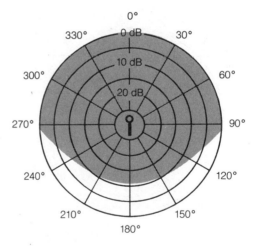

4-17 Wide-angle cardioid polar diagram

(see 4-16). The wide-angle cardioid has a less directional pickup pattern than does the cardioid (see 4-17). Supercardioid and hypercardioid polar patterns are more directional with areas of acceptance at the front, and maximum rejection at the rear sides (see 4-18 and 4-19). There is often confusion about the differences between supercardioid and hypercardioid mics—it may appear from the diagrams that they pick up and reject sound at almost the same points. In fact, the supercardioid mic has good sound rejection at the sides and fair sound rejection at the rear. The hypercardioid is more highly directional, having better side rejection but poorer rear rejection.

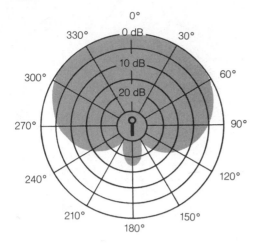

4-18 Supercardioid polar diagram

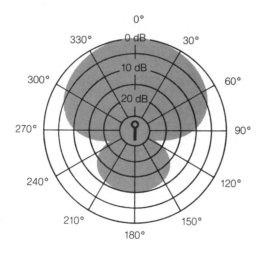

4-19 Hypercardioid polar diagram

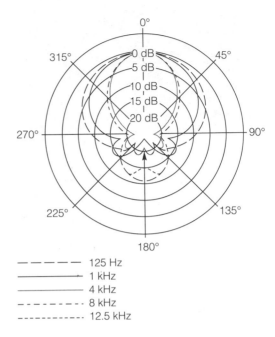

———— 125 Hz
———— 1 kHz
———— 4 kHz
-------- 8 kHz
----------- 12.5 kHz

4-20 Polar pattern indicating differences in directionality at certain frequencies. Notice that the lower the frequency, the less directional the pickup.

More highly directional polar patterns than the hypercardioid are also available for pinpoint pickup at a distance, such as the ultracardioid shotgun mic and the parabolic microphone system. But, generally, the effective frequency response of these microphones is not wide enough for music recording.

The polar diagrams shown here are ideals. In actual use, a microphone's directional sensitivity varies with frequency—the higher the frequency, the more directional a mic becomes. Even some omnidirectional microphones positioned at an angle to the sound source tend not to pick up higher frequencies coming from the sides and rear, thus making the nondirectional pattern somewhat directional at these frequencies. Figure 4-20 shows an example of a polar pattern indicating frequency response.

Pickup pattern also affects a microphone's "reach"—that is, the working distance from the microphone the sound source can be and still remain on mic (see 4-21).

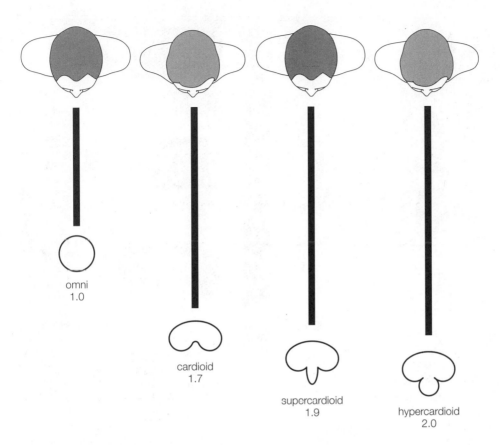

4-21 Differences in relative working distances between omnidirectional, cardioid, supercardioid, and hypercardioid microphones

4-22 Multidirectional microphone with five pickup patterns: omnidirectional, wide-angle cardioid, cardioid, hypercardioid, and bidirectional. This microphone also has a 3-position bass roll-off (flat, 200 Hz, and 500 Hz) and a 3-position pad (0, –10dB, and –20 dB). See "Proximity Effect" and "Overload" later in this chapter.

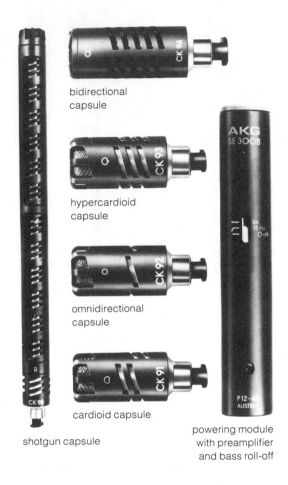

bidirectional
capsule

hypercardioid
capsule

omnidirectional
capsule

cardioid capsule

shotgun capsule

powering module
with preamplifier
and bass roll-off

4-23 Example of a system microphone

Multidirectional Microphones

Microphones with a single directional response have one fixed diaphragm (or ribbon). By using two diaphragms and a switch to select or proportion between them, a microphone can be made **multidirectional** (or **polydirectional**), providing two or more pickup patterns (see 4-22).

System Microphones

Another multidirectional mic of sorts is the **system microphone**, which uses interchangeable heads or capsules, each with a particular pickup pattern, that can be mounted onto a common base (see 4-23). Because these systems are capacitors, the power supply and preamplifier are in the base, and the mic capsule simply screws into the base. Any number of directional capsules—omnidirectional and bidirectional, cardioid, supercardioid, and hypercardioid—can be interchanged on a single base.

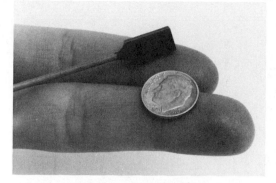

4-24 Lavalier microphone. When lavalier mics are used in studio recording, they are usually mounted on the musical instrument.

a   b

4-25 Contact microphones, also called acoustic pickup mics. (*a*) Bidirectional contact mic used for low- to mid-frequency pickup. (*b*) Cardioid mic used for mid- to high-frequency pickup. These particular contact mics are designed for acoustic string instruments.

Special Purpose Microphones

Some microphones have been developed to meet a particular need. The better known of these special purpose mics used in studio recording are the stereophonic, middle-side, soundfield, and boundary microphones. They are discussed next.

4-26 Stereo microphone with two separate capsules. The upper capsule in this model can be turned 360 degrees, in 10-degree increments. The pattern selectors on the microphone body can be set to *R* for remote control of the capsule configurations.

Two other special purpose mics sometimes employed in studio situations are the **lavalier** and **contact** microphones. They are usually mounted on a musical instrument to pick up the resonance of its surface vibrations (see 4-24 and 4-25).

Stereophonic Microphones

Stereophonic (*stereo*) **microphones** are actually microphone capsules with electronically separate systems housed in a single case (see 4-26).

The stereo mic has two distinct elements. The lower element is stationary, and the upper one rotates 180 to 360 degrees,

4-27 Middle-side microphone and matrix controller

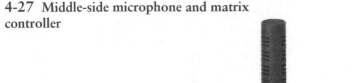

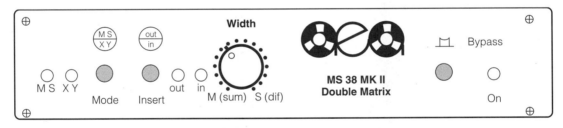

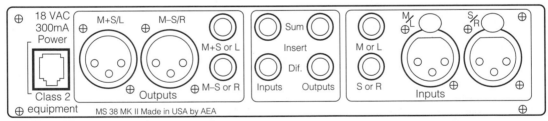

4-28 Another matrix controller, front and rear views

depending on the mic, to facilitate several different stereo pickup patterns. Some stereo mics can be remote controlled.

Middle-Side (M-S) Microphones

The **middle-side** (*M-S*) **microphone** consists of two mic capsules housed in a single casing. One capsule is designated as the mid-

position microphone aimed at the sound source to pick up mostly direct sound; it is usually cardioid. The other capsule is designated as the side-position microphone. It is usually bidirectional with each lobe oriented 90 degrees laterally to the sides of the sound source to pick up mostly ambient sound. The outputs of the cardioid and bidirectional capsules are combined into a sum-and-

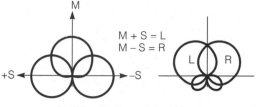

$$M + S = L$$
$$M - S = R$$

(M + S) = L and (M − S) = R
In summed mono [L + R]
the S component disappears
(M + S) + (M − S) = 2M

4-29 M-S pickup pattern and capsule configuration

difference matrix through a controller (see 4-27, 4-28, and 4-29).

The systems in 4-27 and 4-28 make it possible to remote control the ratio of mid-to-side information to adjust the stereo width of the direct-to-ambient sound. It is also possible to produce left-right (XY) information. In addition to its advantage in recording stereo sound, the M-S microphone's matrixed stereo signal is completely mono-compatible (see Chapters 11 and 16).

Soundfield Microphone System

Another concept in multidirectional sound pickup is the **soundfield microphone system**—four capacitor microphone capsules shaped like a tetrahedron and mounted on a single casing. The outputs of the various capsules can be combined into different matrices by using a specially designed control unit (see 4-30 to 4-32). This approach has been given the name **ambisonic** sound, which means the sound can be picked up from all three dimensions. The addition of vertical or height information to the sonic depth and breadth from a single microphone assembly makes sound quite spacious and localization very realistic.

4-30 Soundfield microphone and its control unit

Another microphone system somewhat similar to the soundfield, developed by Digital Arts, is the AGM MR-1. The AGM MR-1 is a complete recording chain that can deliver 20-bit digital, discrete four-channel sound. It consists of the four-capsule microphone and is capable of analog to digital conversion, matrix processing of the four microphone channel signals, stereo reduction encoding, and a variety of two-channel formats at the output.

Boundary Microphones

When a microphone is placed near a reflective surface, such as a wall, floor, or ceiling, time differences between the early-arriving direct waves reaching the mic and the later-arriving indirect waves create a *comb-filter effect*—additive and subtractive phase shifts that give sound an unnatural, hollow coloration (see 4-33). The **boundary micro-**

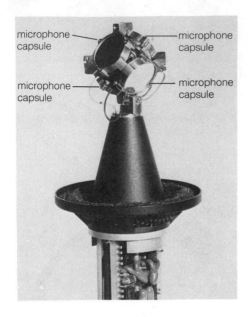

4-31 Four rotating capsules of the soundfield microphone

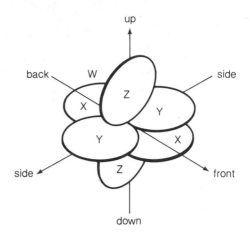

4-32 Pickup arrays of the soundfield microphone system
W = omnidirectional pattern—Left Front + Right Rear + Right Front + Left Rear
X = bidirectional pattern—(front-to-back)
LF + RF − (LR + RR)
Y = bidirectional pattern—(side-to-side)
LF + LR − (RF + RR)
Z = bidirectional pattern—(up-and-down)
LF + RR — (RF + LR)

phone solves this problem by shortening the delay of the reflected sound so that it arrives at the mic at the same time as the direct sound (see 4-34). The boundary, or pressure zone, is defined as the .04- to .08-inch area within which the microphone diaphragm must be placed to move any comb-filter effect out of the audible frequency band.

Most boundary microphones are mounted on rectangular, square, or circular plates. These shapes, and in some cases the microphone mounting itself, tend to create linear distortion in the frequency response. To avoid this problem, some boundary microphones come in a triangular shape with the microphone inset in the plate and off center (see 4-35).

Boundary microphones have an electret transducer. Their pickup pattern is hemispheric, directional, or stereophonic (see 4-36). Their response is open and, in suitable acoustics, spacious.

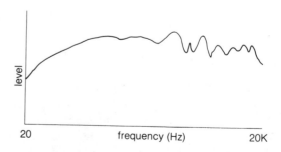

4-33 Comb-filter effect. Delayed reflected sound combined with direct sound can create this effect.

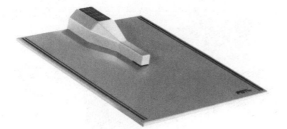

4-34 Boundary microphone

4-35 Triangular-shaped boundary microphone with mic inset into the plate.   This particular configuration is designed to avoid the linear distortion common to some other types of boundary microphones.

Frequency Response

A microphone's frequency response is the range of frequencies that it reproduces at an equal level, within a margin of ± 3 dB. That is, at a given level, a frequency will not vary, louder or quieter by more than 3 dB.

A microphone's *response curve* is displayed in a graph with the vertical line indicating amplitude (dB) and the horizontal line indicating frequency (Hz) (see 4-37). It shows the tonal balance of the microphone pickup at a designated distance from a sound source, usually 2 or 3 feet.

When the curve is reasonably straight or **flat**, response has little coloration; all frequencies are reproduced at the same level.

But flat is not necessarily desirable. In looking at a response curve it is important to know for what purpose the microphone was developed and what your sonic requirements are.

In 4-37, for example, the bass begins "rolling off" at 150 Hz, there is a boost in the high frequencies between 4,000 and 10,000 Hz, and the high end rolls off beyond 10,000 Hz (see the next section). Clearly, this particular microphone would be unsuitable for instruments such as the bass drum, organ, and cello because it is not very sensitive to the lower frequencies from these instruments. It is also unsuitable for high-frequency sound sources, such as the female singing voice, cymbals, and the pic-

4-36 Boundary mics with (*a*) cardioid pickup and (*b*) stereo pickup. The stereo boundary mic is a PZM™ (Pressure Zone Microphone) called SASS™, for Stereo Ambient Sampling System. It uses two boundary-mounted mics, with a foam barrier between them, to make each mic directional.

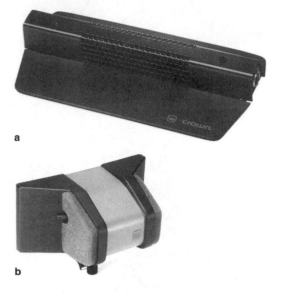

a

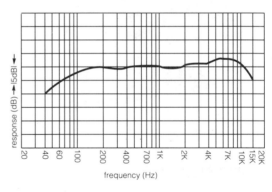

b

colo, because it is not that sensitive to their higher frequencies or harmonics. The microphone, however, was not designed for these purposes—it was designed for the speaking voice. And for this purpose it is excellent. Reproduction of frequencies through the critical upper bass and midrange is flat, the slight boost in the upper midrange adds presence, and the roll-offs in the bass and treble are beyond the ranges of most speaking voices.

Sound Response

A number of sound response characteristics provide important information about a microphone's sound quality. They are frequency response, proximity effect, overload, maximum sound pressure level, sensitivity, self-noise, signal-to-noise ratio, and humbucking.

Proximity Effect

When most bidirectional and unidirectional microphones are placed close to a sound source, bass frequencies increase in level rel-

4-37 Response curve of the Electro-Voice 635A mic

ative to midrange and treble frequencies. This response is known as **proximity effect** or *bass tip-up* (see 4-38).

Proximity effect is most pronounced in pressure-gradient (ribbon) microphones—mics in which both sides of the diaphragm are exposed to incident sound. Response is generated by the pressure differential, or gradient, between the sound that reaches the front of the diaphragm relative to the sound that reaches the rear of the diaphragm. As

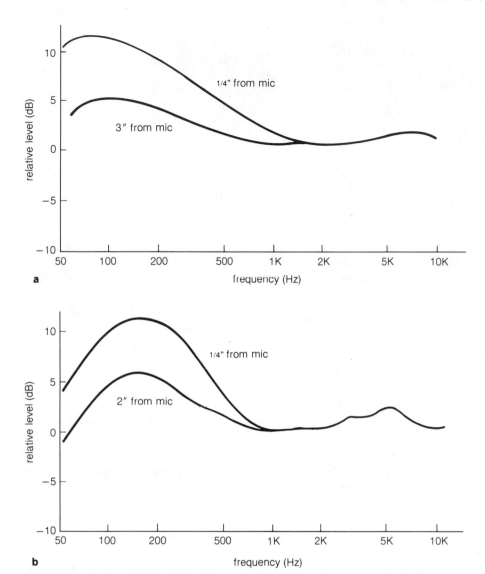

4-38 Proximity effect: (*a*) a typical cardioid moving-coil mic and (*b*) a cardioid capacitor mic.

mic-to-source distance decreases, acoustic pressure on the diaphragm increases. Because pressure is greater at lower frequencies and the path between the front and rear of the diaphragm is short, bass response rises.

Response of directional microphones is, in part, pressure-gradient and, therefore,

also susceptible to proximity effect, but not to the extent of ribbon mics. Omnidirectional microphones are not subject to proximity effect.

Proximity effect can be a blessing or a curse, depending on the situation. For example, in close-miking a bass drum, cello, or

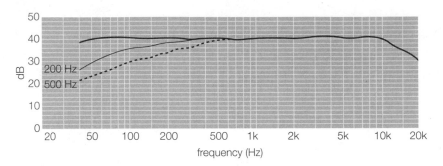

4-39 Bass roll-off curves of the microphone in Figure 4-22

thin-sounding voice, proximity effect can add power or solidity to the sound source. Where a singer with a deep bass voice works close to the mic, proximity effect can increase boominess, masking middle and high frequencies.

To neutralize unwanted proximity effect (rumble, or 60-cycle hum), most microphones susceptible to the proximity effect include the feature, called **bass roll-off**, of a limited in-mic equalizer (see 4-22). When turned on (switch is in one of these positions: ⌐ or /), the roll-off attenuates bass frequencies several decibels from a certain point and below, depending on the microphone, thereby canceling or reducing any proximity effect (see 4-39).

Because bass roll-off has so many advantages, it has become a common feature even on microphones that have little or no proximity effect. In some models bass roll-off has been extended to include several different frequency settings at which attenuation can occur or different levels of attenuation at the same roll-off frequency (see 4-40 and 4-41).

Another way to reduce proximity effect is to use a multiple-entry directional microphone, because these mics have some distance between the rear-entry low-frequency ports and the sound source. At close mic-to-source distances, however, most multiple-

entry microphones have some proximity effect.

To avoid proximity effect at close working distances down to a few inches, directional microphones have been designed that are frequency independent. Such mics use two transducers, one to process high frequencies, the other to process low frequencies. This *two-way system* design also produces a more linear response at the sides of the microphone.

Sometimes, a greater-than-normal proximity effect is desirable. For this reason, single-entry directional microphones with extended increase in the bass are often used to enhance bass frequencies further (see 4-42).

Overload

All microphones will distort if sound levels are too high—a condition identified as **overload**—but some mics handle it better than others. Moving-coil and capacitor microphones are not as vulnerable to distortion caused by excessive loudness as are ribbon mics. Moving-coil mics can take high levels of loudness without internal damage. Do not use ribbon mics when there may be overload, however, for you risk damaging the element.

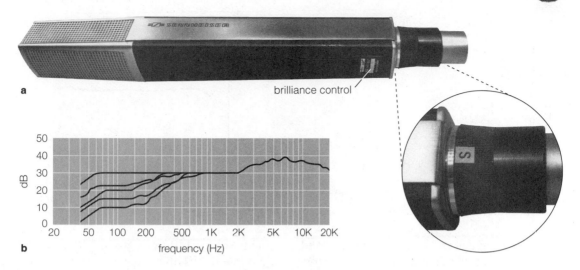

brilliance control

4-40 (*a*) **Five-position roll-off control and** (*b*) **its effect on bass response.** S = Speech, M (not shown) = Music. This particular microphone also has a brilliance control. The response curve in (*b*) shows the curve when the high-frequency boost is switched into the pickup.

Front   Back

4-41 Microphone with 16 different low-frequency response adjustments

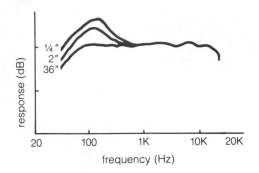

4-42 Proximity effect of the single-entry microphone shown in Figure 4-11

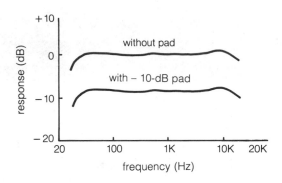

4-43 Effect of a –10 dB pad on response

In the capacitor system, although loud sound pressure levels may not create distortion at the diaphragm, the output signal may be great enough to overload the electronics in the mic. To prevent this, many capacitors contain a built-in pad. Switching the pad into the mic system eliminates overload distortion of the mic's preamp, thereby reducing the output signal several decibels (see 4-22).

A pad and a bass roll-off are not the same. A bass roll-off attenuates only the low frequencies and is found on all three types of professional microphones. A pad, which is found on many capacitor mics, reduces the overall microphone level (see 4-43).

Maximum Sound Pressure Level

Maximum sound pressure level (SPL) is the level at which a microphone's output signal begins to distort, that is, produces a 3 percent *total harmonic distortion (THD)*. **Harmonic distortion** occurs when an audio system introduces harmonics into the output signal that were not present originally. If a microphone has a maximum sound pressure level of 120 dB-SPL, it means that the mic will audibly distort when the level of a sound source reaches 120 dB-SPL. A maxi-

mum SPL of 120 dB is good, 135 dB is very good, and 150 dB is excellent.

Sensitivity

Sensitivity measures the voltage a microphone produces (dBV), which indicates a microphone's efficiency. Sensitivity does not affect a mic's sound quality, but it can affect a recording's overall sound quality. The lower the output voltage, the less sensitive the microphone. The less sensitive the microphone, the closer it has to be to a sound source to maintain decent signal-to-noise ratio (see the "Signal-to-Noise Ratio" section) or the more level gain the signal needs at the console, or both. Increased level often means increased noise. Ribbon and small moving-coil mics have low sensitivity (–85 dBV); larger moving-coil mics have medium sensitivity (–75 dBV); capacitor mics have high sensitivity (–65 dBV).

Self-Noise

Self-noise is the electrical noise, or hiss, a microphone (or any electronic device) produces. Self-noise measurement is in dB-SPL, A-weighted. A fair self-noise rating is around 40 dB-SPL; a good rating is around 30 dB-SPL; an excellent rating is 20 dB-SPL or less.

Signal-to-Noise Ratio

Signal-to-noise ratio (S/N) is the difference between the signal and the noise levels in an electronic component.[*] In relation to microphones, S/N is actually not a ratio but a difference between sound pressure level and self-noise. For example, if the microphone's SPL is 94 dB and the self-noise is 30 dB-SPL, the signal-to-noise ratio is 64 dB. The higher the S/N, the more noise-free the signal. An S/N of 64 dB is fair, 74 dB is good, and 84 dB and higher is excellent.

Humbucking

Humbucking is not so much a response characteristic as it is a feature built into many microphones. Hum is an ever-present concern in audio, in general, and in microphone pickup, in particular. To minimize this problem microphones are designed with a **humbuck circuit**—a circuit that reduces hum by several dBs. It is built into the microphone system and requires no special operation to activate it.

The amount of hum reduction varies with the microphone. The information is included in the *specification sheet* that comes with each microphone, as does most of the information discussed so far. As with all printed information about audio equipment, however, use it only as a guideline; use your ears to determine how much hum is getting through.

---

[*]The difference between the sound a sound system records or reproduces and the inherent system noise generated must be as great as possible. This difference is known as *signal-to-noise (S/N) ratio* and is measured in decibels. Most professional audio systems have S/N ratios of at least 55 to 1. (Some are as wide as 96 to 1.) This means that it is possible to produce 55 dB of signal when the system generates 1 dB of noise. S/N ratios actually are expressed in negative numbers; hence, an S/N ratio of −55 to 1 is better than an S/N ratio of −50 to 1.

Microphone Accessories

Microphones come with various accessories. The most commonly used are windscreens and pop filters, shock mounts, cables, connectors, and microphone mounts.

Windscreens and Pop Filters

A **windscreen** and **pop filter** are designed to deal with distortion that results from blowing sounds caused by breathing and wind, the sudden attack of transients, the hiss of sibilant consonants like "s" and "ch", and the popping plosives of consonants like "p" and "b". (In practice, the terms *windscreen* and *pop filter* are used interchangeably, but for clarity of discussion here they have been given slightly different significance.)

Windscreens are mounted externally and reduce the distortion from blowing and popping but rarely eliminate it from particularly strong sounds (see 4-44). A pop filter is built in and most effective against blowing sounds and popping (see 4-45). It allows very close microphone placement to a sound source, with little risk of this type of distortion.

Windscreens also slightly affect response, somewhat reducing the crispness of high frequencies. Many directional microphones with pop filters are designed with a high-frequency boost to compensate for reduced treble response.

Pop filters are found mainly in moving-coil, newer ribbon, and some capacitor microphones. Unidirectional models in particular need pop filters; because of their partial pressure-gradient response, they are more susceptible to breath and popping noise than are omnidirectional mics. (They are also more likely to be used closer to a sound source than are other mic types.) An omnidirectional mic is about 15 dB less sensitive to wind noise and popping than a unidirectional microphone of similar size.

a   b

4-44 Windscreens. (*a*) Various windscreens for conventional microphones. (*b*) Stocking (fabric) windscreen designed for use between the sound source and the microphone.

pop filter

4-45 Built-in pop filter

Another way to minimize distortion from sibilance, transients, blowing sounds, and popping is through microphone placement. These techniques are discussed in Chapter 12).

Shock Mounts

Because solid objects are excellent sound conductors, the danger always exists that unwanted vibrations will travel through the mic stand to the microphone. To reduce noises induced by vibration, you should place the mic in a **shock mount**—a device that suspends and mechanically isolates the microphone from the stand (see 4-46). Some microphones are designed with a shock absorber built in.

Cable

Microphone cable is either **balanced**—consisting of two conductors and a shield—or **unbalanced**—consisting of one conductor with the shield serving as the second conductor. As with all professional equipment, the balanced line is preferred because it is less susceptible to electric noise.

4-46 Various types of shock mounts. See also Figure 4-22.

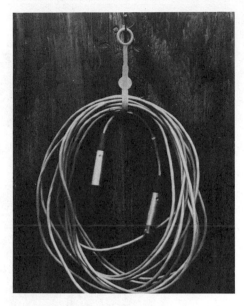

4-47 Microphone cable. To keep cable intact and avoid damage to internal wires and connections, wind and secure it when not in use.

When winding mic cable, do not wind it around your arm, and be careful not to make the angle of the wrap too severe or it can damage the internal wires. It is also a good idea to secure the cable with a clasp especially made for this purpose to prevent it from getting tangled (see 4-47).

Connectors

Most professional mics and mic cable use a three-pin plug that terminates the two conductors and shield of the balanced line. These plugs are generally called **XLR connectors** (X is the ground or shield, L is the lead wire, and R is the return wire). Usually, the female plug on the microphone cable connects to the mic and the three-prong male plug connects to the console (see 4-48).

It is always important to make sure the three pins in all microphones being used in a session are connected exactly the same. If pin 1 is ground, pin 2 is positive, and pin 3 is negative, all mics must be wired in the same configuration; otherwise the mismatched microphones will be electrically out of polarity and will reduce or null audio level.

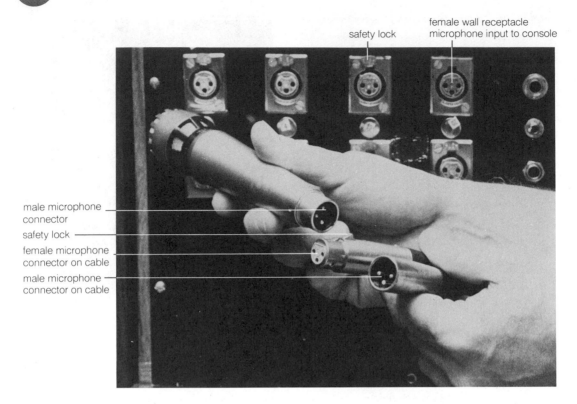

safety lock

female wall receptacle
microphone input to console

male microphone
connector

safety lock

female microphone
connector on cable

male microphone
connector on cable

4-48 Microphone connectors. The female cable connector plugs into the male microphone connector; the male cable connector plugs into the female wall receptacle, which is connected to the microphone input on the console.

Microphone Mounts

Just as there are many types of microphones to meet a variety of needs, many types of microphone mounts (stands) are available for just about every possible application. The more commonly used microphone mounts in studio music recording sessions are displayed in Figures 4-49 to 4-51.

Microphone Care

Poor care of audio equipment adversely affects sound quality—this cannot be stressed enough. Moisture from high humid-

ity or breath can greatly shorten a microphone's life. When moisture is a problem, a windscreen will help protect the microphone element.

Dirt, oil from hands, cigarette smoke, and jarring also reduce microphone efficiency. Microphones should be cleaned and serviced regularly and kept in carrying cases when not in use. Microphones left on stands between sessions should be covered with a cloth or plastic bag but not so tightly as to create a condensation problem. The working environment should be temperature and humidity controlled, kept clean, and vacuumed.

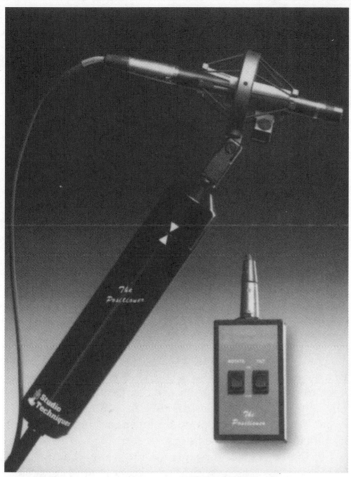

4-49 Special microphone mounts: (*a*) stereo microphone mount, (*b*) remote panner mount and control module.

a

b

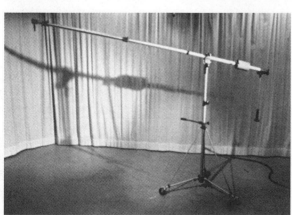

4-51 Boom

4-50 Floor stands

CONSOLES

If the control room can be considered the heart of a sound studio, then the mixing console or **board** is the nerve center. At the console, signals flowing from microphones, electric and electronic musical instruments, and tape recorders are amplified, balanced, combined, monitored, and routed for recording. All consoles perform these basic functions.

They may also perform additional functions, such as **equalization**—altering a sound's harmonic structure; stereo panning—positioning sound in a left-to-right spatial perspective between two loudspeakers; reverb send and return—feeding sound to and retrieving it from an external reverberation source; limiting and compressing—controlling a sound's dynamic range; inboard **patching**—rerouting assigned signal paths within the console; computer-assisted operation; and all-digital signal processing. As this list suggests, consoles vary in complexity, from the comparatively straightforward consoles used in radio broadcasting to the elaborate multichannel production consoles used in music recording.

At first glance the more elaborate consoles, with their dozens, sometimes hundreds, of controls, may appear intimidating. But regardless of design, most multichannel recording consoles have two things in common: four control sections—input, output, master, and monitor—and a prescribed signal flow. Signals from a sound source, such as the microphone, feed to the **input section,** which routes them to the output section. The **output section** routes the signals to the multitrack tape recorder. The **master section** contains, among other things, the master output bus(es) that route the final mix (for

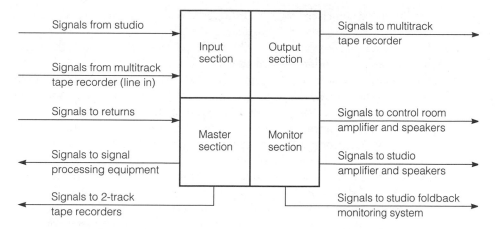

Signals from studio →	Input section	Output section	→ Signals to multitrack tape recorder
Signals from multitrack tape recorder (line in) →			
Signals to returns →	Master section	Monitor section	→ Signals to control room amplifier and speakers
← Signals to signal processing equipment			→ Signals to studio amplifier and speakers
← Signals to 2-track tape recorders			→ Signals to studio foldback monitoring system

5-1 Generalized diagram of the four sections of a split-section console and their input and output feeds

example, 2-mix, for stereo) to the two-channel tape recorder. The **monitor system** enables the signals to be heard (see 5-1). Once you understand the signal flow of each system and how they interrelate, learning console operation is relatively straightforward. Of course, the more complex the console design, the more time it takes to master.

Analog Multichannel Production Consoles

The basic differences between the analog and the digital production console are in the way signals are processed and routed. These differences are more easily explained once the operational features of the analog multichannel production console are understood.

In-Line Versus Split-Section Consoles

In the first generation of multichannel production consoles, the input, output, master, and monitor sections were separate. Such consoles are referred to as **split-section consoles**. Today, multichannel recording consoles combine several input/output functions into one input/output (I/O) section. These consoles are called **in-line consoles** because signal flow in the input and output sections has been brought vertically "in a line." The design change greatly improved recording consoles functionally and ergonomically.

The multichannel console was developed to permit greater sonic control over individual sound sources. Its evolution also goes hand in hand with the development of the multitrack audiotape recorder (see Chapters 6 and 7). As the multitrack tape recorder became capable of handling more and more tracks, the multichannel console had to be expanded to process additional channels of information.

In a multichannel recording session it is customary to record a separate sound source on each track of a multitrack tape recorder. Often during recording, little, if anything, is done to the sound by way of equalization (EQ), panning, reverberation, and other signal processing. Signal processing more often occurs during **mixdown** when all tracks are combined into one (mono), two (stereo), or more tracks. During recording, therefore, some of the console may go unused.

Moreover, with a split-section console, if a producer wishes to get an idea of how something will sound with equalization, for example, without being recorded, the appropriate module must be patched to the monitor system—a procedure that can be time-consuming and cumbersome (see "Patching" later in this chapter). Unless the module is patched, the signal and the processing will be routed to the master output and recorded because effects can only be routed into the signal flow of the input module, or bypassed.

Furthermore, if a split-section console has, say, 24 inputs and 16 master outputs, in most recording sessions it would be rare that all master outputs would be used at the same time even if all inputs were used simultaneously. For example, if 24 inputs were mixed—assigning 2 to each master output, which would be unlikely because usually a master output is used to mix more than 2 inputs—it would require just 12 master outputs. This leaves 4 unused master outputs in a 16-output console. Because the 24 inputs are usually fed directly to the 24 separate tracks of the multitrack tape recorder, there is little need for the master outputs during recording. Thus, during multitrack recording, the master outputs are just taking up space.

The in-line console solves both the wasted space and signal delegation problems by combining the various functions of the input and output sections into a single input-output (I/O) section. Each I/O section contains one input and one output module. The I/O design makes it possible to route a signal from, say, the input of I/O channel 4 either directly to track 4 of the multitrack tape recorder or to the master output(s). The signal is then routed back into channel 4's input section, passing through the equalizer (and/or other effects modules) for delegation (if desired) to either the monitor section or the master section. Such signal routing is possible during both recording and mixdown.

In other words, the I/O section EQ and other signal processing can be delegated to the monitor system for auditioning without affecting the signal being sent to the multitrack tape recorder. At the mixdown, the output from the I/O section can be delegated to feed a signal from the multitrack tape recorder to the mono, stereo, or more master outputs. The in-line console, therefore, requires only a few master outputs rather than 8, 16, or 24.

Input/Output Specifications

Two indications of a console's layout and capabilities are the number of input sources it can accommodate at the same time and the number of discrete signals it can output at its master bus. A **bus** is a common junction of several different signal paths. Consoles are often specified by their number of inputs and master outputs. For example, a 6 × 1 (or 6-in, 1-out) console has 6 inputs and 1 master output; a 6 × 2 (or 6-in, 2-out), 6 inputs and 2 master outputs; a 32 × 16 (or 32-in, 16-out), 32 inputs and 16 master outputs. Clearly, a 6 × 1 console is limited to situations requiring few sound sources to input and one-channel, or **monophonic** (*mono*), output. A 6 × 2 console is still limited to a few sound sources, but it is capable of a two-channel, or **stereophonic** (*stereo*), output. By contrast, a 32 × 16 split-section console could be used for most large-scale recording assignments requiring any number of input/output configurations. In-line recording consoles may have a three-number specification, such as 36 × 8 × 2, which indicates 36 inputs, 8 submasters (for submixes, in which selected I/O channels are combined before they reach the master outputs, where all signals are combined), and 2 master outputs.

The In-Line Console

Although features of the in-line console differ from model to model, the basic design includes four main sections—input/output, master, monitor, and communications. Each section, however, may include some functions belonging to another section. Instead of input, output, and monitor functions being grouped in discrete sections, they are scattered around the multichannel recording console. For example, the I/O section, in addition to its input and output controls, includes selected monitor controls as well.

In-Line Console Functions

Most multichannel in-line recording consoles share certain typical functions. Some consoles may have fewer or more features and, depending on the design and manufacturer, the sequence of functions, signal flow, and terminology may differ somewhat. Following is a description of the typical functions of the four main sections of in-line recording consoles.

Input/Output Section

During recording, the input/output section processes and delegates incoming signals and sends them out to the multitrack tape recorder. During mixdown, the I/O section processes signals from the multitrack tape recorder and routes them to the master section where they are combined into one (mono), two (stereo), or more channels and sent to the master tape recorder.

■ *Microphone-line input selector.* Generally, two types of signal sources are fed to input modules: low-level, such as microphones, and high-level, such as tape recorders. The microphone-line input selector controls which signal source enters the input section.

■ *Microphone preamplifier.* A microphone signal entering the console is weak. It requires a mic preamplifier to increase its voltage to a usable level.

A word about mic preamps in consoles. Whether the audio is analog or digital, each component in the signal flow must be as noise-free as possible. Given the low-noise, high-sensitivity, and high-SPL specifications of many of today's microphones, it is important that the mic preamp be capable of handling a mic's output without strain. If the console's preamp is inadequate to meet this requirement, then it is necessary to use an outboard mic preamp.

Inboard or outboard, a good-quality mic preamp must deliver high gain, low circuit noise (hiss), high *Common-Mode Rejection Ratio* (CMRR)—the ratio between signal gain and interference rejection—freedom from radio-frequency (RF) interference, and freedom from ground-induced buzz or hum.

Console preamps may be located many feet from a microphone. The more circuitry a signal navigates, the greater the chance for increased noise. Placing a mic preamp in close proximity to a microphone and amplifying mic signals to the required levels before they travel very far dramatically reduces noise. A mic preamp should be stable at very low and/or very high gain settings. CMRR values should be at least 80–90 dB at crucial frequencies, such as 50–60 Hz, and above 10 kHz, not just at 1 kHz, the only frequency at which many mic preamps are measured.

- *Phantom power*. Just ahead of the microphone preamplifier is the **phantom power supply** (48 volts DC). When activated it provides voltage for capacitor mics, thus eliminating the need to bother with batteries.

- *Trim*. The **trim** is a gain control that changes the input sensitivities to accommodate the nominal input levels of various input sources. Trim boosts the lower-level sources to usable proportions or prevents overload distortion in higher-level sources.

- *Overload indicator*. The **overload indicator** is a light-emitting diode (LED) that flashes when the input signal is approaching or has reached overload and is clipping. In some consoles the LED flashes green when the input signal is peaking in the safe range, and red either to indicate clipping or to warn of impending clipping.

- *Pad*. A **pad** reduces the power of a signal. On a console it is placed ahead of the mic input transformer to prevent overload distortion of the transformer and mic preamplifier. It is used when the trim, by itself, cannot prevent overload in the mic signal. The pad should not be used otherwise because it reduces signal-to-noise ratio.

- Channel assignment switches. This is a group of switches on each I/O channel used to direct the signal from that channel to one or more outputs; or several input signals can be combined and sent to one output. For example, assume three different microphone signals are routed separately to channels 1, 3, and 11 and the recordist wishes to direct them all to channel 18. By pressing assignment switch 18 on channels 1, 3, and 11, the recordist can feed the signals to channel 18's active combining network and then on to tape track 18. An active combining network (ACN) is an amplifier at which the outputs of two or more signal paths are mixed together to feed a single track of a tape recorder. To save space, the assignment switches are sometimes paired, either alternately—1 and 3, 2 and 4, and so on—or adjacently—1 and 2, 3 and 4, and so on. Usually odd numbers are left channels and even numbers are right channels.

- *Direct switch*. The direct switch connects the channel signal to the channel output, directing the signal to its own track on the tape recorder, bypassing the channel ACN and thus reducing noise. For example, using the direct switch routes the signal on, say, channel 1 to tape track 1, the

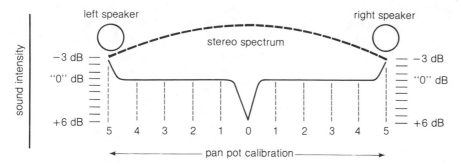

left speaker

right speaker

stereo spectrum

sound intensity

−3 dB —
"0" dB —
+6 dB —

−3 dB
"0" dB
+6 dB

5   4   3   2   1   0   1   2   3   4   5

← pan pot calibration →

5-2 Pan pot's effect on sound placement. Values for sound intensity and calibration will vary with the console.

signal on channel 2 to tape track 2, and so on.

■ *Equalizer and filter.* An **equalizer** is an electronic device that alters a signal's frequency response by boosting or attenuating selected portions of the audio spectrum. A **filter** alters frequency response by attenuating frequencies above, below, or at a preset point. Most production consoles have separate equalizer controls for selected frequencies grouped in the low, middle, and high ranges. Filters are usually high-pass and low-pass. (Equalizers and filters are discussed in Chapter 8.)

■ *Channel/monitor control.* The channel/monitor control switches the equalizer, and usually selected *send* functions (see below), into either the channel signal path to the tape recorder or the monitor signal path to the monitor section.

■ *Polarity reversal control.* **Polarity** (sometimes referred to as *phase*) **reversal** is a control that inverts the polarity of an input signal 180 degrees. It is used to reverse the polarity of miswired equipment, usually microphones, whose signal

is out of phase with the signal from a piece of similar equipment correctly wired. Sometimes, intentional polarity reversal is helpful in canceling leakage from adjacent microphones or in creating electroacoustic special effects by mixing together out-of-phase signals from mics picking up the same sound source.

■ *Pan pot.* A **pan pot** (short for *panoramic potentiometer*) is a control that can shift the proportion of sound to any point from left to right between two output buses and, hence, between the two loudspeakers necessary for reproducing a stereo image (see 5-2). A **potentiometer**, or **pot** (rhymes with hot), is a device that regulates the level coming from a preamp. If you want the signal louder in one bus than in the other, the pan pot varies the relative levels being fed to each of the two output buses. This facilitates the positioning of a sound source at a particular place in the stereo field between two loudspeakers.

■ *Cue send (pre- or postfader).* Cue send is a monitor function that routes a signal from an input channel to the headphone, or foldback, system. **Foldback** is a monitor system that feeds signals from the console to the headphones. The cue-send volume control adjusts the level of the headphone signal before it is sent to the master cue sends in the monitor module.

At the input channel the cue send can be assigned before or after the channel fader. Before, or prefader cue, means that the volume control at cue send is the only one affecting the channel's cue send level. After, or postfader cue, means that the main channel fader also affects the cue-send level. In the postfader mode the volume control at cue send is still operational but the main channel fader overrides it.

Pre- and postfader controls add flexibility by providing a suitable headphone mix to performing musicians. For example, if the musicians were satisfied with their headphone mix and did not want to hear channel-fader adjustments being made during recording, cue send would be switched to the prefader mode. On the other hand, if the musicians did want to hear changes in level at the channel fader, cue send would be switched to the postfader mode.

■ *Reverb (or echo) send (effects send, aux send) (pre- or postfader)*. The reverb send control feeds the input signal to an external reverberation system (see Chapter 8). Some consoles call this feature *echo send*. But echo is a misnomer because reverberation, not echo, is the effect usually being achieved.

After the "dry" reverb send signal reaches the reverb system, reverb is added and it returns "wet" to the reverb return in the master section for mixing with the main output. The wet signal may also feed to a monitor return system.

Reverb send may be called *effects send* or *aux* (for *auxiliary*) *send*. Regardless of what this function is called, it can be used to send an input signal to a reverb system or to another external signal processor. Moreover, it can be used to create a submix if the console lacks a submaster section.

The send function also has pre- and postfader controls. Therefore, any signal can be sent from before or after the channel fader.

■ *Solo and prefader listen (PFL)*. Feeding different sounds through several channels at once can create an inconvenience if you want to hear one of them to check something. It is not necessary to shut off or turn down all the channels except the one you want to hear, however, because each input module has a **solo** control. Activating it automatically cuts off all other channels feeding the monitor system; the solo has no effect on the output system. More than one solo can be pushed to audition several channels at once and still cut off the unwanted channels.

The solo function is usually prefader. On some consoles, therefore, it is called **prefader listen** (*PFL*). In consoles with both solo and prefader listen functions, PFL is prefader and solo is postfader.

■ *Mute (channel on/off)*. The mute function, also called *channel on/off*, turns off the signals from the I/O channel. During mixdown when no sound is feeding through an input channel for the moment, it shuts it down or mutes it. This prevents unwanted channel noise from reaching the outputs.

■ *Channel and monitor faders*. The channel and monitor **fader** controls are pots, sliding or rotary: one to control the channel

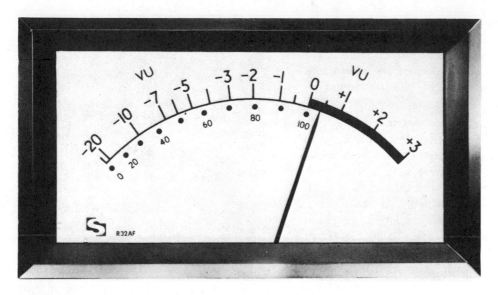

5-3 Volume unit (VU) meter

level of the signal being recorded, the other to control its monitor level. (A fader, or pot, may also be called an *attenuator*, or *gain* or *volume control*.) During recording, channel levels to the multitrack recorder are set for optimal signal-to-noise ratio. That is, levels are set to reach or slightly exceed 0 VU (see Meters, next item). Level balances are made during mixdown. To enable the recordist to get a sense of what the balanced levels will sound like, the monitor faders are adjusted to taste, with no effect on the sig-nal being recorded. Most consoles have a control that, if desired, reverses the assigned channel and monitor fader functions.

■ *Meters.* Most multichannel production consoles have a volume indicator for each input channel to indicate the level (voltage) of the postfader signal. The meter most commonly used in this country is the **volume unit (VU) meter** (see 5-3).

The VU meter is uniquely suited to the sound medium. Unlike most devices that measure voltage, the VU meter responds to changes in electric energy in a mammer similar to the way that the human ear responds to changes in acoustic energy. It "perceives" average sound level rather than momentary peaks. Its unit of measurement is the *volume unit*, which is closely related to the ear's subjective impression of loudness.

Two calibrated scales are on the face of the VU meter: a percentage of modulation scale and a volume unit scale. A needle, the volume indicator, moves back and forth across the scales, pointing out the levels. Some consoles use light-emitting diodes, or so-called plasma or bar graph displays, instead (see 5-18). Both the needle and the light-emitting diodes respond to the electric energy passing through the

VU meter. If the energy level is excessively high, the volume indicator will **pin**—slam against the meter's extreme right-hand side. Pinning can damage the VU meter's mechanism, rendering the volume indicator's reading unreliable.

Percentage of modulation is the percentage of an applied signal in relation to the maximum signal a sound system can handle. It is a linear scale defined such that 100 percent of modulation is equal to 0 VU on the volume-unit scale. Therefore, 30 percent of modulation is equal to slightly less than −10 VU, 80 percent of modulation is equal to −2 VU, and so on.

Any sound below 20 percent of modulation is too quiet or **in the mud**, and levels above 100 percent of modulation are too loud or **in the red**. (The scale to the right of 100 percent is red.) As a guideline, the loudness should "kick" between about −5 and +1, although the dynamics of music make such evenness difficult to accomplish, if not aesthetically undesirable. Usually, the best that can be done is to **ride the gain**—adjust the faders from time to time so that, on average, the level stays out of the mud or the red.

The operator should ride the gain with a light, fluid hand and not jerk the faders up and down or make adjustments at the slightest fall or rise in loudness. Changes in level should be smooth and imperceptible because abrupt changes are disconcerting to the listener. (There may be exceptions to this when trying to compensate for different levels when *punching in* [see Chapters 13 and 14], which may require rapid fader movements to avoid use of additional compression.)

When the VU meter is in the red, it is a warning to be cautious of loudness distor-

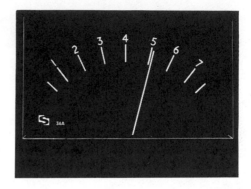

5-4 Peak program meter. A reading of 6 on a ppm is equivalent to 100 percent of modulation on a VU meter. Each scale increment represents a level difference of 4 dB, so that the scale range is −20 dB to +4 dB, if 6 is 0 level. Dual movement ppms with two indicators are for two-channel stereo applications.

tion. All modern consoles are designed with headroom so that a signal peaking a few dB above 0 VU will not distort. **Headroom** is the signal level equipment can take, above working level, before overload occurs. The problem is that although the console may have sufficient headroom, other equipment in the sound chain, such as the tape recorder, may not be able to handle the additional level. (In digital recording there is no such thing as headroom. When you have run out of room, there is nothing left.)

Another instrument used for measuring loudness is the **peak program meter** (**ppm**)—a device with faster ballistics than a VU meter that indicates peaks in level rather than averages (see 5-4). It is used in Europe, and many think it gives a more accurate indication of a signal's actual level of loudness than does the VU meter. The argument is that although humans may not hear momentary peaks in loudness, the electronics do. Therefore, the peak program meter is better insurance against signal distortion. The ppm is calibrated in decibels, not volume units. Some consoles have both VU and ppm meters.

Master Section

The master section contains the master controls for the mixing bus outputs, reverb send and reverb return, master fader, and other functions.

- *Master buses.* After a signal leaves an input/output module it travels to its assigned bus(es). In many consoles these signals may be grouped for premixing at submaster buses before being finally combined at the master bus(es).

  For example, a submaster may be used to group the various input channels dedicated to backup vocals, drums, or keyboards before they are all combined at the master bus(es). There may be any number of submaster buses, but usually there are only a few master buses because most final output signals are mixed down to two-channel stereo or four-channel surround-sound.

- *Master fader.* The master fader controls the signal level from the master bus to the master tape recorder. Generally, it is configured as either a single fader carrying a tandem stereo signal, or a stereo output pair carrying the left and right signals. A console may have two such faders or sets of faders and a mono master fader as well.

- *Reverb (or echo) send (effects send, aux send).* The reverb sends from the I/O channels are first routed to the master reverb sends before being output to the reverb unit or other signal processor.

- *Reverb (or echo) return (effects return, aux return).* Signals routed to the reverb unit, or other signal processor, from the master sends are returned at the master returns and mixed with the main program signal.

- *Level, mute, PFL, solo, and pan pot.* Each master reverb send and return usually has a level control and mute switch. The master returns also usually have PFL, solo, and pan controls.

- *Meters.* Most in-line recording consoles have a VU meter (and/or peak program meter) for each master fader; a mono meter to indicate the level of a summed stereo signal; a phase meter to show the phase relationship between the left and right stereo signals; and metering to display master send and/or return levels. Some consoles also have meters for the control room monitor outputs.

Monitor Section

Monitor functions, such as setting monitor level and panning for each channel, are performed by the I/O module. The monitor module, among other things, allows monitoring of the line or tape input, selects various inputs to the control room and studio monitors, and controls their levels.

- *Line-in/line-out switch.* This switch selects all the I/O channels for either line-input monitoring from the multitrack tape recorder or line-out monitoring from console channel out. Each I/O channel has a line-in/line-out control for individual channel switching, but the monitor line-in/line-out overrides the channel control.

- *Tape select switches*. These switches select a tape recorder (other than multitrack) for direct feed to the monitor system bypassing the I/O controls. There may also be auxiliary (aux) in switches for direct feeds to the monitor system from other sound sources such as a CD player and cassette tape recorder.

- *Send switches*. These switches route signals from the sends to the input of the control room or studio monitors, or both.

- *Mix switches*. These switches select the mix input, that is, mono or stereo, for the monitor system.

- *Speaker select switches*. These switches select the control room or studio loudspeakers for monitoring. There is a level control for each set of loudspeakers. Some monitor sections also have a *dim* switch for the control room monitors. Instead of having to turn the monitor level down and up during control room conversation, the operator can use the dim function to reduce monitor level by 15 dB or more at the touch of a button.

- *Mono switch*. This switch directs a summed mono signal to the control room monitors.

A monitor section may also have a pan pot, mutes for the left and right channel signals to the control room, and a phase coherence switch. The *phase coherence* switch inverts the left channel signal before it combines with the right channel signal. If the stereo signals are in phase, sound quality should suffer and, in particular, the sonic images in the center (between the two loudspeakers) should be severely attenuated. If the phase coherence check improves the mono signal, then there is a problem with the stereo signal's mono-compatibility.

Communications Section

As the terms suggests, the communications section facilitates control room–studio communication. It also contains the modules used for cueing and equipment calibration.

- *Talkback*. The talkback permits the recordist in the control room to speak into a console microphone to the musicians in the studio. The talkback may be directed through the studio monitor, headphones, or slate system (see the next item). Some consoles also have a direct talkback output to the conductor.

- *Slate/talkback*. Most consoles have a talkback to communicate with persons in the studio. Multichannel consoles also have a *slate* feature that automatically feeds to the recording tape anything said through the talkback. It is a convenient way to transcribe information about the name of the recording, the artist, the number of the cut (*take*), and so on.

- *Oscillator*. An **oscillator** is a signal generator that produces pure tones or sine waves (sound waves with no harmonics or overtones) at selected frequencies. On a console it is used to (1) calibrate the console with the tape recorder so their meters indicate the same levels and (2) put reference tone levels on tape recordings (see Chapters 13 and 16).

- *Patch bay*. The inputs and outputs of console components are wired to jacks in the **patch bay**—a central routing terminal—to facilitate the routing of sound through pathways not provided in the normal console design. (See "Patching" later in this chapter.)

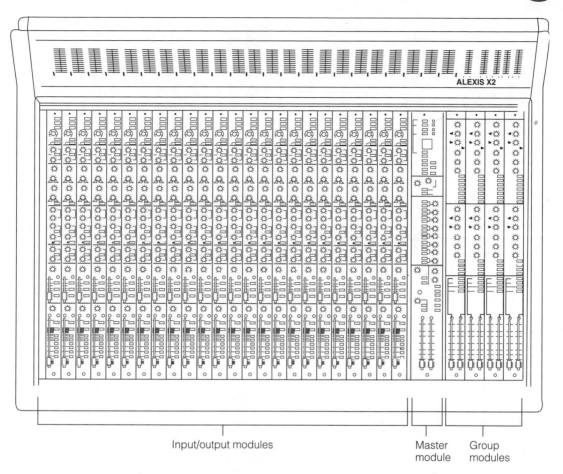

ALEXIS X2

Input/output modules

Master module

Group modules

5-5a Example of a basic in-line console

In-Line Console Flowcharts

As noted earlier, in-line consoles differ in their array of features, complexity, and signal flow. Figure 5-5 should give you an idea of how their basic modules function and interrelate. The purpose of Figure 5-6 is to correlate the functions of selected modules in Figure 5-5b to the way they are symbol-

ized in a flowchart. Learning how to read a flowchart helps you to master console operation more quickly. It also helps you track down operational problems when they occur. However, flowcharts vary in technical complexity. The diagrams a technician requires to install a console are quite different from those a nontechnical person needs to understand signal flow.

Input/output module

Individual **phantom power** switch

Mic/Line switch (both balanced)

Phase reverse on Mic/Line

Mic/Line Gain (60dB range)

Channel/Monitor Reverse:
Selects the source (Tape, or Mic/Line) for both channel and monitor

High-pass filter, 75 Hz

Parametric Equalization

Hi EQ: Shelving type, 12 kHz

EQ to Mon: Patches the shelving EQ into the monitor path

Lo EQ: Shelving type, 80 Hz

Hi Mid Gain: 15 dB

Frequency: 650 Hz to 15 kHz

Bandwidth adjustable 1/6 to 2 octaves

Low Mid Gain: 15dB

Frequency: 45 Hz–950 Hz

Bandwidth adjustable 1/6 to 2 octaves

EQ In: Bypasses channel EQ

Auxiliary Sends

Aux 1-2: A prefader, post-EQ stereo send

Pan: For Aux 1-2

Aux 3/7: Postfader (effect) send

7/8: Assigns Aux 3/4 to Aux 7/8

Aux 4: Postfader send

Aux Source: Selects either the channel or the monitor as the source for the 4 Aux controls above

Aux 5: Postfader send from the channel

7/8: Assigns Aux 5/6 to Aux 7/8

Aux 6: Postfader send from the channel

Monitor

Pan

Peak LED indicator

Solo: Stereo, nondestructive control room solo

L/R: Assigns the monitor output to the stereo mix

Mute: Control manually or via Dynamic Mute Automation

Channel

Pan: between left–right and odd–even groups

Peak LED indicator

Solo: Stereo-in-place, non-destructive control room solo

Mute: Control manually or via Dynamic Mute Automation

Dir (Direct): Selects the source (Direct or Group) of the channel's Tape Out jack

L/R: Assigns the channel to the stereo mix

Group Assign switches (1–8) send the channel signal to the group outputs, which normal to the Tape Outs

Group module

There are two stereo aux returns in each module, for a total of 16 aux return input jacks. Stereo Aux Returns may be used for effect returns or for additional line inputs.

Stereo Aux Return A

Level

Hi EQ: Shelving, 12 kHZ

Lo EQ: Shelving, 80 Hz

Peak LED indicator

Stereo Separation: For combining left/right into mono, or keeping them separated

Balance: Sets left/right balance of the stereo signal

To Aux 1-2: Sends the Stereo Aux Return to the stereo auxiliary mix for headphone monitoring

Assign switches: The upper Stereo Aux Return may be assigned to any of the Groups or directly to the L/R mix

Solo: Stereo, nondestructive control room solo

Mute: Control manually or via Dynamic Mute Automation

Stereo Aux Return B

The Stereo Aux Return B has identical features to the upper return except its output:

Group Masters: Assigns the return to the Group Masters immediately below it only

Group Masters

Assign Left: Sends the Group Output to the Left stereo mix, so it can be used as a subgroup control at mixdown

Assign Right: Sends the Group Output to the Right stereo mix, so it can be used as a subgroup control. If both Assign switches are pressed, the signal will appear in the center of the stereo mix.

PFL: Pre Fade Listen allows the prefader group signal to be heard in the control room via the Solo section

Mute: Control manually or via Dynamic Mute Automation

Group Master Faders
From here, the signals go to the dedicated Group Out jacks and to the Tape Out jacks in their respective channels (Grp. 1 to channels 1, 9, and 17, etc.) if the DIR switch of that channel isn't pressed.

Master module

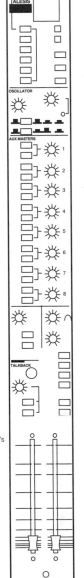

X2 Dynamic Mute Automation includes its own 10,000 event, 100-song sequencer, which can be synchronized to ADAT or to MIDI. Four mute groups can be defined for each song. Data is stored via MIDI SysEx dump.

Solo Mute mutes all other channels except the channels selected, for an alternative method to the X2's nondestructive stereo solo bus

Oscillator provides 100 Hz, 1 KHz, and 10 kHz test tones

Solo Master sets the level of the Solo system

Eight Aux Masters, each with its own AFL (after-fade listen) solo switch and automated mute, control the output of the Aux buses

Studio Level sets the level for the performers' headphones. They can hear either the Aux 1-2 mix or the Control Room source.

The Control Room mix can hear the L/R or Aux 1-2 mixes, or select one of two external stereo inputs. Any Aux send, monitor, group, or channel can be heard in the CR via the SOLO, AFL, and PFL switches.

Phones control the level of the X2's built-in headphone amp

Dim lowers the control room level instantly

Mono allows you to check for mono compatibility

A built-in **Talkback Mic** is for slating recordings and communications to the studio

L/R Masters are the final output controls for mixdown.

5-5b Modular layout of the console in 5-5a

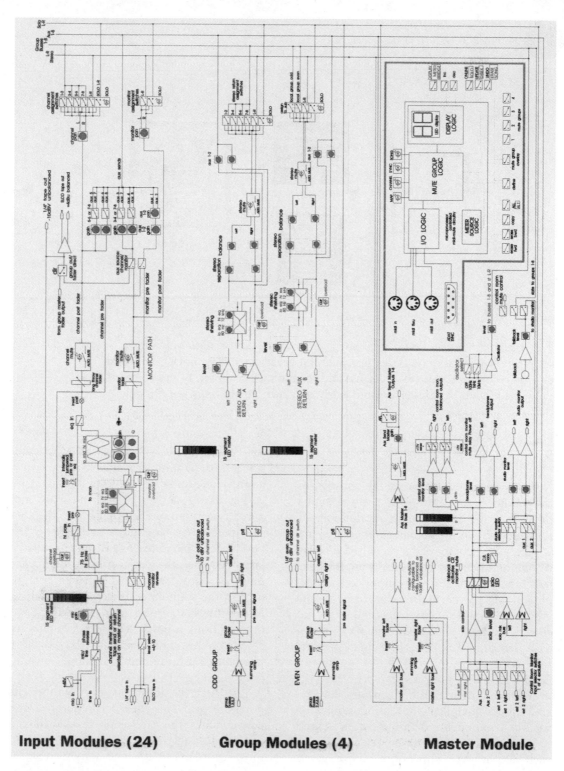

Input Modules (24)   **Group Modules (4)**   **Master Module**

5-6 Block diagrams of the modules in 5-5b

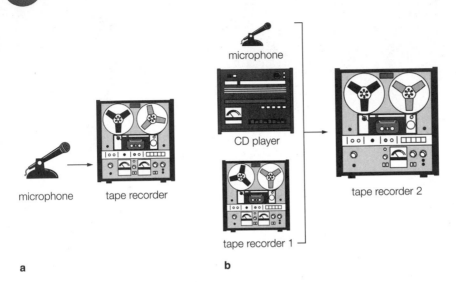

microphone

CD player

microphone

tape recorder

tape recorder 1

tape recorder 2

a

b

5-7 Hard wiring can limit signal flow. In *a*, signal flow can go only one way, so hard wiring makes no difference. In *b*, however, the microphone could feed to tape recorder 1; tape recorder 2 could feed to tape recorder 1, and so on. If these sound sources are hard wired as shown, such flexibility is not possible.

Patching

Regardless of how elaborate the console, or the studio, signal flow—the paths a signal takes from its source to its destination—is restricted by how active components are wired. When components are wired directly to one another (for example, a microphone to a tape recorder, or the output of a microphone, CD player, and tape recorder to the input of another tape recorder), they are considered **hard wired**. The signal can travel only one route (see 5-7). In a small production control room with little equipment, hard wiring may not present a problem.

Multichannel recording consoles, however, require flexibility in routing signals to various components within the console and to and from outboard signal processors, such as limiter-compressors, noise gates,

reverb units, and so on. In these circumstances, the multiple routes a signal may have to take make hard wiring impractical.

Therefore, active components are not wired directly to one another but to the console patch bay or studio patch panel, or both. Each hole in the bay or panel, called a **jack**, becomes the connecting point to the input or output of each electronic component in the sound studio (see 5-8). **Patching** is the interconnecting of these inputs and outputs using a **patch cord** (see 5-9; also see 5-13). In this context a patch bay is more like an old-fashioned telephone switchboard.

But such flexibility is not without its potential problems. In a well-equipped and active facility the patch bay could become a confusing jungle of patch cords. In all studios, regardless of size and activity, a signal

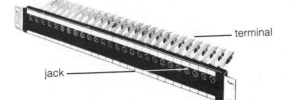

5-8 Patch panel with a row of jacks

terminal

jack

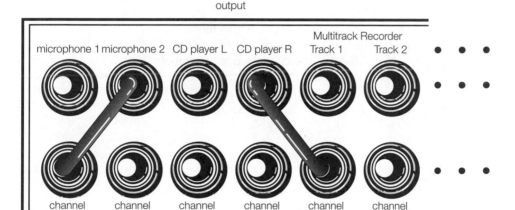

output

microphone 1 microphone 2 CD player L CD player R Track 1 Track 2

Multitrack Recorder

channel channel channel channel channel channel

Input

5-9 Use of patch panel. Any sound source wired to the patch panel can be connected to any other one with a patch cord plugged into the appropriate jacks.

travels some paths more often than others. For example, it is more likely that a signal in a console will travel from mic (or line) input to pan pot to equalizer to delegation control to fader than directly from mic (or line) input to output bus. It is also more likely that a signal will travel from mic to console to tape recorder than directly from one tape recorder to another.

As a way of both reducing the clutter of patch cords at the patch bay and simplifying production, terminals wired to certain equipment can also be wired or *normaled* to

one another. A *normal* connection is one that permits a signal to flow freely between components without any patching. To route a signal through components that have terminals not normaled or wired to one another, patch cords are put in the appropriate jacks to *break normal*—that is, interrupt the normal signal flow—thus rerouting the signal (see 5-10).

The ability to reroute a signal is also advantageous when equipment fails. Suppose a microphone is plugged into studio mic input 1, which connects directly to

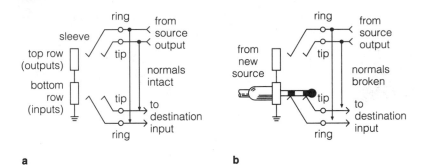

a   b

5-10 Normaling. (*a*) With no patch cords inserted, ouput of source equipment is automatically normaled to the input of another piece of equipment (tip = high, ring = low, sleeve = shield [ground; ⊥ symbol for ground]). (*b*) When a patch cord is inserted in the bottom-row (input) jack, the normals are interrupted, breaking the original signal routing. The new source signal will now feed the destination.

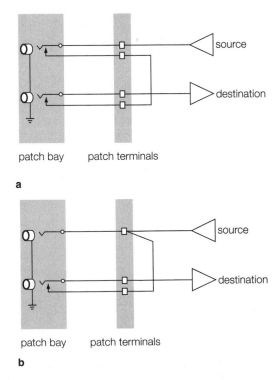

patch bay   patch terminals

a

patch bay   patch terminals

b

5-11 (*a*) **Full-normal and** (*b*) **half-normal patch configurations**

console channel 1, and channel 1 becomes defective. With all inputs and outputs connected at the patch bay, the defective console channel 1 can be bypassed by patching the output from studio mic input 1 to any other working console channel.

Some other features of patch bays include the following:

■ *Input/output.* Most patch bays are wired so that a row of input jacks is directly below a row of output jacks. By reading a patch bay downward it is possible to get a good idea of the console's (or studio's) signal flow.

■ *Full-normal and half-normal.* Input jacks are wired so that a patch cord always interrupts the normal connection. These connections are called *full-normal.* Output jacks may be wired as either full-normal or *half-normal*—connections that continue rather than interrupt signal flow. Hence, a half-normal connection becomes a junction rather than a switch (see 5-11).

- *Multiple*. Most patch bays have special jacks called **multiples** (or *mults*) that are wired to one another instead of to any electronic component. Multiples provide the flexibility to feed the same signal to several different sources at once.

- *Tie line*. When the only patch bay in a control room is located in the console, the other control room equipment, such as tape recorders, CD players, and signal processors have to be wired to it in order to maintain flexibility in signal routing. **Tie lines** in the patch bay facilitate the interconnecting of outboard devices in the control room. When a control room has two patch panels, one in the console and one for the other control room equipment, tie lines can interconnect each patch panel. The tie line is also used to interconnect separate studios, control rooms, or any devices in different locations. Figure 5-12 displays and details one type of patch bay.

General Guidelines for Patching

1. Do not patch microphone-level signals into line-level jacks and vice versa. The signal will be barely audible in the first instance and will distort in the latter one.

2. Do not patch input to input or output to output.

3. Unless jacks are half-normaled, do not patch the output of a component back into its input, or feedback will occur.

4. When patching microphones, make sure the fader controls are turned down. Otherwise, the loud popping sound that occurs when patch cords are inserted into jacks with the faders turned up could damage the microphone or loudspeaker element.

Plugs

While we are on the subject of patching, something more should be said about the plugs on the end of the patch cords. The plugs most commonly used in professional facilities are the *¼-inch phone plug* and the *bantam* (or mini) *phone plug* (see 5-13). Both plugs route sound from one terminal to another. The bantam plug is a smaller version of the ¼-inch phone plug and was designed for the smaller jack panels. These plugs are either unbalanced—tip and sleeve—or balanced—tip, ring, and sleeve (see 5-14). An unbalanced audio cable has two conductors: a center wire and a braided shield surrounding it. A balanced audio cable has three conductors: two center wires and a braided shield. The balanced line is preferred for professional use because it is not as subject to electrical interference.

Console Automation

The mixdown can be exacting and tedious. It requires dozens of tape replays and hundreds of adjustments to get the right equalization, reverberation, blend, spatial balance, timing of inserts, and so on. Comparing one mix with another is difficult unless settings are written down (which is time-consuming) so that controls can be returned to previous positions if necessary. It is not uncommon to discard a mix because someone forgot to adjust one control or decided after a few days to change a few settings without recording the original positions. Then the controls have to be set up all over again. Mixing down one song can take many hours or even days.

Much of this tedium has been eliminated from the mixdown by automated consoles that provide the means to store and retrieve

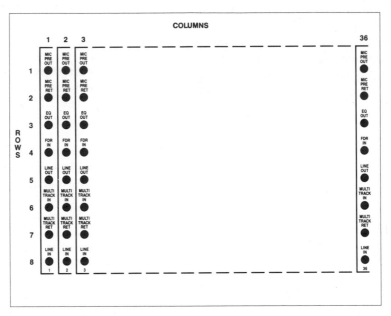

Upper Patch Bay Section

Row 1   MIC PRE OUT: Microphone Pre-amplifier output patch. Normalized to the MIC PRE RET.

Row 2   MIC PRE RET: Microphone Pre-amplifier return. This is the input point for the Channel path on the I/O module. Normalized from MIC PRE OUT.

Row 3   EQ OUT: Post-Equalizer output patch. Normalized to FDR IN.

Row 4   FDR IN: Fader input patch. Normalized from EQ OUT (the Equalizer is pre-Fader).

Row 5   LINE OUT: Provides access to the Channel line output. Normalized to MULTITRACK IN.

Row 6   MULTITRACK IN: Allows connection to be made to the Multitrack input. Normalized from LINE OUT.

Row 7   MULTITRACK RET: Patch point from the Multitrack output. It is normalized to LINE IN.

Row 8   LINE IN: Provides access to the line input. Is normalized from MULTITRACK RET.

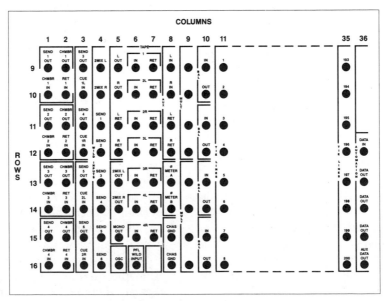

Lower Patch Bay Section

5-12 One type of console patch bay and its jack assignments

Columns 1 and 2

Columns 1 and 2 are arranged in four sets of four jacks each, these being used to provide outputs from Sends 1, 2, 3, and 4 to echo chambers or other effects units.

Each set of four jacks is assigned as follows:

SEND OUT: Provides access to signals from the Send Bus. Is normalized to CHMBR IN.
CHMBR IN: Is for connection to the effects unit input. Is normalized from SEND OUT.
CHMBR OUT: Is for connection from the effects unit output.
RET IN: Is the input jack for the echo return.

Column 3

The patch jacks in Column 3 are used to make inter-connections from Send Buses 3, 4, 5, and 6 to cue inputs 1 and 2. The SEND OUT jacks provide access to the bus signals, and the CUE IN jacks are the cue signal input points. The patches are normalized as detailed below:

Row 1 SEND 3 OUT is normalized to Row 2 CUE 1L

Row 3 SEND 4 OUT is normalized to Row 4 CUE 1R

Row 5 SEND 5 OUT is normalized to Row 6 CUE 2L

Row 7 SEND 6 OUT is normalized to Row 8 CUE 2R

Column 4

The eight jacks in Column 4 are used to accommodate external "wild" inputs to 2-Mix or Sends. Each individual jack is labeled with its specific destination.

Column 5

Rows 1 through 7 of Column 5 are assigned to 2-Mix and stereo functions, and Row 8 is assigned to the Test Oscillator. The patch function for each row is listed below:

The assignments for Rows 1 through 4 (2MIX PATCH) are:

Row 1   L OUT: Provides a pre-Fader, left stereo channel patch point. Normalized to L RET.
Row 2   R OUT: Same as L OUT, but for right stereo channel. Normalized to R RET.
Row 3   L RET: Reinsertion point for left stereo signal. Normalized from L OUT.
Row 4   R RET: Same as L RET, but for right stereo signal. Normalized from R OUT.

Rows 5, 6, and 7 are assigned as follows:

Row 5   2MIX L OUT: Post-Fader patch point for left stereo channel. Picks up the 2-Mix left channel signal at a point immediately preceding the tape recorder input. Normalized to TAPE 2L IN, TAPE 3L IN and TAPE 4L IN.
Row 6   2MIX R OUT: Same as 2MIX L OUT, but for right stereo channel. Normalized to TAPE 2R IN, TAPE 3R IN and TAPE 4R IN.
Row 7   MONO OUT: Post-Fader patch point for Mono signal. Picks up the signal at point immediately preceding the tape recorder input. Normalized to TAPE 1 IN.
Row 8 (OSC) is assigned to the Test Oscillator, and provides an output from the Oscillator for external use.

Column 6

Rows 1 through 7 of Column 6 are assigned to tape recorder input patches, and Row 8 is assigned to PFL wild input.

The TAPE IN jacks provide patches for tape recorder inputs, and are normalized in the following manner:

1 IN is normalized from MONO OUT.

2L IN, 3L IN, and 4L IN are normalized from 2MIX L OUT.

2R IN, 3R IN, and 4R IN are normalized from 2MIX R OUT.

ROW 8 (PFL WILD INPUT) provides a direct input to the PFL amplifier.

Column 7

Rows 1 through 7 of Column 7 provide return patches for the tape recorder output. The TAPE RET jack functions are listed below:

1RET—Return from Mono tape recorder.

2L RET, 3L RET, and 4L RET—Returns from left stereo channels.

2 R RET, 3R RET, and 4R RET—Returns from right stereo channels.

Row 8 (S.V. INPUT) is reserved for a future option.

Column 8

The first four rows of Column 8 (AUX jacks) provide a means of inserting auxiliary inputs into the Monitor system. The AUX RET jacks are wired to the AUX selection switches on the Monitor module.

Rows 5 and 6 (PHASE METER A and PHASE METER B) allow external signals to be patched to the console phase meter.

Rows 7 and 8 (CHAS GND) provide chassis ground points which can be used for grounding any desired point on the Patch Bay.

Column 9

Two sets of MULT (multiple) jacks are provided in Column 9. These afford a means of supplying up to three outputs from a single input. When a signal is patched into any one of the jacks in Rows 1, 2, 3, or 4, it becomes available at the other three jacks in the group. The second group (Rows 5, 6, 7, and 8) are used for the same purpose.

Column 10

Four pairs of BAL IN/BAL OUT JACKS are available in Column 10. These provide access to four balancing transformers which are normally used to isolate console circuits from external devices.

Columns 11 through 35

The tieline jacks in Columns 11 through 35 are used to connect to external devices

Column 36

This column is used for patching tape-based Automation data functions.

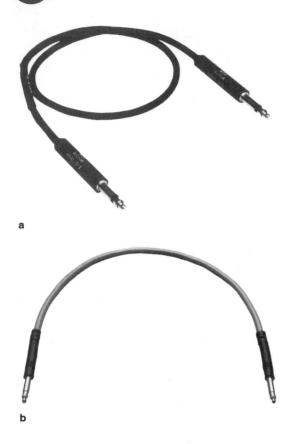

5-13 Patch cords with (*a*) ¼-inch phone plugs and (*b*) bantam (mini) phone plugs

5-14 (*a*) Unbalanced and (*b*) balanced phone plugs

data to recreate any level setting made during a mix.

Console automation also allows the free grouping of signals. Several channels can be assigned to and controlled by one fader without concern for the number of channels available to a given multichannel fader.

To automate a console there are three basic requirements: faders that can generate the required control voltages that represent the fader position; a circuit called a **voltage controlled amplifier** (**VCA**) that can vary the output signal level in response to the changing voltages supplied by the fader; and a place to store the automation data, which may be one track on a multitrack tape but is more likely a computer disk.

It is the VCA that has made console automation possible. The VCA is a special type of amplifier that is used to decrease level, unlike conventional amplifiers that become unstable if operated with loss. It is regulated by an external direct current (DC). Moving the fader varies the DC voltage. The greater the applied DC voltage, the greater the attenuation of the amplifier.

Operating Modes

Most console automation systems have four basic operating modes, write, mute-write, read, and update, although some systems do not specifically use these terms (see 5-15). All functions may be used independently on any or all channels.

- *Write mode.* The **write mode** is used to create an automated mix. In the write mode, the automation system monitors and stores data from the faders. Only current fader movements are stored in the write mode.

- *Mute-write mode.* The **mute-write mode** is generally used either during the building of the mix or as the final mix is play-

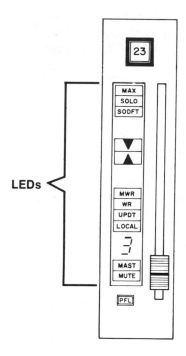

LEDs

MAX indicates that no more gain is available in the channel

SOLO indicates that the fader is in SOLO via the automation SOLO function

SODFT indicates that the fader is in Solo Defeat and will not be affected by an automation SOLO of another fader

Down Arrow indicates that the fader must be moved down to reach the null point. (The null point is the position at which the fader is set, intentionally or not, at the beginning of an update pass through the mix.)

Up Arrow indicates that the fader must be moved up to reach the null point. When both arrows are lit, the fader is at the null point

MWR indicates that the channel is in the Mute Write mode

In MWR, the mute switch controls the mute circuitry

WR puts the automation system in the Write mode for that channel. The MWR and WR modes are independent of each other. This allows the operator to rewrite the Mute switch assignments without affecting the VCA data already written

UPDT puts the automation system in the Update mode for that channel. When the WR and UPDT LEDs are not lit, the channel is in the READ mode. Similarly, the channel is in MUTE READ when the MWR LED is not lit. In READ, the faders and mute switches on the console are inoperative

LOCAL indicates that the channel is no longer under the control of the automation system master fader

The lighted number ("3" in this illustration) indicates the VCA grouping to which the channel (23) has been assigned

MAST indicates that the Group Master fader is controlling all other channels with that VCA grouping number

MUTE indicates that the mute circuitry is active

PFL (Prefader Listening) is a momentary switch that places the prefader audio signal on the PFL bus.

5-15 Channel fader, with automation features. (LED = Light Emitting Diode.)

ing. It is usually not written at the same time that fader movements are being written. Mute-write can be used with all other modes except the read mode.

- *Read mode.* The **read mode** plays back or recalls the stored automation data. In the read mode, the console's faders are inoperative. They take their control voltage information only from the stored data on the disk or tape to reproduce the "recorded" fader movements in real time.

- *Update mode.* The **update mode** allows the operator to read the stored information at any time and make changes by simply moving the appropriate fader. A new data track is generated from the original data track that is being read with the changes that have been made.

Types of Automation Systems

Four types of console automation systems in use are the voltage-controlled automation, software-controlled automation, moving-fader automation, and MIDI-based automation.

- *Voltage-controlled automation.* In voltage-controlled automation, fader levels (and other functions) are regulated by voltage-controlled amplifiers, or by **digitally controlled amplifiers (DCAs)**. A DCA is an amplifier whose gain is remotely controlled by a digital control signal. In a typical VCA-equipped console, faders vary the DC control voltage that changes the VCA's gain in relation to the fader movement. This control voltage is digitized and stored in binary form for later retrieval. In addition to fader levels, it is possible to automate channel and group mutes, solo functions, and in-board signal processors, such as the equalizer and compressor (see Chapter 8).

  Consoles not equipped for automation can be automated with a VCA- or DCA-equipped add-on unit. The unit plugs into the console's patch bay in series with the signal of each channel. Add-on console automation units are also available using computer software systems (see the next section) and MIDI controls (see "MIDI-based automation").

- *Software-controlled automation.* Software-controlled automation uses specially designed computer software programs for console automation. Adjustments are made through *virtual faders* displayed on a video monitor. A *virtual* control is simulated on a computer monitor screen and adjusted at the computer keyboard or with a mouse (see 5-19). Upscale programs, in addition to automated level control, also allow automated control of all in-board signal processing, such as equalization, panning, compression, and effects.

- *Moving-fader automation.* With moving-fader, also called *flying-fader*, automation, instead of using DC voltage to control a VCA, a small servo-motor is attached to the fader. As the control voltages are regenerated, the motor is activated and moves the fader automatically; no hand-operated assistance is necessary. It is possible to automatically control one fader or groups of faders at the same time.

- *MIDI-based automation.* MIDI is a communications protocol. In Musical Instrument Digital Interface, the *Digital* refers to a set of instructions in the form of digital (binary) data, like a computer program, that must be interpreted by an electronic sound-generating, or -modifying, device, such as a synthesizer, that can respond to the instructions. *Interface* refers to the hardware connection that permits the control signals generated by one device to be transmitted to another device. MIDI does not produce or generate sound. Rather, it is a specified system of digital commands and hardware interface that allows musical instruments and other devices to communicate with each other.

  In the same way that MIDI can automate musical instuments and signal processors, for example, it can also be used to automate console operations, such as fader levels, send and return levels, EQ, and pans. MIDI-automated consoles may physically resemble consoles with conventional automation or may be "black boxes" with input and output

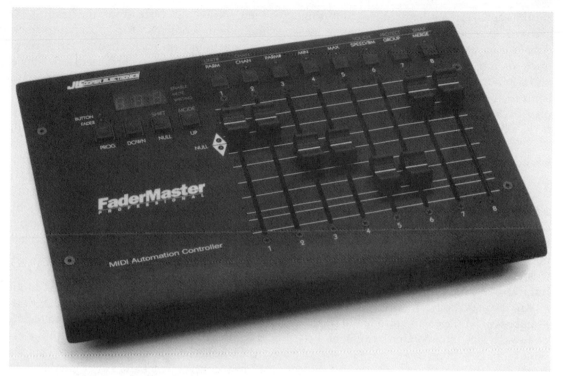

5-16 MIDI automation controller. This model facilitates controlling, mixing, and editing with MIDI-controlled consoles, hard disk recorders, signal processors, and samplers.

jacks. These boxes may use either a "virtual" console computer graphic interface or dedicated controllers with slides and knobs that control the box through MIDI commands (see 5-16).

Two methods are used to translate slider and knob changes to MIDI: *snapshot control* and *continuous control*. With snapshot control, the automation system takes an instant reading of the console settings for recall from storage. With continuous control, each console setting is assigned to a specific MIDI continuous controller. Any movement of these controls transmits corresponding MIDI continuous controller messages.

MIDI console automation has limitations handling the large amounts of data that other types of automation do not have. But because many conventional console automation systems are so complex, recordists are turning to MIDI-based automation systems as a simpler alternative.

Disadvantages of Console Automation

Console automation has greatly facilitated the record keeping and accuracy of mixing; it has made the engineer's arms "longer". But automation has its disadvantages.

Automation systems tend to be confusing, even to experienced operators. Some systems are so complex that it is easy to lose track of the many operations necessary to perform a mix, which defeats the purpose of console automation. Some systems may not play back exactly what the operator wrote. If the mix is complex, a difference of a few dBs, overall, may not be perceptible. That would not be the case, however, in more subtle mixes.

Automation systems, like all computer systems, are vulnerable to crashing. Getting the system operational again, even assuming that you had made a backup copy of the mix before completion, often involves a frustrating loss of production time and continuity, to say nothing of the financial cost.

An aesthetic concern with automation is "sameness." Unless an automated mix is done with skill, its dynamics can sound the same from beginning to end.

Assignable Consoles

The ever-increasing demands that modern audio production is placing on console design have begun to create an ergonomic nightmare. Even as sound designers call for more in-board functions and greater operational flexibility, the growing use of outboard equipment necessitates still more auxiliary console controls. Consoles are becoming too complex and unwieldy for one-person operation. Additionally, regardless of how large or small the console, an operator can deal with only a few controls at any one time. Therefore, most of the console, most of the time, simply represents wasted space.

A relatively new concept in console design seems to have successfully addressed these problems. Instead of the traditional individual controls for channel-to-track routing found on each channel strip, these functions have been centralized into single sets, with no input and output modules in the conventional sense.

The assignable concept can be provided in two approaches. In one configuration, instead of each input module carrying its own set of functions, only one control module is used. This system works in combination with a group of push-button controls, each one corresponding to an input channel. This means that instead of routing a signal through an existing input channel and making individual adjustments, such as EQ, cue and reverb send, and bus assignment at that channel, the various controls of an input channel are grouped into separate, centralized panels. From these panels a signal is assigned to a channel, processed, and routed. Routing assignments are entered into a central control panel and stored on disk.

A second configuration uses as many modules as there are input channels. But each module has only one control fader that works in conjunction with a group of function buttons. All required effects are distributed among the function buttons. In this system, you choose a module and assign one or more functions to the control fader of that particular module. In both assignable approaches, a given control set may be used to perform either the same set of functions for a variety of channels or different functions for a single channel.

The assignable console design has several advantages over large, conventional production consoles: (1) It makes many more operations possible in a more compact chassis; (2) an operator can remain in the central listening location without having to move back and forth to adjust controls; (3) signals can be handled more quickly and easily

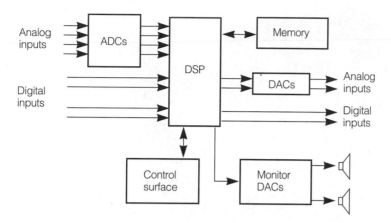

5-17 Generalized diagram of a digital audio console. (ADC = analog-to-digital converter; DAC = digital-to-analog converter; DSP = digital signal processing)

because functions are grouped and, with fewer controls, there are fewer operations to perform; and (4) the reduced number of controls lessens the chance of error and makes console layout easier on the eye.

Digital Consoles

The digital mixing console has been designed using the assignable concept and is available in three configurations. One configuration is actually an analog console that is digitally controlled. The signal path is distributed and processed in analog form, but the console's control parameters are maintained digitally (see 5-17).

The all-digital console uses two approaches. The analog input signal is first encoded into a digital signal, or it is directly accepted as digital information. In either case, the data are distributed and processed digitally. The output might either be decoded

back into analog or remain in digital form, depending on its destination. A third type of digital mixer uses computer software that configures the computer hardware into a "virtual" console.

The digital console has several advantages over its all-analog counterpart: (1) A greater number of operations are possible in a streamlined chassis; (2) there is greater flexibility in signal processing and routing; (3) more data can be stored; (4) in-board patch panels are unnecessary; and (5) distortion and noise are reduced significantly, especially in the all-digital system (see 5-18).

"Virtual" Consoles

As the term suggests, a "virtual" console is not a console per se, but an integrated system that combines a hard-disk computer and specialized software to record stereo or multitrack audio direct to disk. Instead of

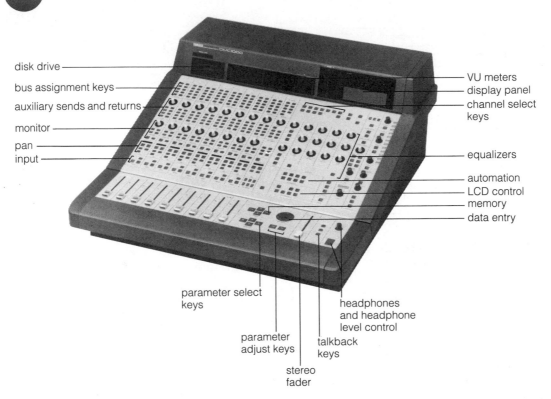

disk drive
bus assignment keys
auxiliary sends and returns
monitor
pan
input

VU meters
display panel
channel select keys

equalizers

automation
LCD control
memory
data entry

parameter select keys

parameter adjust keys

stereo fader

talkback keys

headphones and headphone level control

5-18 All-digital console. In this model, signals are digitized before entering the console. Although there are 9 fader contols, it can be regarded as a 22-input console, with 10 buses, 4 auxiliary buses configured in the following way: 8 mono input channels; 3 stereo input channels; 8 monitor channels; 8 program buses; one stereo bus; 4 auxiliary buses (2 mono and 2 stereo). All sends are available on all 22 inputs. The console is fully automated and the data can be stored in the console's in-board disk drive. Relevant numerical and graphic information is shown on the console's display panel. Display information includes Word Clock, which provides information about the console's digital setup; EQ graphic representation of a channel's equalization response; Effect Parameter displays the settings of an effect, such as reverberation; Automation Track Edit displays automation status.

feeding a sound source to a conventional console, it is fed directly to the computer. The console controls are displayed on the computer monitor—faders, EQ, panning (see 5-19). The controls are usually maneuvered by a mouse.

The number of channels a "virtual" console can handle depends on the capacity of the hard disk. For example, a system may

provide 4 channels per hard disk. Therefore, if you require 16 channels for recording, a total of four hard drives are necessary. Although each channel has a dedicated input and output on the computer, or computer interface, once a track has been recorded, any number of tracks can be processed (see also "Hard Disk Recording" in Chapter 7).

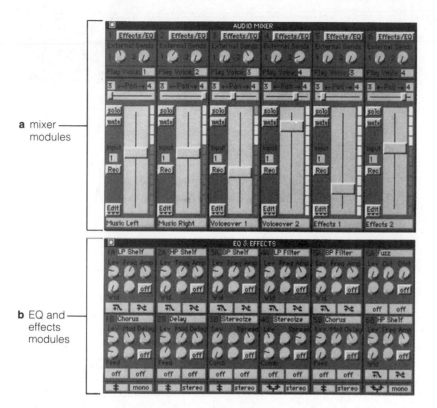

a mixer modules

b EQ and effects modules

5-19 Example of a "virtual" console's display screen. (*a*) Each Mixer Module controls the panning, level, EQ/Effect, etc. for every virtual track. External Sends route signals for additional processing. Each track has its own prefader VU meter. The Edit button takes you to the playlist to arrange regions, spot effects, and create crossfades. (*b*) Every track has two real-time EQ and Effects Modules including Low Shelf EQ, High Shelf EQ, Peak/Notch EQ, Chorus, Delay, Stereoization, and Distortion options. All Parameter Control knobs can be automated.

Analog Recording

It is difficult to overestimate the role of magnetic recording. Most of what you hear and see in media today is prepared, stored, and transmitted by magnetic recording systems.

Until relatively recently, all audio magnetic recording was done on audiotape or magnetic film—for many years in the analog format and, beginning in the early 1980s, in the digital format, as well. Today, the newest formats accomplish digital audio recording using disk-based systems. No audiotape is involved at all. In fact, so much already has been made of tapeless recording that tape has been pronounced an endangered species.

Actually, what the proliferation of recording formats has demonstrated is that none, yet, is the panacea; each one has its advantages and disadvantages. Overall, the benefit of so many recording formats is the wide range of systems made available to professional and nonprofessional alike. The drawbacks, especially to the professional, are the incompatibility among the various systems and the cost of either changing from one format to another or having to accommodate several formats at once.

It will be a while before the marketplace decides which audio recording systems go and which stay. In the meantime, tape-based and disk-based recording will be with us for the foreseeable future.

Tape-Based Audio Recording

In audiotape recording, electrical signals are converted into magnetic signals at the recording stage and encoded onto tape. At the playback stage these taped magnetic signals are reconverted into electrical signals. This process is accomplished in two different ways: using the analog method or the digital method. This chapter covers the analog method.

Analog Audio

In *analog* recording, the waveform of the signal being processed resembles the waveform of the original sound; they are analogous. Or

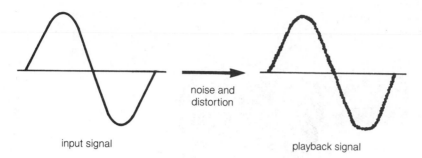

input signal   noise and distortion   playback signal

6-1 Representation of the analog recording process

Table 6-1   Recording times for open-reel analog tape. Times are not exact because extra tape is provided to spool around the take-up and feed reels.

Reel Size (inches)	Tape Thickness (mils)	Tape Length (feet)	Playing Time (minutes)			
			30 ips	*15 ips*	*7½ ips*	*3¾ ips*
5	1.5	600		7.5	15	30
5	1	900		11.25	22.5	45
7	1.5	1,200	7.5	15	30	60
7	1	1,800	11.25	22.5	45	90
7	.5	2,400		30	60	120
10.5	1.5	2,500	16.6	33.3	66.6	133.2
14	1.5	5,000	33.3	66.6	133.3	266.4

to put it another way, the frequency and amplitude of an electrical signal change continuously in direct relationship to the original acoustical sound waves; the signal is always "on." If these continuous changes were examined, they would reveal an infinite number of variations, each instant different from any other adjacent instant. During processing, noise—electrical, electronic, tape—may be added to the signal. Hence, the processed signal is analogous to the original sound plus any additional noise (see 6-1).

Analog Audiotape Recording

Although the digital tape recording process is entirely different (see Chapter 7), the tape

and tape recorders used in analog and digital recording have a number of features in common, which are discussed throughout the chapter.

Physical Characteristics of Audiotape

We tend to take tape for granted, perhaps because it is so familiar and easy to obtain. This attitude is a mistake because tape stores the record of your creative output. Therefore, to avoid using inferior, defective, or inappropriate tape, you must be aware of the properties and composition of your storage medium (Table 6.1).

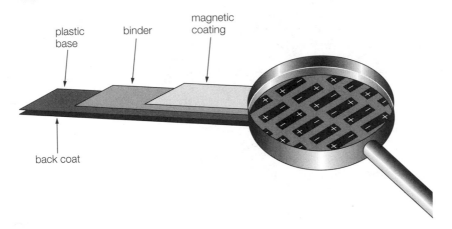

plastic base

binder

magnetic coating

back coat

6-2 The four layers that make up audiotape and the random distribution of magnetic domains on the microscopic magnetic particles

Composition

Audiotape is a thin plastic ribbon consisting of (1) hard, needlelike magnetic particles composed of iron (ferric) oxide, chromium dioxide, cobalt, or pure metal particles; (2) a plastic base material that supports the oxide; (3) a binder of synthetic varnish that holds the magnetic particles and adheres them to the base; and (4) a back coating to reduce slippage and buildup of magnetic charges (see 6-2).

Magnetic Particles and Magnetism

Tape recording is made possible by the ability of the magnetic particles to store electromagnetic impulses. Certain metallic compounds are magnetized when exposed to a field of force such as magnetic or electric current. In tape recording, the electric current flows through the record head of the tape recorder creating the magnetic field that *polarizes* the magnetic particles on the tape—arranges them into patterns—as they pass across the head. The arrangement of these polarized particles is the magnetic analog of the original sound.

Plastic Base

The plastic material most commonly used for a tape's backing is **polyester**, also called **Mylar**™. Polyester is strong, supple, and resistant to temperature extremes as well as humidity. Its one significant drawback is that it stretches when placed under too much tension or when used too often. Once a tape is stretched, so is the recording.

To reduce the possibility of stretching, (1) use only the highest-quality tape, (2) make sure that tape recorders have the proper tension when spooling, and (3) use new tape for each project.

Dimensions

Two physical dimensions of magnetic audiotape are thickness and width. Knowing a tape's thickness helps to determine (1) how much tape can be spooled onto a reel,

(2) how long it will play, and (3) how vulnerable a magnetic signal on one layer of tape will be to a magnetic signal on an adjacent layer.

Thickness   Most audiotape comes in four thicknesses, measured in **mils** (thousandths of an inch): 1½, 1, ½, and ¼ mil. (These measurements are taken from the plastic base. Actually the plastic base plus the magnetic coating is slightly thicker.) A tape's thickness determines how much can be spooled onto a given size of reel. For example, the most common open-reel sizes are 7, 10½, and 14 inches.

A 7-inch reel of analog tape holds 1,200 feet of 1½-mil tape, 1,800 feet of 1-mil tape, or 3,600 feet of ¼-mil tape. The more tape on a reel, the longer the playing time (see Table 6-1).

One-quarter-mil tape may look like the best buy, but not for professionals. They prefer 1½-mil tape for two reasons: (1) it is the thickest and most durable tape and is therefore least likely to crease, snap, stretch, or shrink; and (2) the **print-through** is considerably lessened. Print-through usually occurs in storage, when a signal from one layer of tape "prints" a low-level replica of itself on an adjacent layer. When the tape is played back, you can hear both signals, one strongly and one faintly. The thicker the tape, the less chance of sound "spilling" from layer to layer. Other factors that affect print-through are discussed later in this chapter.

Width   Open-reel audiotape is available in four widths: ¼, ½, 1, and 2 inches (see 6-3).

Magnetic Properties of Audiotape

Much of the tape used in music recording has been designed to provide particular

6-3 Open-reel audiotape in ¼-, ½-, 1-, and 2-inch widths

response characteristics. For example, the type normally used to record popular music is **high-output tape** capable of handling higher levels than is standard tape. The louder recording levels make print-through more noticeable, however. **Low-output tape** is used to preserve program material for long periods of time with reduced print-through. But low-output tape must be used on a tape recorder set up to handle it. If it is used on a machine set up for high-output tape, distortion can occur. (See "Bias" later in this chapter.)

Several measures are used to determine how suitable a tape is for a particular recording. Three ways to determine a tape's ability to retain magnetic information are to check (1) how strong a force field must be to change the magnetic charge of a given particle, (2) how well the tape retains magnetization once the force field is removed, and (3) how great an output level the tape can reproduce. The terms used to describe these measures are *coercivity*, *retentivity*, and *sensitivity*.

Coercivity

Coercivity indicates the magnetic force (current) necessary to erase a tape fully. It is measured in oersteds—units of magnetic intensity. Analog open-reel tapes that are used professionally usually have oersted measurements between 360 and 380. The oersted measurements of digital open-reel tapes are in the 700s. Digital audio cassette tape is 1,500 oersteds. (See "Open-Reel Digital Audiotape" in Chapter 7.)

The higher the coercivity, the more difficult it is to erase the tape. A tape recorder should be able to completely erase the tape being used. If it does not, some part of a previously recorded signal may be heard with a newly recorded signal.

Retentivity

Retentivity is a measure of the tape's magnetic field strength remaining after an external magnetic force has been removed. Retentivity is measured in **gauss**—a unit of magnetic density. A higher gauss rating means greater retentivity, which, in turn, indicates that a tape has a greater potential output level. Greater is not necessarily better; what is better depends on what you are recording and why. Gauss ratings between 1,200 and 1,700 are typical in professionally used open-reel tapes, analog and digital. Digital audio cassette tape has gauss ratings between 2,300 and 2,500.

Sensitivity

Sensitivity is similar to retentivity in that it indicates the highest output level a tape can deliver; however, sensitivity is measured in decibels, and the test must be made against a reference tape. If the maximum output level of a reference tape is 0 dB and the output of the tape you are testing is + 3dB, that means your tape is capable of handling 3 dB more loudness before it *saturates*—becomes fully magnetized.

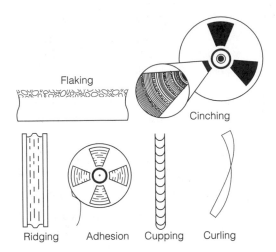

6-4 Common problems caused by poorly made tape

High-Output Tape

Because high levels of loudness are an inherent part of popular music, **high-output tape** helps combat noise buildup on multitrack machines. Its increased retentivity and sensitivity can take higher sound levels than standard tape before saturation occurs.

Tape Defects

Most tape defects are the product of inferior manufacturing, and it is false economy to try to save money by purchasing such tape. To make the point emphatically: *Do not use cheap tape!*

Following are several results of using cheap tape (see 6-4):

- *Dropout*—sudden, irregular drops in sound level caused by poor distribution or flaking of the magnetic coating
- *Cinching*—slippage between the tape layers due to loose packing (also known as *windowing*)

- *Ridging*—a bulge or depression, seen after winding, caused by deformed layer(s) of tape
- *Adhesion*—one tape layer sticking to another
- *Cupping*—deformation of the backing due to expansion of the magnetic coating and base
- *Curling*—twisting of tape when it hangs due to a problem in the binding between plastic and magnetic coating

Each of these defects adversely affects the sound quality, to say nothing of accelerated tape head and machine wear.

Care of Tape

Because the entire tape-recording process ultimately depends on the tape, it is important to exercise proper care when handling and storing magnetic tape.

Handling

1. Never handle the tape surface, front or back. The oil from a fingerprint can catch dust and grime that can damage the tape surfaces. If touching the tape cannot be avoided, use lint-free gloves. This is especially important when using digital tape.

2. Do not smoke or eat in the tape area. Smoke and food particles can contaminate the tape and also cause damage.

3. Carry the tape reel by the hub.

4. Trim damaged tape ends to avoid depositing debris on the tape transport and recording heads.

5. Always store tape in a dust-proof container when it is not in use.

6. Do not stack tapes on top of one another. Store tapes vertically so they will be supported by the hub.

scattered wind

6-5 Scattered wind. Individual tape strands are exposed and vulnerable to damage.

7. Keep tape away from heat-generating equipment and magnetic fields when not in use.

Storage

If you intend to keep a recording for any length of time, take the following precautions against alteration of the magnetically encoded signal:

1. Use low-print-through tape 1½ mils thick.

2. Store the tape in a controlled environment, between 60 and 75 degrees Fahrenheit and 40 and 60 percent humidity.

3. Wind the tape **tails out**—with the end of the recording on the outside of the reel. Then if print-through does occur, the weaker signal or decay will be post-echo (transferred into the stronger signal), thus masking the print-through, instead of pre-echo (before the signal), thus being audible.

4. Beware of exposed edges that result from *scattered wind* or *stepping* of tape due to uneven winding (see 6-5).

5. If the tape is in long-term storage, try to wind and rewind it at least once a year as an added precaution. Even if print-through has occurred, rewinding can reduce it somewhat.

Open-Reel Audiotape Recorders

Open-reel audiotape recorders, and audiotape recorders (ATRs) in general, have three essential elements: (1) the tape transport system, (2) magnetic heads, and (3) record and playback electronics. You may consider the recording tape as a fourth element.

Tape Transport System

Tape transports have different features, but they are all designed to pull the tape across the magnetic heads at a constant speed and tension without causing fluctuations in the tape movement. In a typical *tape transport system*, a tape is prepared for record or play by placing it on the feed reel, threading it past the tape guide, across the head assembly, and between the *capstan* and *pinch roller*, through another tape guide to the take-up reel (see 6-6).

Although Figure 6-6 shows a 2-channel, 2-track tape recorder, most of its features are also found on multitrack tape recorders. The multitrack ATR is discussed later in this chapter.

Capstan and Pinch Roller

The heart of the transport system is the **capstan**—a precision drive shaft that regulates the tape speed. When you put the machine in "Play," the tape is forced against the motor-driven shaft by the **pinch roller**. The pinch roller is usually rubber, and as the spinning capstan comes into contact with it, the capstan drives the roller and the two together pull the tape.

Feed (Supply) and Take-Up Reels

The feed and take-up reels are also driven by motors. Electric current feeding these motors controls the tension on each reel so that (1) tape will not spill as it is pulled by the capstan and pinch roller, and (2) tape maintains optimal contact with the heads without stretching.

Tension (Reel-Size) Control

Although electric current to the feed and take-up motors keeps the torque on the reels constant, it does not control differences in tension created when tape winds from one size reel to a different size reel. Older-model professional recorders that are designed to take different size reels have a **tension** or **reel-size switch** so the tape wind from reel to reel is constant regardless of tape distribution and reel sizes. Newer-model professional ATRs use a microprocessor for reel tension control.

Safety Control

Professional ATR transports incorporate a safety control that stops the transport when it senses the absence of tape along the guide path because the tape ran out or broke. The control may be a light beam interrupted by the presence of tape in its path, or the control may be incorporated in the tape-tension sensor. Because the safety control stops the transport without turning off the entire recorder, it cuts down on machine wear and tear.

Tape Guides

Tape guides are used to position the tape correctly on the heads and as it winds from the feed to the take-up reel.

Wow and Flutter

Constant tape movement and tension are critical to acceptable recording. If a problem develops with some part of the tape trans-

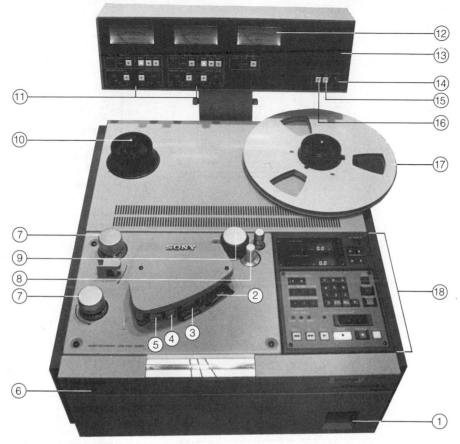

(1) Tape recorder on/off control
(2) Playback head
(3) Record head
(4) Erase head
(5) Time code head
(6) Headphone jack
(7) Tape guides
(8) Capstan
(9) Pinch roller
(10) Feed reel

(11) Meter housing and controls for channels 1 and 2
(12) Time code VU meter
(13) Monitor speaker
(14) Volume control for monitor speaker
(15) Track 2 Select assigns audio channel 2 to the monitor speaker
(16) Track 1 Select assigns audio channel 1 to the monitor speaker
(17) Take-up reel
(18) Transport control panel

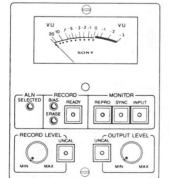

Meter Housing and Controls

ALN Selected: LED indicates whether the channel is selected during alignment operation.

RECORD: Bias and Erase LEDs indicate whether the Bias and Erase signals are active, which they are during recording. RECORD READY is pressed to put the channel into the record mode.

MONITOR: Repro, Sync, and Input buttons select from where the output of the audio channel will come—playback head, time code head, or record head.

RECORD LEVEL: Volume control adjusts record level when UNCAL(ibration) is off. In the CAL mode, the record level is internally preset.

OUTPUT LEVEL: is similar to the RECORD LEVEL but adjusts for output level.

6-6 Tape recorder with an open-loop transport system and its functions

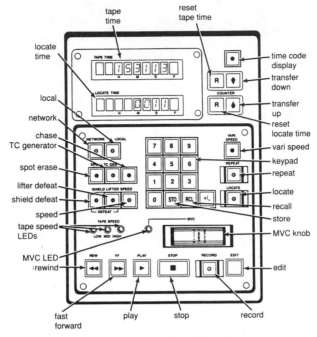

Transport Control Panel and Its Functions

REWIND puts the transport into fast rewind

FAST FORWARD puts the transport into fast forward

PLAY starts the tape at the selected speed

STOP stops the tape

RECORD pressed together with PLAY (and with the RECORD READY LED on the meter housing controls lit) puts the tape recorder into the record mode

EDIT puts the transport into the Dump Edit mode by turning off the take-up reel

MVC (Manual Velocity Control) Knob shuttles the transport from fast to slow wind in either rewind or forward

KEYPAD permits entering of specific values into the LOCATE TIME DISPLAY and is used in conjunction with STO (Store) and RCL (Recall) for search-to-cue operation

STORE stores in a memory the numbers punched into the KEYPAD

RECALL recalls the stored numbers from the memory

LOCATE causes the transport to fast wind from the location shown in the TAPE TIME display to the location shown in LOCATE TIME display

REPEAT causes the tape recorder to play a segment of tape repeatedly

VARI SPEED varies the selected tape speed by ± 50 percent

RESET LOCATE TIME resets locate time display

RESET TAPE TIME resets tape time display

TRANSFER UP causes the value shown in the LOCATE TIME display to be loaded into the TAPE TIME display

TRANSFER DOWN causes the value shown in the TAPE TIME display to be loaded into the LOCATE TIME DISPLAY

TIME CODE DISPLAY displays TAPE TIME in time code — hours, minutes, seconds, and frames

TAPE TIME displays the tape time either in hours, minutes, and seconds or in time code

LOCATE TIME displays the locate time

LOCAL mode keeps tape recorder control at the transport control panel (or at a parallel remote control)

NETWORK mode transfers tape recorder control to a network (serial remote control) and disables the transport control (or parallel remote control)

CHASE mode slaves the tape recorder to an external time code source

TC GENERATOR selects the internal time code generator

SPOT ERASE disables the record head with the erase head on so that tape can be erased with no bias frequency from the record circuitry

LIFTER DEFEAT disables the tape lifters so the tape passes over the heads in any fast wind mode

SHIELD DEFEAT deactivates the head shields during Play or Record

SPEED selects high (30 ips), medium (15 ips), or slow (7½ ips) tape speed

TAPE SPEED LEDs indicate which tape speed has been selected

MVC LED indicates that the MVC has been selected

6-6 (continued)

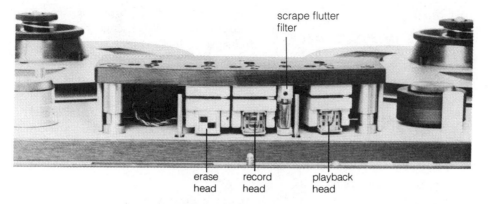

scrape flutter
filter

erase   record   playback
head   head   head

6-7 Audiotape recorder with three magnetic heads. These are half-track heads (see Figures 6-12 and 6-13).

port system, the sound may take on wow or flutter. **Wow** is instantaneous variations in speed at moderately slow rates caused by variations in the tape transport, and perceived as frequency changes; **flutter** is generally the result of friction between the tape and heads or guides resulting in amplitude changes.

Most professional open-reel ATRs come with **scrape flutter filters** to reduce flutter. Scrape flutter filters are installed between the heads to reduce the amount of unsupported tape, thereby restricting the degree of tape movement as it passes across the heads (see 6-7).

The lower the wow and flutter specification, the better. Although it is beyond the scope of this book to explain the following wow and flutter measurements, .05 percent WRMS (weighted root mean square) is very good; .04 percent WRMS is excellent.

Tape Speeds

Five speeds generally are used in analog audiotape recording: 1⅞, 3¾, 7½, 15, and 30 inches per second (ips). (A sixth speed, ¹⁵⁄₃₂ ips, is used with logging tape—tape used

for transcribing the oral record of a broadcast station's program day and for communications recording in emergency agencies and security institutions.) In analog recording the faster the speed, the better the frequency response and signal-to-noise ratio. Many ATRs operate at two, three, or four speeds.

Professionals usually use 7½ ips as a common speed when distributing or airing tape recordings, but they often work at 15 or 30 ips for improved sound quality and ease of editing. In any case, do not use speeds lower than 7½ ips. To give you an insight into the relationship between speed and sound quality, a top-quality professional tape recorder may have a frequency response to 20,000 Hz at 15 ips; at 7½ ips response may reach 15,000 Hz, and at 3¾ ips it may only go as high as 10,000 Hz. A record/play frequency response of 40 Hz–18 kHz is considered excellent for an open-reel analog ATR.

Faster speeds also make it easier to edit tape (see Chapter 14). The more tape that passes across the heads per second, the more spread out the sound is on the tape. (A speed of 1⅞ ips is standard for analog audio cassette recorders. Digital ACRs run at ¼ ips.)

Tape Transport Controls

Several different controls operate the tape transport system (see 6-6).

- *On-off switch.* This control turns the electric power to the tape recorder on or off.

- *Selectable speed control.* Most professional recorders operate at more than one speed. This control selects the speed.

- *Variable speed control.* Some two- and three-speed recorders have a control that adjusts the tape speed to a rate that is ± 5 percent to 50 percent of the machine's set speeds. This **variable speed control** comes in handy when you want to change the pitch of a sound for special effect or to correct slight anomalies in pitch resulting from AC voltage changes or batteries that gradually lose power during recording. The variable speed control also permits a shortening or lengthening of material that may be desirable and acceptable if the change in frequency and rate is unimportant.

- *Play.* This control activates the tape transport in the play mode.

- *Record.* This control activates the erase and record electronics. To avoid accidental erasure, it usually will not work unless you also press the "Play" button.

- *Fast forward and rewind.* These controls disengage the capstan/pinch roller and wind or rewind the tape at high speed. In either mode, tape lifters hold the tape away from the heads to avoid the increased friction that would rapidly wear both tape and heads, and to mute the annoying high-pitched squeal that comes from running the tape at high speed. If that high-pitched squeal is loud enough, by the way, it can damage the tweeter(s) in a loudspeaker (see Chapter 9).

- *Stop.* This control stops the feed and take-up reels and disengages the pinch roller from the capstan.

- *Edit control.* This control allows you to spool off unwanted tape without the take-up reel turning. For **edit control** press "Edit" to disengage the take-up reel while allowing the rest of the tape transport to continue functioning.

Magnetic Heads

The heads of a tape recorder are small electromagnets. These magnetic heads are transducers; they convert electric energy into magnetic energy during recording or magnetic energy back into electric energy during playback.

Most professional tape recorders have at least three heads: erase, record, and playback (see 6-7). A good way to identify them is to remember that the erase head is always closest to the feed reel, the record head is in the middle, and the playback head is closest to the take-up reel.

Machines with four heads use the fourth head as a sync head for *SMPTE time code* (see 6-6 and Chapter 14). Older-model two-channel, two-track ATRs may dedicate the fourth head as a four-track playback head.

Bias

Before we examine the function of each magnetic head, we need to discuss **bias**. The response of magnetic particles on recording tape (and magnetic film) is nonlinear—their magnetic energy is not a perfect analog of the signal from the record head. A method is needed to force the magnetic properties of the particles as the audio current directs.

The force is a high-frequency current several times that of the highest recorded frequency and, therefore, far above the frequency limits of human hearing (100,000 Hz and higher). This high-frequency current, referred to as **bias current**, is added to the audio signal during recording. It affects the magnetic tape particles so that they respond and conform to the audio signal. During playback the bias frequency is not reproduced because the playback head is unable to read such high frequencies.

In addition to making magnetic recording linear, the strength of the bias current also affects frequency response, distortion, and signal-to-noise ratio. A particular amount of bias current will work best with a particular type of recording tape. It is critical, therefore, that the tape recorder you use has been *biased* for the specific tape that you are using. Otherwise, a bias current set too high results in loss of high frequencies, and one set too low results in increased distortion and background noise. Always check with a technician to be sure.

Types of Heads

Erase Head The **erase head** is activated during recording. Its function is to neutralize the polarities of the magnetic particles—to remove sound from the tape with a high-frequency current before the tape passes across the record head.

Bulk Erasers Another way to erase tape is with a **bulk eraser** (also known as a **degausser**)—a large magnet that can erase an entire reel at once (see 6-8). It is fast and easy to use but generally gives a poorer signal-to-noise ratio than does the erase head. When using a bulk eraser with no conveyor belt, take the following precautions:

1. Keep the tape (and your watch) away from the demagnetizer when it is turned on or off, because the tape could get a

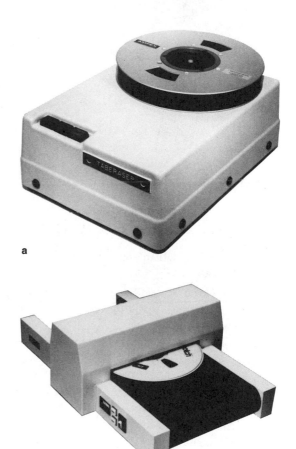

a

b

6-8 High-quality bulk erasers. (*a*) This model erases open-reel tapes from 150-mil to 2-inch widths, as well as cartridges, cassettes, and magnetic film. The erase field electronically diminishes at the end of each 20-second cycle. A fan blower protects the eraser from overheating damage. (*b*) High-energy bulk eraser for high-coercivity tapes.

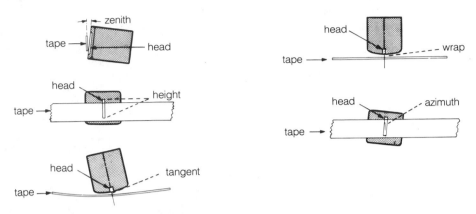

6-9 Five alignment adjustments made to a magnetic head

surge of magnetism that may be difficult to neutralize.

2. Before (and after) degaussing, slowly move the tape into (and away from) the bulk eraser's field.

3. Rotate the tape over the degausser slowly at a rate not more than 2 inches per second. Faster rates will leave residual magnetism on the tape. Do not scrape the tape too hard or jerk it across the surface of the bulk eraser; these actions will reduce signal-to-noise ratio and increase background noise in the form of a swishing sound. Make sure the passes include both sides of the entire reel.

4. Make sure you know the use time of the demagnetizer; some of them tend to heat up quickly and will burn out if left on too long.

Record Head   The **record head** transduces electric energy into the magnetic force that magnetizes the tape. It carries two signals: the record bias current and the audio current—the signal fed to the recorder from the original sound.

Playback Head   The **playback head** transduces the magnetic field from the tape back into electric energy.

Head Care

Magnetic heads require very careful treatment. The slightest change in their alignment, any accumulation of dust, dirt, or magnetic particles, scratches, wear, or overmagnetizing will adversely affect sound quality.

Aligning the Heads   Whether or not you align the heads, you should be aware of what adjustments are made and some problems that can result when the heads are out of alignment. There are five adjustments (see 6-9):

■ **Zenith.** The vertical angle of the heads is important to maintain uniform tape tension across the entire width of the tape-to-head contact. If a head is tilted and the top or bottom portion applies greater pressure to the tape than the other, it causes the tape to *skew*—ride up or down

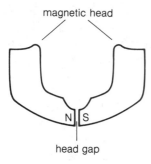

6-10 The poles and
head gap of a magnetic
head

6-11 Head demagnetizer

on the head. In less severe cases the lack of pressure can cause degraded performance.

- **Height.** The heads must present themselves to the tape at exactly the right height. Otherwise, the result could be signals that are only partially recorded or reproduced, crosstalk between tracks, more noise, or poor erasure.

- **Tangency.** The head-to-tape contact at the head gap must be at the right pressure. The head gap is the space between the poles of a magnetic head (see 6-10). The farther forward the head, the greater is the pressure. Too little or too much pressure noticeably degrades a signal by reducing high-frequency response and causing dropout.

- **Wrap.** The angle at which the tape curves around the head must ensure proper contact at the gap. Without firm tape-to-head contact, as with poor tangency, there is sound dropout and high-frequency loss.

- **Azimuth.** Adjustment of the gap must be exactly perpendicular to the length of the tape. Heads that are not in azimuth alignment record and reproduce out-of-phase stereo signals.

It is difficult to visually spot heads that are out of alignment, but you can hear many of the problems caused by misaligned heads. Most studios have a routine schedule of preventive maintenance that includes head alignment. If you are getting poor sound from a tape recorder, have a technician check the heads. As for the other aspects of head care, you can handle them yourself.

Demagnetizing the Heads   Before you use a tape recorder (and once or twice during long sessions), make sure the heads are free from any magnetization that may have been left from previous use. When heads build up enough permanent magnetism, they can partially erase a recording; higher frequencies are particularly susceptible. Recordings so affected sound "muddy"; they often lack presence and brilliance.

You can demagnetize heads with any of several demagnetizers available (see 6-11). Select one that does not produce too strong a magnetic field, however, or it can permanently magnetize a head instead of demagnetizing it. Turn off the tape recorder before demagnetizing. Also, turn the demagnetizer on and off away from the heads; otherwise, the surge or cut in power could leave remnant magnetization on the heads. Make sure, too, that the demagnetizer does not touch or scrape the heads, or they could be scratched and permanently damaged. An etched head acts like sandpaper in scraping magnetic particles off tape.

Cleaning the Heads   Dust, dirt, and magnetic particles collect on the heads and tape guides even in the cleanest studios. Some of these particles are abrasive; when the tape picks them up and drags them across the heads, they can scratch both the magnetic coating and the heads. If these particles build up sufficiently, sound quality suffers noticeably. For example, if oxide particle buildup is 1 one-thousandth of an inch on the playback head, a recording running at 15 ips will have a loss of 55 dB at 15 kHz.

The best preventive maintenance is to clean the heads and tape guides each time you use a tape recorder. Dense-packed cotton swabs and an approved head cleaner or easy-to-obtain and inexpensive denatured alcohol will do. Try not to use isopropyl alcohol or rubbing alcohol because they can leave a film on the head, and they contain water.

Use one cotton swab for each head and guide (two if the cotton turns brown) and swab the head gently. Special head cleaner is available, but it may be too potent for some heads and dissolve part of the plastic. Check with a technician if you are in doubt. A rubber cleaner is better for pinch rollers because alcohol could swell and crack the rubber.

Electronic Alignment

Another important procedure in a tape recorder's preventive maintenance is **electronic alignment** (or **calibration**). In fact, in music recording studios it is not uncommon for machines to be aligned before sessions start each day. Because specifications such as bias requirements, frequency response, and sensitivity vary so from one tape formulation to another, audiotape recorders have various electronic adjustments so that they all operate at a given standard. Without such a standard, tapes recorded on one ATR may not have the identical response as a recording made on another ATR.

The National Association of Broadcasters (NAB) has established standards for 3¾ ips, 7½ ips, and 15 ips that are in use throughout the United States and much of the world. Europe conforms to the DIN standard set by Deutsche Institute Norme. The Audio Engineering Society (AES) has established the standard for 30 ips.

To perform a physical alignment, you need the appropriate alignment tape. Although alignment tapes are available in various track-width and tape-speed formats, they contain the same reference measurements:

- *Standard reference level.* Standard reference level is a 700 Hz or 1 kHz tone recorded at a standard reference level.

- *Azimuth adjustment tone.* The azimuth adjustment tone is 15 kHz for a duration of 30 seconds.

- *Frequency response.* Frequency response is calibrated using tones at 12 kHz, 10 kHz, 7.5 kHz, 5 kHz, 2.5 kHz, 1 kHz, 500 Hz, 250 Hz, 100 Hz, 50 Hz, and 30 Hz.

Playback and record alignment procedures are outlined in Table 6-2.[*] It is worth noting that before electronic alignment can begin, the tape heads must be in proper physical alignment.

Electronics

The *record electronics* receive the audio input to the tape recorder and convert it to the current that flows through the record head. The *playback electronics* take the

---

[*]From David M. Huber and Robert E. Runstein, *Modern Recording Techniques*, 3rd ed. (Indianapolis: Howard Sams, 1989), p. 125.

Table 6-2 Playback and record alignment procedures

Playback Alignment

Thread the playback alignment tape on the machine to be aligned. If the tape was stored tails out, rewind to the head.

A. 15-ips playback alignment for low-noise, high-output tape, using a standard full-track 15-ips alignment tape.

1. Set repro level for 0 VU at 700 Hz.
2. Set high-frequency 15-ips playback EQ for 0 VU at 10 kHz.
3. Reset repro level for –6 VU at 700 Hz.
4. Do not adjust low-frequency playback EQ until after record adjustments.

B. 15-ips playback alignment for regular tape using a standard full-track 15-ips alignment tape.

1. Follow steps given in A, above, but omit A3.

C. 7½-ips playback alignment for low-noise, high-output tape, using a standard full-track 7½-ips alignment tape.

1. Set repro level control so that the 700-Hz tone recorded 10 dB below operating level reads 0 VU.
2. Set 7½-ips high-frequency playback EQ so that the 10-kHz tone reads 0 VU.
3. Do not adjust low-frequency EQ until after record adjustments.
4. Set repro level control so that the 700-Hz tone recorded at operating level reads –6-dB VU.

D. 7½-ips playback alignment for regular tape, using a standard full-track 7½-ips alignment tape.

1. Follow steps C1 through C3.
2. Set repro level control so that the 700-Hz tone recorded at operating level reads 0 VU.

Record Alignment

Thread the tape to be recorded on the machine.

A. For all tapes at 15 ips.

1. Set output selector to the bias position, and set the machine into the record mode on all tracks.
2. Adjust the erase peak control for maximum meter reading.
3. Feed a 1,000-Hz tone into the machine inputs.
4. Set the output selector to repro and, beginning with a low bias setting, increase the amount of bias until the meter reading rises to a maximum. Continue increasing the bias level until the meter reading drops by 1 dB.
5. Feed a 700-Hz tone into all machine inputs at a 0-dB level from the console and set the level control so that the meter on the recorder reads 0 VU.
6. Set the output selector to the input position and adjust the record cal control for a 0-VU meter reading.
7. Set the output selector to repro and feed a 10-kHz tone into all machine inputs at 0-VU level from the console, and set the 15-ips record EQ so that the meter reads 0 VU (at the peak of the meter swing if the needle is unsteady).
8. Feed a 50-Hz tone into the machine inputs at 0-VU level. Adjust the 15-ips low-frequency playback EQ for a 0-VU meter reading.

Table 6-2 (continued)

B. For all tapes at 7½ ips.

1. Follow steps A1 and A2 above.
2. Set the output selector to repro and feed a 500-Hz tone to all the machine inputs. Set all tracks into the record mode and increase the bias level to obtain maximum meter reading. Increase bias so that meter reading drops slightly below the peak reading.
3. Feed a 700-Hz tone at 0 VU to all machine inputs and set the level control for a 0-VU reading on the meter.
4. Set the output selector to input and set the record cal control for a 0-VU reading on the meter.
5. Reduce the setting of the record level control so that the meter reads −10-dB VU.
6. Set the output selector to repro and adjust the repro level control for a 0-VU reading on the meter.
7. Feed a 10-kHz tone into the machine inputs at 0 VU and adjust the 7½-ips record EQ to obtain a meter reading of 0 VU.
8. Feed a 50-Hz tone into the machine inputs at 0 VU and adjust the 7½-ips low-frequency playback EQ for a 0-VU meter reading.
9. Feed a 700-Hz tone into the machine inputs at 0 VU, set the output selector switch to input, and adjust the record level control for a reading of 0 VU on the meter.
10. Reduce the repro level control to approximately the position set with the operating level tone on the playback alignment tape. Then switch the output selector to the repro position and adjust the repro level control for a 0-VU meter reading. (Follow step 10 in the order stated to prevent pinning and possibly damaging the VU meters on the tape machine.)

---

signal from the playback head and amplify it into the voltage, which is then sent to the output of the tape recorder.

The electronics also equalize the record and playback signals so that it is possible to achieve a flat frequency response with magnetic tape. Because analog recording is not linear, during recording the low and high frequencies are boosted to improve their signal-to-noise ratio. During playback, the playback head output rises 6 dB per octave. To compensate for this rise, playback equalization falls 6 dB per octave. Playback equalization also attenuates the bass to compensate for the bass boost during recording.

Total Transport Logic

Modern tape recorder transport designs incorporate *Total Transport Logic (TTL)* using microprocessor monitoring and control over transport functions. In older ATRs,

for example, to stop a tape in fast forward or rewind by pressing the "Stop" button meant risking stretching the tape. To prevent tape damage it was necessary to "rock" the tape to a stop by engaging the fast forward mode when the tape was in rewind and vice versa. When the tape slowed, it was safe to press the "Stop" button. With TTL, the recorder "rocks" the transport until stopping is safe. Also, a shuttle control makes it possible to shuttle tape at various speeds in either direction (see 6-6).

Features of Audiotape Recorders

Audiotape recorders have various features that increase flexibility in their use.

Tracks and Track Widths

Professional analog open-reel audiotape recorders come in 1-, 2-, 4-, 8-, 16-, and

a

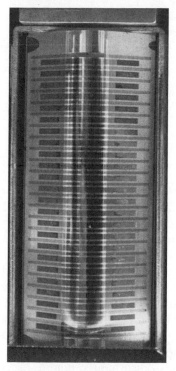
b

6-12 (*a*) **8-track headstack for 1/2-inch tape and** (*b*) **24-track headstack for 2-inch tape.** In the 24-track headstack, track width is .037. See also Figure 6-13.

24-channel/track formats. The amount of surface area on each head (or **headstack**, as it is called on multitrack heads) used for recording or playback varies with the size of the head (see 6-12). Between each head is a **guard band** that reduces considerably the chance of magnetic information from one head affecting the magnetic information on an adjacent track.

Do not confuse *channel* with *track*; these terms are not synonyms. A **channel** is a conduit through which signal flows. The path the signal makes on the tape is the *track*. See 6-13 for a graphic explanation of the relationship between channel and track in analog recording.

Narrow-Gauge Formats

Analog tape recorders are also available with a narrow-gauge headstack. Narrow-gauge headstacks make it possible to record more tracks on ¼-, ½-, and 1-inch tape—as many as 8 tracks on ¼-inch tape, 8 or 16 tracks on ½-inch tape, and 16 or 24 tracks on 1-inch tape.

Narrow-gauge formats were developed for industrial-grade and nonprofessional audio production. Their main advantage is greater multitrack capability at a lower cost because narrow-gauge ATRs are considerably less expensive than conventional analog multitrack machines. Their main disadvantages are generally poorer sound quality and greater risk of crosstalk.

Selective Synchronization (Sel Sync)

Multitrack recorders were developed to permit greater control of the sound sources during recording and playback by making it possible to assign each one to its own track. Multitrack recorders also make it possible to record various sound sources at different

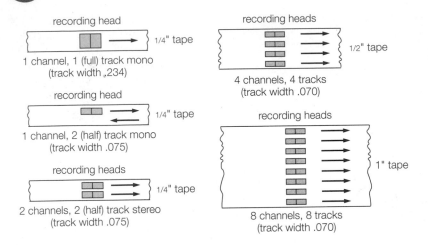

6-13 Channel and track formats of selected standard-gauge open-reel analog recorders. A 24-channel, 24-track headstack is displayed in Figure 6-12.

times by **overdubbing**—recording new material on open tracks and synchronizing it with material on tracks already recorded. The technology that facilitates this production technique is called by the copyrighted term **Sel Sync** (short for *selective synchronization*). It was developed by Ampex (the innovator was guitarist Les Paul).

Under normal conditions, if you first recorded, say, only the instrumental accompaniment to a vocal, the vocalist would have to listen to the recording (through headphones) to synchronize the words to the music. A distance of a few inches separates the record and playback heads, however. This will create a delay between the music and the lyrics as they are played back together (see 6-14). To eliminate this delay, Sel Sync uses the record head as a playback head for the previously recorded tracks and plays them in sync with the new material being recorded (see 6-15; also see the section on overdubbing in Chapter 13).

Tape Timing

Professional tape recorders are equipped with a tape timer (see 6-6). It provides an easy way to locate recorded material. The tape timer is wound by a tape guide roller with revolutions that are converted to inches per second. It reads out in hours, minutes, seconds, and, in many ATRs, in frames.

Another means of keeping tape time is by using **SMPTE** (**longitudinal**) **time code**, a feature on most new ATRs. Time code, which also reads out in hours, minutes, seconds, and frames, codes each "frame" of audiotape with a different number. Time code is also used to synchronize tapes (see Chapter 14).

Auto-Locator

Even with a timer, locating specific cue points on a tape can be time-consuming. An accessory that is part of most professional

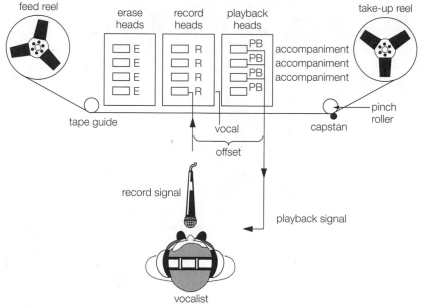

incorrect

6-14 Overdubbing without Sel Sync. This method creates an offset between the sound being played back and the sound being recorded.

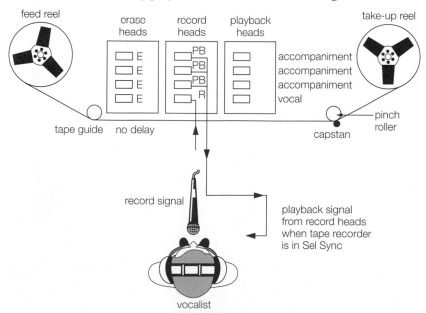

correct

6-15 Overdubbing with Sel Sync. Playback and record are synchronized.

multitrack ATRs makes it possible to program cues and store them in a memory. At the touch of a few buttons, the tape transport automatically spools to a precise location on the tape. This function is commonly known as *auto-locator* (see 6-6). Most auto-locators have remote control.

With an auto-locator, specific cue points on a tape are coded and entered into a memory using a keypad. The code is a number in tape time or in SMPTE time code and, usually, switchable between the two. To recall the cue point from memory, you re-enter the coded number into the keypad. To make the auto-locator shuttle the tape to the desired position, you press the "Search" button. At that point, the transport will either stop, place itself into "Play", or cycle. Cycling "loops" the tape between two cue points in a play-relocate-play sequence.

Cassette Tape Recorders

The cassette tape recorder has made tape recording accessible to virtually anyone, anywhere. But because of the analog cassette's mediocre sound quality, its format (the tape's small size), and its slow playing speed, it is not used in professional music recording—except, perhaps, to make quick copies of rough mixes or for temporary demo recordings.

The digital audiocassette tape recorder (R-DAT), however, has become part of the professional recording scene because, despite the tape's even smaller size and slower playing speed, it delivers digital-quality sound. The R-DAT is discussed in Chapter 7.

DIGITAL RECORDING

Compared to analog recording, digital recording greatly increases dynamic range and virtually eliminates noise, distortion, crosstalk, wow and flutter, print-through, and degeneration of sound quality in tape-to-tape dubbing. Despite these advantages, digital recording has not made the analog format obsolete. The best analog recording produces a dynamic range of 80 dB to 90 dB. Given that many recordists prefer analog's "warmer" colorings to the "edge" in digital sound, the two formats should coexist for some time to come.

Digital Audio

Instead of using an analogous relationship between the acoustic sound and the electronically processed signal, **digital recording** uses a numerical representation of the audio signal's actual frequency and amplitude. In analog, frequency is the time component, amplitude is the level component. In digital, sampling is the time component, quantization is the level component.

Sampling

Sampling takes periodic samples (voltages) of the original analog signal at fixed intervals and converts them into digital data. The rate at which the fixed intervals sample the original signal each second is called the **sampling frequency**. For example, if the sampling frequency is 48 kHz that means samples are taken 48 thousand times per second, or each sample period is 1/48,000 of a second. Because sampling and the component of time are directly related, a system's sampling rate determines its upper frequency limits. Theoretically, the higher the sampling rate, the greater a system's frequency range.

It was determined several years ago that if the highest frequency in a signal were to be digitally encoded successfully, it had to be sampled at a rate at least twice its frequency.* In other words, if high-frequency response in digital recording is to reach 20 kHz, the sampling frequency must be at

---

*This concept was developed by a Bell Laboratories researcher named Harry Nyquist. To honor this discovery, the sampling frequency has been named the *Nyquist frequency*.

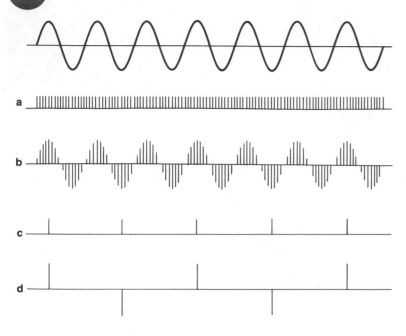

7-1 Sampling. A signal (*a*) sampled frequently enough (*b*) contains sufficient information for proper decoding. (*c*) Too low a sampling rate (*d*) loses too much information for proper decoding.

least 40 kHz. Too low a sampling rate would cause loss of too much information (see 7-1).

Think of a movie camera that takes 24 still pictures a second. A sampling rate of 1/24 second seems adequate to record most visual activities. Although the camera shutter closes after each 1/24 second and nothing is recorded, not enough information is lost to impair perception of the event. A person running, for example, does not run far enough in the split second the shutter is closed to alter the naturalness of movement. If the sampling rates were slowed to one frame a second, the running movement would be quick and abrupt; if it were slowed to one frame every minute, the running would be difficult to follow.

For practical and economic reasons, digital audio today uses essentially four sampling rates: 32, 44.056, 44.1, and 48 kHz. Thirty-two kHz is the international sampling rate used for broadcast digital audio. Because maximum bandwidth in broadcast transmission is 15 kHz, 32 kHz is sufficient. For laser disc, compact disc, and digital tape recording, however, 44.056, 44.1, and 48 kHz, respectively, are used.

Aliasing

If frequencies higher than the Nyquist frequency (half the sampling frequency) are sampled, they will be reflected back into the audible bandwidth, generating inharmonic pitches. This unwanted condition is known as *aliasing* (also called *foldover error*). For example, if a 32-kHz signal is sampled with a 50-kHz sampling rate, it will produce an 18-kHz alias frequency.

To prevent aliasing, a signal is first fed through a **low-pass filter** before analog-to-digital conversion. A low-pass filter filters out high frequencies at a set point, allowing the frequencies below that point to pass. This input filter is sometimes called the *anti-aliasing* filter.

To compensate for the high-frequency filtering in anti-aliasing, systems use sampling rates higher than twice the highest frequency. For example, a system with a bandwidth of 15 kHz is sampled at a rate of 32 thousand samples a second; a system with a bandwidth of 20 kHz may be sampled at 44.1 or 48 thousand samples a second.

Many people believe that higher sampling frequencies are necessary to realize fully the potential of digital sound. A solution to this problem is oversampling. **Oversampling** raises the sampling rate in a digital system to improve audio quality without using appreciably more storage space.

Quantization

As samples of the waveform are taken, these voltages are converted into discrete quantities and assigned a value. This process is known as **quantization**. The assigned value is in the form of *bi*nary dig*its* (*bits*). Most of us learned math using the Decimal, or Base 10, system, which consists of ten numerals, 0 through 9. The Binary, or Base 2, system uses two numbers, 0 and 1. In the conversion of an analog signal to digital, when the voltage is off, the assigned value is 0; when the voltage is on, the assigned value is 1.

A quantity expressed as a binary number is called a *digital word*. Ten is a 2-bit word,

101 is a 3-bit word, 11010 is a 5-bit word, and so on. Each N-bit binary word produces 2^N discrete levels. Therefore, a 1-bit word produces 2 discrete levels—0, 1; a 2-bit word produces four discrete levels—00, 01, 10, 11; a 3-bit word produces eight discrete levels—111, 110, 101, 100, 011, 010, 001, 000, and so on. So the more quantizing levels there are, the longer the digital word must be. The longer the digital word, the better the sonic resolution. For example, the number of discrete voltage steps possible in an 8-bit word is 256, in a 16-bit word it is 65,536, and in a 20-bit word it is 1,048,576 steps. The greater the number of these quantizing levels the more accurate the representation of the analog signal (see 7-2).

This raises a question, however. How can a representation of the original signal be better than the original signal itself? Assume that the original analog signal is an ounce of water with an infinite number of values (molecules). The amount and "character" of the water changes with the number of molecules; it has one "value" with 500 molecules, another with 501, still another with 2,975, and so forth. But all together, the values are infinite. Moreover, changes in the original quantity of water are inevitable: Some of it may evaporate, some may be lost if poured, and some may be contaminated or absorbed by dust or dirt.

But what if the water molecules were sampled and then converted to a stronger, more durable form? In so doing, a representation of the water would be obtained in a form from which nothing would be lost. Sufficient samples would have to be obtained, however, to make sure that the character of the original water was maintained.

For example, suppose the molecule samples were converted to ball bearings and a quantity of 1 million ball bearings was a sufficient sample. In this form, the original

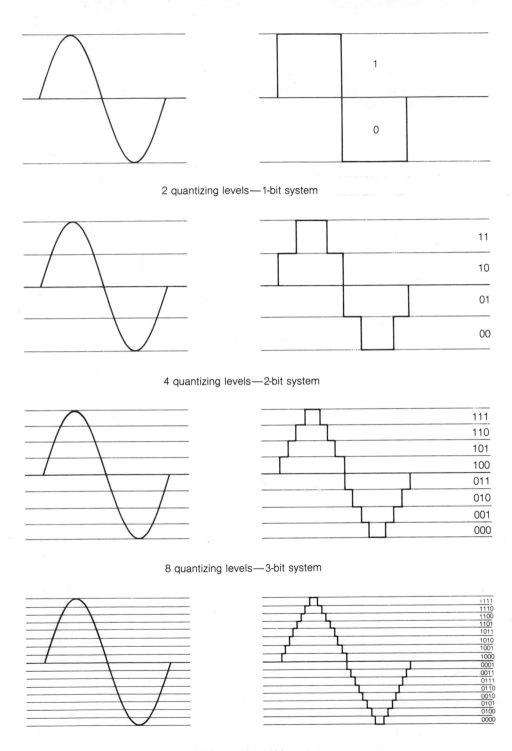

2 quantizing levels—1-bit system

4 quantizing levels—2-bit system

8 quantizing levels—3-bit system

16 quantizing levels—4-bit system

7-2 Quantizing. As the number of quantizing levels increases, the digital representation of the analog signal becomes more accurate.

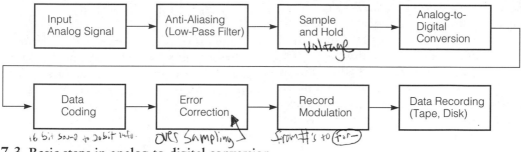

7-3 Basic steps in analog-to-digital conversion

water is not vulnerable to evaporation or contamination from dust and dirt. Even if a ball bearing is lost, they are all the same; therefore, losing one ball bearing does not affect the content or quality of the others.

In quantizing the analog signal into discrete binary numbers (voltages), noise, known as *quantizing noise*, is generated. The signal-to-noise ratio in an analog-to-digital conversion system is 6 dB for each bit. It has been generally agreed, at least for now, that a 16-bit system is sufficient to deal with quantizing noise (although some digital formats may use a 20-bit system). This, therefore, gives digital sound a signal-to-noise ratio of 96 dB (6 dB × 16-bit system), which is significantly better than anything most analog recording can produce.

The Digital Recording/ Reproduction Process

The digital recording/reproduction process essentially involves two complementary procedures in the encoding and decoding of a signal.

The Recording Process

Converting analog signals into a digital format for recording occurs in five basic steps: anti-aliasing, sample and hold, analog-to-digital conversion, signal coding, and data storage (see 7-3).

You will recall that in order to keep unwanted high frequencies from aliasing— becoming audible when the analog signal begins its passage through the digital sampling system—they are rolled off using a low-pass filter. The process is called *anti-aliasing*.

After anti-aliasing, a *sample and hold* circuit temporarily holds the analog voltage level for the duration of a single sample period. This allows enough time for the analog-to-digital converter to generate a digital word that corresponds to the sampled voltage.

During analog-to-digital conversion, the signal is sampled and quantized in a remarkable operation. For example, in a 16-bit system at a sampling rate of 48 kHz, as the signal is sampled and held, 16 successive approximations are performed within 1/48,000 of a second.

Once the signal has been converted into digital form it is coded. This process involves data coding, error correction, and record (or data) modulation. *Data coding* prevents ambiguity by making it easier to identify the beginning of each digital word in the bit stream. Data coding serves much the same purpose as spaces between words in a sentence. *Error correction* is necessary to minimize the effect of storage defects. Because digital data are packed at very high density, storage defects are inevitable. These defects would degrade the quality of digital audio, especially with digital audiotape recorders and compact disc formats. The data error rate for hard disks and optical disks is very low. Error correction minimizes the number of errors during the storage process. *Record (or data) modulation* is the final processing of digital data before storage. Although the data are in the form of 1s and 0s, binary code is not an efficient way to store data. Therefore, the data are modulated and stored as pulses of magnetic energy. Data may be stored onto any recording medium such as tape, compact disc, or floppy, hard, or optical disk.

The Reproduction Process

The basic steps in the digital reproduction process are demodulation, error correction, digital-to-analog conversion, sample and hold, and low-pass filtering.

Demodulation performs three important functions. (1) It amplifies the signals, which are at a very low level. (2) It takes the waveforms, which are inevitably distorted by the conversion process, and reshapes them into their original modulated states. (3) It returns the modulated signals into their original binary form of 1s and 0s. *Error correction* compensates for errors introduced during storage. In *digital-to-analog conversion* the digital word is converted to an analog voltage that is analogous to the original signal before sampling. The *output sample and hold* circuit removes irregular signals, called *switching glitches*, from the reproduction chain. *Low-pass filtering* at the output, also known as *anti-imaging filtering*, smoothes any nonlinearity in the final waveform that was introduced by the digital sampling process.

Open-Reel Digital Audiotape

There are several essential differences between the types of audiotape used for analog and digital recording. First, digital tape does not have to be as thick as tape used for analog recording; the magnetic coating, in particular, does not need to be as thick. In the analog system, varying signal strengths recorded on the tape correspond to the different levels from the input signal. To a great extent, the thickness of the oxide coating determines the tape's signal-to-noise ratio. Moreover, saturating the tape with too much signal must be avoided.

In digital recording the sampling frequency is constant, and at each sample the tape is saturated with a series of pulses. There is no resultant distortion because the digital system only has to deal with the presence (1) or absence (0) of a pulse. Therefore, tape thickness is not a factor in the tape's ability to reproduce dynamic range.

The total thickness of digital tape (base, back, and magnetic coating) is about ½ mil less than the analog tape used professionally (which is 1½ mil). This, plus the sampling rates, affects recording times on the various-size open reels (see Table 7-1).

Second, the coercivity of nonmetal tape used for digital recording is about twice that of analog tape. Greater coercivity is needed to retain the very short wavelengths of the higher frequencies and the densely packed digital information, which is about 10 times that stored in analog recording.

Third, any tape requires care in handling, but digital tape requires more care than analog tape. It is essential that the working area be as free from dust and dirt as possible. Moderate temperature and low humidity should be kept within ranges of ±10 percent. Oils from the hands can cause degradation

Table 7-1 Recording times for open-reel digital tape

Format	Sampling Rate (kHz)	Tape Speed (ips)	Tape Width (inches)	Playing Time (minutes) per Reel Size			
				7-inch	10½-inch	12½-inch	14-inch
DASH-S (slow)	44.1	6.89	¼	69	139	208	
	48	7.5	¼	63	127	191	
Twin-DASH (slow and medium)	44.1	13.67	¼	34	69	104	
	48	15	¼	31	63	95	
DASH-F (fast)	44.1	27.56	½				65
	48	30	½				60
PD (Pro Digi)	44.1 48	7.5	¼				240
	44.1 48	15	¼				120
	44.1 48	30	½				60
	44.1 48	30	1				60

of the quality of both the magnetic and back coatings. If tape is soiled, it should be wiped gently with a soft cloth. Tape recorder heads must be completely dry from cleaning liquids before digital tape is used.

Digital Audiotape Recorders

Digital audiotape recorders are divided into two categories: stationary head and rotary head.

Stationary Head Digital Audio Recording

In the early stages of the digital audio revolution, as manufacturers rushed to the marketplace with their "unique" digital ATR designs, the need to standardize became clear almost at once. About the only things the digital ATRs had in common were their operational functions, such as "Play," "Record," "Fast Forward," and so on, functions similar to those in analog ATRs.

Some digital ATRs operated at the familiar speeds of 7½, 15, and 30 ips, but others ran at such speeds as 22½, 25, 35, or 45 ips. Head configurations, tracks formats, sampling rates, and other technical specifications differed. In short, most designs were incompatible with one another. Fearing chaos, and at the urging of the Audio Engineering Society (AES), some companies agreed to attempt to standardize digital formats. Although the results, so far, are less than satisfactory, at least stationary head digital tape recording now has greater design and format compatibility.

Formats

Two formats are currently being used by most companies producing stationary head

Track Density and Channel Numbers				
Tape Width	1/4"		1/2"	
Track Density	Normal	Double	Normal	Double
Digital Tracks	8	16	24	48
Aux. Tracks	4	4	4	4
Digital Audio Channels — Fast	8	16	24	48
Digital Audio Channels — Medium	TWIN DASH 2	8	—	24
Digital Audio Channels — Slow	2	4	—	—

Tape Speed and Sampling Rate			
Sampling Rate	Tape Speed		
	Fast	Medium	Slow
48kHz	30 ips	15 ips	7.5 ips
44.1kHz	27.56 ips	13.78 ips	6.89 ips

7-4 DASH formats

digital ATRs: the **DASH** (**Digital Audio Stationary Head**) format used by Sony, Studer, and Tascam; and the **PD** (**Professional Digital** or **Pro Digi**) format used by Otari.

DASH Format   The DASH format is not so much one format as it is a family of formats. It specifies sampling frequency, tape format, track geometry, packing density, and error correction for 2-channel to 48-channel digital tape recorders using ¼-inch or ½-inch tape, respectively (see 7-4).

A stereo DASH single-density recording on ¼-inch tape actually records 12 tracks on the tape (see 7-5). In the slow speed, 8 digital audio tracks would be used for 2 audio channels. At medium speed the 8 digital tracks are used for either 4 audio channels or, in the Twin-DASH format, 2 audio channels (Twin-DASH was developed to increase error protection in heavy-duty usage). At fast speed the 8 digital audio tracks could be used for 8 audio channels. There are 4 auxiliary tracks for stereo analog cue track

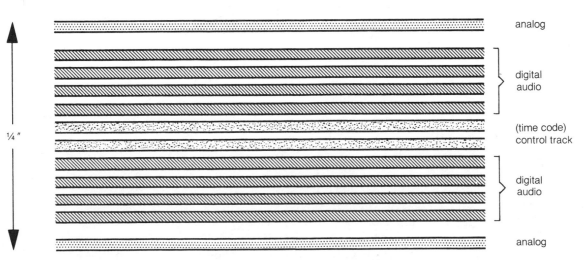

analog

digital audio

(time code) control track

digital audio

analog

¼ "

7-5 Twelve tracks of a DASH single-density recording on ¼-inch tape

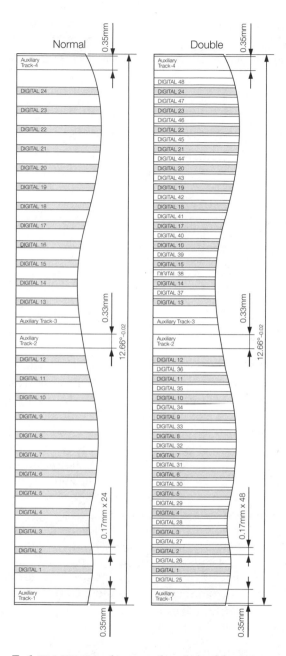

7-6 DASH ½-inch normal and double-density formats

recording and for a time-code track and a control track. With DASH ½-inch tape using fast speed in the single-density mode, for example, 28 tracks are recorded: 24 digital audio tracks and 4 auxiliary tracks for cue, time code, and control track recording (see 7-6).

Double-density recording, known as DASH II, packs more digital audio channels and tracks onto the ¼- and ½-inch tape. Using thin-film heads instead of the conventional ferrite heads makes this possible.

PD Format There are several differences between the DASH and PD formats. Although most are too technical for discussion here, listing a few should provide at least a superficial understanding of their dissimilarities.

One difference is that the PD format supports three tape widths: ¼-inch for stereo recording; ½-inch for 16-channel recording; and 1-inch for 32-channel recording. One-quarter-inch machines operate at 7½ ips, encoding data in high-bit density, and at 15 ips, encoding data in high- or low-bit density. One-half-inch and 1-inch machines operate at 30 ips with medium-bit data density (see Table 7-2).

Another important difference between PD and DASH is the absence of a specific control track in PD. A *control track* is used to provide information for tracking control and tape speed. PD integrates this information on each main data track.

The ¼-inch format consists of 10 tracks: 8 digital audio tracks (6 for audio-signal data and 2 parity tracks for error correction) and 2 auxiliary tracks (1 analog track for tape cueing and 1 analog track for time code) (see 7-7). One-half-inch and 1-inch PD-formatted tape recorders encode 24 and 45 tracks, respectively.

Table 7-2   Pro Digi formats

	PD 2-channel *high rate*	PD 2-channel *low speed*	PD 2-channel *high speed*	PD 16-channel	PD 32-channel
Tape Speed (ips)	15	7.5	15	30	30
Tape Width (inches)	¼	¼	¼	½	1
Sampling Ftequency (kHz)	96	48 and 44.1	48 and 44.1	48 and 44.1	48 and 44.1
Quantization (linear PCM)	16- or 20-bit	16- or 20-bit	16- or 20-bit	16-bit	16-bit
Number of Tracks	12	12	12	24	45
Tracks per Channel	4	4	4	1.25	1.25
Bit Density (thousands of bits per inch)	40	40	20	29.9	29.9

subtrack 4	cue left channel
subtrack 3	cue right channel
main track 8	
main track 7	
main track 6	
main track 5	two channels
main track 4	of digital audio
main track 3	
main track 2	
main track 1	
subtrack 2	aux digital
subtrack 1	time code

7-7 Pro Digi ¼-inch track format

Head Configuration

In digital audio, using the conventional analog head configuration—erase, record, playback—would make editing, particularly cut-and-splice editing (see Chapter 14), synchronous recording, and overdubbing, as well as other operations, extremely difficult. Recording and reproducing digital information requires head functions and head configuration different from those in analog. There are several arrangements in digital audio, but two examples should illustrate the point.

In one ¼-inch stereo design there is an advanced or forward record head—the **write head**—and playback head—the **read head**. The **write-sync head** is a second record head next to the playback head. There is no erase head. An operation called *overwriting* is used instead. The first recording head is used during normal recording; the second one is used to synchronize new audio with prerecorded audio. The distance between the playback head and the sync head is adjusted to match the decoding and encoding delay of the two heads. Some digital ATRs may also have an analog head to facilitate cut-and-splice editing and performance of conventional erase, record, and playback functions (see 7-8).

In one digital multichannel design there are erase, record-1, playback, and record-2 (sync) heads (see 7-9). The record-1 and playback heads are used for playback after record, and the playback and record-2 heads are used for sync recording.

Stationary Head Digital Audiocassette Recorders

The **stationary head digital audiotape recorder (S-DAT)** uses a fixed, instead of a rotating, head. Until recently, it was not

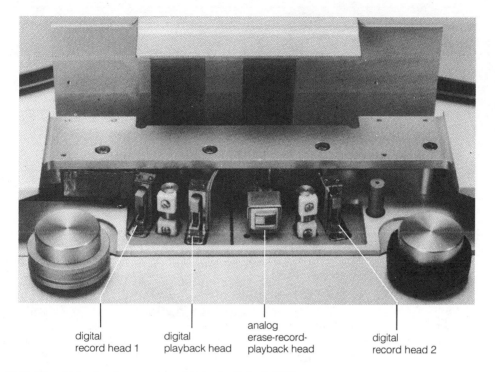

digital
record head 1

digital
playback head

analog
erase-record-
playback head

digital
record head 2

7-8 Head block of one type of ¼-inch digital ATR

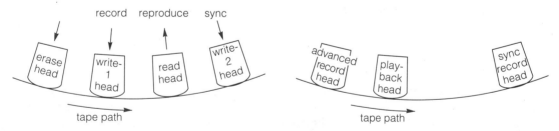

7-9 Head blocks for two different multichannel digital ATRs

given much of a chance against R-DAT, discussed in the next sections. The main problems with S-DAT are the limited recording time per cassette and mechanical problems with the fixed head design in relation to the sonic requirements of digital audio. One viable use of S-DAT was designing the concept into a multitrack digital recorder and integrating it into a console (see 7-10). But recording time per cassette is only about 20 minutes with the system shown in 7-10.

The Dutch conglomerate Philips, developer of the compact analog cassette, has also developed its digital successor: the **digital compact cassette** (DCC). It was introduced for the consumer market, but it holds

tape housing

7-10 S-DAT digital mixer/recorder

implications for the project studio in a stationary head design. Although it has a fixed head, the DCC's coding, tape formulation, and mechanism differ significantly from the earlier S-DAT design. The DCC records and plays back 18-bit stereo digital audio, supports three sampling frequencies (48 kHz, 44.1 kHz, and 32 kHz), has a dynamic range of 105 dB, and produces CD-quality audio. Signal-to-noise ratio can be as wide as 90 dB.

The DCC runs at 1⅞ ips, the same as analog cassette. It is similar to the chrome-type tape used in video, with a cobalt-treated magnetic coating that is slightly narrower and thinner than R-DAT tape. The digital compact cassette records bidirectionally (the tape cannot be turned over; the tape recorder heads invert at the end of a side). The casing sizes of the DCC and compact analog cassette are the same. The single head combines both digital and analog transducing, which makes it possible to play back analog cassettes. There is no erase head; you rerecord over the previous track. Tape time of up to 120 minutes per digital compact cassette is possible.

Rotary Head Digital Audio Recording

Storing video information on tape requires a different recording system than the one used to record sound in fixed-head formats. Due to the considerable bandwidth it takes to store video, very high tape speeds are necessary. In a stationary head format the tape speed would have to be many times faster than the 30 ips of today's fastest ATRs, and it would take thousands of feet of tape to make a video recording. Therefore, instead of increasing longitudinal tape speed in video recording, the videotape head rotates at very high speed (2,000 revolutions per minute in rotary head digital audiotape recording). This creates the tape-to-head velocity essential for the wide bandwidth to store video information without requiring faster longitudinal tape speeds. This technique is called **helical scanning**, due to the somewhat spiral shape of the tape when it is threaded around the head assembly (the Greek word for spiral is *helix*).

Helical videotape recording has made it possible not only to record picture on tape but also to produce digital sound on audio-cassette (and on videocassette). Today, digital audio on cassette can be produced in stereo and multitrack.

Rotary Head Digital Audio Recorders

The **rotary head digital audiocassette recorder** (**R-DAT**) has the wide dynamic range, low distortion, and immeasurable wow and flutter common to digital audio. Although the R-DAT uses cassette tape, it equals or exceeds many standard digital specifications.

R-DATs usually operate at two sampling frequencies: 44.1 kHz and 48 kHz. Many R-DATs include a third sampling frequency of 32 kHz. A few also use 44.056 kHz. Recording and playback can be done at all sampling rates. Originally, 44.1 kHz was a playback-only mode to discourage unlawful copying of prerecorded digital audiocassette tapes and compact discs. Consumer units still cannot duplicate this sampling rate in the record mode. Many professional R-DATs, however, do provide recording at 44.1 kHz.

Most R-DAT recorders have a longitudinal tape speed of about ⅓ ips, one-sixth the speed of analog cassette recorders. The very slow speed does not affect sound quality, however, due to the high speed of the head drum and digital processing of the audio signal. Digital audiocassettes are available in different lengths up to 2 hours.

R-DAT specifications provide for four record/playback modes: standard record/play speed; record/play option 1; record/play option 2; and record/play option 3. Standard record/play records two (stereo) channels using the 48 kHz sampling rate. This speed must be supported in all R-DAT equipment. Record/play options 1, 2, and 3

provide for the 32 kHz sampling rate. In option 1, two (stereo) channels are provided with 16-bit linear quantization. Option 2 also supports two (stereo) channels, but tape speed is half that of most R-DATs and has a resolution of only 12 bits that is nonlinear—the amplitude steps are not all the same size. All this results in reduced sound quality but increased tape time, up to 4 hours. Option 3 is a combination of options 1 and 2. Speed and data rate are the same as in option 1, but fidelity is comparable to option 2 because this mode uses four channels instead of two. The chief advantage of option 3 is that it enables four-channel multitrack recording.

R-DAT has other advantages. For example, the encoding of nonaudio data permits automatic cueing to a particular selection, skipping over selections, and numbering selections. In addition, a high-speed search function facilitates quick search-to-cue spooling. R-DAT machines are available in portable, lightweight cassette-size units, as well as in relatively compact, conveyable studio models (see 7-11 and 7-12).

Aligning an R-DAT

R-DATs are designed to correct errors due to noise, slight mistracking, and dropout. But if there is significant mistracking, error correction cannot handle it and the audio mutes. The following is intended to give you an idea about some concerns related to R-DAT alignment.

In helical recording, the upper part of the spinning drum carries the heads. The lower part is stationary and guides the lower edge of the tape around the drum. The tape does not touch the upper or lower drum surface. It is prevented from rising by a series of guides that are adjusted to contact the top edge of the tape and hold it in place along

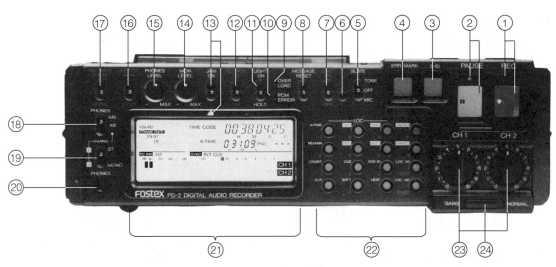

Front Panel Description

(1) REC key/LED: Starts recording. The LED illuminates during recording

(2) REC PAUSE key/LED: Pauses recording. The LED illuminates while in pause mode

(3) S-ID key: Records a START .D while recording

(4) ERROR MARK key: Records an ERROR MARK while recording

(5) SLATE switch: Records a 1kHz slate tone, or the sound picked up by the internal microphone on both audio channels

(6) SLATE MICROPHONE: A condenser type microphone

(7) LIMIT switch: Switches the internal limiter on/off

7-11   R-DAT recorder/reproducer and its functions

(8) MESSAGE RESET switch: Clears the error message currently shown on the LCD

(9) OVER LOAD LED: Illuminates when the microphone or line signal is clipped (CH1 and CH2)

(10) PCM ERROR LED: Lights green when the BER (block error rate) is greater than 1% and red when the BER is greater than 10% (1 block = 288 bits; 1 track = 196 blocks)

(11) LIGHT switch: Switches on the internal lights for viewing the cylinder drum and the LCD side light

(12) TC MONITOR switch: Monitors the TC using the internal speaker and headphones (TC = time code)

(13) JAM switch: Synchronizes the tape recorder's internal TC generator with the external TC source, allowing you to disconnect the external TC and let the tape recorder's internal TC generator continue striping the tape (free-run mode)

(14) MONITOR LEVEL: Adjusts the volume of the monitor speaker

(15) PHONES LEVEL: Adjusts the volume of the headphones

(16) METER switch: Selects the source for the LCD bargraphs: INPUT or follow the REC MON switch

(17) REC MON switch: Selects the monitor source: INPUT or REPRO. During recording REPRO allows off tape "confidence" monitoring

(18) PHONES MODE switch: Selects the headphones mode: MONO/STEREO, LEFT only/RIGHT only, MS mono/MS stereo

(19) PHONES ST/MONO: Used in conjunction with the PHONES MODE switch

(20) PHONES JACK: Headphone connection

(21) LCD: See detail on the following page.

(22) FUNCTION KEYS: See detail below.

(23) CH1 CH2 Record level controls: Adjusts the level of signal recorded on to tape

(24) GANG/NORMAL LEVER: Gangs the record level controls together, or normal allows independent channel record level setting

Function Keys

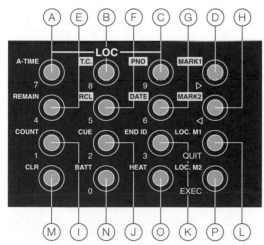

(A) A-TIME LOCATE key: Enters an A-TIME value that is to be used for locating

(B) TC LOCATE key: Enters a TC value that is to be used for locating

(C) PNO LOCATE key: Enters a PNO that is to be used for locating (PNO = program number)

(D) MARK 1 / >> key: Stores the current A-TIME value in memory as MARK 1. Also used as the right cursor key when entering or editing numeric values

(E) TAPE REMAIN key: Shows the remaining time on tape

(F) RCL key: Sets the real time clock. TC generator start time. PNO starting number and edit MARK 1 & 2

(G) DATE DISPLAY key. Displays the current date and time. When playing a tape, the date information recorded in the sub code will be displayed

(H) MARK 2 / << key: Stores the current A-TIME value in memory as MARK 2. Also used as the left cursor key when entering or editing numeric values

(I) COUNTER key: Uses a linear tape counter instead of A-TIME

(J) CUE key: Cue mode: monitor off tape during F.FWD and REWIND

(K) END-ID REC key: Records an END ID while recording

(L) LOC-M1 / QUIT key: Locates to the MARK 1 A-TIME value. Also used as the QUIT key when using the soft functions

(M) CLR key: Resets the linear tape counter. Sets numeric values to zero when in edit mode and resets the peak hold function when using manual reset mode

(N) BATTERY CHECK key: Checks the battery voltage under any load condition

(O) HEATER key: Pre-heats the cylinder drum to prevent dewing

(P) LOC-M2 / EXECUTE key: Locates to the MARK 2 A-TIME value. Also used as the EXECUTE key when using the soft functions

LCD

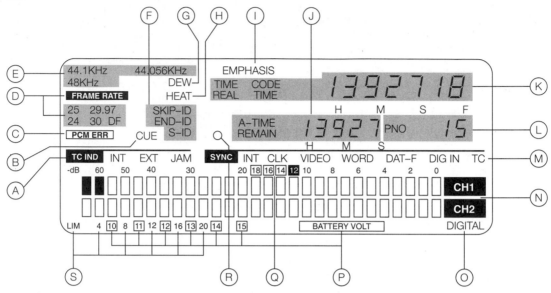

(A) TC mode indicator: Indicates the TC source: INT, EXT, or JAM operation

(B) CUE mode indicator: Indicates that CUE mode is on

(C) PCM ERROR indicator: Flashes when a PCM error occurs

(D) FRAME RATE indicator: Indicates the currently selected TC frame rate

(E) SAMPLING FREQ indicator: Indicates the currently set sampling frequency

(F) SKIP-, END-, S-ID indicator: Indicates the type of ID marker that is recorded, or being recorded on tape

(G) DEW indicator: Indicates that dew has been detected on the tape transport

(H) HEATER indicator: Indicates that the internal heater is on

(I) EMPHASIS indicator: Indicates that the EMPHASIS switch is on

(J) A-TIME field: Displays the A-TIME

(K) TIMECODE field: Displays the TC value

(L) PNO field: Shows the current PNO

(M) SYNC mode indicator: Indicates the current SYNC mode: INT CLK, VIDEO, WORD, DAT-F, DIG IN or TC

(N) Bargraph level meters: While recording these meters show the level of the signal being recorded to tape. During playback they show the signal level recorded on the tape

(O) DIGITAL INPUT indicator: Indicates that a digital input signal corresponding to the consumer (SP DIF) or professional (AES/EBU) is connected at the DIGITAL IN connector

(P) BATTERY VOLTAGE: Shows when the battery check function is being used

(Q) REFERENCE LEVEL marker: Shows the current setting of the reference level marker

(R) ERROR MARK indicator: Indicates that an ERROR MARK has been recorded onto tape

(S) LIMITER indicator: Indicates that the limiter is currently on

7-11 (continued)

Top Panel

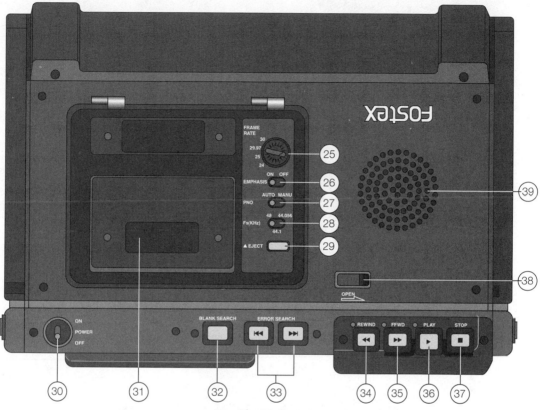

Top Panel Description

(25) FRAME RATE selector: Sets the TC frame rate of the INT TC generator

(26) EMPHASIS switch: Records an analog source with emphasis

(27) PNO switch: Records program numbers either MANUALLY by pressing the S-ID key, or AUTOMATICALLY when recording is started

(28) Fs SELECT switch: Sets the sampling frequency for analog recording

(29) EJECT key: Ejects the cassette

(30) POWER SWITCH: Switches on the power

(31) Tape transport and cover: Tape insertion slot and protective cover

(32) BLANK SEARCH key: Searches for an END ID, or if there is no END ID, the blank section of tape after the last recording

(33) ERROR SEARCH keys: Searches for ERROR MARKS

(34) REWIND key: Starts rewind mode. Press once for slow (× 5), or twice for fast (× 100). Repeated pressing will toggle between slow and fast rewind

(35) F.FWD key: Starts fast forward mode. Press once for slow (× 5), or twice for fast (× 100). Repeated pressing will toggle between slow and fast forward

(36) PLAY key: Starts play mode

(37) STOP key: Stops all tape transport modes. Press once for pause mode and twice for stop mode. Repeated pressing will toggle between pause and stop mode

(38) Protective cover open lever: Opens the protective cover

(39) MONITOR SPEAKER: Internal speaker used for monitoring

7-11 (continued)

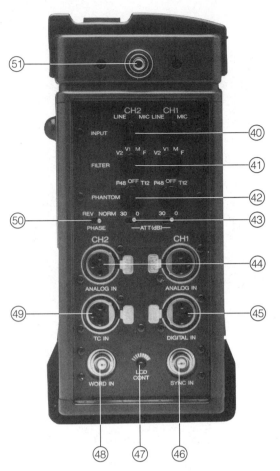

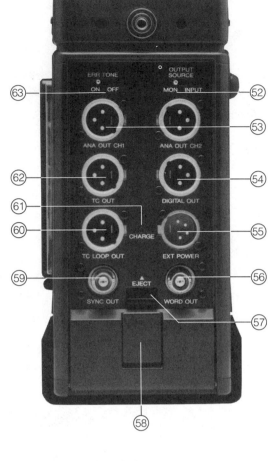

Right Side Panel Description

(40) INPUT switch: Selects microphone or line for analog recording

(41) FILTER switch: Selects a filter type for microphone recording

(42) PHANTOM switch: Phantom powering for condenser type microphones

(43) ATT switch: Input gain attenuator for microphone recording

(44) ANALOG IN: Balanced analog-input signal connection

(45) DIGITAL IN: Digital input connection for AES/EBU professional and consumer (SP DIF) formats

(46) SYNC IN: Synchronizing-video, or DAT frame input connection

(47) LCD CONTRAST: Adjusts the contrast of the LCD display

(48) WORD SYNC IN: Synchronizing-wordclock input connection

(49) TC INPUT: Balanced external TC input connection

(50) PHASE switch (CH 2): Reverses the phase of CH 2 microphone input

(51) Shoulder strap fixing stud: Shoulder strap fixing point

Left Side Panel Description

(52) ANALOG OUTPUT SOURCE: Sets the output source to INPUT or MON

(53) ANALOG OUT: Balanced analog-output signal connection

(54) DIGITAL OUT: Digital output connection for AES/EBU professional and consumer formats

(55) EXT POWER: External power supply connection

(56) WORD SYNC OUT: Wordclock output connection

(57) BATTERY EJECT lever: For removing the Ni-Cd battery

(58) BATTERY DOOR open button: Opens the door of the battery compartment

(59) SYNC OUT: Video-frame sync pulse output connection

(60) TC LOOP OUT: Balanced output of TC applied at the TC INPUT connection

(61) CHARGE INDICATOR: Lights red during normal charging, and green during trickle charging

(62) T.C. OUTPUT: Balanced TC output connection

(63) ALARM TONE switch: Sounds a 1kHz error tone in the following situations: PCM error, input amplifier clipping, and battery low charge condition

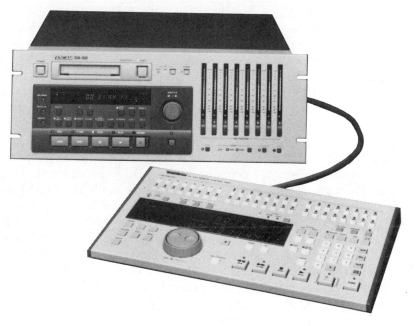

7-12 Multitrack R-DAT with remote controller. This model has 8 tracks and can record 108 minutes on a standard 120-minute Hi-8mm videotape (see "Multitrack R-DAT Recording on Videotape" later in this chapter). A single cable can lock up and synchronize two machines for 16-track recording. This **modular digital multitrack (MDM)** approach allows up to 16 of these R-DATS to be interlocked providing 128 tracks (in 8-track increments) of recording capability. In addition to the usual transport functions such as Play, Record, and so on, there are controls for tape shuttle, sample rate selection, locator points, Rehearse and Auto-punch, clock source selection, time code generate/record, and soft-keys that are used in conjunction with a display button that allows the setting of preroll and crossfade times.

7-11 (concluded) (opposite)

the way. Of particular importance are the entry and exit guides. If they are not properly adjusted, the tape will not track correctly as it passes around the drum's scanner. A reference tape is used for alignment of the guides.

Proper tape tension is also important to alignment because it affects track angle and, therefore, must be checked before adjustments to the drum are made. Usually a specially designed cassette with a tension gauge built into each hub is used. The amount of tension is read off a scale in the body of the cassette. Tension is adjusted for normal play, reverse, and shuttle.

Proper track spacing in Record is determined by checking the frequency-generating wheel on the capstan shaft to make sure the frequency is correct. This is done in the Record mode with a scratch tape.

Tracks can be recorded at the proper angle and spacing. However, if the timing is off, a tape recorder will be able to play its own tapes, but those tapes may not play back accurately on another machine. Recording begins when a sensor generates a pulse once for each revolution of the scanner. A timing reference tape is used to adjust the relative timing between the event on the reference tape and the sensor pulse. Properly adjusted, tracks are recorded in the right place along the helical sweep. Improper adjustment reduces the interchangeability of the recorded tape from the original R-DAT to another R-DAT.[*]

Cleaning an R-DAT

The importance of having a regular equipment maintenance schedule cannot be over-

emphasized. With R-DATs, that is almost as easily done as said; there are cleaning tapes especially made for them. These tapes are nonabrasive, gentle to the heads, and good at removing small, loose particles in the tape path. It is wise to clean your R-DAT after about 20 hours of use. It takes 5 to 10 seconds to run a cleaning tape.

Cleaning tapes usually will not remove grime and debris that get into the nooks and crannies of the small working parts. To do this, you have to get inside the R-DAT and clean the tape path and heads, if you are technically able. This requires removing the tape elevator assembly, which, on some R-DATs, is cumbersome. For this operation use a lint-free lens cleaning cloth, a chamois, a foam-tipped cleaner dipped in an approved VCR cleaning solvent, or a small, round wooden stick soaked in VCR cleaning solvent. The wood should be strong enough to dislodge the debris but not hard enough to scratch the drum surface. Do not use anything that could clog the tape path and heads, such as cotton swabs, tissue, or cotton cloth.

R-DAT Audiocassette Tape

Digital audiocassette tape (DAT) is about ½-inch wide, slightly wider than the standard analog audio cassette. Tape thickness is similar to that of a 90-minute analog cassette (30 microns). The cartridge itself is half the size of an analog cassette, and the length of tape in a cartridge is one-fourth that of an analog cassette. Most digital audiocassette tape is metal particle, not lower than 1,500 oersteds.

Although the tape is enclosed in a plastic cartridge, its thinness and the density of encoded information (114 million bits per square inch) make the tape and data

---

[*]Based on "Get in Line," by John Watkinson, *Studio Sound*, December 1993, p. 45.

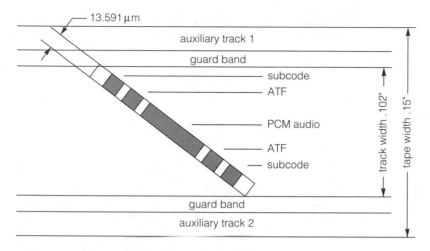

7-13 Tape pattern of an R-DAT recorder. Actual digital audio data are recorded on the center portion of the tape. The width of each data bit is 13.591 microns, about one-tenth the thickness of a human hair. The ATF (automatic track finding) pilot signal is used for servo track alignment. Subcode data enable rapid program access.

extremely susceptible to damage from dirt, dust, and mishandling, especially because the track width of the encoded data is about one-tenth the thickness of a human hair (see 7-13).

Bulk erasing cannot totally eliminate the recorded signal on the high-density DAT surface. A recorded signal can be completely removed only by rerecording.

Many R-DATs have a moisture prevention cutoff to help protect the tape. Any moisture entering the unit from the tape stops the recorder, which then heats up to evaporate the moisture. When the unit is dry, it begins to function again.

Problems with DAT

It is natural to assume that because the digital recording process converts analog signals into a more durable format, the sonic results are relatively invariable, regardless of the digital cassette tape used. Such is not the

case. Qualitative differences exist among the various brands of DAT, just as they do among the various makes of R-DATs.

■ *Wear.* The R-DAT's rotary head spins at 2,000 rpm. Over time, this can create a molecular breakdown that could lead to tape shedding and head clogging. As pointed out earlier, interference with tape-to-head contact is of much greater consequence in digital recording than it is in analog recording due to the densely packed digital information, among other things.

■ *Error concealment.* During error correction in R-DATs, concealment is used to help negate random and burst errors. A *random error* results from either tape noise or noise from an external source. A *burst error* can be due to defects in the tape coating, head-to-tape contact problems, or sullied or creased tape. If there are too many errors to be corrected, the system tries to conceal them rather than to fail by generating inner (C1) and outer (C2) codes. C1 errors are a measure of a DAT's normal errors that have passed the first error correction level and may be correctable at the C2 level. The more inner code errors that are passed on for outer code correction, the greater the possibility of increase in the tape's error rate and, hence, for audible errors. Certain makes of DAT are better able to deal with C2 concealment than others.

- *Cassette shells*. Like cassette tape, the plastic cassette tape shell is also subject to wear. A worn tape shell could create audible error-rate variations caused by problems with tape rotation, accelerated tape wear, debris that could roughen the running of the tape, timing errors, and tape vibration.

- *Erasure*. Some DATs have a higher remnance. **Remanence** is residual magnetization from a previous recording after erasure. In rerecording, this could create a significant error rate.

- *Aging*. Because an increasing number of recordings are being mastered onto DAT, tape aging has become a concern. When DAT is in good condition, digital copies can be made with no sonic degradation. But if a DAT has deteriorated, the inevitable increased error rate creates a loss in sound quality that would be quite audible.

Storage in a scrupulously controlled cool-temperature and low-humidity environment is necessary. Warm temperatures and high humidity accelerate tape deterioration. Indeed, high humidity can lead to water penetration into the gaps of wound tape after long storage periods, causing tape layers to stick or the magnetic particles to rust, or both. Rusting is particularly notable because R-DATs are subject to buildup of condensation, and unless the tape's magnetic particles are protected in some way rusting could be accelerated.

Multitrack R-DAT Recording on Videotape

So far, the size of digital cassette audiotape has not been conducive to more than two-channel stereo encoding. The option 3 mode, discussed previously, offers four-channel recording. At 32 kHz, however, fidelity is not up to professional standards. By employing the video track on videocassette tape (Hi8 and S-VHS are most commonly used) with its greater width, compared to DAT, it is possible to use R-DATs for multitrack recording (see 7-12). Recording times vary from roughly 15 to over 100 minutes per cartridge, depending on the tape format and hardware used.

Disk-Based Audio Systems

In recent years, many new tape recording systems, particularly digital systems, have emerged. The entry of several different types of disk-based audio systems has made "progress" in magnetic encoding of audio bewildering. The good news is that these new systems have revolutionized the quality, random access, and editing of audio materials. The bad news is that many of these systems are complex, and with so many already on the market—most of them incompatible with one another—and more surely to come, audio producers face the dilemma of which system(s) to choose, how long it (they) will be around, and how cost-effective their choice(s) will be.

Disk-based audio production has already reached the point where entire books have been devoted to the subject (see the Bibliography). In this section, only the systems that have come into use in music recording or that have a reasonable near-future chance of doing so are discussed.

Recordable Compact Discs

Until recently, the **compact disc (CD)**, like its predecessor the phonograph record, was a play-only disc. But unlike the phonograph record, which was encoded mechanically, the CD is encoded optically. Optical technology has made it possible to develop the recordable compact disc, usually abbreviated **CD-R**, short for *compact disc-record*, or, sometimes, **CD-WO**, short for *compact disc-write only*.

The CD-R makes the compact disc somewhat similar to recording tape in that it has unlimited playback, but it can only be recorded on once and cannot be erased. Even false starts are there for good. Hence, many users assemble their audio on DAT and then transfer it to CD-R.

The CD-R conforms to the standards document known as the "Orange Book." According to this standard, data encoded on a CD-R do not have to be recorded all at once but can be added to whenever the user wishes, making it more convenient to produce sequential audio material. CD-Rs conforming to the Orange Book standard, however, are not compatible with standard CD players. To be playable on any standard CD player, CD-R must conform to the "Red Book" standard, which requires that a table of contents file (TOC) be encoded onto the disc.* A TOC file is written at the start of the disc and includes information related to subcode and copy prohibition data, index numbering, and timing information. The

TOC, which is written onto the disc after audio assembly, tells the CD player where each cut starts and ends. Once it is encoded, any audio added to the disc will not be playable on standard CD players due to the write-once limitation of CD-R.

One answer to this problem is to use preformatted TOC tracks of different lengths, depending on the amount of TOC data to be encoded. Audio program data can be written on the first available track and continue to be written uninterrupted across track boundaries until the recorder is stopped. The disadvantage to this approach, however, is that preformatting reduces disc time for program material.

There are two broad, basic categories of CD-R systems: stand-alone and computer-based. Both systems contain an audio data encoder and disc recorder. The stand-alone CD-R system also contains all other necessary data processing and is, therefore, self-contained (see 7-14 and 7-15). Computer-based systems use the computer, among other things, to generate subcode data. In either system, various analog and digital tape formats can be used as a source for CD recording.

CD-R has revolutionized music premastering and mastering by making it convenient and relatively inexpensive for the recordist to produce a finished, customized music CD at the end of a recording and mixdown session (see Chapter 16).

---

*In addition to the Orange and Red Book standards, there are Yellow, Green, White, and Blue Book standards. The *Yellow Book* format describes the basic specifications for computer-based CD-ROM (Compact Disc-Read Only Memory). The *Green Book* format describes the basic specifications for CD-I (Compact Disc-Interactive). The *White Book*, sometimes referred to as *CD-K* (Karaoke), describes basic specifications for full-motion, compressed video discs. The *Blue Book* format provides specifications for a high-density compact disc (HDCD) format.

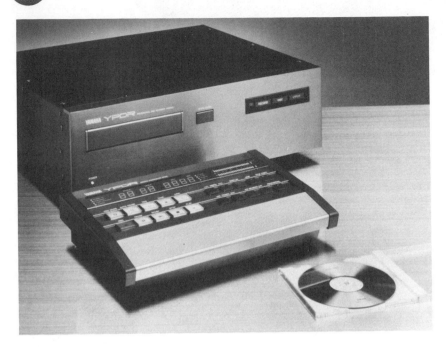

7-14 CD cartridge recorder with remote control

Magneto-Optical Recording

Magneto-optical (MO) recording, like magnetic digital tape recording, uses tiny magnetic particles to encode digital information. But unlike magnetic tape recording: (1) the MO recording medium is disc-based, (2) instead of magnetic heads to orient the particles a laser beam is used; and (3) orienting the magnetic particles requires heating them to extremely high temperatures. Magneto-optical recording has made it possible to produce erasable compact disc recording (abbreviated **CD-E**, for *compact disc-erasable*, or **CD-MO**, for *compact disc-magneto-optical)*. The magneto-optical disc is also called by the more colorful term *floptical*.

The CD-E's main advantages are that it can be used like tape due to its write-many, read-many (WMRM) format and that it is two-sided to increase playing time. Its main disadvantages are that it is not interchangeable with ordinary CD players; that, even with two-sided recording, playing time is limited; and that it is expensive. Also, MO drives are slow, and it takes careful design and software optimization to record and play back CD quality sound. This problem has begun to improve, however (see 7-16).

Mini Disc (MD)

A potentially far-reaching development in magnetic-optical recording is **mini disc**™ (**MD**™), a compact disc that stores more than an hour of digital-quality audio, with a dynamic range of 105 dB, on a 2.5-inch-wide CD (see 7-17). The MD system uses two types of media: magneto-optical media for recordable blank discs, and CD-type optical media for prerecorded software. The MD is Sony's answer to the Philips DCC.

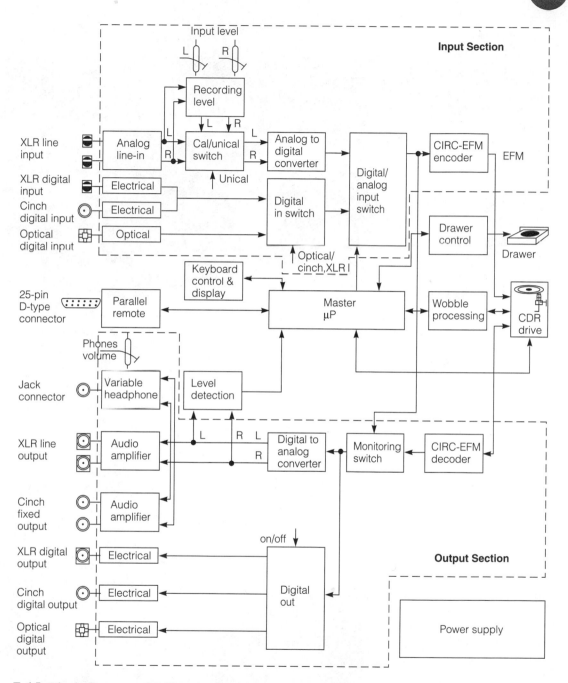

7-15 Block diagram of a CD recorder

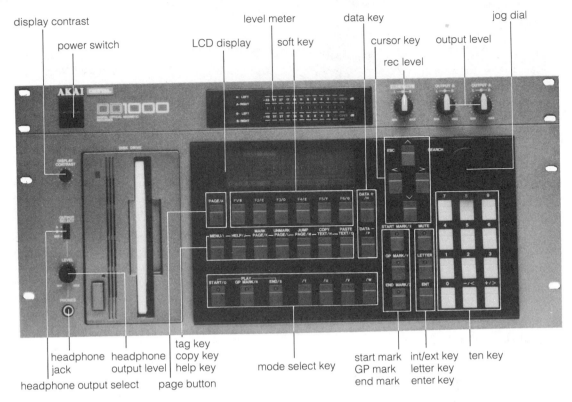

display contrast
power switch
LCD display
level meter
soft key
data key
cursor key
rec level
output level
jog dial

headphone jack
headphone output level
headphone output select
tag key
copy key
help key
page button
mode select key
start mark
GP mark
end mark
int/ext key
letter key
enter key
ten key

7-16 Magneto-optical disc recorder

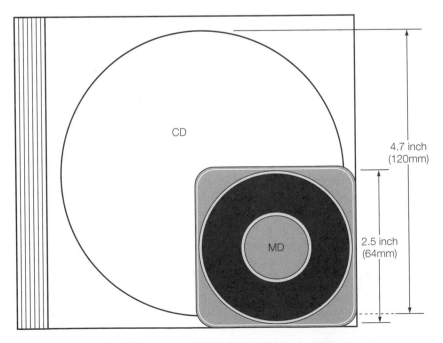

CD

MD

4.7 inch
(120mm)

2.5 inch
(64mm)

7-17 Comparison between mini disc and compact disc

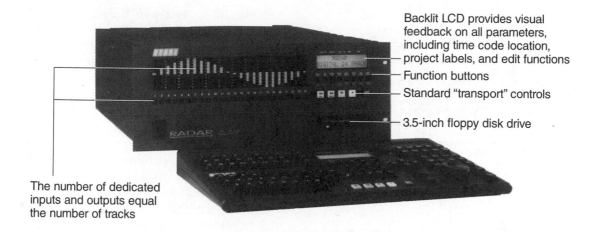

Backlit LCD provides visual feedback on all parameters, including time code location, project labels, and edit functions

Function buttons

Standard "transport" controls

3.5-inch floppy disk drive

The number of dedicated inputs and outputs equal the number of tracks

7-18 Multitrack random access digital audio hard-disk recorder with remote control. This unit can be configured as an 8-, 16-, or 24-track recorder/editor. Multiple units can be combined for 48 or more synchronized tracks.

Intended for the consumer market, it has potential for project studios because of its CD-quality audio, fast random access of encoded information, and easy portability. But its data-reduction scheme limits its use for critical recording, to say nothing of the affordability of full-pulse code-modulated (PCM) R-DATs.

Hard-Disk Recording

What once took various types of equipment—console, tape recorder(s), and signal processors, to name the most obvious—located in different areas of the control room to produce a finished music recording, now can be done at a central location with a hard-disk recorder (see 7-18).

Hard-disk recording resembles tape recording in that it encodes, stores, and reproduces a signal on a few or several different tracks. But there the resemblance ends. Unlike tape recording, hard disk

recording has a different, more versatile channel-track configuration; information access is nonlinear, random, and quick; storage capacity can be far greater; most hard disk recording systems also include nonlinear editing capability (see Chapter 14); and many incorporate digital signal processing (DSP) (see Chapter 8).

On a professional, analog open-reel tape recorder, one input, output, and channel are dedicated to each track. Once a track has been magnetically encoded, that information is tied to that track. It cannot be moved to another track or slipped out of time without being rerecorded.

With hard disk recorders, which are available in two-, four-, or multichannel configurations, channels are not directly linked to inputs, outputs, and tracks. Once the computer-based audio data are recorded and stored, they can be assigned to any output(s) and moved in time. For example, a hard-disk recorder may have four inputs,

Virtual
tracks

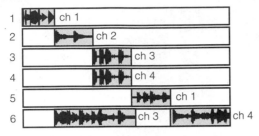

7-19 Example of how virtual tracks can be assigned to any output channel

eight outputs, 16 channels, and 256 tracks. This means that up to four inputs can be used to record up to four channels at one time; up to eight channels at one time can be used for internal mixing or routing; up to 16 channels (*real tracks*) are simultaneously available during playback; and up to 256 separate **soundfiles**[*] can be maintained and assigned to a *virtual track*. Any track can be assigned to any output channel(s) and slipped along that channel or across channels (see 7-19).

Digital Audio Workstation

The main differences between a **digital audio workstation** (**DAW**) and a standard hard-disk recording/editing system are that a DAW is expandable, and it is integrated with and networked to a collection of devices, such as other audio, video, and

MIDI sources, within or between facilities (see 7-20 and 7-21). A digital audio workstation incorporates a variety of functions, depending on its sophistication and cost.

In addition to its expandability and control and communications over various internal and external systems, a DAW can provide multichannel audio recording, mixing, and replay; digital signal processing (DSP); nonlinear editing; real-time synthesis and interaction; quick, random access retrieval; high-speed backup and archiving; removable media or background off-loading; sizable information storage capacity; and data reduction (compression) to reduce the disk storage space required.

A DAW's systemwide communication with other external devices is facilitated through the distribution of standard digital interfaces such as **AES/EBU**, **SPDIF**, **SCSI**, or **MIDI**. *SMPTE* or **MIDI time code** (**MTC**) can be used for timing and synchronization (see Table 7-3).

Digital Audio Networking

Recording has come a long way since the days when overdubbing provided a way to manipulate time and space. Signal processing added to that capability with effects such as delay, reverberation, time compression, and pitch shifting. Digital technology provided the means to access data randomly and nonlinearly. Workstations facilitated speedy interstudio interchange of encoded, digital-quality audio. Now, through telephone lines, a recording can be produced in real time between studios across town or across the country with little or no loss in audio quality, and at relatively low cost.

Integrated Services Digital Network (**ISDN**) is a public telephone service that allows cheap use of a flexible, wide-area, all-

---

[*]Audio that is encoded onto the disk takes the form of a soundfile. The soundfile contains information about the sound such as amplitude and duration. When the soundfile is opened, on most systems that information is displayed on a monitor screen.

7-20 Digital audio workstation

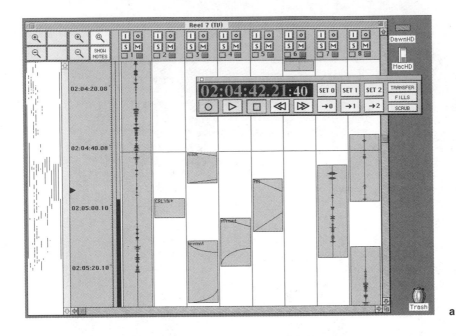

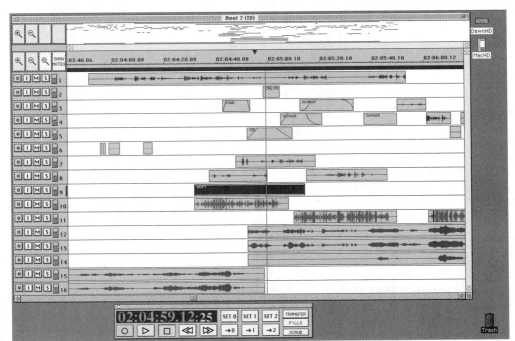

7-21 Mixview windows. (*a*) Vertical mixview window. (*b*) Horizontal mixview window. (*c*) Horizontal mixview expanded for editing. (*d*) Mixview track sheet window.

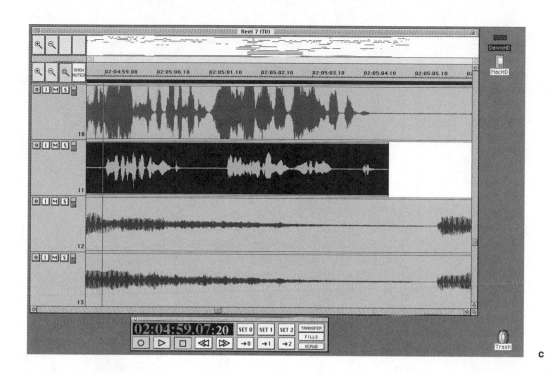

c

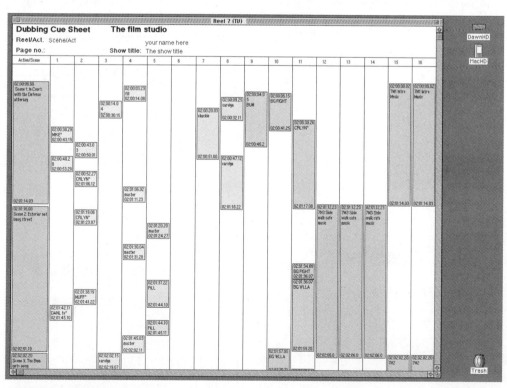

d

7-21 (continued)

Table 7-3 Standard digital interfaces

■ The *AES/EBU* interface is a professional digital audio connection standard specified jointly by the Audio Engineering Society and the European Broadcast Union. Its standard calls for two audio channels to be encoded in a serial data stream and transmitted through a balanced line using XLR connectors.

■ *SPDIF (Sony/Philips Digital InterFace)* is the consumer version of the AES/EBU standard. It calls for an unbalanced line using phono connectors. SPDIF is implemented on consumer digital audio equipment such as CD players.

■ *SCSI (Small Computer Systems Interface,* pronounced "scuzzy") is the standard for hardware and software command language. It allows two-way communication between, primarily, hard disk and CD-ROM drives to exchange digital data at fast speeds. SCSI can also be used with other components, such as scanners.

• *SMPTE (Society of Motion Picture and Television Engineers) time code* encodes individual frames of a tape or film with a unique number, defined in hours, minutes, seconds, and frames. (Each frame is 1/30 of a second.) SMPTE time code allows synchronization between two or more devices—audio, video, film, sequencers, drum machines, and other time-reliant equipment (see Chapter 14).

■ *MIDI time code (MTC)* provides a way to implement SMPTE time code, representing real-time locations, through a MIDI system for synchronization purposes (see Chapter 14).

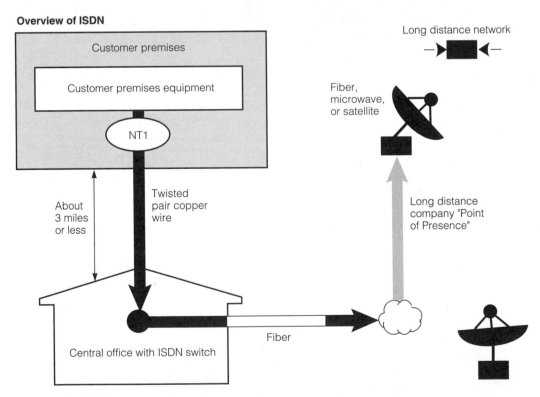

7-22 Long distance recording. Note: NT1 is a network terminator; it protects the network from electrical malfunctions. CDQ2000ED code enables you to send a cue mix to an artist in another location, delay the mix sent to your monitors, not delay the received artist's solo signal, mix the two, give direction, and make production judgments in real time. RS232 is an asynchronous port.

The export (artist) side of a link

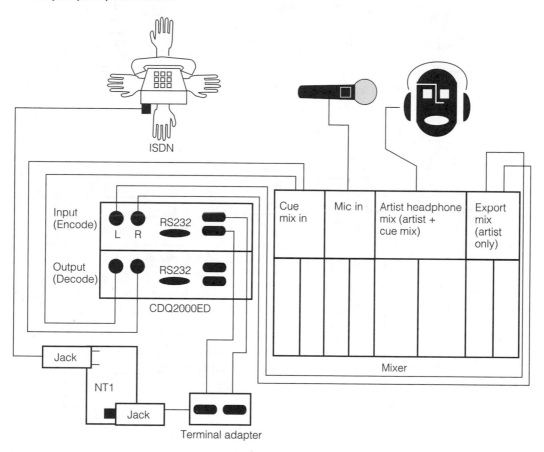

ISDN

Input
(Encode)
L R
RS232

Output
(Decode)
RS232

CDQ2000ED

Jack

NT1

Jack

Terminal adapter

Cue mix in	Mic in	Artist headphone mix (artist + cue mix)	Export mix (artist only)

Mixer

7-22 (continued)

digital network (see 7-22). With ISDN, it is possible to have a vocalist in New York, wearing headphones for the foldback feed, singing into a microphone whose signal is routed to a studio in Los Angeles. In L.A., the singer's audio is fed through a console, along with the accompaniment from, say, the L.A. studio (it could be from elsewhere), and recorded. When necessary, the singer in N.Y., the accompanying musicians, from wherever, and the recordist in L.A. can communicate with each other through a talk-back system. In other words, ISDN makes it possible to do a conventional recording session from different locations in real time. And unlike much of today's advanced technology, ISDN is a relatively uncomplicated service to use.

The import (producer) side of a link

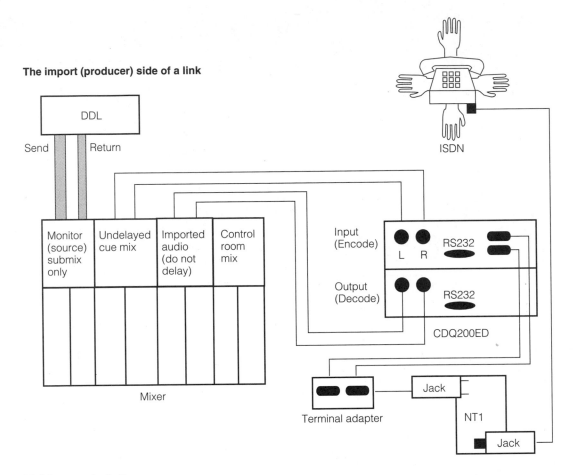

7-22 (concluded)

SIGNAL PROCESSING

Signal processors are devices used to alter some characteristic of a sound. Most signal processors can be grouped into four categories: spectrum processors, time processors, amplitude processors, and noise processors. A **spectrum processor,** such as the equalizer, affects the spectral balances in a signal. A **time processor,** such as a reverberation or delay device, affects the time interval between a signal and its repetition(s). An **amplitude processor,** such as the compressor-limiter, affects a signal's loudness. A **noise processor,** such as the Dolby system, does not alter a signal as much as it makes the signal clearer by reducing the noise added in analog recording.

Some signal processors can be assigned to more than one category. For example, the equalizer also alters a signal's amplitude and, therefore, can be classified as an amplitude processor as well. The flanger, which affects the time of a signal, also affects its frequency response. A de-esser alters amplitude and frequency. Moreover, various signal-processing functions may be combined in a single unit that can be delegated to, say, time compress, delay, pitch shift, and/or flange a signal. The signal processors discussed in this chapter are categorized according to their primary function.

Their specific applications are discussed in Chapter 13, "The Recording Session" and Chapter 15, "The Mixdown."

Spectrum Signal Processors

Spectrum signal processors include equalizers, filters, and psychoacoustic processors.

Equalizers

The best-known and most often used signal processor is the **equalizer**—an electronic device that alters frequency response by increasing or decreasing the level of a signal at a specific portion of the spectrum. This alteration can be done in two ways: by boost or cut (also known as *peak* or *dip*) or by **shelving.**

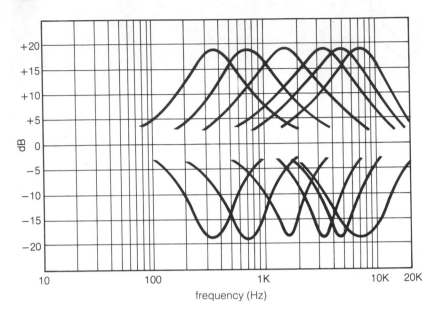

8-1 Bell or haystack curves showing 18-dB boost or cut at 350, 700, 1,600, 3,200, 4,800, and 7,200 Hz

Boost/cut increases or decreases the level of a band of frequencies around a **center frequency**, the frequency at which maximum boost or cut occurs. This type of equalization is often referred to as *bell curve* or *haystack* due to the shape of the response curve (see 8-1).

Shelving also increases or decreases amplitude but gradually flattens out or shelves at the maximum selected level when the chosen (turnover) frequency is reached. Level then remains constant at all frequencies beyond that point (see 8-2).

The number of frequencies on equalizers varies. Generally, the frequencies are in full-, half-, and third-octave intervals. If the lowest frequency on a full-octave equalizer is, say, 50 Hz, the other frequencies ascend in octaves: 100 Hz, 200 Hz, 400 Hz, 800 Hz, 1,600 Hz, and so on, usually to 12,800 Hz. A half-octave equalizer ascends in half octaves. If the lowest frequency is 50 Hz,

the intervals are at or near 75 Hz, 100 Hz, 150 Hz, 200 Hz, 300 Hz, 400 Hz, 600 Hz, and so on. A third-octave equalizer would have intervals at or near 50 Hz, 60 Hz, 80 Hz, 100 Hz, 120 Hz, 160 Hz, 200 Hz, 240 Hz, 320 Hz, 400 Hz, 480 Hz, 640 Hz, and so on. Obviously, the more settings, the better the sound control—but at some cost. The more settings on an equalizer (or any device, for that matter), the more difficult it is to use correctly, because technical problems such as ringing, phasing, and so on may be introduced.

Two types of equalizers are in general use: fixed frequency and parametric.

Fixed-Frequency Equalizer

The **fixed-frequency equalizer** is so called because it operates at fixed frequencies usually selected from two (high and low) or three (high, middle, and low) ranges of the

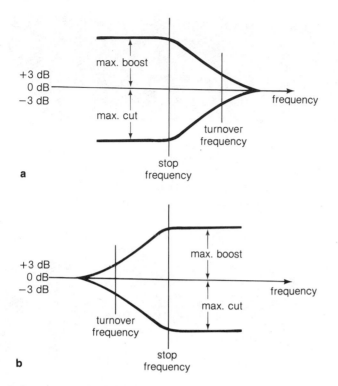

8-2 (*a*) **Low-frequency shelving equalization and** (*b*) **high-frequency shelving equalization.** The turnover frequency is that frequency where the gain is 3 dB above (or below) the shelving level—in other words, the frequency where the equalizer begins to flatten out. The stop frequency is the point where the gain stops increasing or decreasing.

frequency spectrum. Each group of frequencies is located at a separate control, but only one center frequency at a time per control may be selected. At or near each frequency selector is a level control that boosts or cuts the selected center and band frequencies. On consoles, if these controls are concentric to save space, the outer ring chooses the frequency, and the inner ring increases or decreases level.

A fixed-frequency equalizer has a preset bandwidth—a range of frequencies on either side of the center frequency selected for equalizing that is also affected. The degrees of amplitude to which these frequencies are modified forms the bandwidth curve. If you boost, say, 350 Hz a total of 18 dB, the bandwidth of frequencies also affected may go to as low as 80 Hz on one side and up to 2,000 Hz on the other. The peak of the curve is 350 Hz—the frequency that is boosted the full 18 dB (see 8-1). The adjacent frequencies are boosted also but to a lesser extent, depending on the bandwidth.

8-3 Two-channel, third-octave graphic equalizer. This particular model provides a scale switch that allows a choice of either a 12-dB boost/cut or a high-resolution 6-dB boost/cut for each channel; a filter control that switches a 30-Hz subsonic filter in or out of each channel; and an input level control that facilitates interfacing each equalizer channel with the output signals of other equipment.

8-4 Two-channel parametric equalizer. In this particular model, the outer concentric controls of the four larger dials in the top row of each channel adjust the level of the boost or cut, and the inner concentric controls adjust the bandwidth of the affected frequencies. The four larger dials in the bottom row of each channel select frequencies for four overlapping frequency ranges: low frequency (LF), 20–500 Hz; middle-low frequency (MLF), 80–1,600 Hz; middle-high frequency (MHF), 315–6,300 Hz; high frequency (HF), 1–20 kHz. Each channel also has a high-pass filter, variable from 20 to 315 Hz, and a low-pass filter, variable from 2 to 20 kHz (see "Filters" in this chapter). The "cascade" function can change the two-channel four-band configuration into a one-channel eight-band configuration. The parametric equalizer shown here is also a notch filter (see "Notch Filter" later in this chapter).

Because each fixed-frequency equalizer can have a different fixed bandwidth and bandwidth curve, it is a good idea to study the manufacturer's specifications before you use one.

Usually, the high- and low-fixed frequency equalizers on consoles are shelving equalizers. The midrange EQs are center-frequency boost and cut equalizers.

Graphic Equalizer

The **graphic equalizer** is a type of fixed-frequency equalizer. It consists of sliding, instead of rotating, controls that boost or attenuate selected frequencies. It is called *graphic* because the positioning of these controls gives a graphic display of the frequency curve set. (The display does not

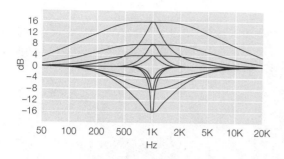

8-5 Selectable bandwidths of the parametric equalizer shown in 8-4. In this particular model, the boost curves are broad and the cut curves are tight. Many parametric equalizers use the same range of adjustment for the boost and cut curves.

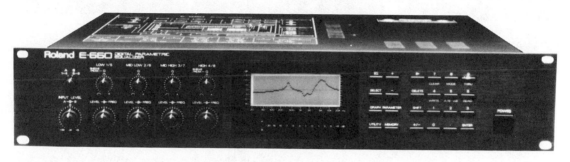

8-6 Digital programmable parametric equalizer. This particular model has 99 storage memories for individual curves, each nameable and recallable at the touch of a button. The frequency bands allow control from 30 Hz to 20 kHz, in increments of one hertz. Level in each band is adjustable up to +12 dB.

include the bandwidth of each frequency, however.) Because each frequency on a graphic equalizer has a separate sliding control, it is possible to use as many as you wish at the same time (see 8-3).

Parametric Equalizer

The main difference between a **parametric equalizer** (see 8-4) and a fixed-frequency equalizer is that the parametric has continuously variable frequencies and bandwidths. Because the parametric equalizer's frequencies and bandwidths are continuously variable, it is possible to change a bandwidth curve by making it wider or narrower, thereby altering the frequencies affected and their levels (see 8-5). This provides greater

flexibility and more precision in controlling equalization (EQ).

The digital programmable parametric equalizer can store and recall several different EQ settings and bandwidths either separately or simultaneously (see 8-6).

For example, in a vocal, if one word sounds too bassy, another too harsh, and still another both too shrill and lacking in low end, the appropriate frequencies and bandwidths can be programmed to correct these problems, and the corrections can be stored in a memory. During playback the equalizer will automatically make the ap-propriate EQ changes at the precise points in the lyric. For the word that is too shrill and lacking in low end, two different EQ settings can be programmed for the same instant. Also if,

8-7 Stereo paragraphic equalizer

say, the accompaniment re-quires EQ changes, different EQ settings can be pro-grammed and stored in the same equalizer without disturbing the settings for the vocal (up to the equalizer's storage limit).

Paragraphic Equalizer

A **paragraphic equalizer** combines the sliding controls of a graphic equalizer with the flexibility of parametric equalization (see 8-7).

Filters

A **filter** is a device that attenuates certain bands of frequencies. The difference be-tween attenuating with an equalizer and attenuating with a filter is sometimes con-fusing, because both reduce a frequency's loudness. There are generally two differ-ences. First, with an equalizer attenuation affects only the selected frequency and the frequencies on either side of it, whereas with a filter all frequencies above or below the selected frequency are affected. Second, an equalizer allows you to vary the amount of the drop in loudness; with a filter, however, the drop is preset and usually steep.

The most commonly used filters are high-pass, low-pass, bandpass, and notch filters.

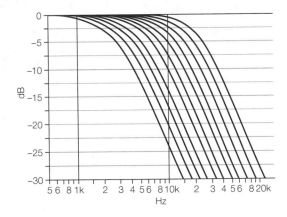

8-8 Curves of the low-pass filter in 8-4

High- and Low-Pass Filters

A **high-pass (low-cut) filter** attenuates all frequencies below a preset point; a **low-pass (high-cut) filter** attenuates all frequencies above a preset point (see 8-8).

Suppose, in a recording, that there is a bothersome rumble between 35 and 50 Hz. If a high-pass filter is set at 50 Hz, all fre-quencies below that point are cut and the band of frequencies above it continues to pass—hence the name "high-pass" (low-cut) filter.

The low-pass (high-cut) filter works on the same principle but affects the higher

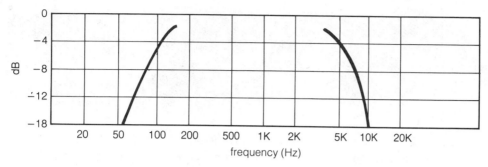

8-9 Band-pass filtering. The frequencies below 120 Hz and above 5,000 Hz are sharply attenuated, thereby allowing the frequencies in the band between to pass.

frequencies. If there is tape hiss in a recording, you can get rid of it by setting a low-pass filter at, say, 10,000 Hz. This cuts the frequencies above that point and allows the band of frequencies below 10,000 Hz to pass through. But you should keep in mind that *all* sound above 10 kHz—the program material along with the tape hiss—will be filtered.

Band-Pass Filter

A **band-pass filter** is a device that sets high- and low-frequency cutoff points and permits the band of frequencies between to pass (see 8-9). Band-pass filters are used more for corrective purposes than for creative purposes.

Notch Filter

A **notch filter** is a filter used mainly for corrective purposes (see 8-4 and 8-5). It can cut out an extremely narrow band, allowing the frequencies on each side of the notch to pass. For example, a constant problem in audio is AC (alternating current) hum, which has a frequency of 60 Hz. A notch filter can remove it without appreciably affecting adjacent frequencies.

Psychoacoustic Processors

A **psychoacoustic processor** is designed to add clarity, definition, overall presence, and life or "sizzle" to program material. Some units add odd and even harmonics to the audio, tone-generated from 700 Hz to 7 kHz; others are fixed or program-adaptive high-frequency equalizers. A psychoacoustic processor might also achieve its effect by adding comb filtering and by introducing narrow-band phase shifts between stereo channels. One well-known psychoacoustic processor is the Aural Exciter® (see 8-10).

Another type of psychoacoustic processor acts like a dynamic equalizer on low-level signals. It brings out quiet details without affecting louder sounds, disturbing the overall sense of dynamics, or increasing noise (see 8-11).

Time Signal Processors

Time signal processors are devices that affect the time relationships of signals. These effects include reverberation, delay, and pitch shifting.

8-10 Aural exciter®, a well-known psychoacoustic processor. The SPR (Spectral Phase Refractor) function corrects the bass delay inherent in the recording process to restore clarity and openness, and increases the apparent bass level without adding bass boost. Harmonics mixing is adjustable to whatever level is desired. Null Fill is a tuning adjustment. Used in conjunction with the Peaking and Tune controls, it adds the flexibility to enhance most types of audio sources.

8-11 Another type of psychoacoustic processor acts like a dynamic equalizer. This particular psychoacoustic processor acts on low-level signals while leaving the high-level signals untouched.

Reverberation

Reverberation, you will recall, is created by random, multiple, blended repetitions of a sound or signal. As these repetitions decrease in intensity, they increase in number. Reverberation increases average signal level and adds depth, spatial dimension, and additional excitement to the listening experience.

A common principle is basic to reverberation and, hence, reverb systems. Think of what it takes to produce an echo: A sound has to be sent, hit a reflective object, and then bounce back. In the parlance of audio, the sound sent is **dry**—without reverb—and the sound returned is **wet**—with reverb.

Actually, as defined, there is a difference between echo and reverb. Echo is one or, at most, a few discrete repetitions of a sound (or signal); reverb consists of many blended repetitions (see Chapter 3). To produce either, the dry sound must be sent, reflected, and returned wet.

The *reverberation (reverb) unit* is a device that artificially reproduces the sound of different acoustic environments such as a large hall, small room, auditorium, nightclub, and so on. Three types of reverberation systems are in popular use: (1) the so-called acoustic echo chamber, which is more accurately an acoustic reverb chamber, (2) plate reverberation, and (3) digital reverb. A fourth type of reverberation device, the spring reverbera-

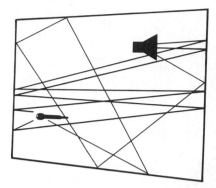

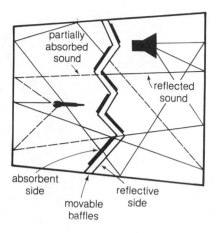

8-12 Sound in an acoustic chamber. The sound feeding from a loudspeaker bounces around the chamber off highly reflective walls and into a microphone. The dead sides of the microphone and loudspeaker are opposite each other to reduce direct sound and avoid feedback.

8-13 Movable baffles. Using these gobos with absorbent and reflective sides in various arrangements can alter the acoustics in an acoustic chamber.

tion unit, used to be widely used because it was available in many models and relatively inexpensive. It has been supplanted by digital reverb in popularity, availability, and cost effectiveness. In spring reverb, the dry signal activates a driver that vibrates coiled springs, then a pickup senses the motion and feeds the wet signal from the springs to the console. Controls on the reverb unit vary the reverb time.

Acoustic Chamber

The *acoustic chamber* is the most natural and realistic of the four types of reverb because it works on acoustic sound in an acoustic environment. It is a room with hard, highly sound-reflective surfaces and nonparallel walls to avoid flutter echo—multiple echoes at a rapid, even rate—and standing waves—apparently stationary waveforms created by multiple reflections

between opposite, usually parallel, room surfaces (see 8-12, sound in an acoustic chamber). It usually contains a directional microphone (two for stereo), placed off room center, and a loudspeaker, usually near a corner at angles to or back-to-back to the mic to minimize the amount of direct sound picked up by the mic(s). The dry sound feeds from the console through the loudspeaker, reflects around the chamber, is picked up by the mic(s), and is fed back wet into the console for further routing.

Reverb times differ from chamber to chamber. Generally, however, reverb time should be about 3½ seconds at 500 Hz, and about 1¼ seconds at 10,000 Hz. Reverb times can be varied by using movable acoustic baffles (gobos) (see 8-13).

Although an acoustic chamber creates very realistic reverberation, it is the most expensive of the reverb systems. It must be at least 2,000 cubic feet in size (too small a room is poor for bass response) with spe-

driver —
pickup —
pickup —
— pickup
— steel plate
— frame

8-14 Reverberation plate

cially treated surfaces; it must be isolated; and it must contain professional-quality microphones and loudspeaker. Arranging the baffles to produce appropriate reverb times can also be time-consuming and costly. Even with a chamber, studios use other reverb devices to provide additional sonic alternatives.

Plate Reverberation

The *reverberation plate* is a mechanical-electronic device consisting of a thin steel plate suspended under tension in an enclosed frame (see 8-14). It is large and heavy and requires isolation in a separate room. A moving-coil driver, acting like a small speaker, vibrates the plate, thus transducing the electric signals from the console into mechanical energy. A contact microphone (two for stereo) picks up the plate's vibrations, transduces them back into electric energy, and returns them to the console. The multiple reflections from the vibrating plate create the reverb effect.

A characteristic of plates is long reverb times (more than two seconds) at high frequencies that produce a crisp, bright decay. Plates, however, are susceptible to overload. With louder levels, low frequencies tend to increase disproportionately in reverb time compared to the other frequencies, thus muddying sound. Rolling off the unwanted frequencies will help, but be careful—too much roll-off reduces a sound's warmth.

Reverb Plates are no longer manufactured commercially. But because of their unique quality of reverberation, many studios construct their own. A few companies provide kits for this purpose.

Digital Reverberation

Digital reverberation, the most commonly used today, is accomplished electronically. The analog signal, when fed into the circuitry and digitized, is delayed for several milliseconds. The delayed signal is then recycled to produce the reverb effect. The process is repeated many times a second,

8-15 Digital reverberation and effects system

with amplitude reduced to achieve decay. After processing, the signal is reconverted into analog.

High-quality digital reverb units are capable of an extremely wide range of effects, produce high-quality sound, and take up very little room.

Some digital reverb systems can simulate a variety of acoustical and mechanical reverberant sounds such as small and large concert halls, bright- and dark-sounding halls, small and large rooms, and small and large reverb plates. With each effect it is also possible to control individually the attack; decay; diffusion (density); high-, middle-, and low-frequency decay times; and other sonic colorings.

Programmable digital reverb systems are also available. They come with prepro-

grammed effects but also permit newly created effects, not previously in the memory, to be programmed and stored for reuse. This provides an almost limitless variety of reverberant effects (see 8-15 and 8-16).

Choosing a Reverberation System

When you choose a reverberation system, personal taste notwithstanding, the system should sound natural. The high end should be bright and lifelike, and the low end should not thicken or muddy the sound. Good diffusion is essential; repeats should be many and random. There should be an absence of flutter, twang, "boing," and tinniness.

A good test to check for muddy sound is to listen to a vocal. If the reverb system

BANK	PROGRAMS									
	1	2	3	4	5	6	7	8	9	10
1. HALLS	Large Hall	Large + Stage	Medium Hall	Medium + Stage	Small Hall	Small + Stage	Large Church	Small Church	Jazz Hall	Auto Park
2. ROOMS	Music Club	Large Room	Medium Room	Small Room	Very Small	Lg. Wood Room	Sm. Wood Room	Large Chamber	Small Chamber	Small & Bright
3. WILD SPACES	Brick Wall	Buckram	Big Bottom	10W — 40	20W — 50	Metallica	Silica Beads	Inside Out	Ricochet	Varoom
4. PLATES	A Plate	Snare Plate	Small Plate	Thin Plate	Fat Plate					
5. EFFECTS	Illusion	Surfin'	Vocal Whispers	Doubler	Back Slap	Rebound	Elinar	Sudden Stop	In The Past	Tremolo L & R
6. SAMPLING	Forward/ Reverse	Rate Changer	Mono 3 s	Mono 6 s	Stereo 3 s	Dual Sampler				
7. DRUM SAMPLER	Mono 3 s	Mono 6 s	Stereo 3 s							
8. DOPPLER	Doppler	Band-wagon								
9. SO WHAT ELSE?	The In/Out	Twin Delays	Stereo Adjust							

8-16 Programs of the reverb system displayed in 8-15

makes the lyrics more difficult to understand, then the unit is not clear or transparent enough. To check for density and randomness of the early reflections, try a transient sound like a sharp drumbeat or handclap. Poorer reverb systems will produce a sound like an acoustic flutter. To check for randomness of the later reflections, listen to a strong male voice completely wet—with no dry feed from the reverb send on the console. If the lyrics are clear, then the combined wet and dry signals will probably be muddy.

Delay

Delay, *echo*, and *reverberation* are terms often wrongly used interchangeably; nevertheless, their psychoacoustical effects differ. As we have said, reverb is formed by multiple, random, blended repetitions that occur after a sound is emitted. The time between repetitions is imperceptible. Echo is a reflected sound of about 50 milliseconds (1/20 second) or longer of the original sound. The time between echoes is perceptible. The time between reflections is the delay.

By manipulating delay times it is possible to create a number of sonic effects (see the section on uses of delay). Generally, delay can be produced with a tape recorder or electronically with an analog or digital delay unit.

Tape Delay

The oldest and perhaps least expensive way to produce delay is by using a tape recorder with separate record and playback heads. With the machine in record and set to monitor playback, the console (or sound source) feeds the signal to the record head. As the

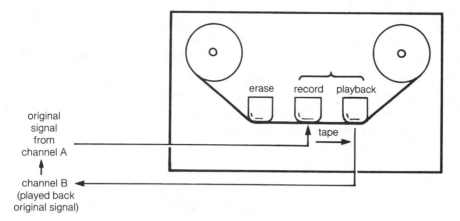

8-17 Tape delay. To produce tape delay manually, feed a signal through one channel to a tape recorder that is in the record and playback modes at the same time. When the signal reaches the playback head, feed it to another channel, then back again to the original channel, the tape recorder, the second channel, and round and round.

tape passes to the playback head a split second later, the signal is reproduced and returned to another channel, usually at the console. The signal path then continues round and round; the tape speed and the distance between the heads determine the amount of delay (see 8-17). The slower the delay, the more deliberate and discernible the repeat. A slow-repeating echo—about ½ second between repeats—creates a haunted house or outer-space effect. Faster delays generate more cascading sounds.

At 3¾ ips the delay is roughly half a second, assuming the record and playback heads are the typical 2 inches apart. At 7½ ips the delay is ¼ second; at 15 ips, it is ⅛ second; and at 30 ips it is 1⁄16 second. You can obtain an even greater range of effects by changing these fixed times using a variable-speed recorder.

You can also create a variety of sound intensities by coordinating the loudness controls on the console and tape recorder, because different levels of loudness also change the sonic character of delay. Make sure to coordinate these settings, however, because in most reverb and delay systems the "return" is noisier than the "send." Set "send" at a higher level and "return" to taste. It is common practice to set the level of the "returns" lower than the level of the "sends."

In addition to the electronic noise a signal generates as it passes through the channels, the tape produces noise. As the number of repeats in the delay increases, the signal-to-noise ratio decreases. For these reasons tape delay, although it produces a variety of effects for almost no extra cost, may not always create clean delay.

Electronic Delay

Electronic delay is produced using an analog or digital delay device.

Analog Delay An analog delay device performs the same function as tape delay, but it

8-18 Digital delay. This particular unit can produce a delay of up to 4.5 seconds set in 0.1 steps from 0 to 10 milliseconds (ms) and in 1 ms steps for periods over 10 ms. Eight different programmable memories can store the settings of delay time, feedback level, output level, modulation rate, modulation, and feedback phase. Frequency response is 10 Hz–17 kHz for delay times up to 1,500 ms and 10 Hz–8 kHz for delay times up to 4,500 ms.

does so electronically. Basically, the input signal is fed to the circuitry, which samples it several thousand times a second. These samples are stored in a long series of capacitors and stepped along from one capacitor to the next until the signal reaches the output as a delayed copy of the original input signal. Delay times can be selected. The variety of delay times available depends on the delay unit.

Digital Delay   Digital delay converts the analog signal to digital information at the input and reconverts it back into analog at the output. After conversion at the input, the signal is fed to a memory that stores it. After the selected amount of delay time, it is read out. It is then converted back to analog and sent to the output. As with analog delay, the amount and number of delay times vary with the unit (see 8-18).

Analog Versus Digital Delay   The attributes of analog and digital delay are different; each has its advantages and disadvantages. Analog units are less expensive and warmer sounding. They are especially good at creating sound effects, particularly flanging effects (see the section on flanging). The stepped delays in the analog process are smaller than in digital delay and can be hastened or slowed more conveniently. A significant problem, though, is that, with delays

of about 80 milliseconds and longer, signal-to-noise ratio drops dramatically. Also, the longer the delay time, the worse the high-frequency response.

Digital delays have become the delay unit of choice, pretty much replacing analog delays. They offer better signal-to-noise ratio, less distortion, improved high-frequency response with longer delay times, and a more extensive array of effects. They are also excellent for pre-reverb delay (see the information on delay with reverberation).

Uses of Delay

Delay has a number of creative applications. In-studio, the delay effects most frequently used are to double, chorus, and slap back sound and to create more realistic reverberation.

- *Doubling.* One popular use of delay is to fatten sound. The effect gives an instrument or voice a fuller, stronger sound and is called **doubling**. It is created by setting the delay around 15 to 35 milliseconds. These short delays are like early sound reflections and lend a sense of openness or ambience to dead-sounding instruments or voices.

  Doubling can also be done live by recording one track and then overdubbing the same part on a separate track in synchronization with the first track. Because it is not possible to repeat a performance exactly, variations in pitch, timing, and room sounds add fullness or openness to sound. By continuing this process it is possible to create a chorusing effect.

- *Chorus.* The **chorus effect** is achieved by recirculating the doubling effect. The delay time is about the same as in doubling—15 to 35 milliseconds—but is repeated. This effect can make a single voicing sound like many and add spaciousness to a sound. Two voices singing in a relatively dead studio can be made to sound like a large choir singing in a cathedral by chorusing the original sound.

- *Slap back echo.* A **slap back echo** is a delayed sound that is perceived as a distinct echo, much like the discrete Ping-Pong sound emitted by sonar devices when a contact is made. Slap back echo can be created with delay times of around 35 milliseconds or more.

- *Delay with reverberation.* In an acoustic situation there is a definite time lag between the arrival of direct waves from a sound source and the arrival of reflected sound. In some reverb systems there is no delay between the dry and wet signals. Therefore, by delaying the input signal before it gets to the reverb unit, it is possible to improve the quality of reverberation, making it sound more natural. Some reverb systems have a delay line of their own.

Flanging

Flanging is a time-delay effect that gets its name from the way in which it was first produced. The same signal was fed to two different tape recorders and recorded simultaneously. The playback from both was fed to a single output, but one playback was delayed, usually by applying some pressure to the flange of the supply reel to slow it down. The sonic result is a kind of swishing sound that has many uses in creating special effects for music recording and sound effects for TV and film.

Today, these effects are produced electronically (see 8-19). The delay time is automatically varied from 0 to 20 milliseconds. Ordinarily, the ear cannot perceive time differences between direct and delayed sounds that are this short. But due to phase cancellations when the direct and delayed signals are combined, the result is a series of peaks and dips in the frequency response (called a *comb filter*), which creates a filtered tone quality that sounds swishy, hollow, and spacey.

Flanging can be "positive," meaning that the direct and delayed signals have the same polarity. Or it can be "negative," meaning that these two signals are opposite in polarity. Negative flanging can create strong, sucking effects like a sound being turned inside out. Flanging can also be "resonant." That is, by feeding some of the output back into the input, the peaks and dips will be reinforced creating a "science fiction"-type effect.

Phasing

Phasing and flanging are similar in the way they are created except that phasing uses a phase shifter instead of a time-delay circuit. The peaks and dips are more irregular and farther apart than in flanging. Sonically, this results in something like pulsating, wavering vibrato or the undulating sound produced by playing an instrument underwater. Phasing is produced electronically (see 8-20).

Morphing

Morphing is the continuous, seamless transformation of one effect (aural or visual) into

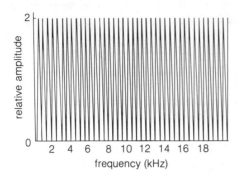

2-millisecond delay

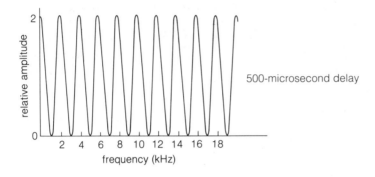

500-microsecond delay

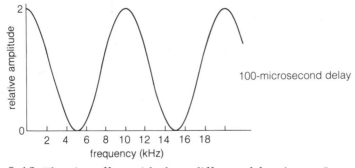

100-microsecond delay

8-19 Flanging effect with three different delay times. In flanging, the direct signal and the output of the delay line are combined. Varying the delay time produces the flanging effect.

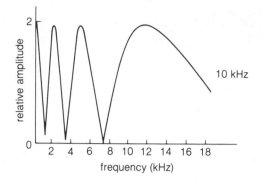

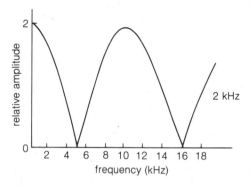

8-20 Phasing effect at two resistances.
In phasing, the direct signal and the output of a phase shift network are combined. The phasing effect is produced as the cancellations move up and down the audio bandwidth.

another. For example, in Michael Jackson's video, *Black and White*, a Chinese woman transformed into an Afro-American man who transformed into an Irishman who transformed into an Hispanic woman, and so on. In *Terminator II*, the silver "being" could melt, slither through cracks, and transform into various objects. These effects are more than sophisticated dissolves (the sonic counterpart of dissolve is crossfade). Morphing is a complete parametric and algorithmic restructuring of two completely different and independent effects. Because most audio morphing effects are delay-based, audio morphing devices can be classified as time signal processors (see 8-21).

Pitch Shifting

A **pitch shifter** is a device that changes the pitch (frequency) of a signal. It is used to correct minor off-pitch problems, create special effects, or change the length of a program without changing its pitch. The latter function is called **time compression**. Some pitch shifters can change frequencies over a couple of octaves without changing duration, allowing you to harmonize an input signal. For example, if a singer delivers a note slightly flat or sharp, it is possible to raise or lower the pitch so that it is in tune. To create harmony, the input signal can be mixed with the harmonized signal at selected pitch ratios (see 8-22).

As a time compressor, a pitch shifter can shorten recorded audio material with no editing, no deletion of content, and no alteration in pitch (see 8-23).

Amplitude Signal Processors

Amplitude processors are devices that affect dynamic range. These effects include compressing, limiting, and expanding a signal.

Compressors and Limiters

Earlier, we discussed dynamic range, comparing a human's ability to perceive an extremely wide range of sound levels with the inability of typical analog recording to reproduce little more than half that range. There are two reasons for this limitation. First, the analog tape medium can handle

a

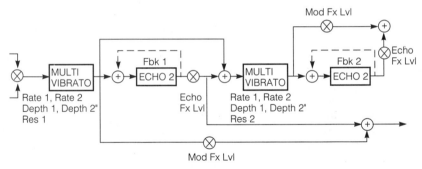

Mosaic A —a dual modulator with the left input chased by quarter-note echoes, and the right input chased by quarter-note triplet echoes.

Mosaic B —produces a deep, resonant multivibrato effect with very tight echoes

b

ORBITS A/B: the sound of a cabinet containing two rotary speakers. Morph rates are set to simulate the inertial drag when the speakers are sped up or slowed down.

CENTRIFUGE A: produces spinning, vowel-like sounds. Envelope controls rate and depth—hit a note hard, and the effect freezes until the note begins to fade away.

AEROSOL A: a deep "over the top" flanger that sprays your sounds across stereo space. Envelope control of rates can be added, as well as cascade echo effects.

CHOIR A: a lush multivoice chorus with echo rhythms that become more dense as they repeat. Envelope "ducks" chorus depths, so the effect grows stronger as the notes fade away.

BLEEN A/B: dramatic with short percussive sounds like muted guitar, vibes, or individual drums. In BLEEN A, Envelope controls pitch sweeps that dive into a pool of swirling echoes. In BLEEN B, polyrhythmic echoes mutate into ring modulation as they bounce from side to side.

FRACTAL B: an effect that devours itself. Loop echo with a twist. When you play a melodic line, the individual notes eventually stack up to form a chord.

c

8-21 Audio morphing™ processor   (a) Example of how the processor transforms one effect into another (b). Selected presets of the processor (c).

#	Preset Name	Algorithm	Description
623	PITCH QUANTIZE	DIATONIC SHIFT	This program quantizes the input to the nearest chromatic interval.
624	SUSPENSE	MULTI-SHIFT	Echoes are shifted to create suspenseful harmonies.
625	THIRD & FIFTH	DIATONIC SHIFT	Generates an 'in-key' 3rd and 5th above the input.
626	THIRD & OCTAVE	DIATONIC SHIFT	This generates a diatonic 3rd above and an octave below the input.
627	TWELVE STRING	MULTI-SHIFT	Provides an octave down and a micro-pitch-shift, simulating a twelve string guitar.
628	VIBRATO	MULTI-SHIFT	Instant vibrato at the press of a button.
629	VOICE SHIFT	STEREO SHIFT	This STEREO SHIFT program is optimized for pitch shifting program material whose main content is spoken voice.
630	ALIENS	REVERSE SHIFT	Transforms voice into a rough, alien-like sound.
631	ANTI-AMBIENCE	REVERSE SHIFT	This is a reverb-like sound created from REVERSE SHIFT. Sounds great on guitar.
632	AUTOPANNER	SWEPT COMBS	Produces automatic stereo (left<->right) panning.
633	AVANTE-GARDE	REVERSE SHIFT	A REVERSE SHIFT effect that generates descending chromatic lines.
634	BACKWARDS	REVERSE SHIFT	Turns the input around in one-second chunks.
635	BAND PAN	BAND DELAY	Rhythmically, panned and delayed, with its own band pass filter.
636	BAND SLAP	BAND DELAY	A stereo slap effect using two bands that are fed back. One band is tuned higher.
637	BANDSWEEPRAND	BAND DELAY	A random-pitched set of bands that are delayed and pass from left to right in the stereo field.
638	BAND SWEEP	BAND DELAY	Upward sweeping bands passing from left to right.
639	BIZARREMONIZER	LAYERED SHIFT	Generates a bizarre, upward sweeping pitch shift.
640	CANNONS	REVERSE SHIFT	A unique sweeping sound that's great on drums. Try playing a tom solo through this.
641	CRITICAL BAND	PATCH FACTORY	A close approximation to Fletcher/Munson bandpass curves. Use to brighten signals, or key compressors and gates to frequencies to which our ears are most sensitive.

8-22 (*a*) **Harmonizer**® and (*b*) **examples of preset programs of this Harmonizer.** This particular unit, in addition to pitch shifting, is also capable of flanging, delay, reverberation, and tone generation. There are four ways to enter data: with the keypad, what Eventide calls the Knob, the Up/Down buttons, and MIDI. The key pad is used when you know the preset values or the parameter values (delay times, for example) you wish to use. Punch them in and hit enter. The Knob is used to dial up an existing program and fine-tune its parameters. The Up/Down keys are used to "nudge" a parameter value or to scroll through the presets. The MIDI function facilitates entering MIDI data into the Harmonizer. The Soft Keys affect the various programs in different ways; their functions are labeled on the character display.

	Leave titles at 1X to avoid VTR jitter	Compress boring dialog 20%			More boring dialog—Compress 20%		Compress 10% to increase excitement	
1:27:00								
Original Play Time	5:00	15:00	20:00	10:00	15:00	5:00	15:00	2:00
Program Material	Titles	Action	Dialog	Fight Scene	Dialog	Action	Action	Credits

		Compress 10% to increase excitement	Compress 5% to pick up pace		Don't compress or expand		Leave credits at 1X to avoid VTR jitter	
1:16:30								
New Play Time	5:00	13:30	16:00	9:30	12:00	5:00	13:30	2:00
Program Material	Titles	Action	Dialog	Fight Scene	Dialog	Action	Action	Credits

8-23 Example of time compression of an event sequence

only a certain amount of information before reaching its "threshold of pain" and becoming saturated. Second, at its "threshold of hearing," the tape's noise level is often as loud as, or louder than, the information. Before the development of certain signal-processing devices, the only way to control the program level was to ride the gain—manually control loud sound surges to prevent them from going into the red, and raising the level of quiet passages to lift them above the noise floor. Today, most sound designers use electronic devices called *compressors* and *limiters* to keep a signal automatically within the dynamic range that a medium can handle (and also for other sonic purposes that will be discussed later) (see 8-24 and 8-25).

Compressors

The compressor is a processor whose output level increases at a slower rate as its input level increases. Compressors usually have four controls—for compression ratio, compression threshold, attack time, and release time, each one of which can affect the others.

The **compression ratio** establishes the proportion of change between the input and output levels. The ratios are usually variable, and depending on the compressor, there are several selectable points between 1.1 to 1 and 20 to 1. If you set the compression ratio for, say, 2 to 1, it means that for every 2-dB increase of the input signal, the output will increase by 1 dB; at 5 to 1, a 5-dB increase of the input signal increases the output by 1 dB. This is how sound with a dynamic range greater than a tape can handle is brought to usable proportions.

The **compression threshold** is the level at which the compression ratio takes effect. You set it based on your judgment of where compression should begin. (For an idea of the relationship between compression ratio and threshold, see 8-26.) There is no way to predetermine what settings will work best for a given sound at a certain level; it is a matter of listening and experimenting.

Attack time is the length of time it takes the compressor to react to the signal being compressed. Attack times, which usually range from 0.25 to 10 milliseconds, can enhance or detract from a sound. If the attack time is long, it can help to bring out

8-24 Compressor/limiter (single channel)

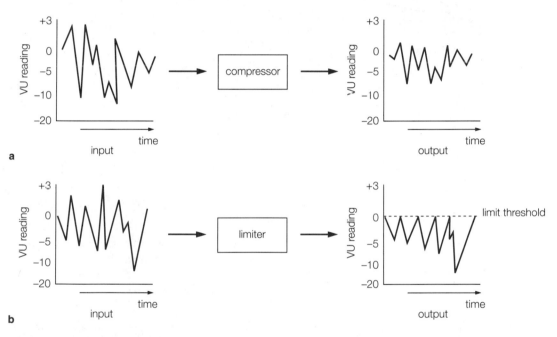

8-25 Effect of (*a*) compression and (*b*) limiting

percussive attacks, but if it is too long, it can miss or overshoot the beginning of the compressed sound. If the attack time is too short, it reduces punch by attenuating the attacks, sometimes producing popping or clicking sounds. When it is controlled, however, a short attack time can heighten transients and add a crisp accent to sound. Again, set attack time by using your ear.

Release time (or *recovery time*) is the length of time it takes a compressed signal to return to normal. Release times vary from 50 milliseconds to several seconds. It is perhaps the most critical variable in compression because it controls the moment-to-moment changes in the level and, therefore, the overall loudness. Generally, the purpose of the release-time function is to

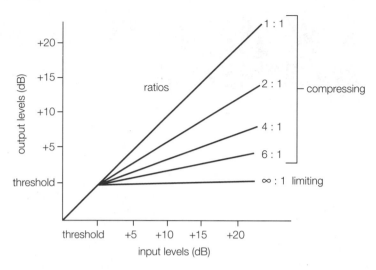

8-26 A representation of the relationship of various compression ratios to a fixed threshold point. The graph also displays the difference between the effects of limiting and compressing.

make the variations in loudness level caused by the compression imperceptible. Longer release times are usually applied to music that is slower and more legato (that is, smoother and more tightly connected), and shorter release times to music that is fast.

This is not to suggest a rule, however; it is only a guideline. In fact, various release times produce various effects. Some enhance sound; others degrade it, as the following list of potential effects suggests. For example:

1. A fast release time combined with a close compression ratio makes a signal seem louder than it actually is.

2. Too short a release time with too wide a ratio causes the compressor to pump or breathe. You actually hear it working when a signal rapidly returns to normal after it has been compressed and quickly released.

3. A longer release time smooths a fluctuating signal.

4. A longer release time combined with a short attack time gives the signal some of the characteristics of a sound going backward. This effect is particularly noticeable with transients.

5. A release time longer than about half a second for bass instruments prevents harmonic distortion.

6. Too long a release time creates a muddy sound and can cause the gain reduction triggered by a loud signal to continue through a soft one that follows.

Limiters

The **limiter** is a compressor whose output level stays at or below a preset point regardless of its input level. It has a compression ratio between 10 to 1 and infinity; it puts a ceiling on the loudness of a sound at a preset level (see 8-26). Regardless of how loud the input signal is, the output will not go above this ceiling. This makes the limiter useful in situations where high sound levels are frequent or where a performer or console operator cannot prevent loud sounds from going into the red.

The limiter has a preset compression ratio but a variable threshold; the threshold sets the point where limiting begins. Attack and release times, if they are not preset, should be relatively short, especially the attack time. A short attack time is usually essential to a clean-sounding limit.

Unlike compression, which can have little effect on the frequency response, limiting can cut off high frequencies. Also, if you severely limit a very high sound level, the signal-to-noise ratio drops dramatically.

De-essers

Some compressors are equipped with a filter to help control the stronger, more annoying high-frequency sounds around 3,200 Hz such as "s," "z," "ch," and "sh." The filter, called a **de-esser**, is frequency-selective and handles the highly sibilant signals without affecting the rest of the sound.

A more sophisticated application of this principle is the *relief stressor* (or *enlarger*). Instead of compressing frequencies in a preset bandwidth, it tracks the sibilance and compresses it where it occurs.

Uses of Compressors and Limiters

Compressors and limiters have many applications, several of which are listed here.

1. Compression minimizes the wide changes in levels of loudness caused when a performer fails to maintain a consistent mic-to-source distance.

2. Compression smooths the variations in attack and loudness of instruments with wide ranges or wide sound pressure levels, such as the guitar, bass, trumpet, French horn, and drums.

3. Compression can improve the intelligibility of a vocal in an analog tape recording that has been rerecorded, or dubbed, several times.

4. Compression reduces apparent noise if the compression ratios are close. Wider ratios add more noise.

5. Compression creates the effect of moving a sound source back in relation to the noncompressed sound sources. This may or may not be desirable depending on the overall spatial balance.

6. Limiting prevents high sound levels, either constant or momentary, from saturating the tape.

7. The combination of compression and limiting can add more power or apparent loudness to sound.

Expanders

An **expander**, like a compressor, affects dynamic range (see 8-27 and 8-28). But whereas a compressor reduces it, an expander increases it. Like a compressor, an expander has variable ratios and is triggered when sound reaches a set threshold level. However, the ratios on an expander are the inverse of those on a compressor: 1 to 2, 1 to 3, and so on. At 1 to 2 each 1 dB of input expands to 2 dB of output; at 1 to 3 each 1 dB of input expands to 3 dB of output. Because an expander is triggered when a signal falls below a set threshold, it can be

8-27 Expander/noise gate

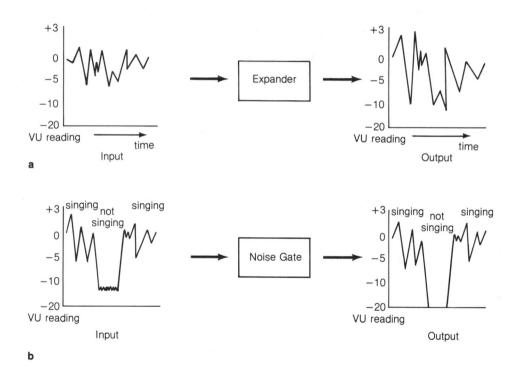

b

8-28 Effect of (*a*) expansion and (*b*) noise gating.   Without noise gating, ambient noise is masked during singing and audible when singing is not present. Noise gating eliminates the ambient noise when there is no singing.

used as a **noise gate** to reduce or eliminate unwanted low-level noise from amplifiers, ambience, rumble, tape hiss, and leakage from one microphone to another.

Assume, for example, that you have two microphones, one for a singer and one for an accompanying piano. When the singer and pianist are performing, the sound level will probably be loud enough to mask unwanted low-level noises. But if the pianist is playing quietly and the vocalist is not singing, or vice versa, the open, unused microphone may pick up these noises.

An obvious solution to this problem is to turn down the pot when a microphone is not being used, cutting it off acoustically and electronically. But this could become hectic for a console operator if there are several sound sources to coordinate. A better solution would be to set the expander's threshold level at a point just above the quietest sound level that the vocalist (or piano) emits. When the vocalist stops singing, the loudness of the sound entering the microphone falls below the threshold point and shuts down, or *gates*, the mic.

The key to successful noise gating is in the coordination of the threshold and ratio settings. Because there is little difference between the low level of a sound's decay and the low level of noise, you have to be wary that in cutting off noise, you do not cut off program material also. Always be careful when you use a noise gate: Unless it is set precisely, it can adversely affect response.

Noise gates are also used to create effects. Shortening decay time of the drums can produce a very tight drum sound. Taking a 60-Hz tone and feeding it so that it is keyed or triggered by an electric bass can produce not only a simulated bass drum sound but also one that is synchronized with the bass guitar.

Noise Signal Processors

Of the many links in the sound chain, analog tape is a major cause of noise. Noise processors are designed to reduce that noise.

As discussed in Chapter 2, the dynamic range of human hearing is 120 db-SPL and beyond. In Chapter 7, we pointed out that the best analog recording produces a dynamic range of 80–90 dB. Much analog recording is in the 65–70 dB range, half as much as humans are capable of hearing (see 8-29). Recording at high levels could improve dynamic range but it could also increase distortion. And there is the problem of tape noise.

Tape Noise

The inherent unevenness of a tape's magnetic coating, even in the highest-quality tapes, always leaves a slight polarization of the magnetic particles in the coating after erasure, regardless of how complete erasure is. Each time a tape is used, some of the magnetic coating is worn away, thus decreasing the signal-to-noise ratio. Poor dispersion of the magnetic particles creates sound dropout and noise. Residual magnetization after erasure, due either to an improper erase current or to poor bulk-erasing technique, increases tape noise. A problem with the record current will result in a recording that is not uniformly magnetized. A tape recording made at a level that is too quiet will underpolarize the magnetic particles, thereby creating hiss. Multitrack tape brings an associated increase in tape noise.

To improve dynamic range and reduce noise, the signal must be processed before it is encoded on tape and after it is decoded from tape. Such a process is called *double-ended noise reduction*. Noise reduction that

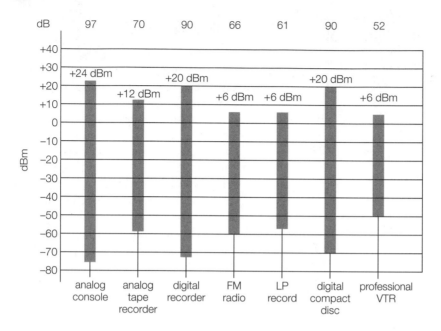

8-29 Dynamic ranges of various audio devices in dBm (an electrical measurement of power) and in dB

occurs either just before recording or just after playback is called *single-ended noise reduction.*

Double-Ended Noise Reduction

As mentioned in the previous section, a compressor can process noise "before the fact," during recording, and the expander can process noise "after the fact," during playback. During recording, the input signal is compressed—that is, dynamic range is reduced. Where quiet passages occur in the sound, they are recorded at a higher-than-normal level. During playback the signal is expanded—returned to its original dynamic range—but with one difference. The level is reduced, and so is the noise, in all of the places where it was increased during recording (see 8-30).

Using the compressor and expander for noise reduction is an exacting and time-consuming job. It is also expensive. It involves setting the appropriate thresholds and ratios on each unit for each tape track being produced; a 24-track recording would require 24 compressors and 24 expanders to reduce overall tape noise. Therefore, the double-ended process of noise reduction has been incorporated into a single unit called a **compander** (from its functions, compression and expansion). The compander is more popularly known as a *noise reducer.*

In double-ended noise reduction, a tape encoded with noise reduction must be decoded during playback. If it is not, the increased signal and noise level that was encoded during recording will be annoyingly perceptible. The most commonly used double-ended noise reduction systems are

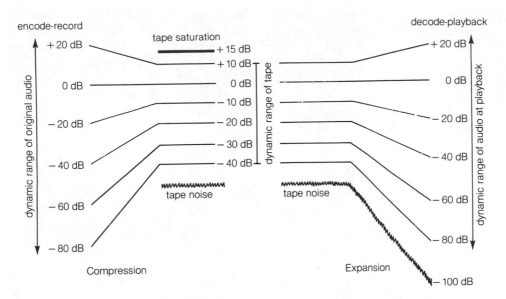

8-30 **How one type of noise reducer decreases noise in a tape recording**

Dolby and dbx. The systems are not compatible, so tapes made with one are not interchangeable with the other. Because Dolby is, by far, the more widely used of the two systems for music recording, it is the system considered here.

The Dolby System

Dolby has a number of systems currently in use. The one most prevalent in professional music recording is *SR (Spectral Recording)*.

SR uses the principle of least treatment to the audio signal (see 8-31). At the lowest levels or when no signal is present, SR applies a fixed gain/frequency characteristic that reduces noise and other low-frequency disturbances. Noise reduction is applied to those regions that contain low- and medium-level signal components. Similar to the response of the human hearing system, SR responds to changing amplitudes in various regions of the frequency spectrum,

rather than to instantaneous variations in the signal's overall waveform. To put it another way, SR changes the gain only by the amount required and only at frequencies where the change is needed, thereby achieving as nearly optimum a level as possible at all frequencies. SR increases dynamic range as much as 24 dB at high frequencies and 10 dB at low frequencies, increasing headroom to the point where the risk of under-recording analog tape and over-recording digital tape is reduced considerably.

Other Dolby systems are the S, B, and C. Dolby S noise reduction is based on the SR process. It is less complex and less costly than SR and was designed for the audiocassette. The Dolby B system is used for less critical noise reduction in home tape recorders. It reduces high-frequency noise 10 dB above 8 kHz and has no operating effect on lower-frequency noises. Dolby C, for audiocassettes, reduces noise 20 dB across a wider range than Dolby B, acting

8-31a Dolby SR noise reduction system for a 24-track analog tape recorder

down to 100 Hz.

Single-Ended Noise Reduction

Double-ended noise reduction systems do not remove noise from a signal; they prevent it from entering. Single-ended noise-reduction systems work to reduce existing noise from a signal or recording. Generally, single-ended noise reduction senses the level of the incoming signal. When the level falls below a certain threshold, high frequencies in the low-level signal are reduced progressively, thereby reducing the level of hiss. High-level signals are not processed.

The noise gate can be considered as a single-ended noise reducer. When a particular threshold is set and the signal level falls below that threshold, the noise gate shuts down, thereby preventing unwanted noise from passing through. Of course, if the threshold level is not set carefully, program information may also be prevented from coming through. Another type of single-ended noise reducer is shown in 8-32.

Digital Signal Processing

With the advent of the hard-disk recorder and digital audio workstation (see Chapter 7) has come **digital signal processing (DSP)**. Thanks to the use of algorithms—programs that perform complex calculations according to a set of controlled parameters—it is possible to perform almost any signal-processing function digitally in a self-contained unit. EQ, limiting, compression, expansion,

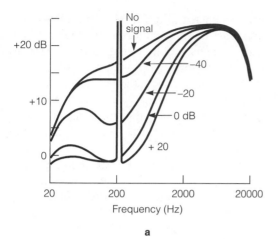

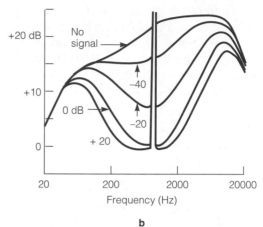

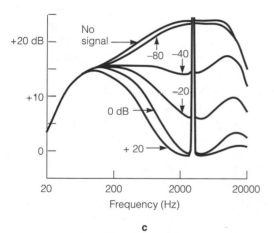

8-31b Examples of Dolby SR noise reduction at (*a*) 200 Hz, (*b*) 800 Hz, (*c*) 3000 Hz

8-32 Single-ended noise reducer. Single-ended noise reducers can be connected just prior to the input of a master tape recorder and also enable individual channels from a mixer to be processed independently. They can be connected to process reproduced sounds during playback, as well.

pitch shifting, delay, and so on can be accomplished at the touch of a few buttons, some movements of a mouse, or with strokes of a light-pencil (see 8-33). Settings can be stored in a memory for almost instant retrieval at any time.

Noise Reduction with Digital Signal Processing

Another advantage of DSP is its considerable potency in noise reduction, particularly during conversion of analog recordings to digital. Virtually any unwanted sound can be eliminated.

In addition to the conventional noise reduction associated with Dolby, for example, digital noise reduction can act on other noises as well. One system uses three main tools: manual de-clicking for removal of clicks, pops, thumps, electrostatic ticks, and other impulse noises; production de-clicking and de-crackling for automatic click and scratch detection and removal; and broad-band de-noising to eliminate hiss, surface noise, and unwanted background noise. For example, it is possible to take a sample of a hiss or hum, isolate it in a section as small as half a second, and then take a signature of it. Analysis is done on all frequency components of that noise, and the signature is digitally removed from the digital audio signal that contained it. If the problem is a 60-cycle hum, each one of the frequencies associated with the 60 cycles is attenuated by the exact multiple of the hum. The desirable part of the signal remains undisturbed. The frequency components contributing to the hum are brought down.

Clicks and pops can be removed manually, one at a time, or automatically. The area to the left and right of the click or pop is analyzed to determine what frequencies in the signal are present. The gap that results from the removal of the click or pop is filled with appropriate synthesized material. De-crackling is a more intensive de-clicking operation that interpolates and removes thousands of clicks and pops per second.

The system is particularly effective at removing constant, steady noises. For example, in a vocal track with high-level background noise from lights, ventilating fans, and studio acoustics, 85 percent of the noise can be removed without affecting voice quality.

Extolling the virtues of DSP in general and digital noise reduction in particular should not lead to the mistaken conclusion that they are panaceas in the world of signal processing. In audio, as in life, there is always a trade-off.

For example, in noise reduction you have control over three parameters and have to be aware of the balances among them. You have to consider the amount of noise being removed from the signal, the amount of signal being removed from the program material, and the amount of new sonic colorations being added to the signal.

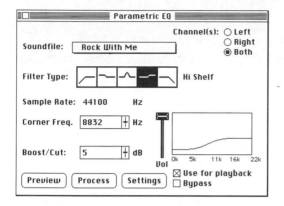

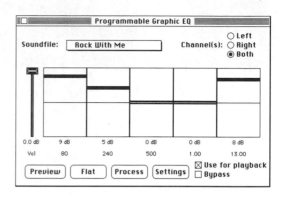

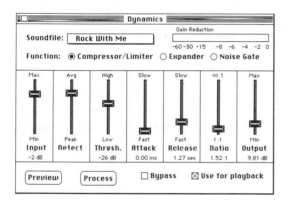

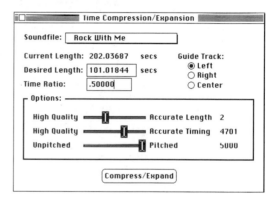

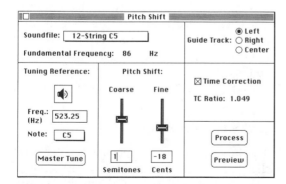

8-33 Examples of DSP menus

9

Loudspeakers and Monitoring

Each component in the sound chain is important; but no matter how good the components are, when you listen to their product, you hear only what the loudspeaker can reproduce. To put it another way, the quality of every sound you evaluate, analog or digital, is based on what you hear from the loudspeaker. The tendency is to underestimate the importance of the loudspeaker, perhaps because it is the last link in the sound chain. There may be a subconscious correlation between last and least. This attitude is aesthetically fatal.

The point seems straightforward: Always use the best loudspeaker. But which is best? Is it the most expensive, the largest, the loudest, the one with the widest, flattest frequency response, or the one suitable for symphonic music or hard rock? Although a loudspeaker is critical to any audio operation, choosing the best one for your needs is anything but a straightforward procedure. It involves several decisions; each influences later decisions, and most are mainly subjective.

In deciding which loudspeaker is "best," you should look at several factors: frequency response, linearity, amplifier power, distortion, output-level capability, sensitivity, polar response, arrival time, and phasing. Placement also affects the sound. These factors will be discussed later in the chapter.

Like the microphone, the loudspeaker is a transducer, but it works in the opposite direction. Instead of changing acoustic energy into electric energy, it changes electric energy back into acoustic energy. But unlike microphone usage, only one type of loudspeaker is in common use: the **moving-coil loudspeaker**.

Loudspeaker Systems

The function of a loudspeaker is to convert the electrical energy that drives it into mechanical energy and in turn to acoustic energy. Theoretically, a loudspeaker should be able to reproduce all frequencies linearly—that is, have an output that varies proportionately with the input. In reality, this does not happen. A loudspeaker that is large enough to generate low-frequency sound waves most likely will not be able to reproduce the high frequencies efficiently. Conversely, a speaker capable of reproducing the shorter waves may be incapable of reproducing the longer wavelengths.

To illustrate the problem, many radio and television receivers contain a single speaker; even many stereo radios and tape recorders contain only one loudspeaker in each of the two loudspeaker enclosures. Because a single speaker has difficulty coping with the entire range of audible frequencies, a compromise is made: The long and short wavelengths are sacrificed for the medium wavelengths that a single midsize loudspeaker can reproduce more efficiently. Therefore, regardless of a recording's sound quality, a receiver with just one loudspeaker cannot reproduce the sound with full-frequency response.

Crossover Network and Drivers

To widen the loudspeaker's frequency response and make reproduction of the bass and treble more efficient, the **crossover network** was created. Also, individual speaker elements, called *drivers*, were developed to handle the different physical requirements necessary to emit the long, powerful bass frequencies and the short, more directional treble frequencies.

The crossover network divides the frequency spectrum between the low and high frequencies. The actual point, or frequency, where the bass and treble divide is called the **crossover frequency**. A driver large enough to handle the low frequencies is dedicated to the bass, and a driver small enough to handle the high frequencies is dedicated to the treble. Informally, these drivers, or loud-

speakers, are called the **woofer** and the **tweeter**. Low- and high-frequency drivers are contained in a single cabinet. The size of the drivers is related to the power output of the loudspeaker system.

If a loudspeaker system divides the frequency spectrum once, it is called a **two-way system loudspeaker**. The crossover frequency in a two-way system is in the neighborhood of 1,500 to 2,000 Hz. The frequencies below the crossover point are assigned to the woofer, and the frequencies above the crossover are assigned to the tweeter. A loudspeaker may have more than one driver for each frequency range (see 9-1).

A loudspeaker system that uses two crossover frequencies is called a **three-way system loudspeaker** (see 9-2), and one that has three crossover frequencies is called a **four-way system loudspeaker** (see 9-3). Three-way systems divide the frequency spectrum at roughly 400 to 500 Hz and 3,500 to 5,000 Hz. Four-way systems divide it at anywhere between 400 to 500 Hz, 1,500 to 2,000 Hz, and 4,500 to 6,000 Hz.

Passive and Active Crossover Networks

Two types of crossover networks are used in loudspeakers: passive and active. In a passive crossover network the power amplifier precedes the crossover (see 9-4). This design can create certain problems: Output level at the crossover frequency is usually down by a few dB; intermodulation distortion is more likely to occur, particularly at loud levels; harmonic distortion may be heard in the high frequencies.

In an active crossover network, the crossover precedes two power amps and operates at low power levels. One amp receives the low-frequency signals and drives the woofer; the other amp receives the high-frequency signals and drives the tweeter.

9-1 Two-way system loudspeaker with two woofers and a dome tweeter

9-2 Three-way system loudspeaker with two woofers, midrange driver, and a horn-type tweeter to widen the dispersion of the high frequencies

9-3 Four-way system loudspeaker with two 15-inch woofers, 10-inch midbass, midrange, and high-frequency horn-loaded tweeters

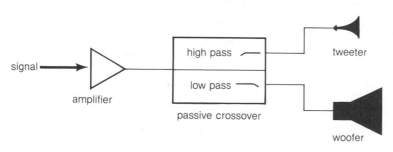

9-4 Monitor system with a passive crossover

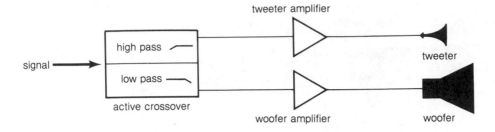

9-5 Biamped system with an active crossover

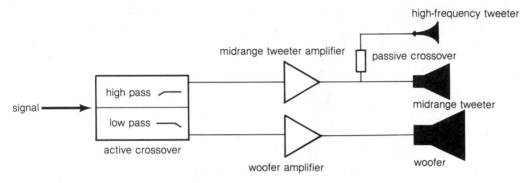

9-6 Biamped monitor system with both active and passive crossovers

This is known as a *biamplification*, or *biamped*, system (see 9-5). An active crossover network has several advantages over a passive one. It reduces distortion, and if distortion should occur in either the woofer or the tweeter, it will not be transferred to the other component. Power is more efficiently used because a lower-power amp can drive the tweeter, which requires less power than the woofer. Both woofer and tweeter have their own power amp. Transient response is better, especially in the lower frequencies.

Three-way system loudspeakers can be triamped, meaning that each speaker is driven by its own amp. If a three-way system is biamped, a passive crossover is added before the tweeter to create the three-way design (see 9-6).

Horns

A *horn* couples the loudspeaker enclosure to the air in an environment and provides control over the sound dispersion of a particular freqency range. Various types of horns are displayed in Figure 9-7.

Selecting a Monitor Loudspeaker

Loudspeakers are like musical instruments in that they produce sound. They are not like purely electronic components such as consoles, which can be objectively tested and rationally evaluated. No two loudspeakers ever sound quite the same. Comparing the same make and model loudspeakers in one room only tells you what

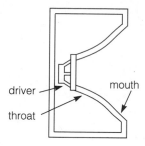

Front-Loaded Horn

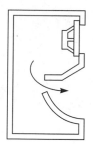

Rear-Loaded Horn

Front-loaded horn. Located in front of the loudspeaker. A front-loaded horn is a specific reference to a low-frequency horn enclosure because most front-loaded horns are high frequency.

Rear-loaded horn. A low-frequency horn located at the rear of the loudspeaker.

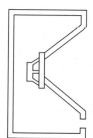

Combination
Front-Rear-Loaded Horn

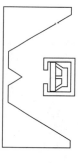

W-Horn

Combination front-rear-loaded horn. A low-frequency horn in which the horn is in the front of the loudspeaker and the rear is reflex loaded. In a bass reflex loudspeaker enclosure, the speaker's rear wave emerges through a port (vent) to reinforce the low frequencies.

W-horn. An enclosure for low frequencies in which two folded horns direct the sound forward.

9-7 Various types of horns

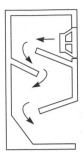

Folded Horn

Folded horn. Low-frequency horn that curves around the inside of the cabinet to achieve a greater effective horn length in a smaller enclosure.

Rate of flare is exponential rather than linear.

Exponential Horn

Exponential horn. Low or high-frequency horn in which the horn's flare rate follows an exponential curve.

Radial Horn

Radial horn. High-frequency horn with curved inner surfaces that flare open at an exponential rate to create a partially spherical wavefront.

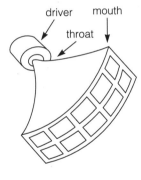

driver   mouth
throat

Multicellular Horn

Multicellular horn. High-frequency horn divided into cells or compartments for greater directivity.

9-7 (*continued*) **Various types of horns**

they sound like in that acoustic environment; in another room they may sound altogether different. Furthermore, a loudspeaker that satisfies your taste might be unappealing to someone else's taste. Thus, it is extremely difficult to suggest guidelines for selecting a studio monitor. Nevertheless, all loudspeakers used for professional purposes should meet certain requirements.

Frequency Response

Evaluating **frequency response** in a loudspeaker involves two considerations: (1)

how wide it is and (2) how flat, or linear, it is. Frequency response ideally should be as wide as possible, from at least 40 Hz to 16,000 Hz. But the relationship between the sound produced in the studio and the sound reproduced through the audience's receiver/loudspeaker becomes a factor when selecting a monitor loudspeaker.

For example, TV audio can carry the entire range of audible frequencies. You may have noticed during a televised music program, however, that you see certain high- and low-pitched instruments being played, but you hear them only faintly or not at all. Overhead cymbals are one example. Generally, their frequency range is between 300 and 12,000 Hz (including overtones), but they usually begin to gain good definition between 4,500 and 8,000 Hz, which is well within the frequency of television transmission. However, the highest response of many home TV receivers is about 6,000 Hz, which is below a good part of the cymbals' range.

Assume you wish to boost the cymbal frequencies that the home TV receiver can barely reproduce. Unless you listen to the sound over a monitor comparable in output level and response to the average TV speaker, you cannot get a sense of what effect the boost is having.

Due to the differences between the potential sound response of a medium and its actual response after processing, transmission, and reception, it makes sense to choose at least two types of studio monitors. One should provide both wide response and enough power to reproduce a broad range of sound levels, and the other should have response and power that reflect what the average listener hears. Many music recording studios use three sets of monitors to check sound: (1) low-quality loudspeakers with only midrange response and limited power output, such as those in portable and car radios and cheap tape decks; (2) average-quality loudspeakers with added high and low response, such as moderately priced component systems; and (3) high-quality loudspeakers with a very wide response and high output capability.

Linearity

The second consideration in evaluating frequency response in a loudspeaker is how linear it is—regardless of a loudspeaker's size, power requirements, or wideness of response. **Linearity** means that frequencies being fed to a loudspeaker at a particular loudness are reproduced at the same loudness. If they are not, it is very difficult to predetermine what listeners will hear. If the level of a 100-Hz sound is 80 dB going in and 55 dB coming out, some—if not most—of the information may be lost. If the level of an 8,000-Hz sound is 80 dB going in and 100 dB coming out, the information may be overbearing.

Loudspeaker specifications include a value that indicates how much a monitor deviates from a flat frequency response, either by increasing or decreasing level. This variance should be no greater than ±3 dB.

Amplifier Power

To generate adequately loud sound levels without generating distortion, the loudspeaker amplifier must provide sufficient power. At least 30 watts for tweeters and 100 watts for woofers is generally necessary. Regardless of how good the rest of your loudspeaker's components are, if the amplifier does not have enough power, it is as if you were trying to power a large boat with a small outboard motor—efficiency suffers considerably.

There is a commonly held, seemingly plausible, notion that increasing amplifier power means a proportional increase in loudness; for example, that a 100-watt amplifier can play twice as loud as a 50-watt amplifier. In fact, if a 100-watt and a 50-watt amp are playing at top volume, the 100-watt amp will sound only slightly louder. What the added wattage gives is clearer and less distorted reproduction in loud sonic peaks.

Distortion

Discussion of amplifier power leads naturally to consideration of **distortion**—appearance of a signal in the reproduced sound that was not in the original sound. Any component in the sound chain can generate distortion. Because distortion is heard at the reproduction (loudspeaker) phase of the sound chain, regardless of where in the system it was generated, and because loudspeakers are the most distortion-prone component in most audio systems, it is appropriate to discuss briefly the various forms of distortion—intermodulation, harmonic, transient, and loudness—here.

Intermodulation Distortion

The loudspeaker is perhaps most vulnerable to **intermodulation distortion**. Intermodulation distortion (IM) results when two or more frequencies occur at the same time and interact to create combination tones and dissonances that are unrelated to the original sounds. Audio systems can be most vulnerable to intermodulation distortion when frequencies are far apart, as when a piccolo and a baritone saxophone are playing at the same time. Intermodulation distortion usually occurs in the high frequencies because they are weaker and more delicate than the low frequencies.

Wideness and flatness of frequency response are affected when IM is present. In addition to its obvious effect on perception, even subtle distortion can cause listening fatigue.

Unfortunately, not all specification sheets include percentage of IM, and those that do often list it only for selected frequencies. Nevertheless, knowing the percentage of IM for all frequencies is important to loudspeaker selection. A rating of .5 percent IM or less is considered good for a loudspeaker.

Harmonic Distortion

You will recall that **harmonic distortion** occurs when the audio system introduces harmonics into a recording that were not present originally. Harmonic and IM distortion usually happen when the input and output of a sound system are **nonlinear**—that is, when they do not change in direct proportion to each other. A loudspeaker's inability to handle amplitude is a common cause of harmonic distortion. This added harmonic content is expressed as a percentage of the total signal or as a component's *total harmonic distortion* (THD).

Transient Distortion

Transient distortion relates to the inability of an audio component to respond quickly to a rapidly changing signal such as percussive sounds. Sometimes transient distortion produces a ringing sound.

Loudness Distortion

Loudness (or **overload**) **distortion** arises when a signal is recorded or played back at a level of loudness that is greater than the sound system can handle. The clipping that results from loudness distortion creates a fuzzy, gritty sound.

Output-Level Capability

Overly loud signals give a false impression of program quality and balance; nevertheless, a loudspeaker should be capable of reproducing loud sound levels without distorting, blowing fuses, or damaging its components. An output capability of 110 dB-SPL is desirable for studio work. Even if studio work does not often call for very loud levels, the monitor should be capable of reproducing them, because it is sometimes necessary to listen at a loud level to hear subtlety and quiet detail.

Sensitivity

Sensitivity is the on-axis sound pressure level a loudspeaker produces at a given distance when driven at a certain power (about 3.3 feet with 1 watt of power). A monitor's sensitivity rating gives you an idea of the system's overall efficiency. Typical ratings range from 84 dB to over 100 dB.

In real terms, however, a sensitivity rating of, say, 90 dB indicates that the loudspeaker could provide 100 dB from a 10-watt input and 110 dB from a 100-watt input, depending on the type of driver. The point is that it is the combination of sensitivity rating and power rating that tells you whether a monitor loudspeaker will be loud enough to suit your production needs. Generally, a sensitivity rating of 93 dB or louder is required for professional applications.

Polar Response

Polar response indicates how a loudspeaker focuses sound at the monitoring position(s). Because it is important to hear only the sound coming from the studio or the tape without interacting reflections from the control room walls (vertical surfaces) and ceiling or floor (horizontal surfaces), dispersion must be controlled (see Chapter 3).

Bass waves are difficult to direct because of their long wavelengths. Therefore, bass traps and other low-frequency absorbers are included in control room design in order to handle those bass waves not focused at the listening position.

Frequencies from the tweeter(s), on the other hand, are shorter and easier to focus. The problem with high frequencies is that, as the wavelength shortens, the pattern can narrow. Therefore, the **coverage angle**, defined as the off-axis angle or point at which loudspeaker level is down 6 dB compared to the on-axis output, may not be wide enough to include the entire listening area (see 9-8).

9-8 JBL Bi-Radial™ horn monitor loudspeaker. This model is designed to provide constant vertical and horizontal polar coverage.

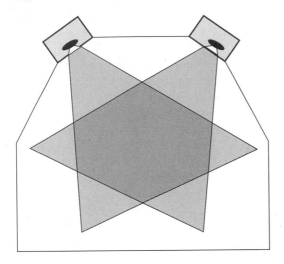

9-9 Desirable radiation angle of monitor loudspeakers

To help in selecting a loudspeaker with adequate polar response, specifications usually list a monitor's horizontal and vertical coverage angles. These angles should be high and wide enough to cover the listening position and still allow the operator or audience some lateral movement without seriously affecting sonic balance (see 9-9).

Arrival Time

Even if coverage angles are optimal, unless all reproduced sounds reach the listening position(s) at relatively the same time they were produced, aural perception will be impaired. When you consider the differences in size and power requirements among drivers and the wavelengths they emit, you can see this is easier said than done.

In two-, three-, and four-way system loudspeakers the physical separation of each of the speakers in the system causes the sounds to reach the listener's ears at different times. Loudspeaker systems exist that are time-accurate within 1 millisecond or less (see 9-10). Arrival times different by more than 1 millisecond are not acceptable in professional applications.

Phasing

Sometimes, although dispersal and arrival time are adequate, sound reaching a listener may not be as loud as it should be, or the elements within it may be poorly placed. For example, a rock band may be generating loud levels in the studio, but the sounds in the control room are, in relative terms, not so loud; or a singer is supposed to be situated front and center in a recording, but is heard from the left or right loudspeaker.

These problems may be the result of out-of-phase loudspeakers: One loudspeaker is pushing sound outward (compression), and the other loudspeaker is pulling sound inward (rarefaction). Phase problems can occur between woofer and tweeter in the same loudspeaker enclosure or between two separate loudspeakers. In the latter case it is usually because the connections are not wired properly (see 9-11 and 9-12). If you think sound is out of phase, check the VU meters. If they show a similar level and the audio still sounds skewed, then the speakers are out of phase. If they show quite different levels, then the phase problem is probably elsewhere.

Monitor Placement

Where you place monitor loudspeakers also affects sound quality, dispersal, and arrival time. Loudspeakers are often designed for a particular room location and are generally positioned in one of four places: (1) well toward the middle of a room, (2) against or flush with a wall, (3) at the intersection of two walls, or (4) in a corner at the ceiling or on the floor. Each position affects the

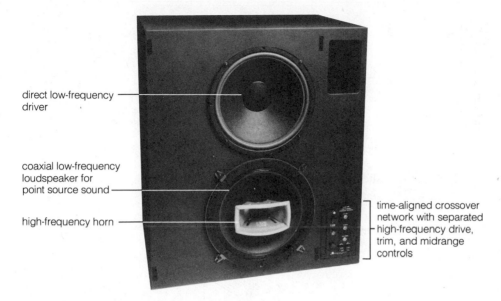

direct low-frequency driver

coaxial low-frequency loudspeaker for point source sound

high-frequency horn

time-aligned crossover network with separated high-frequency drive, trim, and midrange controls

9-10 The UREI time-aligned™ loudspeaker. This loudspeaker is designed to ensure precise arrival times. Instead of separate transducers to handle high, middle, and low frequencies, which could cause stereo imaging to "smear," the UREIs use a coaxial loudspeaker—literally two speakers in one—to cover the full audio range.

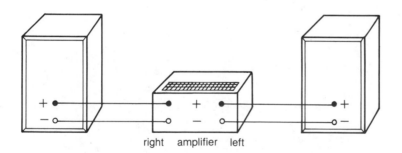

right   amplifier   left

9-11 Properly wired loudspeakers. These loudspeakers will reproduce in phase.

sound's loudness and dispersion differently.

A loudspeaker hanging in the middle of a room radiates sound into what is called a *full sphere* (or *full space*), where—theoretically—the sound level at any point within a given distance is the same (see 9-13). If a loudspeaker is placed against a wall, the wall concentrates the radiations into a *half sphere*, thereby theoretically increasing the sound level by 3 dB. With loudspeakers mounted at the intersection of two walls, the radiation angle is concentrated still more into a *one-quarter sphere*, thus increasing the sound level another 3 dB. Loudspeakers placed in corners at the ceiling or on the floor radiate in a *one-eighth*

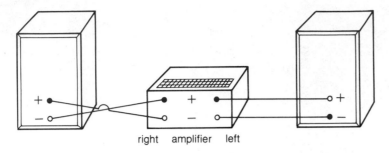

9-12 Improperly wired loudspeakers. These loudspeakers will reproduce out of phase.

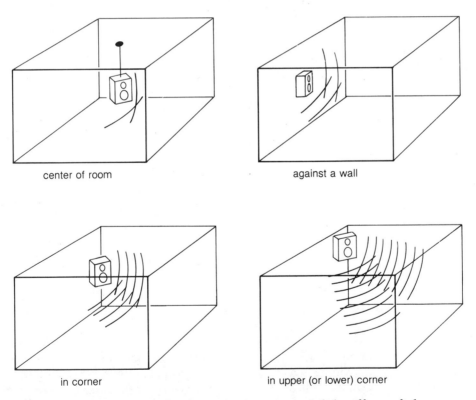

center of room

against a wall

in corner

in upper (or lower) corner

9-13 Four typical loudspeaker locations in a room and the effects of placement on overall loudness levels

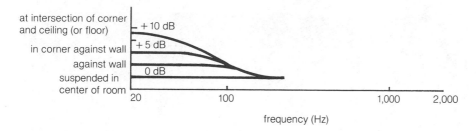

9-14 An example of the effects of loudspeaker placement on bass response

sphere, generating the most concentrated sound levels in a four-walled room. A significant part of each increase in the overall sound level is due to the loudness increase in the bass (see 9-14).

For informal listening, one of these monitor positions is not necessarily better than another; placement may depend on a room's layout, furniture placement, and/or personal taste. In professional situations it is preferable to flush mount loudspeakers in a wall or soffit. The most important thing in monitor placement is to avoid any appreciable space between the loudspeaker and the wall, and any protrusion of the loudspeaker's cabinet edges. Otherwise, the wall or loudspeaker cabinet edges, or both, will act as secondary radiators degrading frequency response. Flush-mounting also improves low-frequency response through avoiding back-wall reflections.

Near-Field Monitoring

Even in the best of monitor–control room acoustical environments, the distance between wall-mounted loudspeakers and the listening position is often wide enough to generate sonic discontinuities from unwanted control room reflections. To reduce these unwanted reflections another set of monitors is placed on or near the console's meter bridge (see 9-15).

Near-field monitoring reduces the audibility of control room acoustics by placing loudspeakers close to the listening position. Moreover, near-field monitoring improves source localization because most of the sound reaching the listening position is direct; the early reflections that hinder good source localization are reduced to the point where they are of little consequence. At least, that is the theory. In practice, problems with near-field monitoring still remain (see 9-16).

Near-field monitoring became a vital link in the sound chain in the last decade, but it is not new. What limited its use for so long was the absence of good-quality small loudspeakers. Now, small loudspeakers that meet the requirements of near-field monitoring are readily available. Among those requirements are a uniform frequency response from about 70 to 16,000 Hz (especially smooth response through the midrange), a sensitivity range from 87 to 92 dB, sufficient amplifier power, and good vertical dispersion for more stable stereo imaging.

Adjusting Monitor Sound to Room Sound

As important as the "ear" and personal taste are to monitor selection and evaluation, it is critical to obtain an objective measure of the correlation between monitor sound and room sound. This is done using a

9-15 Near-field monitors on console's meter bridge

real-time analyzer—a device that displays response curves on an instantaneous basis (see 9-17). Real-time analysis should be taken at different amplitudes.

When problems with frequency response show up, particularly serious ones, avoid the temptation to offset them with equalization. For example, if control room acoustics boost loudspeaker sound 6 dB at 250 Hz try not to equalize the monitors by, in this case, attenuating their response 6 dB at 250 Hz. Aside from adding noise by running the signal through another electronic device, an equalizer can change the phase relationships of the audio that passes through it.

To deal with discontinuities in monitor–control room interface, look to the source of the problem and correct it there. You may have to change or modify the monitor, monitor position, power amplifier, sound-diffusing materials, or impedance mismatch between sections of the monitor system. Whatever it takes, "natural" provides a truer sonic reference than "artificial," especially if the recording has to be evaluated or further processed in a different control room.

Evaluating the Monitor Loudspeaker

The final test of any monitor loudspeaker is how it sounds. Although the basis for much of the evaluation is subjective, there are guidelines for determining loudspeaker performance.

■ Sit at the designated listening position—the optimal distance away from and between the loudspeakers (see 9-18). This position should allow some front-to-back and side-to-side movement without altering perception of loudness, frequency response, or spatial perspective. It is important to know the boundaries of the listening position(s) so that all sound can be monitored on-axis within this area.

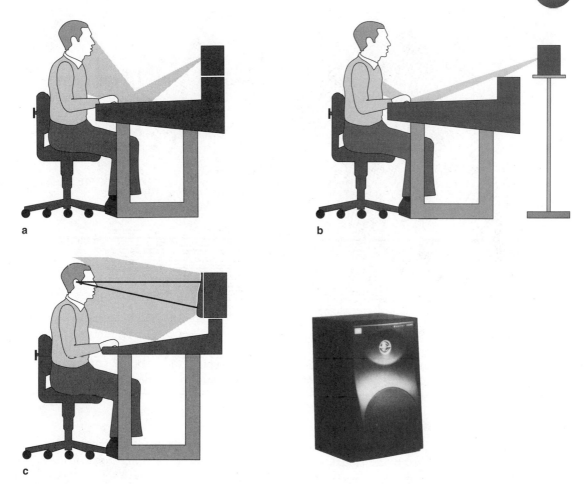

9-16 Near-field monitoring. (*a*) If a meter bridge is too low, early reflections will bounce off the console, degrading the overall monitor sound reaching the operator's ears. (*b*) One way to minimize this problem is to place the near-field monitors a foot or so in back of the console and cover the meter bridge with absorptive material. (*c*) The curved design of this near-field monitor was intended, among other things, to direct the shorter wavelengths away from the listening position.

■ Use familiar material for the evaluation. Otherwise, if some aspect of the sound is unsatisfactory, you will not know whether the problem is with the original material or with the loudspeaker.

■ In listening for spatial balance, make sure the various sounds are positioned in the

same places relative to the original material. If the original material has the vocal in the center (in relation to the two loudspeakers, assuming a stereo recording), the first violins on the left, the bass drum and bass at the rear center, the snare drum slightly left or right, and so on, then these should be in the same spatial posi-

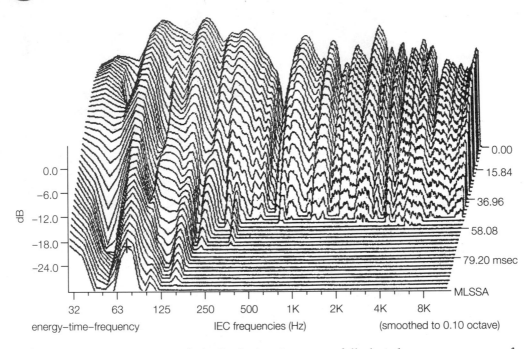

9-17 Real-time spectrum analysis displaying (in a waterfall plot) the response curve of a room with a broad notch from 350 to 550 Hz, caused by destructive reflections

tions when the material is played through the monitor system. As an additional test, put the monitor system into mono and check to make sure that the sound seems to be coming from between the two loudspeakers. Move toward the left and right boundaries of the listening position. If the sound moves with you before you get near the boundaries, reposition the monitors. Then recheck their dispersion in both stereo and mono until you can move within the boundaries of the listening position without the sound following you or skewing the placement of the sound sources. If monitor repositioning is necessary to correct problems with side-to-side sound placement, be sure it does not adversely affect front-to-back sound dispersion to the listening position (see 9-9 and 9-18).

■ In evaluating treble response, listen to the cymbal, triangle, flute, piccolo, and other high-frequency instruments. Are they too bright, crisp, shrill, or dull? Do you hear their upper harmonics?

■ In testing bass response, include instruments such as the tuba and bass, as well as the low end of the organ, piano, bassoon, and cello. Sound should not be thin, boomy, muddy, or grainy.

■ Assess the transient response, which is also important in a loudspeaker. For this, drums, bells, and triangle provide excel-

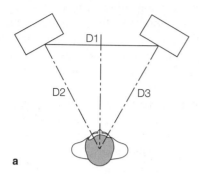

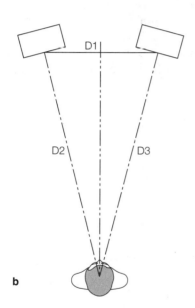

9-18 To help create an optimal travel path for sound from the loudspeakers to the listening position, carefully measure the loudspeaker separation and the distance between the loudspeakers and the listening position. In (*a*), the distance between the acoustic center (between the loudspeakers) and the listening position is equal. In this arrangement, head movement is restricted somewhat, and the stereo image will be emphasized or spread out, heightening the sense of where elements in the recording are located. Shortening D2 and D3 will produce a large shift in the stereo image. In (*b*), the distance between the acoustic center and the listening position is about twice as long. With this configuration, the movement of the head is less restricted and the stereo image is reduced in width, although it it more homogeneous. The more D2 and D3 are lengthened, the more monaural the stereo image becomes (except for hard left and hard right panning).

lent tests, assuming they are properly recorded. Good transient response reproduces a crisp attack with no distortion or breakup.

Other important elements to evaluate, such as intermodulation, harmonic, and loudness distortion, were touched upon earlier in this chapter. (See also Chapter 15.)

Monitoring in an Unfamiliar Control Room

When you do a session in a facility you have not worked in before, it is essential to become thoroughly familiar with the interaction between its monitor sound and room sound. A relatively quick and reliable way to get an objective idea of that interaction is to do a real-time analysis. It is also crucial to put the real-time analysis into perspective with reference CDs and your ears.

Reference CDs can be commercial recordings with which you are entirely familiar or discs specially designed to help assess a listening environment, or both. You must know how a commercial recording sounds in a control room whose monitors and acoustics you are intimately familiar with to use it as a test CD—to determine the sonic characteristics of and between the monitors and acoustics—in a strange environment. For example, if you know that a recording has clear high-end response in your own control room but the high end sounds thinner in another control room, it could indicate, among other things, that the other studio's monitors have inadequate treble response; the presence of harmonic distortion; a phase problem; the room's mediocre sound diffusion; or any combination of these factors.

CDs specially produced for referencing are also available. They are variously designed to test monitor and/or room response to a particular instrument, such as the drums; individual or groups of instruments, such as the voice and clarinet, or strings, brass, and woodwinds; various sizes and types of ensembles, such as orchestras, jazz bands, and rock groups; room acoustics; spatial positioning; and spectral balances (see the Bibliography).

P A R T

3

PREPRODUCTION

Planning the Recording Session

For the recordist trying to capture the nuances of sound—timbre, tonal balance, blend, and so on—recording live music is a most demanding challenge. The ways to shape the sound of music are as infinite and individual as music itself. Because there can be no firm rules about music production, and because artistry in recording technique never compensates for lack of artistry in musicianship, you must trust your creative judgment and your ear throughout the production process.

That process starts well before you enter the studio, in **preproduction**, when you evaluate the music, decide how you are going to record it, and work out the budgeting. In the second stage of the process, **production**, the music is recorded. In the final stage, **postproduction**, the music is processed, edited, and mixed into its final form. Each phase in the production process is important to the successful outcome of a music recording. Perhaps the most critical stage, however, is preproduction because as it goes, so usually goes the rest of the production.

Murphy's Law states that if something can go wrong, it will. The proposition may appear facetious, but during production Murphy seems to be everywhere. If a session requires nothing more than recording a vocal direct-to-master, do not underestimate Murphy's uncanny knack to somehow loosen a connection in the microphone cable, miswire the pins in the XLR connector, vary the voltage to the tape recorder, tie up the singer in traffic, or see to it that the singer has a raw throat. Although these predicaments might overstate the case, the basic caution stands: Each detail in a production must be worked out in advance to thwart Murphy. Murphy is costly and frustrating. His only benefit is in the comic relief sometimes provided by the unexpected. But the unexpected is to be avoided if possible, and that is why preproduction is so important.

Because recording music can run from the simple to the complex and involve from a few persons to several, this discussion of preproduction applies to creative planning in general and not to the relating of a particular task to a designated title or function (see Chapter 1).

Preparation

Being prepared goes a long way toward making the most of studio time and ensuring a successful recording session. Although each session is different, the following list of preparatory procedures serves most situations.

Purpose of the Session

Why are you doing the recording in the first place? Is it for a demonstration (demo) tape, an album, a "sketch pad" for ideas, or a segment of a larger project being worked out piece by piece? Or will the recording be mixed with other elements, such as dialogue and sound effects tracks in a film sound track? In all instances you want a recording to sound as good as possible; but the purpose and pressure in producing, for example, a demo compared to an album are different.

If a demo is to show off musicianship, good production and sound quality are important but not vital; performance is. If the demo's purpose is to market a new song, then production should be spare to better spotlight the song; overproduction may convey the impression that the songwriter is trying to hide deficiencies in the music. If the recording is for commercial release, music, musicianship, production, and sound quality all must be top-notch.

Knowing the Studio

Make sure the musicians know what your facility can do. Recording studios vary greatly in their acoustics and equipment.

The acoustics of a room have to be considered in relation to the music being recorded. For example, rock usually requires a relatively "dead" studio, otherwise the loud SPLs would swim in reverberation. But such a studio would render the sound of a jazz or classical music ensemble lifeless (see Chapter 3). Certainly, reverberation devices can be used to add acoustics during the mixdown, but most jazz and classical music producers prefer natural to artificial acoustics.

The equipment has to be capable of meeting the demands of the session. If a session requires certain microphones, a given number of mic inputs, console automation, several compressors and noise gates, and a digital 24-track tape recorder, the studio must have the hardware in place. If the musicians are savvy about signal flow diagrams, a convenient way to display a studio's capability and flexibility is to show them one, preferably simplified (see 10-1). That said, keep in mind that the more you tell a client about how you "make the magic," the more it gives the client to think about.

Knowing the Musicians

If it is at all possible, get to know the musicians. Become familiar with their music and playing styles. Establish a rapport with them and convey your interest in ensuring that their recording will be well-produced and receive caring attention. Make sure they understand that your job is to transfer their "vision" to tape, not transform it.

Note any personal or musical idiosyncrasies. A musician may like to hum along while playing or tap a foot to the beat. These sounds cannot be made if they are picked up by the microphone. An instrument may squeak, buzz, ring, or click. Such

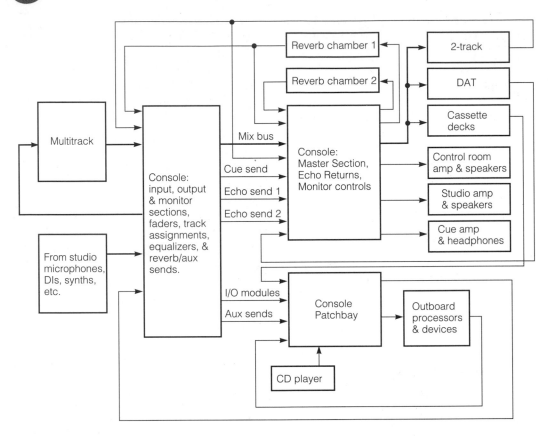

10-1 Signal flow in a typical control room

sounds may be masked in a concert, but in a studio they will be audible. Some musicians warm up fast and give a better performance early in a session; others take a while to get hot. There are musicians who perform better without thinking about interpretation, and there are those who must consider every phrase. One performer may need constant encouragement; another may require more frequent breaks because of fatigue.

A recording session usually involves a not insignificant investment in time and money. Although business is business, the chance for a successful outcome is improved if you like the artists you are working with and the music impassions you.

Handling the Client

Another advantage in getting to know clients beforehand is that you have a better insight into how to deal with them during the session. For example, if they are skittish about the vagaries of technology, do not call in the maintenance team at the first sign of technical trouble—try to work around it until a break in the session. Even then, take a good look at the problem before summoning help to avoid being accused of wasting time. If the client wants to attempt several experiments, try to anticipate what will and will not work, with the understanding that over a long period of time no one will be able to tell the difference. Then there is the problem of the degree to which a client wants to get involved in the engineering. On one hand, it is disconcerting, if not confusing, with too many "cooks in the kitchen"; the session can get out of control, especially when adjustments are being made without coordination or the awareness of the engineer, or both. On the other hand, some clients are worth indulging because their insight can make hands-on involvement helpful to the creative process. When clients know what they want, give it to them. Keep in mind that you are making a musician's record, not an engineer's.

Before Setting Up

Make up a project sheet detailing personnel and equipment assignments. Diagram instrument and microphone placement (see 10-2). Make sure the studio and control room are clean before musicians and production personnel enter. All console controls should be in neutral or off. Tape recorders should be aligned, and the heads demagnetized and cleaned. Put all equipment and furniture not being used in the session out of the studio. Not only is unnecessary equipment and furniture stacked to the side unsightly, it also affects acoustics.

If the session calls for the studio drum set or piano to be used, make sure they are tuned and placed. If you know what instruments are being assigned to which channels (and submixers if you are doing submixes), label the console with this information. Determine channel assignments, submixes,

foldback feeds, and so on before the session begins. It not only saves time during production but helps to organize board operations more quickly.

Setting Up

Have all equipment and furniture in place before the musicians arrive. The advice is obvious, but as it sometimes is with the obvious, it's overlooked. The following is a checklist of the more important items to attend to.

- Microphones should be mounted on the appropriate stands, roughly in position—precise placement may have to wait until the musicians are in place—and plugged into their designated console inputs.

- Check the roll off, pad, and directional setting (of multipattern mics) to make sure they are in the proper position.

- Test the microphones, one at time, to make sure they are working, sounding as they should, and feeding the correct channels on the console and tracks on the tape recorder. It is better to do this as you plug in each one (with the fader down, remember). That way, if there is a problem, it is easier to track.

- As much as you are able to, set up the console. Label assigned faders, monitor controls, and meters. A color, or some other graphic, scheme may help to highlight routing assignments.

- If signal processing is being used, particularly reverb, check each channel, dry and wet, for noise. That way, if noise is present, it is easier to determine if the problem is in the signal processor.

- Do all necessary patching.

- Calibrate the equipment. Make sure the VU meters on the console and on the tape

air PROJECT SHEET

PRODUCER	CLIENT				DATE		JOB Nº
ENGINEER					TIME BOOKED	FROM	TO
ASSISTANTS	FRESH START	REC	O/D	MIX	LOCATION		ARTIST

SESSION LINE UP	MACHINE DETAILS

		HEADPHONES	CLICKS

ANALOGUE

	MULTITRACKS	2 TRACKS
FORMAT		
SPEED		
CURVE		
DOLBY		
LEVEL		
TAPE TYPE		
TONE DETAILS		

EQUIPMENT HIRINGS

EQUIPMENT	HIRE COMPANY	RATE	BILLING WHO ?	AIR P/O Nº

DIGITAL

	MULTITRACKS	2 TRACKS
FORMAT		
SAMPLE RATE		
T.C. REF.		

PICTURE REQUIREMENTS

VIDEO / FILM FORMAT

LOCK TO PICTURE

OUTBOARD & MICROPHONE REQUIREMENTS	ADDITIONAL INFORMATION

10-2 Example of project sheet

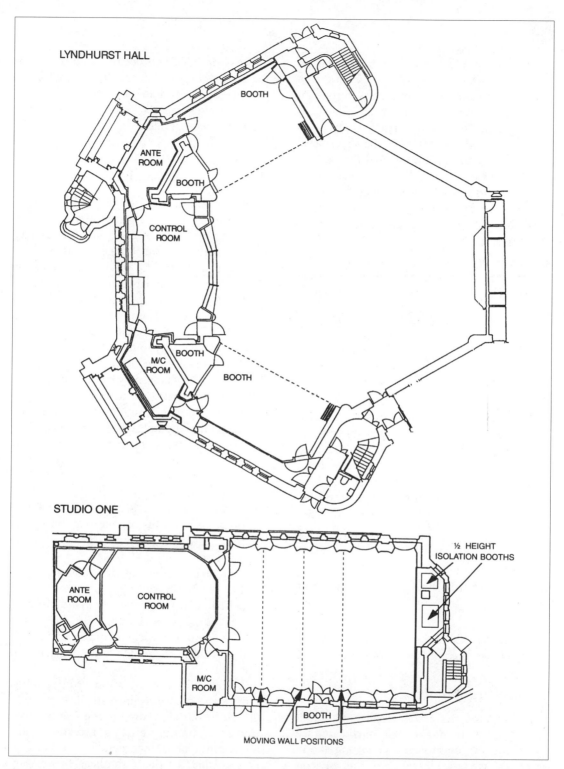

LYNDHURST HALL

BOOTH

ANTE ROOM

BOOTH

CONTROL ROOM

M/C ROOM

BOOTH

BOOTH

STUDIO ONE

½ HEIGHT
ISOLATION BOOTHS

ANTE ROOM

CONTROL ROOM

M/C ROOM

BOOTH

MOVING WALL POSITIONS

10-2 (*continued*)

recorder are adjusted or calibrated to show the same readings. **Calibration** adjusts equipment parameters into conformance with a known standard. If equipment is not calibrated, you have no idea, in this case, whether the signal level passing through the console is the same as the one being recorded, and vice versa. This could result in a poor signal-to-noise ratio, a signal being over- or undermodulated, or a signal being out of stereo balance.

■ Mount the tape on the tape recorder. Spool and respool new tape to ensure proper layering and to check for defects.

■ If you are using time code, record it on the entire tape.

■ Test the tape recorder in Record and Playback, with noise reduction if you are employing it.

■ Check the foldback system and each studio and control room headset. Headsets should be as airtight as possible against the head to prevent bleedthrough to open microphones. If loudspeakers are being used for foldback instead of headsets, make sure the microphone has been positioned at the null point (see Chapter 13).

■ Listen to the control room and studio monitors for noise, distortion, sound quality, and stereo balance.

■ Set up chairs, music stands, the conductor's podium, whatever the session requires.

■ Have tool kit and test equipment at the ready just in case. Remember Murphy.

Session Ergonomics

One way to offset the sterility of studio recording is to make the musicians feel cared for and comfortable. Lighting should be conducive to a pleasant working environment, warm yet functional. Seating should be easy on back and bottom, and placement of chairs should not cramp the musicians. Music stands should be within easy reach and the music easy to see. Use headphones that are comfortable to wear.

Recording Plan and Schedule

Time is money. Plan the quickest and most economical way to produce the session. Remember: In production make it as easy on yourself (and your budget) as possible.

Draft a recording plan and schedule. Decide the order of songs to be taped. Perhaps start with an easy piece to get the musicians warmed up and into the session, then do the most difficult song second to get it out of the way while the talent is still fresh. Instead of recording one song at a time, the musicians may prefer to do each song in sections, recording the rhythm tracks of all the songs first and then the accompaniments followed by the vocals.

Another advantage to drafting a recording plan is that everyone concerned has an idea of when particular voicings will be recorded and about how long the process will take. If the vocalist, for example, records last and is not needed until, say, 3 hours into the session, waiting could be boring and draining. If a particular musician is needed on a certain day, confirm availability before scheduling.

Schedule break times to avoid listening fatigue and "restore ears." If the session involves union musicians, union regulations will stipulate the length and frequency of breaks.

Decide whether any effects will be added during the recording instead of at the mixdown. If so, make sure the musicians understand that once an effect is recorded it usually cannot be unrecorded. If effects are to be recorded, set them up ahead of time and do whatever patching is necessary.

Consider whether the music lends itself to direct-to-two-track recording. The advantages of direct-to-two-track recording, compared to multitrack recording, are that it is simpler; is less expensive, because there is little or no mixdown time required; captures the vitality of a live performance; and is less time-consuming. A multitrack recording takes four to six times longer to produce than a direct-to-two-track recording.

Make sure the musicians are thoroughly rehearsed before they get to the studio. Studio time is too expensive to waste working out performance problems. It also puts an additional drain on an already demanding situation. Top-of-the-line musicians are less of a problem in this regard than are musicians in the formative stage or a group that has not worked together long.

Studio Awareness

If the musicians are new to studio work, make them aware of session procedures. Studio recording is tedious, demanding, exacting, tiring work. Moreover, the ways in which the ensemble is recorded—overdubbing, positioning of musicians, use of isolation booths—differ greatly from playing before an audience. Musicians caught unaware could perform poorly, wasting time and money.

Sheet Music or Chord Charts

Study the sheet music or chord charts. If they do not exist or if you do not read music, thoroughly familiarize yourself with the music by listening to rehearsals before the recording session and make reference charts (see 10-3).

Track Assignments

Make the track assignments. In multitrack sessions know the voicing or group of voic-

ings to be recorded on each track. It usually does not make much difference which elements are assigned to which track, but it is a good idea to record information that is particularly valuable or difficult to rerecord on the inside tracks of the tape, away from the outer edges. Sometimes, the edges can fray from scraping against improperly aligned tape guides or the sides of defective tape reels. On an 8-track tape, this would damage tracks 1 and 8; on a 16-track tape, tracks 1 and 16 could be lost; and so on. Deciding which tracks are more important depends on the recording, but it is usually obvious. Drums are trickier to record than, say, trumpets; it would be more difficult to rerecord a soloist who has flown in for a session than to rerecord performers who live in the vicinity; a vocalist usually requires more time and attention than most instruments.

It is also helpful to put the same instruments or groups of instruments on adjacent tracks, such as the various components of a drum set, strings, woodwinds, and rhythm instruments. This makes it easier to see and coordinate their relative levels and processing (see 10-4).

Physical Demand

Anticipate the physical demand. Be well rested and well fed before the session. Avoid exposure to loud sounds and prolonged listening to music. And no alcohol or drugs! They affect perception and make it impossible to hear and evaluate sound with any consistency.

Cost and Budget

Although business matters are beyond the purview of this book, whatever the creative and aesthetic rewards, music recording is a business. Session cost, budget, and payment should be agreed to before a session begins.

SONG - " . . . "

FORM	Reel Time
Tape starts	00 00
Intro	00 10
Verse 1	00 28
Verse 2	00 56
Chorus 1	01 24
Bridge	01 55
Verse 3	02 20
Chorus 2	02 48
Outro	03 19
End	03 25

a

SONG - " . . . "

Tape starts	Intro	Verse 1	Verse 2	Chorus
00 00	A1	B1	B2	C1
	00 10	00 28	00 56	01 24
Bridge	Verse 3	Chorus 2	Outro	End
D1	B3	C2	E1	
01 55	02 20	02 48	03 19	03 25

b

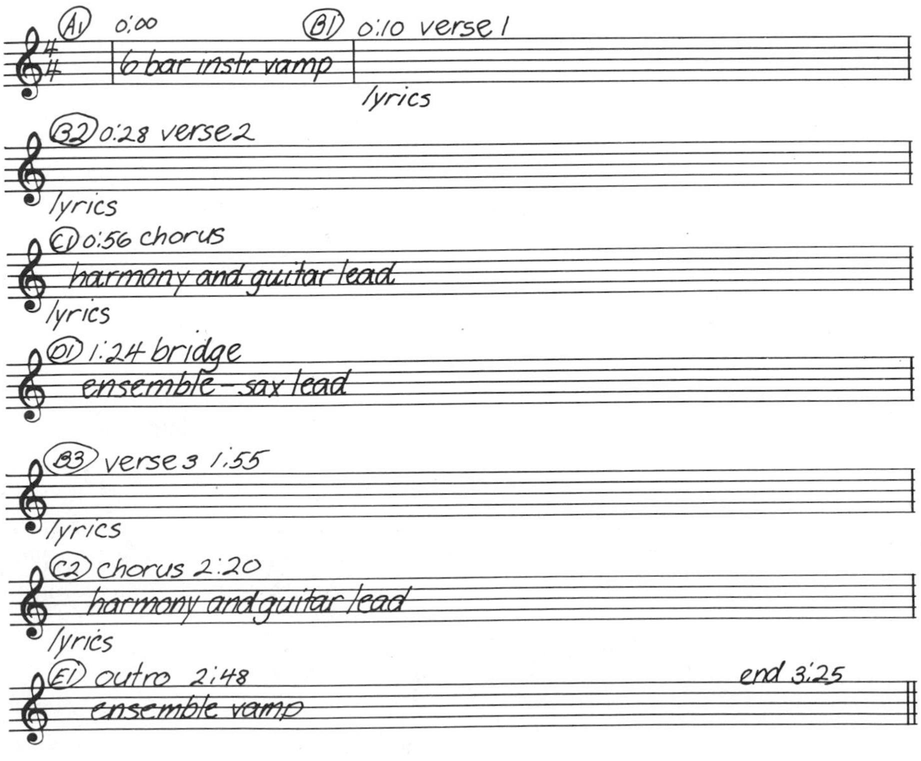

c

10-3 Three ways to chart or blueprint a pop song for recordists who do not read music

BASS | BASS DRUM | SNARE/ HI HAT | TOMS | LEFT OVER-HEAD DRUMS | RIGHT OVER-HEAD DRUMS | LEAD GUITAR | RHYTHM GUITAR | BACKGROUND VOCAL | LEAD VOCAL

10-4 Making track assignments. Putting similar instruments or groups of instruments on adjacent channels makes it easier to coordinate console operations.

All things considered (personnel, tape and other materials, maintenance, scope of the project, and so on), a session for a multi-track album, demo grade, typically runs roughly an hour for every minute of final product. Album-grade work (assuming good, well-rehearsed musicians that are doing material they are familiar with) runs anywhere from 5 to 10 hours for every minute of final product.

PRODUCTION

DISTANT MIKING: ENSEMBLES

In studio recording there are two basic microphone techniques: (1) **distant miking**—using two or a few microphones (or capsules) to record an entire ensemble—and (2) **close miking**—placing a microphone relatively close to each sound source or group of sound sources in an ensemble. (Close miking is covered in Chapter 12.) The technique you choose depends on several factors: the spatial environment you wish to create, the studio acoustics, the complexity of the music and arrangement, the type of music, whether the instruments are all acoustic or a combination of acoustic and electric, and whether it is necessary that all musicians record at the same time. Generally, distant miking is used more in ensemble recording and close miking is used more in pop music recording. Each approach has its advantages and disadvantages (see Tables 11-1 and 11-2).

Distant Miking

Usually, distant miking is employed when all sounds or voicings in an ensemble have

to be, or can be, recorded at the same time and it is important to do so in natural acoustics to preserve the ensemble sound. Orchestral and choral music and certain types of jazz are examples of music that use distant miking.

Distant miking of music attempts to reproduce the aural experience that audiences receive in live concerts, whether the recording is made in a studio or in a concert hall. Different techniques are used in distant miking, but they all have three main goals: (1) to ensure that each instrument is reproduced in the same relative location as it was during recording; (2) to reproduce reverberation as it would be heard from a particular seat, such as in the center of the hall, or toward the front or rear of the hall; and (3) to achieve the same musical blend that is heard by the conductor.

Basic Considerations in Distant Miking

Five considerations in distant miking are (1) critical distance, (2) air loss, (3) phase, (4) localization, and (5) stereo-to-mono compatibility.

Table 11-1 Advantages and disadvantages of distant miking

Advantages	Disadvantages
More closely reproduces the way we hear in an acoustic environment	Requires adjustment of the microphones and may even require repositioning the musicians, in studio recording, to accomplish the music blend
Requires fewer mics and so fewer faders to control; reduces electronic noise	Requires a retake by all musicians for a mistake by one, because all instuments are recorded at once
Can record entire ensemble at the same time	
May spark performance from interaction because everyone plays at once	Makes it difficult to isolate instruments for solos
	Requires a recording environment with excellent acoustics

Table 11-2 Advantages and disadvantages of close miking

Advantages	Disadvantages
Allows greater control of each element in the recording	Makes it difficult to create the nuances of each sound's interaction with the other sounds and with the acoustic environment
Increases separation of sound sources	Requires artificial production of acoustics and spatial placement
Usually means multitrack recording, so musicians can be recorded separately, a few musicians can do the work of several, and a mistake by one musician does not always require rerecording the entire ensemble	Increases phasing problems
	Means greater effort and more time for mixdown

Critical Distance

The **inverse square law** states that as the distance from a sound source doubles, loudness decreases in proportion to the square of that distance (see 11-1). But in an enclosed space such as a recording studio or concert hall, where acoustics are fairly evenly distributed, this is not quite the case. There is a point where sound no longer loses loudness. At this point, known as the **critical distance**, the amount of energy the microphone receives from the direct sound source and from the room reflections is equal. A mic placed in front of the critical distance is in the room's direct and reverberant sound field; a mic placed beyond the critical distance is in the room's reverberant sound field. Locating a room's critical distance, which must be done before mics are situated, is accomplished by using various technical methods, as well as your ear.

Air Loss

Air loss relates to the friction of air molecules as sound waves move across distance through an elastic medium. All frequencies begin converting to heat, but higher frequencies convert faster. The result is that the farther from a sound source you get, the duller the sound becomes. On the one hand, this works for you because music is not meant to be heard with your ear at, say, the bridge of a violin or under the lid of a piano. On the other hand, a microphone too far from an ensemble will reproduce a dull, lifeless sound.

Phase

Stereo microphones improperly placed relative to the angle or space between them, or to their distance from an ensemble in relation to a room's acoustics, can create sound

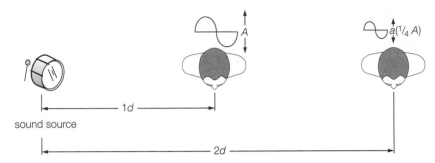

11-1 Illustration of the inverse square law. As the distance (*d*) from a sound source doubles, loudness (*A*) decreases in proportion to the square of that distance.

cancellations. These phasing problems result from the sound waves reaching the microphones at significantly different times.

Localization

Localization is the accurate reproduction of the instruments—front-to-back and left-to-right—in relation to their placement during recording. If the angle or distance between the stereo pair of microphones is too narrow, sound will be concentrated toward the center (between two loudspeakers) and the stereo image will lack breadth. If the angle or distance between the stereo pair is too wide, sound will be concentrated to the left and right with insufficient sound coming from the center. This condition is often referred to as "hole in the middle" (see 11-2).

Stereo-to-Mono Compatibility

When a mono version is being made from a stereo recording, the type of microphone array used directly affects compatibility of the two formats. Therefore, it makes sense to discuss stereo-to-mono compatibility in the context of the three types of miking used for

distant music recording—coincident, near-coincident, and spaced.

Coincident Miking

Coincident miking, also called **X-Y miking,** employs two matched, directional microphones mounted on a vertical axis—with one mic diaphragm directly over the other—and angled apart to aim approximately toward the left and right sides of the ensemble. The degree of angle depends on the width of the ensemble, the mics' distance from the group, and the pickup pattern of the microphones: The greater the angle between the microphones, the wider the stereo image. (Remember that too wide an angle creates a hole in the middle.) If the stereo pair is cardioid, the included angle may be from 90 to 135 degrees. If it is hypercardioid, the included angle must be narrower—because the on-axis pickup is narrower—to ensure a balanced center image. The frontal lobe of coincident hypercardioids can extend to 130 degrees (see 11-3 and 11-4). Due to the hypercardioid's tighter pattern, however, a stereo pair can be placed farther away from the sound source than can cardioids.

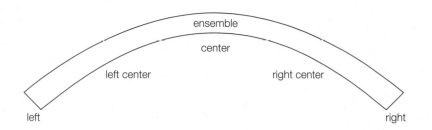

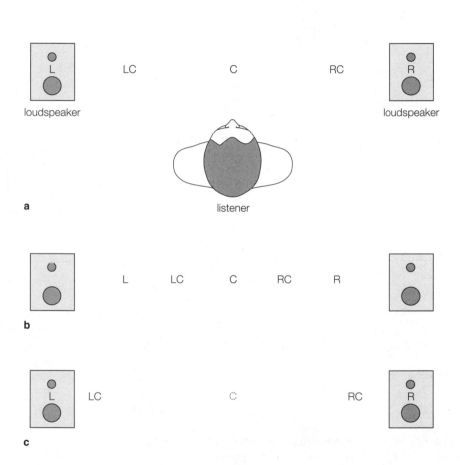

11-2 Location of elements in an ensemble during recording (*top*).
(*a*) If the stereo microphones are in optimal proximity to each other
and to the ensemble, stereo imaging during playback should be accurate.
(*b*) If the stereo microphones are at too narrow an angle or spaced too
close to each other, stereo imaging will be too narrow. (*c*) If the stereo
microphones are at too wide an angle or spaced too far apart, stereo
imaging will be too wide to the left and right, creating a "hole in the
middle."

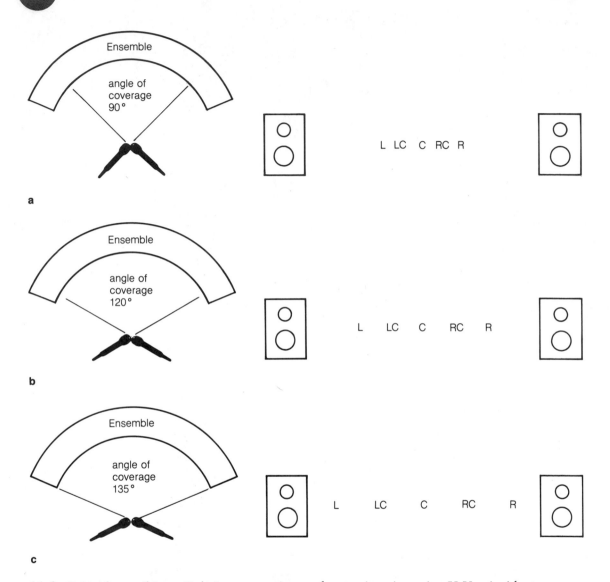

11-3 Coincident miking. Relative comparisons of stereo imaging using X-Y coincident angles of (*a*) 90 degrees, (*b*) 120 degrees, and (*c*) 135 degrees.

A stereo pair must be matched to ensure a uniform sound, and the mics should be capacitors. Miking at a distance from the sound source, particularly with classical music, requires high-output/high-sensitivity microphones, and capacitors are the only type of microphone that meets this requirement. Moreover, the microphone preamps should be high-gain, low-noise.

Another coincident technique utilizes a crossed pair of bidirectional microphones with a useful frontal lobe of 90 degrees– 45 degrees to the left of center and 45 degrees to the right of center (see 11-5). This approach, the earliest of the X-Y techniques, is also called the **Blumlein technique** (named

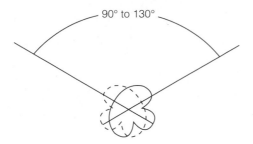

11-4 Coincident hypercardioid microphone array

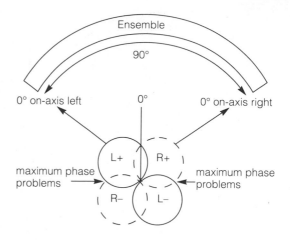

11-5 Blumlein technique. Two coincident bidirectional microphones are positioned at a 90-degree angle.

after British scientist Alan Blumlein, who developed the technique in the early 1930s). Because the later development of the M-S (middle-side) approach (described in the following paragraphs) was a direct result of Blumlein's research, the bidirectional X-Y array is also known as the double M-S.

The stereo microphone provides the same coincident pickup as the stereo pair but with two directional microphone capsules housed in a single casing. The upper element can rotate up to 180 degrees relative to the lower element. Some stereo mics enable control of each capsule's polar pattern (see 4-26).

The M-S (middle-side) technique most commonly uses two coincident microphones in a single housing; separate microphones also may be used. One mic, which can be either cardioid or omnidirectional, depending on the mic-to-source distance and spread of the ensemble, is aimed toward the ensemble; the other mic, which is bidirectional, is aimed at the sides. Whether the mic capsules are in one housing or separate, M-S miking requires matrixing to sum and

difference the mics' outputs to provide the discrete left and right channels (see 4-29). Unlike most X-Y miking, M-S lets you change the stereo spread during or after recording by adjusting the middle-to-side ratio.

Coincident microphone arrays produce level (intensity) differences between channels and minimize differences in arrival time. This has two sonic advantages: (1) Localization of instruments between the loudspeakers is sharp, and imaging corresponds to their placement during recording, giving you a conductor's balance; and (2) the stereo signals are mono-compatible because the two microphones occupy almost the same space, meaning their signals are in phase at all frequencies. With M-S miking all it takes to make it mono-compatible is to cancel the sides, which means the middle information is really mono-identical.

Although coincident miking provides sharp imaging and mono compatibility, it tends to lack spaciousness and sounds flat and dry. The Blumlein pair rectifies this problem somewhat, but the center imaging

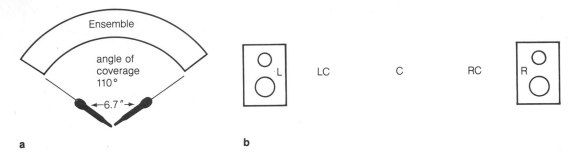

11-6 (*a*) ORTF array and (*b*) its effect on stereo imaging

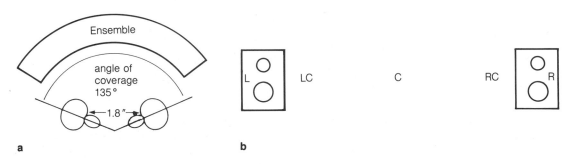

11-7 (*a*) Stereo 180 array and (*b*) its effect on stereo imaging

is not as strong as it is with M-S and more directional X-Y miking. Near-coincident techniques address these shortcomings.

Near-Coincident Miking

Near-coincident miking angles two directional microphones, spaced horizontally, a few inches apart. The few inches of difference between the near-coincident and coincident arrays add a sense of warmth, depth, and "air" to sound. The mics are close enough to retain intensity differences between channels at low frequencies, yet far enough apart to have sufficient time delay between channels for localization at high frequencies. The stereo spread can be increased or decreased with the angle or space between the mics. The time delay between channels creates a problem, however: The greater the delay, the less the chance of stereo-to-mono compatibility.

A number of different approaches to near-coincident miking have been used with varying results. Among the better known are the ORTF, NOS, DIN, stereo 180, and Faulkner arrays.

The **ORTF** (Office de Radiodiffusion-Television Française, the French broadcasting system) **microphone array** mounts two cardioid microphones on a single stand spaced just under 7 inches apart at a 110-degree angle, 55 degrees to the left and

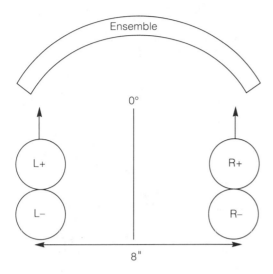

11-8 Faulkner bidirectional microphone array

right of center (see 11-6). The mics can also be crossed. The **NOS** (Nederlandsche Omroep Stichting, the Dutch broadcasting organization) **microphone array** places two cardioid microphones at a 90-degree angle about 12 inches apart. The **DIN** (Deutsche Industrie-Norm, the German standard) **microphone array** also places the stereo pair at a 90-degree angle but reduces the distance between the microphones to just under 8 inches. All three arrays produce similar results.

Another method, called the **stereo 180 microphone array**, uses two hypercardioid microphones, with excellent front-to-rear rejection, spaced just under 2 inches apart at a 135-degree angle (see 11-7). It creates the illusion that sound is coming from the sides of the room, or outside the loudspeakers, as well as from between them.

The **Faulkner microphone array** (named after British engineer Tony Faulkner) uses two bidirectional microphones spaced just

under 8 inches apart but facing directly toward the ensemble and placed farther from it than is usual with coincident pairs (see 11-8). This configuration combines the sonic reinforcement of the Blumlein pair with the depth and openness of the near-coincident array.

Spaced Miking

Spaced miking employs two (or three) matched microphones several feet apart, perpendicular to the sound source, and symmetrical to each other along a centerline. Although any pickup pattern can serve, the two most commonly used are omnidirectional, which is the more popular, and cardioid.

Spaced microphones reproduce a more spacious, lusher, bigger sound than any of the near-coincident arrays, but at a cost. Stereo imaging is more diffused and, therefore, less detailed. Instrument locations tend not to be clearly defined and can vary considerably as mic-to-source distance changes. Instruments may cluster left and right at the speakers, blurring the center image. Also, because so much of the sound reaching the mics derives its directional information from time differences (in addition to intensity differences), stereo-to-mono compatibility is unreliable.

Spaced omnidirectional microphones have less off-axis coloration and flatter overall response than cardioids, especially in the low frequencies. Capacitors are almost always used. Spacing is determined by the width of an ensemble and by mic-to-source distance. With omnis, spacing has to be wide enough to reproduce a stereo image. If it is too wide, however, separation is exaggerated and may produce a ping-pong effect between speakers; if spacing is too narrow,

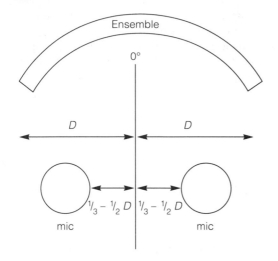

11-9 Spaced omnidirectional microphone array

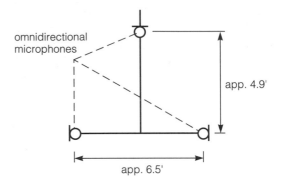

11-10 The Decca Tree

the stereo image will lack breadth. A good place to begin situating each omni is one-third to one-half the distance (D) from the centerline of the ensemble to its outer edge (see 11-9). If this creates a hole in the middle or if center imaging is diffused, a third mic placed between the outer pair should fill the hole and focus the center image. For a center mic to stabilize stereo imaging, however, its output must be split equally to the left and right channels.

Among the best-known miking techniques using three spaced microphones is the **Decca Tree.** Omnidirectional microphones are mounted at the ends of a T-shaped frame (see 11-10). The fixture is usually positioned behind, and a few feet above, the conductor's head. The Decca Tree technique is noted for its warm and enveloping sound.

Spaced cardioid microphones are arrayed similarly to spaced omnidirectionals, but their directionality produces a different sonic outcome. Spaced cardioids tend to emphasize the voicings that are most on-axis.

They also show the effects of coloration, particularly from reverb. Placement is critical to producing acceptable results with any spaced miking, but even more so with cardioids than with omnis. Spaced cardioids do provide a better chance for mono compatibility, however, because each microphone is picking up less common information, reducing the chance of phase cancellations.

Spaced boundary microphones used as the main stereo array have become a popular miking technique since the development of the Pressure Zone Microphone (PZM). Its pickup is similar to that of omnidirectionals, although around the boundary surface the polar pattern is hemispheric. If there is a choice, most recordists prefer using omnidirectional mics due to their superior sound quality.

Comparing Stereo Miking Techniques

A number of studies have been done comparing standard stereo microphone techniques. Condensed excerpts from two of those studies follow in alphabetical order.[*]

- Blumlein (coincident bidirectionals at 90 degrees): Good, sharp stereo imaging

- Blumlein (coincident bidirectionals at 90 degrees with shuffler circuit[**]): Very good stereo imaging and stereo spread

- Coincident cardioids angled 90 degrees apart: Very good stereo imaging, but a very narrow stereo spread

- Coincident cardioids angled 120 degrees apart: Fair stereo imaging with a narrow stereo spread

- Coincident hypercardioids angled 120 degrees apart: Imaging fair because frequencies around 3 kHz have a wider spread than low frequencies

- Coincident hypercardioids angled 120 degrees apart (with shuffler circuit): Excellent stereo imaging and stereo spread

- Middle-side microphone: Lacks spaciousness, intimacy, and warmth

- ORTF (cardioids angled 110 degrees and 7 inches apart): Good stereo imaging but with low frequencies narrowly spread and high frequencies wider spread

- ORTF (hypercardioids angled 110 degrees and 7 inches apart): The same as the ORTF cardioids angled 110 degrees and 7 inches apart but with wider separation

- Two omnis spaced 9½ feet apart: Poor stereo imaging and exaggerated stereo separation

- Three cardioids spaced 5 feet apart: Poor stereo imaging and exaggerated stereo separation at high frequencies

Accent (or Fill) Miking

In some studio orchestral situations **accent, or fill, miking** may be used to supplement overall sound pickup. Weaker-sounding sections of an orchestra, or a soloist, may not be heard as well or at the same time as louder sound sources and sound sources closer to the main microphone array.

The outputs of accent microphones are handled separately from the stereo pair and blended or panned into the stereo field at the position of the sound source it is picking up. There are two dangers in accent miking: (1) If the accent sound is too loud it will stick out; and (2) the time delay between the closer mic-to-source distance of the accent mic(s) and the more distant mic-to-source distance of the main array has to be compensated for, or the sound source(s) picked up by the accent mic(s) will be unblended and perceived as being in front of the ensemble. One way to compensate for this time difference is to delay the signal from the accent mic(s) electronically using a digital delay device. This facilitates the blending of the sound from the accent mic(s) with the overall ensemble. Time delay is a consideration in large studios and concert halls.

Ambience Microphones

Although stereo miking implies two (or three) microphones, accent mics notwith-

---

[*]From Benjamin Bernfeld and Bennett Smith, "Computer-Aided Model of Stereophonic Systems," Audio Engineering Society Preprint, February 1978; and Carl Ceoen, "Comparative Stereophonic Listening Tests," *Stereophonic Techniques Anthology*, Audio Engineering Society, 1986. Also listen to "Demonstration of Stereo Microphone Technique," by James Boyk et al., Performance Recordings: PR-6-CD.

[**]**Shuffling**, or *spatial equalization*, increases spaciousness so that coincident and near-coincident microphone arrays can sound as spacious as spaced microphone arrays. It also aligns the low frequencies and high frequencies of the sounds, thereby creating sharper stereo imaging. Shuffling is accomplished with a low-frequency shelving boost of the L–R (difference) signals and a low-frequency shelving cut of the L+R (sum) signals.

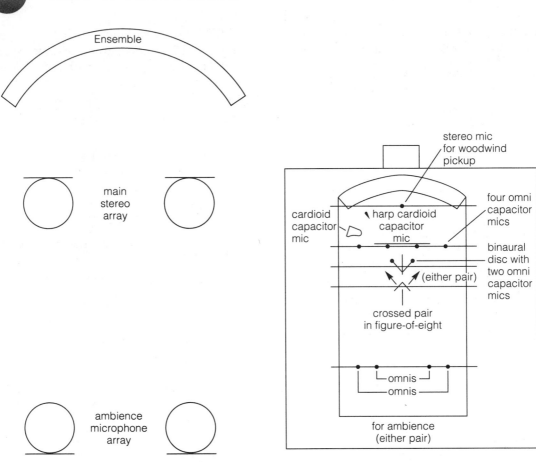

11-11 Two examples of miking ensembles incorporating ambience microphones

standing, more microphones are actually employed, usually for ambience. That is assuming the producer wants natural, instead of artificial, reverberation. **Ambience microphones** add depth and spaciousness to a recording, particularly if the main stereo array is located forward in the direct sound field or if it is coincident. For example, with M-S miking, although the side pickup is dedicated to the room reflections, overall sound is not as spacious as with near-coincident or spaced arrays. By facing an ambience microphone toward the rear of the room, additional reflections not heard by the M-S mic are picked up because the M-S mic is dead at the rear.

Ambience microphones are usually mounted as a stereo pair. If the room can accommodate them omnidirectional mics are preferred, due to their absence of off-axis coloration; otherwise, cardioids are used (see 11-11). If phasing problems are to be avoided, the placement of the ambience microphones is very important.

Three-Dimensional Sound Imaging

Ever since Alan Blumlein's far-reaching experiments with stereo microphone techniques, there have been many other attempts to add the three-dimensional sonic localization and spaciousness of the live listening experience to recorded music. These endeavors fall roughly into two groups: 3-D (three-dimensional) sound and surround sound. Generally, **3-D sound** reproduces three-dimensional aural space—depth, width, and height—through stereo headphones or the conventional, frontally mounted two-loudspeaker stereo array, or both. Some 3-D systems, however, enhance the two-dimensional stereo image—depth and width —by bringing it to the outermost edges of the soundfield on a plane with the listener. **Surround sound** uses at least four loudspeakers, two in front and two behind the listener, to reproduce three-dimensional sound. Some three-dimensional sound systems apply processing during recording; a few of those also apply it during mixdown. Others systems apply processing only during mixdown (see Chapter 15).

Binaural Sound

The best known of the 3-D recording systems is binaural sound. **Binaural sound** is a recording technique that has been around for years. It recreates sound source locations and room ambience that are quite remarkable. It is produced using a **binaural microphone head** (also known as *artificial head* or *dummy head* [*Kunstkopf*] *stereo*). Sound pickup is through omnidirectional capacitor microphones or mic capsules placed in both ear canals of the artifical head (see 11-12).

There are two essential differences between the way a stereo microphone, or stereo pair, "hears" sound and the way humans hear it. (1) With stereo there is no solid object, like the head, between the microphones. When sound comes from the left, particulary in midrange and high frequencies, it reaches the left ear sooner and with greater intensity than it does the right ear. The sound reaching the right ear is delayed, creating a sound shadow. The con-

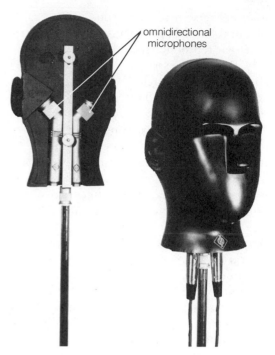

omnidirectional microphones

11-12 Binaural microphone head. Two omnidirectional capacitor microphones mounted in "ear" cavities reproduce binaural sound. To hear the binaural effect, it is necessary to listen with headphones.

verse is also true: Sound coming from the right is louder in the right ear and casts a sound shadow in the left ear. (Sound is also reflected from the shoulders and torso of the listener.) (2) The human ear itself also modifies sound. The folds in the outer ear (pinna) resonate and reflect sounds into the ear canal, causing phase cancellations at certain frequencies. Combined, these head-related transfer functions (HRTF), generally, are the theoretical bases for binaural head construction and recording.

Although binaural sound is an extraordinary listening experience it has not been marketable because it is only possible to get its full effect through stereo headphones;

loudspeakers will not do. That said, binaural recording systems are now available that reproduce something of the binaural listening experience through loudspeakers: the AachenHEAD™ and the computer-based AudioReality™ systems, to name two.

The AachenHEAD, constructed of fiberglass, is a detailed representation of a human head constructed through statistical averaging of variations in real human heads, and features felt hair and shoulders to simulate the characteristics of hair and clothing (see 11-13). The microphones are mounted only a little more than .15 of an inch inside the ear canal to prevent ear canal resonances from being recorded. One striking result of the AachenHEAD system is that the binaural effect is apparent on a conventional stereo loudspeaker array, although headphones are required to hear the full benefits of binaural spatial imaging.

Binaural Miking

To record music binaurally, positioning of the artificial head is critical. It must be situated for optimal overall sound pickup in relation to the ensemble and studio acoustics. Voicings in an ensemble must be clearly localized. Two problems with binaural sound are that directionality is sometimes difficult to perceive and the music is sometimes awash in ambience. Clearly your ear is important in determining where the binaural head is placed, but so are real-time analysis and the measurement systems that some binaural head manufacturers supply.

Transaural Stereo

What makes it difficult to reproduce binaural sound over loudspeakers is the acoustic crosstalk around the head. The left ear hears the signal not only from the left speaker but from the right speaker as well, and with the right ear, vice versa. Using headphones, the left ear hears only the left signal, and the right ear hears only the right signal. With **transaural stereo** a converter cancels the acoustic crosstalk signals, making it possible to reproduce a binaural recording over loudspeakers and get a quasi-binaural sound.

Surround-Sound Recording

Among the surround-sound methods that have been used in recording music are the ambisonic, ITE™/PAR™ (In The Ear/Pinna Acoustic Response), and Dimensional Sound Recording systems (DSM™).

Ambisonic Sound

Ambisonic sound is a method of recording an entire soundfield as defined by absolute sound pressure and three pressure gradients of the left/right, front/rear, and up/down directions. The technique is related to the development of a unique microphone called the soundfield microphone (see Chapter 4). The soundfield microphone contains four mic capsules mounted as a tetrahedron. The outputs of these elements are fed into a matrix network that can be controlled to reproduce a number of different pickups.

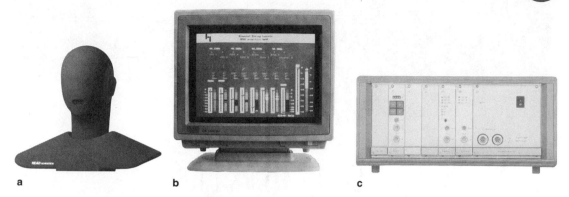

a   b   c

11-13 AachenHEAD binaural recording system, including the (*a*) Dummy Head, (*b*) Binaural Mixing Console, and (*c*) HEADphone Playback

The four outputs, known as the *A-format*, feed the high left-front-right-rear and the low right-front-left-rear information into the matrix network. After the signals are mixed, they are converted into the so-called B-format, from which the signals can be manipulated to produce a variety of pick-ups (see 4-30 to 4-32). The operation is complex, but the resulting three-dimensional sound is worth the trouble, especially because ambisonic sound does not require headphones for listening. It does, however, require four loudspeakers, two in front of the listener and two to the rear.

ITE™/PAR™ (In The Ear/Pinna Acoustic Response)

The ITE™/PAR™ approach to surround-sound recording inserts two probe mics with low noise and wide frequency response and dynamic range in the pressure zone of the eardrum of a human listener during recording. During playback, two loudspeakers are placed in front of the listener, for normal stereo, and two loudspeakers are placed on either side aimed directly at the listener's ears. The function of the side loudspeakers is to mask opposite-ear crosstalk. The result is similar to hearing through headphones and allows the listener to enjoy a surround-sound effect from a binaural recording through conventional loudspeakers.

Dimensional Stereo Recording (DSM™)

DSM™ takes identical, high-quality electret capacitor microphones and mounts them, using rubber loops, to each temple piece of a pair of eyeglasses close to the outer ear canal pointing face-front. DSM recording "hears" live sound with a 360-degree ambient view that is psychoacoustically conditioned by the shape of the listener's head and upper torso and that can be reproduced through surround-sound loudspeakers or stereo headphones.

Close Miking:

Instrument and Voice

Whatever the advantages of distant miking, not much of today's popular music is recorded that way. Many recordists are quite willing to sacrifice the more realistic sense of sonic space for greater control in recording the nuances of each musical element. This means close-miking practically each instrument or group of instruments in an ensemble. Reverberation, spatial positioning, and blend, which occur naturally with distant miking, are lost in close microphone recording and are added artificially in the postproduction mixdown. Positioning, blending, and some processing may be applied to a few instruments during recording.

Close miking is used in most popular music recording for a number of reasons: The difference in loudness between electric and acoustic instruments can be very difficult to balance with distant miking; the sound from each instrument, and sonic leakage from other instruments, is better controlled; a pop music ensemble usually does not have to be recorded all at once; much of pop music is played loudly, with acoustics added in the mixdown, so close miking prevents the music from being awash in reverberation during recording.

Before getting into specific applications of close miking, it may be helpful to recall four important principles:

1. The closer a microphone is to a sound source, the more detailed, drier, and, if proximity effect is a factor, bassier the sound; the farther a microphone is from a sound source, the more diffused, open, and reverberant the sound.

2. The higher the frequency, the more directional the sound wave; the lower the frequency, the more omnidirectional the sound wave.

3. Although close miking may employ a number of mics, more may not always be better. Each additional microphone adds a little more noise to the system, can introduce phase cancellation, and means dealing with another input at the console.

4. Generally, large-diaphragm microphones are more suitable in reproducing low-frequency instruments, and small-diaphragm mics are more suitable in reproducing high-frequency instruments.

Phase: Acoustical and Electrical

Important to any discussion of microphone technique is the subject of phase, acoustical and electrical. Acoustical phase relates to the time relationship between two or more sound waves at a given point in their cycles (see Chapter 2). Electrical phase relates to the relative polarity of two signals in the same circuit.

Acoustical Phase

If sound sources are not properly placed in relation to microphones, sound waves can reach the mics at different times and be out of phase. For example, sound waves from a performer who is slightly off center between two spaced microphones will reach one mic a short time before or after they reach the other mic, causing some cancellation of sound. Perceiving sounds that are considerably out of phase is relatively easy: When you should hear sound, you hear little or none. Perceiving sounds that are only a little out of phase, however, is not so easy.

By changing relative time relationships between given points in the cycles of two waves, a **phase shift** occurs. Phase shift is referred to as *delay* when it is equal in time at all frequencies. Delay produces a variety of "out-of-phase" effects that are useful to the sound designer (see Chapters 8 and 15). To detect unwanted phase shift, however, listen for unequal levels in frequency response, particularly in the bass and mid-range; for slightly unstable, wishy-washy sound; or for a sound source that is slightly out of position in relation to where it should be in the aural frame.

One way to avoid phase problems with microphones is to follow the **three-to-one rule**—place no two microphones closer together than three times the distance between one of them and its sound source. If one mic is 2 inches from a sound source, the nearest

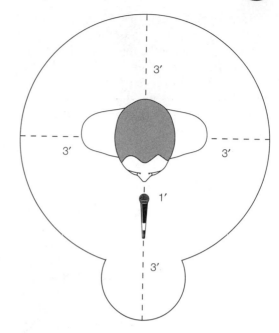

12-1 The three-to-one rule. Most phasing problems generated by improper microphone placement can be avoided by placing no two microphones closer together than three times the distance between one of them and its sound source.

other mic should be no closer to the first mic than 6 inches; if one mic is 3 feet from a sound source, the nearest other mic should be no closer than 9 feet to the first; and so on (see 12-1).

If a sound source emits loud levels, it might be necessary to increase the ratio between microphones to 4 to 1 or even 5 to 1. Quiet levels may facilitate microphone placement closer than that prescribed by a ratio of 3 to 1.

If two microphones are used for one performer, their capsules should be as close to each other as possible and at about a 90-degree angle. This placement creates a wider pickup pattern and permits lateral head movement without phase cancellation. It is useful for stereo recording (see 11-3a).

If two performers using separate directional microphones must work close together, phasing can be minimized by angling the mics away from each other. Make sure the angle is not so severe that the performers are off-axis. Most phasing problems generated by improper microphone placement can be avoided by following the three-to-one rule.

Electrical Phase

The difference between acoustical phase and electrical phase is that signals acoustically in phase are dependent on the behavior of sound waves, whereas signals electrically in phase are dependent on electrical polarity.

A cause of microphones being electrically out of phase is incorrect wiring of the microphone plugs. Male and female XLR connectors used for most microphones have three pins: (1) a ground, (2) a positive pin for high output, and (3) a negative pin for low output. (XLR 5-pin connectors are used for stereo microphones.) Mic cables house three coded wires. All mics in the same facility must have the same number pin connected to the same color wire. If they do not and are used at the same time, they will be electrically out of polarity. It is worth noting that because there is no electrical standard for determining whether pin 2 or 3 should be high, this varies among manufacturers.

To check whether mics are electrically out of polarity, first make sure that both mics are delegated to the same output channel. Adjust the level for a normal reading as someone speaks into a mic. Turn down the pot and repeat the procedure with another mic. Then open both mics to the normal settings. If the VU meter reading decreases when the levels of both mics are turned up, you have an electrical polarity problem.

The obvious way to correct this condition is to rewire the equipment, assuming the problem is not in the mic itself. If there is no time for that, most multichannel consoles have a polarity reversal control that shifts out-of-phase signals by 180 degrees into phase (see 5-5b).

Close Miking

Most of the discussion that follows assumes the use of directional microphones. Remember, the main reasons for close miking are better sonic control of each instrument and reduced leakage. If acoustics and recording logistics permit, omnidirectional (and bidirectional) mics should not be overlooked. The better omni capacitors have extraordinarily wide, flat response, particularly in the lower frequencies, and little or no off-axis coloration. Also, omnis are not as subject to proximity effect, sibilance, plosives, and breathing sounds as are directional mics. Because of the inverse square law, it is possible to close-mike with an omni and still reduce leakage if the instrument's sound pressure level is high enough (see Tables 12-1 and 12-2). The differences detailed in Tables 12-1 and 12-2 notwithstanding, a microphone's suitability must depend on the given situation.

Drums

Perhaps no other instrument provides as many possibilities for microphone combinations, and therefore as much of a challenge, as the drums. Several different components make up a drum set—at least a bass drum, floor (low-pitched) tom-tom, medium- and high-pitched tom-toms, snare drum,

Table 12-1 The omnidirectional microphone

Advantages	Disadvantages
Does not have to be held directly in front of the mouth to provide adequate pickup	Does not discriminate against unwanted sound
Does not reflect slight changes in the mic-to-source distance	Is difficult to use in noisy environments
Gives a sense of the environment	Presents greater danger of feedback in reverberant locations
Is less susceptible to wind, popping, and handling noises	
Is not subject to the proximity effect	
Is natural sounding in rooms with good acoustics	

Table 12-2 The unidirectional microphone

Advantages	Disadvantages
Discriminates against unwanted sound	Must be angled correctly to the mouth or the performer will be off-mic
Gives little or no sense of the environment (which could also be a disadvantage)	May be subject to the proximity effect
Significantly reduces the danger of feedback in reverberant locations	Is susceptible to wind and popping, unless there is a pop filter
	Is more susceptible to handling noises
	Requires care not to cover the ports, if hand-held
	Is less natural sounding in rooms with good acoustics

hi hat cymbal, and two overhead cymbals (see 12-2).

Characteristics

Drums consist of at least one membrane (drumhead) stretched over a cylinder and, usually, a second membrane that resonates with the struck head. Drums produce loud sound levels and steep transients. They are not considered pitched instruments, although drumheads can be tuned to a musical pitch, and the pitch relationships of the floor, medium, and high tom-toms must be maintained. Also, various sonic effects can be achieved by tuning the top and bottom heads to different tensions relative to each other.

It is important that tension be uniform across the head to produce a single pitch. When several pitches are produced simultaneously, the sonic result is dissonance.

Drums radiate sound perpendicular from the heads, particularly the top head. High-frequency transients are most pronounced on axis, perpendicular to the point where the stick hits the drumhead. This is the sound responsible for most of the drum's "kick." Harmonics and overtones are produced from the tension rings, the shell, and the bottom head.

floor tom-tom

high tom-tom

medium tom-tom

overhead cymbals

hi hat cymbal

snare drum

bass drum

12-2 Typical drum set with each drum and cymbal miked

Bass (Kick) Drum The bass drum is the lowest pitched of the drums. Its fundamental frequencies range from 30 to 147 Hz, with harmonics extending from 1 to 6 kHz. It is commonly called the kick drum because it is struck with a beater controlled by the drummer's foot. The drum stands on its side with the "top," or beater, head fac-ing the drummer. The "bottom" head is usually removed or has a hole cut into it because of the low-frequency resonances and very steep transients that the drum can generate. Most of the drum's low frequencies are emitted omnidirectionally, though vibrations from the shell and heads resonate throughout the instrument.

Tom-Toms Tom-toms come in a variety of sizes and pitches, and usually have two heads. They produce the steep transients and radiating characteristics common to most drums. Lower-pitched toms generate more omnidirectional waves; higher-pitched toms generate more directional waves. Because tom-toms are often used to accent a piece, they are tuned to have more sustain than the kick and snare drums.

Snare Drum The snare can be characterized as a tom-tom tuned to a higher pitch and with less sustain. Fundamental frequencies range from 100 to 200 Hz, with harmonics that extend from 1 to 15 kHz. The major difference between a tom-tom and a snare are the chainlike snares, stretched across the bottom head of the instrument, that give the drum its characteristic crispness and high-frequency cutting power.

Cymbals Cymbals are usually round, metal plates shaped like a flattened bell. They may be struck with a hard, wooden drum stick, soft mallet, or brushes. The type of striker used is largely responsible for the sound that is produced: The harder the striker, the greater the number of transient high frequencies produced. Unlike drums, cymbals have a long decay. A cymbal tends to radiate sound perpendicular to its surface, with a ringing resonance near its edge.

A cymbal's pitch is determined by, among other things, size and thickness. Cymbals are also designed to produce different textures: the ring of the ride cymbal or the splash of the crash cymbal to name two common examples.

Generally, their fundamentals range from 300 to 587 Hz. Their harmonics extend from 1 to 15 kHz.

Hi Hat Cymbal The hi hat cymbal is actually two cymbals with the open end of the

12-3 One directional microphone placed at the drummer's position so the mic hears what the drummer hears. The problem is that the drummer does not usually hear a balanced sound.

bells facing each other. A foot pedal, controlled by the drummer, raises and lowers the top cymbal to strike the bottom cymbal, or the top cymbal is struck with a drum stick, or both. Different timbres are generated by varying the pressure and distance between the two cymbals. The hi-hat is integral to the drum sound both for its high frequencies that "cut through" a recording and as a timekeeper. For these reasons the high-frequency transients perpendicular to the contact point and the shimmer from the edges are important.

Miking

Although the drum set consists of several different-sounding instruments, it must be miked so that they sound good individually and blend as a unit. However, drums are miked in many ways (see 12-3 through 12-9). The approach you take will depend on (1) how much sound control you want and (2) what type of music you are recording. Explaining how to deal with sound control is relatively easy: The more components

12-4 Two directional microphones placed over the left and right sides of the set for direct stereo pickup. The danger with this arrangement is that the bass drum may sound too distant.

12-5 Three directional microphones, one each over the left and right sides of the set and one at the bass drum for greater control of its sound. Make sure that the sounds of the snare and hi hat are balanced with the sounds of the rest of the drum set.

12-6 Four directional microphones. Three are placed as suggested in 12-5 and the fourth is placed either on the snare drum or between the snare and the hi hat cymbal. This gives greater control of the snare and the hi hat. The overhead mics, however, may pick up enough of the snare/hi hat sound so that the snare/hi hat mic may be needed only for fill.

12-7 Five directional microphones. Four are placed as suggested in 12-6, and the fifth is placed between the two tom-toms for added control of the tom-toms.

12-8 Two directional microphones for the overhead cymbals and a separate directional mic on each of the other components

12-9 Three ways to mike drums using boundary mics

you want to regulate, the more mics you use (although this can have its drawbacks—possible phasing, for one). Achieving a particular drum sound for a certain type of music involves many variables and is more difficult to explain.

Generally, in rock-and-roll and contemporary music, producers like a tight drum sound for added punch and attack. Because this usually requires complete control of the drum sound, they tend to use several microphones for the drums. In jazz, however, many styles are loose and open; hence, producers are more likely to use fewer drum mics to achieve an airier sound. But remember: A good drum sound begins with the musicianship of the drummer and the quality and tuning of the drum set. No miking technique will save the drum sound of an incompetent drummer or low-quality drum set.

Therefore, before drums are miked, they must be tuned. This is critical to achieving the desired drum sound. Some studios have their own in-house drum set always tuned and ready to go, not only to ensure the drum sound but also to avoid having this necessary and time-consuming procedure cut into recording time.

Tuning the drums is important to the sound of individual drums and also to the overall drum sound. As you might expect, there are many ways to tune a drum set: in fifths and octaves; in thirds; by tapping on the sides of the drum, finding its fundamental pitch and then tuning the head to it; by pitching the bass drum low enough to leave room in the upper bass and midrange for the tom-toms and snare drum. If the bass drum is pitched too high, it pushes too close to the toms, which in turn get pushed too close to the snare drum, making the drum sound smaller. Moreover, by not separating the individual drum

12-10 A directional microphone pointed at the drum head produces a fuller sound. Foam rubber padding is placed in the drum to reduce vibration.

sounds, little room is left for such instruments as the bass and guitar.

One problem with even the best of drum sets is ringing. Damping the drums helps to reduce ringing, and undesirable overtones as well. To damp a bass drum, place a pillow, blanket, foam rubber cushion, or the like, inside the drum (see 12-10). To damp a tom-tom and snare, tape a cotton or gauze pad near the edge of the drumhead so it is not in the way of the beating drumstick. Specially made drum silencers are also available (see 12-14). Because many drummers do not care to have things taped to their drums, another effective way to damp them is with O-rings placed on top of the drumhead. They come in a variety of circumferences for different sizes of drums.

Make sure the damping does not muffle the drum sound. It helps to leave one edge of the damping material untaped so it is free to vibrate. To reduce cymbal ringing, apply masking tape from the underside of the bell to the rim in radial strips or use specially made cymbal silencers.

12-11 A microphone pointed to the side of the drum produces more of the drum's overtones

Where the drum set is placed in a studio also affects its sound. Isolated in a drum booth (to reduce leakage into other instruments' microphones), the overall sound will take on the acoustic properties of the booth. For example, if it is live, the drums will sound live; if the booth is absorptive, the drums will sound tight or dull. On a hard floor the drums sound live and bright. On a carpet they sound tighter and drier. In a corner they sound boomier because the dominant lower frequencies are more concentrated. Often, drums are put on a riser that can resonate to reduce low-end leakage.

Bass (Kick) Drum The bass (kick) drum is the foundation of the drum set because it provides the bottom sound that, along with the bass guitar, supports the other musical elements. Because the bass drum also produces high levels of sound pressure and steep transients, large-diaphragm moving-coil microphones (e.g., AKG D-112, Electro-Voice RE-20) work best.

As for mic placement, the common technique is to use the hole often cut in the front drumhead or remove it entirely and place the mic inside. This usually gives the sound of the bass drum more punch. Pointing the mic perpendicular to the back drumhead produces a fuller sound (see 12-10), and pointing it toward the side of the drum picks up more of the drum's overtones (see 12-11). Placing the mic close to the beater picks up the hard beater sound and, if you are not careful, the action of the beater pedal as well.

When you use the multiple miking technique on the drums, the mics are usually directional to increase sound separation and reduce leakage from the rest of the drum set. An omnidirectional mic can be effective in a bass drum. Placing it in close proximity to a loud sound source usually prevents leakage from the other drums. To separate the bass drum even more, use a low-pass filter, shelving, or parametric equalizer to cut off or reduce frequencies above its upper range. Be careful, though—the perceived punch of the bass drum goes into the midrange frequencies. In fact, boosting from 1,600 to 5,000 Hz adds a brighter, sharper snap to the bass drum sound. The dull, thuddy, cardboard sound the bass drum tends to produce can be alleviated by attenuating between 300 and 600 Hz.

Although recording session procedures are discussed in Chapter 13 and the mixdown is treated in Chapter 15, some brief comments about equalizing during recording are included here. First, equalization should not be used as a substitute for good microphone technique or to correct poor mic technique. Second, if you must equalize, make sure you know exactly what you are doing. Even if mistakes in equalizing during recording can be undone in the mixdown, the additional noise and possible distortion created in passing a signal through an electronic device cannot.

12-13 Miking the high tom (left) and medium tom (right)

12-12 Miking a floor tom

Tom-Toms   As previously stated, tom-toms come in a variety of sizes and pitches. Typical drum sets have three toms: the low-pitched, fuller-sounding floor tom; the middle-pitched medium tom; and the higher-pitched, sharper-sounding high tom.

Although toms produce loud transients (all drums do), they are not as strong as those the bass drum produces; therefore, you can mike them with moving-coil, capacitor, or the more rugged ribbon mics. Placement, as always, depends on the sound you want. Generally, the mic is placed from 1 to 10 inches above the tom and is aimed at the center of the skin. It is usually mounted just over the edge of the rim to avoid interfering with the drummer's sticks (see 12-12 and 12-13).

The mic-to-source distance depends on the low-frequency content desired from the drum sound itself. If it has little low-frequency content, place a directional mic with proximity effect close to the drum skin to boost the lower frequencies. Placing a mic inside the drum gives the best isolation, but it also produces a closed, dull sound. Whatever technique you use, remember the sonic relationships of the toms must be maintained; using the same make and model microphone on each tom helps.

Snare Drum   Of all the components in a drum set, the snare usually presents the biggest problem in miking. Most producers prefer a crisp snare drum sound. Miking the snare drum too close tends to produce a lifeless sound, whereas miking it too far away tends to pick up annoying overtones, ringing, and leakage from the other drums.

Another problem is that the snare drum sometimes sounds dull and thuddy. In this instance the problem is most likely the drum itself. Two ways to add crispness to the sound are to (1) use a mic with a high-frequency boost or (2) equalize it at the

12-14 Miking a snare drum. The pad on the skin of the drum reduces vibrations.

12-15 Miking a snare drum over and under

console. Boosting at around 4,000–5,000 Hz adds crispness and attack. The better alternatives are to retune the drum set and, if that does not work, to replace the drum head(s).

Moving-coil or capacitor microphones work well on the snare drum; the moving-coil mic tends to give it a harder edge, and the capacitor mic tends to make it sound richer or crisper. To find the optimal mic position, begin at a point 6 to 10 inches from the drum head and aim the mic so that its pickup pattern is split between the head and the side of the drum (see 12-14). This picks up the sounds of the snares and the stick hitting the head. To get the snares' buzz and the slight delay of the snares' snap, use two mics: one over and one under the drum (see 12-15).

Hi Hat Cymbal The hi hat cymbal produces two sounds: a clap and a shimmer. Depending on how important these accents are to the music, the hi hat can either share the snare drum's mic or have a microphone of its own. If it shares, place the mic between the hi hat and the snare and adjust the sound balance through placement of the mic (see 12-16). The hi hat, like the snare, can take either a moving-coil or a capacitor microphone.

If the hi hat has a separate mic, the two most common positions for it are 4 to 6 inches above the center stem with the mic pointing straight down (see 12-17) and off the edge (see 12-18). Sound is brightest

12-16 Miking the hi hat cymbal and the snare drum

12-17 Miking over the hi hat cymbal

12-18 Miking at the edge of the hi hat cymbal

12-19 A microphone aimed at the point where the cymbals clap may pick up the rush of air as they come together

over the edge of the cymbal. Miking too close off the center produces ringing, and miking off the edge may pick up the rush of air produced each time the two cymbals clap together (see 12-19). Equalize by rolling off the bass to reduce low-frequency leakage, but only if the hi hat is miked separately. If the mic is shared with the snare drum, rolling off the bass adversely affects the low-end sound of the snare.

Overhead Cymbals   Two types of overhead cymbals are the ride, which produces ring and shimmer, and the crash, which has a splashy sound. In miking either cymbal, the definition of the characteristic sounds must be preserved. To this end, capacitors usually work best; and for stereo pickup, the coincident, near-coincident (see 12-2), or spaced pair can be used (see 12-20). When using the spaced pair, remember to observe the

12-20 A spaced pair of directional microphones to pick up the sound of the overhead cymbals and add spaciousness to the overall sound of the drum set

three-to-one rule to avoid phasing problems. For mono compatibility, however, coincident arrays are safest.

The overhead microphones usually blend the sounds of the entire drum set. Therefore, they must be at least a few feet above the cymbals. If they are too close to the cymbals, the drum blend will be poor, and the mics will pick up very annoying overtones that sound like ringing or gonging, depending on the narrowness of the mic's pickup pattern. If blending the drum sound is being left until the mixdown, and it is important to isolate the cymbals, roll off the low frequencies reaching the cymbal microphones from the other drums.

Acoustic String Instruments

Acoustic string instruments derive their sound from stretched strings, held taught in a frame, that are set into vibratory motion by being bowed, plucked, or struck. As strings do not produce much loudness, the frame, which also vibrates with the strings, serves to amplify and radiate sound. Three variables help determine the pitch of a vibrating string: length, tension, and mass, or thickness. Acoustic string instruments fall into three categories: plucked, bowed, and struck.

Characteristics of Plucked String Instruments

Plucked string instruments include the guitar, banjo, and mandolin. Because the six-string guitar is clearly the most popular of the plucked string instruments, it is considered here. The guitar's six strings are stretched across a hollow body with a flat top and sound hole that resonates the fundamental frequencies and harmonics of the vibrating strings. Fundamental frequencies range from 82 to 988 Hz, with harmonics extending from 1 to 15 kHz.

The guitar has a fingerboard with raised metal frets that divide the effective length of the strings into exact intervals as the strings are pressed down onto the frets. Where the guitar string is plucked affects sound quality because of the relationship between the distance from the point of contact to the ends of the strings. For example, a string plucked close to the bridge contains more high-frequency energy due to the relatively short distance between the point of contact and the bridge. A string plucked farther from the bridge produces a warmer sound due to the presence of more longer wavelengths and, therefore, lower frequencies.

Overall, most high frequencies are near the bridge; the joint between the neck and body produces more lower frequencies; and most lower frequencies are resonated by the back of the guitar and are generated from the sound hole.

What the strings are made of and what is used to pluck them also affect a guitar's sound quality. For example, metal strings tend to sound brighter than nylon, and a string plucked with a pick will be brighter than one plucked with the finger.

Miking Plucked String Instruments

The guitar and mandolin are similar in construction; therefore, miking techniques applicable to one usually produce about the same results with the other. Because the guitar is a dominant instrument today, we will focus on it. The banjo's action is somewhat different and is discussed separately.

Because most of a guitar's sound radiates from the front of the instrument, centering a microphone off the middle of the sound hole should, theoretically, provide balanced sound. But if a mic is too close to the hole, sound is bassy or boomy. If it is moved closer to the bridge, detail is lost. If it is moved closer to the neck, presence is reduced; if it is moved farther away, intimacy is destroyed. On the other hand, if a guitar lacks bottom, mike closer to the sound hole; if it lacks highs, mike closer to the bridge; to increase midrange, aim a mic at the neck.

Plucking creates quick attacks. Using a dynamic mic, which has slower transient response than a capacitor microphone, can slow the attacks and diminish detail, particularly in the guitar's bass frequencies. If a capacitor mic brings out too much crispness, however, a good moving-coil microphone can reduce it. No doubt dozens, perhaps hundreds, of methods have been used to mike the guitar. A few general techniques are discussed here, but keep in mind that many factors affect a guitar's sound, as we noted above.

One way to achieve a natural, balanced sound is to position the microphone about 1 to 3 feet from the sound hole. To set more high- or low-frequency accent, angle the mic either down toward the high strings or up toward the low strings. To brighten the natural sound, place the microphone above the bridge and even with the front of the guitar, because most high-frequency energy is radiated from a narrow lobe at right angles to the top plate (see 12-21 and 12-22). Miking off the twelfth fret, across the strings, produces a sound rich in harmonics.

Another way to achieve natural sound is to place a microphone about 8 inches to 1 foot above the guitar, 1 to 2 feet away, aimed between the hole and bridge. A good-quality capacitor mic reduces excess bottom and warms the sound.

A microphone perpendicular to the sound hole, about 8 inches away, reduces leakage from other instruments but adds bassiness. Rolling off the bass creates a more natural sound. If isolation is critical, move the

12-21 Miking an acoustic guitar. Aiming a microphone at the center of the guitar hole 2 to 3 feet away produces a sound with balanced highs, middles, and lows.

microphone closer to the sound hole. In this position bassiness increases and sound becomes boomy or muddy; bass roll-off definitely would be needed.

A microphone about 4 to 8 inches from the front of the bridge creates a warm, mellow sound, but the sound lacks detail; this lack is beneficial if pickup and string noises are problems.

For a classical guitar, which requires acoustic interaction, place the microphone more than 3 feet from the sound hole. Make sure mic-to-source distance is not too great or the subtleties of the instrument will be diminished.

The banjo differs from the guitar and mandolin because its strings are attached to a head across which sounds are distributed. The fundamental frequency is louder near the center of the head, and the harmonics are louder near the edges.

A microphone placed 1 to 2 feet from the center of the head produces a natural and balanced sound. Sound begins to get bassy closer than a foot from the head's center, and some roll-off is usually necessary; leak-

age is reduced, however. Miking a few inches from the edge of the head produces a brighter sound.

A natural part of most plucked string instruments' sound is the screechy, rubbing noises, called *fret sounds,* caused by the musician's fingering. Some musicians are more heavy-handed than others. When a musician is heavy-handed, it usually brings to a head the problem of whether the fret sounds, which are a natural part of the instrument's sound, should be part of the recording. Personal taste is the determining factor. If you do not care for the fret sounds, mike farther from the instrument or use a supercardioid or hypercardioid mic placed at a slight angle to the neck of the instrument (see 12-23). This puts the mic's off-axis side facing the frets. Make sure the mic's angle is not too severe, or the sound from the instrument will be off-mic. There are also strings specially designed to reduce finger noises and sprays to reduce friction.

12-22 Miking an acoustic guitar. A microphone placed about 6 inches above the bridge and even with the front of the guitar brightens the natural sound of the instrument.

fret

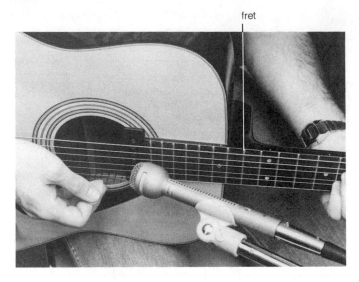

12-23 Microphone placement to reduce loudness of fret sounds. Place the dead side of a supercardioid or hypercardioid mic opposite the guitar's neck to reduce fret sounds without interfering with the overall frequency response.

Characteristics of Bowed String Instruments

The well-known bowed string instruments are the violin, viola, cello, and bass. Bowed string instruments are similar to plucked string instruments in that their strings are stretched above a fingerboard to a bridge mounted on a hollow body that resonates with the vibrating strings. But they have only four strings and no metal frets on the fingerboard; intervals are determined by the placement of the musician's fingers on the fingerboard. Another difference is that the strings are vibrated using a bow drawn across the strings, thereby generating a smoother attack than the attack of a plucked string. The bridge in a bowed instrument is connected to a top plate, or belly, supported by a sound post to the back plate, and is important to the overall sound, as are the f-holes in the top plate that allow

the air inside the body to resonate. The dynamic range of bowed string instruments is not as wide as most other orchestral instruments, nor is their projection as strong (see 12-24).

Violin The four violin strings are tuned to perfect fifths and have a fundamental frequency range of 196–3,136 Hz, with harmonics that extend from 4 to 15 kHz. The violin radiates lower frequencies in a roughly spherical pattern. As frequencies get higher, the violin radiates frequencies about evenly in the front and back, as both the top plate and back plate are designed to resonate with the strings. The highest frequencies are radiated upward from the top plate.

Viola The viola is essentially a larger, lower-pitched version of the violin. The strings are tuned a fifth lower than the violin; their fundamental frequency range is

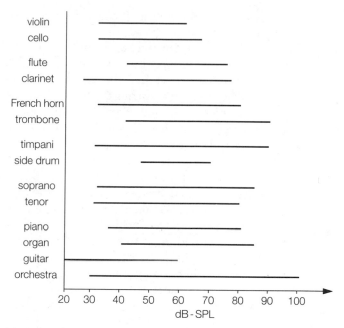

12-24 **Dynamic range of selected musical sound sources**

131 to 1,175 Hz, with harmonics that extend from 2 to 8.5 kHz. The radiating pattern is similar to that of the violin but is less directional due to the viola's lower frequency range.

Cello The cello's strings are tuned a full octave below the viola, with a fundamental frequency range of 65 to 698 Hz and harmonics that extend from 1 to 6.5 kHz. The cello's radiating pattern is more omnidirectional than directional but is affected by the playing position. The cello rests on a spike that is set on the floor. Some vibrations are transmitted to the floor, which reflects and absorbs the sound waves to some degree, depending on the sound absorption coefficient of the floor's material and whether the spike is set into a rubber or wood cup.

Bass The bass strings are tuned in fourths rather than fifths and have a fundamental

range from 41 to 294 Hz, with harmonics extending from 1 to 5 kHz. The bass radiates sound omnidirectionally and, because it is positioned like the cello, the sound is somewhat affected by the floor's material.

Miking Bowed String Instruments

Because the dynamic range of bowed string instruments is not wide, sound has to be reinforced by use of several instruments or multiple miking, or both, depending on the size of the sound required. Overdubbing, discussed in Chapter 13, is another method used to reinforce string sound. The need for reinforcement is compounded by the dearth of competent string players in many communities, to say nothing of the cost of hiring very many of them where they do exist in sufficient numbers.

Individually, miking a violin or viola a few feet above the instrument, aiming the

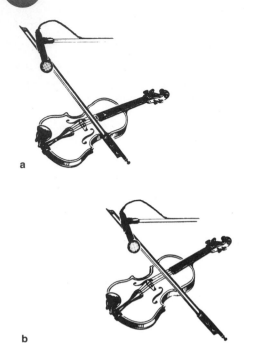

a

b

12-25 Miking a violin or viola.
(*a*) Placing the mic several feet above the instrument, aimed at the front face, tends to produce an open, natural sound. (*b*) To produce a country fiddle sound, place the microphone closer to the bridge but not close enough to interfere with the bowing.

mic at the front face, produces an open, natural sound, assuming fairly live acoustics (see 12-25). Although sound radiation is uniform up to 500 Hz, depending on the microphone, a single mic may not hear sufficient low end and, therefore, not reproduce a robust sound. Miking "over and under" assures that the highs, which are concentrated above 500 Hz and radiate perpendicularly to the sound board, are picked up from above the instrument and the lows are picked up from both above and below. This technique also tends to make one instrument sound like a few and a few sound like several (see 12-26). Overdubbing will accomplish this with greater effectiveness, however.

Miking a few inches from the side or above the strings of a violin produces a country fiddle sound; the closer a microphone is to the strings, the coarser or scratchier the sound. But be careful not to interfere with the musician's bowing when close miking over bowed instruments.

Generally, for either the cello or the acoustic bass, miking off the bridge 2 to 3 feet produces a brighter sound, and miking off the f-hole produces a fuller sound. A contact mic placed behind the bridge produces a closed, tight sound (see 12-27).

With a plucked bass, used in jazz, some producers like to clip a mic to the bridge or f-hole for a more robust sound. A danger with this technique is getting a thin, mid-range-heavy sound instead. Close-miking a plucked bass will pick up the attack. If close-miking also produces too boomy a sound, compress the bass slightly or roll off some of the low end, but beware of altering the characteristic low-frequency sound of the instrument.

Capacitor and ribbon microphones work particularly well with bowed string instruments. Capacitor mics enrich the string sound and enhance detail. Ribbon mics produce a resonant, warm quality, although there may be some loss of high-end detail. As for plucked strings, capacitors are preferred because of their excellent transient response.

Characteristics of a Struck String Instrument

The best-known example of a struck string instrument is the piano. The piano's strings are stretched across a bridge attached to a soundboard that resonates in sympathy with the vibrating strings after they are struck. The strings are struck by hammers

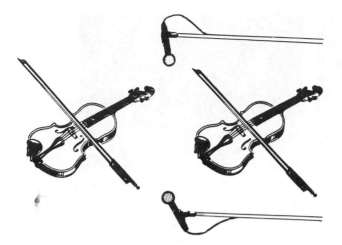

12-26 Enlarging the sound of a violin or viola. Place one microphone several feet over the instrument(s) and one microphone under the instrument(s). This tends to make one instrument sound like a few and a few sound like several.

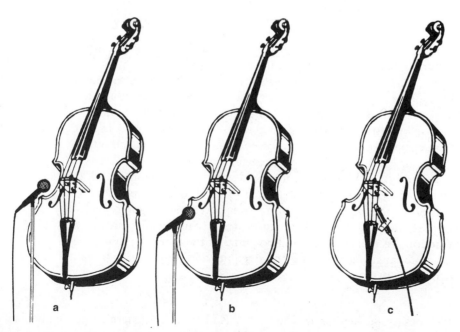

12-27 Three ways to mike a cello or bass. (*a*) Off the bridge produces a brighter sound. (*b*) Off the f-hole produces a fuller sound. (*c*) A mic behind the strings, near or at the bridge, taped to the body of the instrument, produces a more resonant sound, which could also be dull and devoid of harmonics.

a

b

c

12-28 Miking the grand piano. (*a*) Two directional microphones, one pointed at the piano's sounding board mainly to pick up direct sound and another a few feet away facing the raised lid to pick up reflections from the lid, produce a natural sound that is also open and, if acoustics are suitable, spacious. (*b*) One directional microphone above and facing the high strings and one directional microphone above and facing the low strings produce a good stereo blend with more discrete high and low frequencies. Adjust the mics to compensate for the time and intensity differences between the low and high frequencies. (*c*) Positioning microphones just above the hammers adds the "kiss" of hammer and string to the piano sound. In this particular arrangement a ribbon microphone picks up the low-frequency sounds to enhance their warmth, and a microphone with a transparent aural quality picks up the high-frequency sounds to enhance their clarity. This technique may also pick up annoying pedal action. To reproduce the full potential of the piano's frequency response and dynamic range, techniques *b* and *c* require additional mics placed at least a few feet from the piano.

controlled by the keys on the keyboard. The strings continue to vibrate until the key is released and a damper stops the vibration of the string. The piano's fundamental frequency and dynamic ranges are wide (see 12-24).

Radiation is generally perpendicular to the soundboard, primarily upward in a grand piano. The lower-frequency strings will be more omnidirectional; the higher-frequency strings will be located closer to an

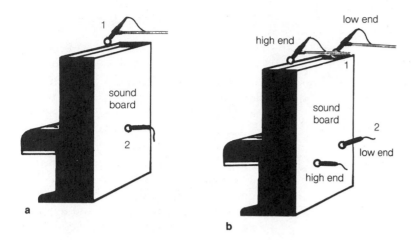

12-29 Miking an upright piano. (*a*) For mono, position a mic over an open top (1) for a natural sound, or behind the soundboard (2) for a fuller, tubby sound. (*b*) For stereo, position two microphones, one for low-end pickup and the other for high-end pickup, over an open top (1) or behind the soundboard (2). Mics also can be placed inside the piano to pick up the hammer sound. When spacing the mics, remember the three-to-one rule.

axis perpendicular to the soundboard. The lid is also a factor in a piano's sound radiation, but directionality depends on the angle at which the lid is open.

Because of the percussive nature of the key striking the strings, timbre is affected by how hard the string is struck. Higher harmonics are more present in strings that are struck hard. Strings struck more gently produce a warmer sound.

Miking Pianos

The piano offers almost unlimited possibilities for sound shaping. More than with many other instruments, however, the character of the piano sound is dependent on the quality of the piano itself. Smaller grand pianos may have dull, wooden low-end response. Old or abused pianos may sound dull or ring or thump. Steinways, generally,

are built to produce a lyrical sound. Yamahas produce crisp sound with more attack. The Bosendorfer aims for additional sonority by adding semitones in the bass range.

Mic technique and signal processing cannot change a piano's voicing from dull to bright, from thin to rich, or from sharp to smooth, but they can alter a piano's existing sound. There are several common miking techniques for the grand piano (see 12-28) and the upright piano (see 12-29).

Although the techniques displayed in Figure 12-28 are among the common ones used in miking a grand piano, they do not address the fact that you have to be some distance from the piano to get its full sound—close distances yield only partial sound—because its dynamic range can be so wide. In studio recording there is the additional problem of leakage in the piano mics

12-30 Miking across the bridge–rail axis. This produces a spacious, full-bodied sound, but at the expense of low end–high end stereo imaging.

from other instruments, thus necessitating closer mic-to-source distances. Because there is more piano sound across the bridge–rail axis than horizontally along the keyboard, try miking along the piano instead of across it (see 12-30). This should reproduce a more spacious, full-bodied sound. But a clear low–high stereo image is sacrificed because the sound is more blended.

Woodwinds

Just as the vibrating string is the acoustical foundation of string instruments, a vibrating column of air is the foundation of woodwind (and brass) instruments. All wind instruments have in common a tube, or cone, through which air is blown generating a standing wave of vibrating air within. In woodwinds the vibrations are produced in the clarinet and saxophone using one reed, in the oboe and bassoon using a double reed, and in the flute and piccolo by blowing across the air hole.

Characteristics of Woodwinds

The pitches of woodwinds are determined by the length of the tube, whether the tube is open at one end (clarinet) or at both ends (flute), and by the opening and closing of the holes in the tube. A tube open at one end has stronger odd-number harmonics: third, fifth, seventh, and so on. A tube open at both ends, and flared or conical tubes (oboe and bassoon) have stronger "normal" harmonics: second, third, fourth, fifth, and so on. The vibrating reed and sound holes generate their own overtones. In general, higher frequencies radiate from the bell, and lower frequencies radiate from the holes.

Flute   The flute is a tube that is held horizontally. The musician blows across a sound hole and controls pitch and timbre by varying the stream of air. Pitch is also determined by opening and closing of the holes in the side of the instrument. Sound radiates from the sound hole, the side holes, and the end of the flute. Fundamental frequencies range from 261 to 2,349 Hz, and harmonics extend from 3 to 8 kHz. Its dynamic range is limited.

Clarinet   The clarinet is a single-reed tube played almost vertically with the bell pointed toward the floor. Its fundamental frequency range is 165–1,568 Hz, with harmonics extending from 2 to 10 kHz. Sound is generated from the mouthpiece and reed, the side holes, and the bell. Reflections from the floor also may affect the clarinet's sound.

Oboe and Bassoon   The fundamental frequencies of the oboe and bassoon are 261–1,568 and 62–587 Hz, with harmonics extending from 2 to 12 kHz and 1 to 7 kHz, respectively. Both instruments, despite their relatively narrow frequency response and limited dynamic range, are comparatively rich in harmonics and overtones. The oboe's sound emanates from the mouthpiece and reed, sound holes, and bell. Like the clarinet, it is played aimed at the floor and may also be affected by sound that is absorbed by and/or reflected from the floor. The bassoon curves upward at its bottom, pointing toward the ceiling. If the ceiling is high enough, the bassoon's overall sound is usually not affected.

Saxophone The family of saxophones includes the soprano, alto, tenor, and baritone. Saxophones have a conical shape with a bell that curves upward (except for the soprano saxophone, which may be straight). The saxophone's sound radiates mostly from the bell, but the sound holes also generate significant detail. Fundamental frequency ranges are roughly as follows: soprano—200–1,100 Hz, alto—138–820 Hz, tenor—100–600 Hz, and baritone—80–400 Hz.

Miking Woodwinds

Woodwind instruments such as the flute, clarinet, and oboe are among the weaker-sounding instruments and have a limited dynamic range. Alto, tenor, and baritone saxophones are stronger sounding. But the higher-pitched woodwinds—flute, clarinet, soprano saxophone—can cut through the sound of more powerful instruments if miking and blending are not properly attended to (or if the recordist intends it).

Because most woodwinds are not powerful instruments, the tendency is to close-mike them; but, due to their sound radiation, this results in an uneven pickup. They should be miked far enough away so the pickup sounds blended and natural.

Because the flute and piccolo (a smaller, higher-pitched version of the flute) radiate sound in shifting patterns sideways and from the instruments' end hole, close miking, or, worse, contact miking, tends to miss certain frequencies and emphasize others. Moreover, dry, less reverberant sound can distort some tonalities.

For the flute, mic-to-source distance depends on the music. For classical music, it should be about 3 to 8 feet; for pop music, about 6 inches to 2 feet. Microphone positioning should start slightly above the player, between the mouthpiece and the end of the instrument. To add the breathy quality of the blowing sound, mike toward the mouthpiece—how close depends on how much breath sound you want. If breath noise is a problem regardless of where the mic is placed, and you want to eliminate it, try placing the microphone behind the player's head, aiming it at the finger holes (see 12-31). This technique also reduces high-frequency content. A windscreen or pop filter reduces unwanted breath noise, too. In miking a flute or any woodwind, be careful not to pick up the sound of the key action.

Microphone positioning for the clarinet and oboe must take into account the narrowing of high frequencies radiating in the vertical plane in front of the player and floor reflections from the bell being aimed downward. Close miking tends to emphasize these disparities. If close miking is unavoidable, position the mic to the side of the bell rather than straight at it. This should smooth most of the sonic anomalies. Miking off the bell also tends to reduce leakage and makes the sound brighter and harder. Another possibility is to mike toward the bottom third of the instrument and far enough away to blend the pickup from the finger holes and bell (see 12-32).

Saxophones radiate more sound from the bell and some sound from the holes. The proportion of sound radiating from holes and bell constantly changes, however, as the keys open and close. Miking saxophones off

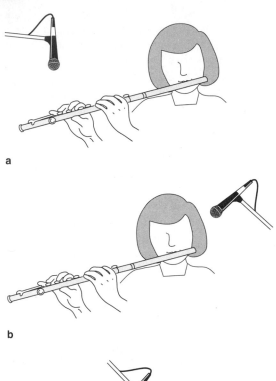

a

b

c

12-31 Miking flute and piccolo. (*a*) Placing a microphone over the finger holes nearer the end of the instrument picks up most of the sounds these instruments emit and does not pick up the breathy sounds that miking the mouthpiece produces. (*b*) Some producers feel that these sounds are part of the instruments' overall aural character, however, and mike the mouthpiece to produce a thinner-textured sound. (*c*) If un-wanted breath sounds persist, place the microphone behind the musician's head and aimed at the finger holes.

12-32 Miking clarinet and oboe. Place a microphone over the finger holes toward the bottom third, because most of the sounds come from this part of the instrument. In miking the keys of any instrument, avoid close mic-to-source distances; otherwise, the sound of the moving keys will be heard.

12-33 Miking a saxophone. Aiming a microphone at the holes from above the bell produces a natural, blended sax sound. Miking too close to the instrument may pick up blowing, spit, or key sounds.

the bell produces a bright, thin, hard sound. Miking too close to the bell further accentuates the high frequencies, making the sound piercing or screechy. Miking off the finger holes adds fullness, presence, and warmth. Aiming a microphone at the holes from above the bell produces a natural, more blended sound (see 12-33).

Brass

Brass instruments—trumpet, trombone, French horn, baritone, tuba—generally are conical and have a cup-shaped mouthpiece; the lips act as a vibrating "reed" when the musician blows into the mouthpiece. The brass are the loudest acoustic musical instruments with the widest dynamic range.

Characteristics of Brass Instruments

Trumpet The fundamental frequency range of the trumpet is 165–988 Hz, with harmonics extending from 1 to 7.5 kHz. In addition to the sound control by lip pressure and tension at the mouthpiece, a series of three valves are used to vary the tube length and, hence, the pitches. Most of the sound radiates from the bell with higher frequencies located on an axis closer to the center of the bell.

Trombone The trombone is the orchestra's most powerful instrument. Its distinctive feature is a slide that is moved in and out to vary the length of the tube and change pitches. (Some trombone models use valves instead of a slide.) The fundamental frequency range is 73–587 Hz with harmonics and a radiation pattern similar to that of the trumpet.

Tuba The tuba is the lowest pitched of the brass instruments with a fundamental frequency range of 49–587 Hz and harmonics extending from 1 to 4 kHz. It uses valves to vary its effective length and emits sounds upward from a wide, curved bell. Higher-frequency harmonics are present at the axis of the bell although, to a live audience, they are not a recognizable component of the tuba's sound because they are generated upward. Most of a tuba's distinctive bass sound is radiated omnidirectionally.

French Horn The French horn is a curved, cone-shaped tube with a wide bell and valves that is played with the bell pointed to the side, or behind, the musician, often with the musicians hand inside the bell for muting. Therefore, the instrument's sound is not closely related to what the live audience hears. Its fundamental range is relatively narrow—87–880 Hz, with harmonics extending from 1 to 6 kHz—but the French horn's sound can "cut through" the sound of louder instruments with wider frequency response.

Miking Brass Instruments

Brass instruments require care in microphone placement and careful attention in adjusting levels at the console because of their loudness and dynamic range. They also emit the most directional sound; high-frequency harmonics radiate directly out of the bell. But the most distinctive frequencies of the trumpet and trombone are in the frequencies around 1,200 Hz and 700 Hz, respectively, which are radiated from the sides of the bell. Below 500 Hz, radiation tends to become omnidirectional. Therefore, close-miking brass instruments with a directional microphone does not quite produce their full frequency response. A directional mic close to and in front of the bell produces a bright, biting quality. Miking at an angle to the bell or on-axis to the side of the bell produces a more natural, mellower, hornlike sound (see 12-34).

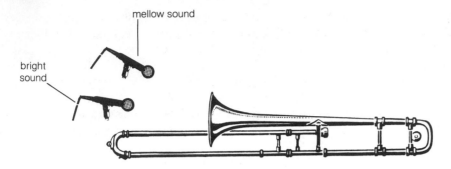

12-34 Miking off the bell. Mike trumpets, trombones, baritones, and tubas at an angle to the bell for a natural, mellower sound, being careful to avoid close mic-to-source distances so the air flow and spit sounds are not heard. Miking in front of the bell produces a brighter sound.

12-35 Miking the French horn. (*a*) To control leakage, place the musician away from the ensemble and the microphone near a soft baffle pointing at the bell. (*b*) If this arrangement creates a blending problem due to the French horn's lack of presence, placing a hard baffle a few feet from the bell should carry the sound to the mic in sufficient proportions.

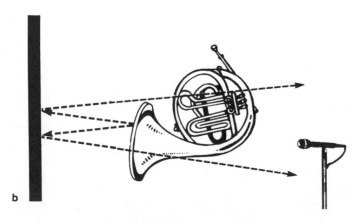

About 1 to 5 feet is a good working mic-to-source distance. Closer placement gives a tighter sound, although miking too close to a brass instrument could pick up spit and valve sounds. More distant placement makes the sound fuller and more emphatic.

For the French horn, a mic-to-source distance of at least 5 feet is recommended. It is not the most powerful brass instrument but, as noted above, it can cut through and overwhelm louder instruments, and its levels fluctuate considerably. To increase control and to minimize French horn leakage, move the instrument away from the ensemble (see 12-35).

In miking brass sections, trumpets and trombones should be blended as a chorus. One microphone for each pair of instruments produces a natural, balanced sound and provides flexibility in the mixdown. If you try to pick up more than two trumpets or trombones with a single mic, it has to be far enough from the instruments to blend them, and the acoustics have to support the technique. Of course, leakage will occur. Mike baritones and tubas individually from above (see 12-36).

The type of microphone you use can also help shape the sound of brass. The moving coil can smooth transient response; the ribbon can add a fuller, warmer tonality; and the capacitor can produce accurate transient response.

Electric Instruments

Electric instruments—bass, guitar, keyboards—generate their sound through an electrical pickup that can be sent to an amplifier or directly to the console. Therefore, three techniques are generally used to record an electric instrument: (1) plugging the instrument into an amplifier and placing a mic in front of the amp's loudspeaker, (2) direct insertion (D.I.), or plugging the

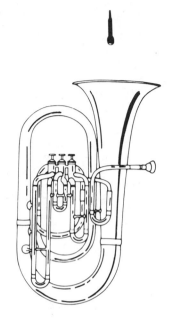

12-36 Miking the baritone and tuba from above the bell

instrument directly into the mic input of the console through a direct box, or (3) both miking the amp and using direct insertion.

Electric instruments are usually high-impedance, whereas professional-quality audio equipment is low-impedance. Not surprisingly, high- and low-impedance equipment are incompatible and produce sonic horrors if connected. The **direct box** is a device that matches impedances, thus making the output of the instrument compatible with the console's input (see 12-37).

Miking Electric Instruments

Although this chapter deals with close-miking technique, it is important to know the differences between miking an amp and going direct. Deciding which method to use is a matter of taste, practicality, and convenience (see Tables 12-3 and 12-4).

Table 12-3   Advantages and disadvantages of miking an amplifier loudspeaker

Advantages	Disadvantages
Adds interaction of room acoustics to sound	Could leak into other mics
Captures more midbass for added punch	Could be noisy due to electric problems with amp
Creates potential for different sound textures	
Gives musician greater control over an instrument's sound output	Level of amp can make it difficult for musicians to hear less powerful instruments
Permits other instrumentalists more chance to hear what the electric instruments are playing so that the acoustic players can interact better with electric instruments	Distortion

Table 12-4   Advantages and disadvantages of direct insertion

Advantages	Disadvantages
Has a cleaner sound	Has a drier sound—no room ambience
Captures more high and low frequencies	May use a transformer, which adds another electronic device to the sound chain
Allows more sound control at the console	Too present
Eliminates leakage	
Does not require an amp	

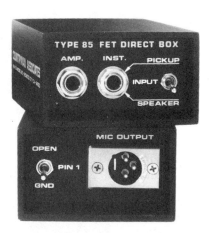

12-37 Direct box. A direct box has an isolated transformer that is less vulnerable to damage, distortion, grounding problems, volume loss, and changes in tone quality. This particular direct box can be battery or phantom powered. To improve sound quality further, many direct boxes are transformerless.

When miking an amp loudspeaker, the moving-coil mic is most often used because it can handle loud levels without overloading. With the bass guitar the directional moving-coil is less susceptible to vibration and conductance, especially with a shock mount, caused when the instrument's long, powerful wavelengths are amplified. Due to its powerful low end the bass is usually recorded direct to obtain a cleaner sound. The fundamental frequency range of the electric bass is 41–300 Hz, with harmonics extending from 1 to 7 kHz.

Recording electric bass presents a particular challenge. If there is too much bass, the mix will sound muddy. This could mask the fundamentals of other instruments and result in a thickening and weighing down of the overall sound. Among the ways to improve clarity are to have the bassist increase treble and reduce bass on the guitar or to equalize in the control room by attenu-

a   b

12-38 Miking an amplifier loudspeaker. (*a*) Aiming a directional microphone at the loudspeaker produces a brighter sound. (*b*) Aiming a directional microphone at an angle to the loudspeaker produces a fuller but less bright sound.

ating around 250 Hz and boosting around 1,500 Hz.

Compression is commonly used in recording the electric bass. It helps to reduce noise, smooth variations in attack and loudness, and tighten the sound. Be careful in setting the compressor's release time. If it is too fast in relation to the decay rate of the bass, the sound will be organlike. A slower release time maintains the natural sound of the instrument. Too slow a release time muddies the sound.

With an electric guitar a directional moving-coil mic adds body to the sound. But if it is necessary to reproduce a subtler, warmer, more detailed sound, a capacitor or one of the more rugged ribbon mics may be used. The fundamental frequency range of the electric guitar is 82–1,319 Hz. When amplified the harmonics extend from 1 to 3.5 kHz; going direct the harmonics range from 1 to 15 kHz.

As for placement, the main challenge is understanding the dispersion pattern of the amplifier's loudspeakers (see Chapter 9). Miking close to and head on the amp produces a strong central lobe that has considerable high-frequency content within the bandwidth of the instrument itself (see 12-38a). Hence, this technique creates an unblended, unbalanced sound. Off-axis miking reduces high-frequency content, and backing the mic farther from the amp produces a more blended, balanced sound (see 12-38b). Also, the decrease in highs gives the impression of a heavier, bassier sound. Hanging a small microphone over the amp emphasizes a guitar's midrange and reduces leakage. If leakage is not a problem, and even if it is, close miking with an omni works well. An omnidirectional microphone has no proximity effect; its response is uniform, so it will pick up various aspects of the loudspeaker dispersion pattern; and the inverse square law will take care of the leakage problem because you are essentially force-feeding the mic from an amp that is producing a high sound-pressure level at a short mic-to-source distance. Use a capacitor or ribbon omni with fast response.

In their continuing effort to achieve new sounds, producers record amp loudspeaker and direct insertion feeds simultaneously. This technique combines the drier, unreverberant but crisp sound of direct insertion with the acoustic coloring of the amplified sound. The amp and D.I. signals should be recorded on separate tracks. This provides

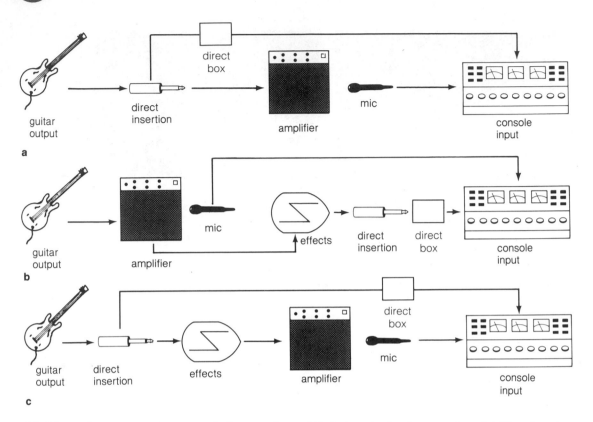

12-39 Techniques used to record direct and amplified signals simultaneously. (*a*) The signals are recorded on separate tracks. (*b, c*) Special effects boxes can be used; *c* shows the usual technique, and *b* illustrates an alternate technique.

more flexibility in the mixdown when the two sounds are combined, or if you decide not to use one of the tracks.

It should be noted that direct recording of guitars does not necessarily guarantee a leakage-free track. If a guitar pickup is near or facing a loud instrument, it will "hear" the vibrations. By turning the musician away from the direct sound waves or by putting a baffle between the instruments, you can reduce leakage.

With the electric guitar, special effects boxes are often used to add to the sonic possibilities (see 12-39). Here, too, the various signals should be recorded on separate

tracks, if possible, to allow flexibility in the mixdown.

Musicians' Amplifiers An amp often produces annoying hum. Using a microphone with a humbuck coil can help reduce hum but not always enough. It also helps to turn up the loudness control on the guitar and turn down the volume on the amp, unless the amp's sound is integral to the guitar's overall sonic quality. Try using guitar cables with extra shielding, or grounding the musician with a wrist or ankle strap when using guitars with single-coil pickups, such as Telecasters and Dan Electros. Moving the musician around the studio until a spot is located where the hum is reduced or disappears is another solution. If it is possible, convince the musician to use a smaller, lower-powered amp than is used in live concerts. There may be a problem here, however, because the change in amp produces a change in sound. If the problem is the AC line, use a ground lift adapter.

Leslie Loudspeaker Cabinet The Leslie amplifier loudspeaker, usually used with an electric organ, is almost an instrument in itself (see 12-40). It is not a loudspeaker in the normal sense but is designed especially to modify sound. It contains a high-frequency loudspeaker (the tweeter) in the upper portion and a low-frequency loudspeaker (the woofer) in the lower portion. The two loudspeaker systems rotate, creating a vibrato effect.

Voice

At its most basic level the human voice acts like a wind instrument. The lungs expel air through the vocal chords, which vibrate and act like a double reed. The voice is then radiated through the larynx and mouth and out into the air. Sound is modified by movement of the tongue, jaw, and lips and also the rate of exhalation. Pitch is determined primarily by the vocal chords and larynx, but mouth, lip, and tongue movements change timbre. The human voice's wide-ranging and complex harmonics and overtones are a product of the mouth, nasal cavity, and chest cavity.

Although the speaking voice has a comparatively limited frequency range, the singing voice does not (see 12-41). And whereas the speaking voice is comparatively straightforward to mike and record, the singing voice can place a severe test on any microphone. The singing voice is capable of

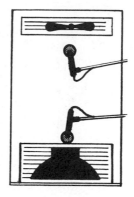

12-40 Miking a Leslie amplifier loudspeaker. One way is with two directional microphones, one to pick up the highs and the other to pick up the lows. The greater the mic-to-source distance, the less the chance of picking up the rotor sounds and increased tremolo and the better the sound blend. To record stereo, use either a top and bottom pair of mixed mics left and right or just single mics panned toward the left and right. If the sound of the rotating horn is desired, place a boundary microphone inside the cabinet.

almost unlimited and subtle variations in pitch, timbre, and dynamic range. There are also plosives and sibilance—annoying popping and hissing sounds—to deal with.

Close-Miking the Voice

Timbre In choosing a vocal mic, the most important consideration is the singer's timbre—how edged, velvety, sharp, mellow, or resonant the voice sounds. The microphone should enhance a voice's attractive qualities and minimize the unattractive. For

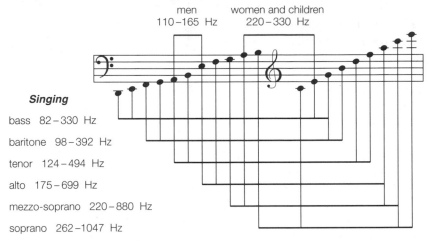

12-41 Fundamental frequency ranges for speech and singing in the human voice. Harmonics in the male singing voice extend from 1 to 12 kHz and in the female singing voice from 2 to 12 kHz.

example, if a voice sounds mellow, a ribbon mic may enhance the mellowness, but if a voice sounds low-pitched, the ribbon mic could muddy its quality. If a voice sounds too sharp or edged, the ribbon mic would smooth the sound, but a moving-coil or capacitor mic could make the voice sound more cutting. A capacitor mic may add richness to a voice that is soft and has little projection; a moving-coil type may help to thin out a voice that sounds too full.

Generally, assuming there are no serious problems with tone quality, most producers prefer to use capacitor microphones for vocals because they can better handle the complicated pattern of harmonics and overtones in the human voice, and overall sound quality is the most natural.

Dynamic Range Controlling the dynamic range—the quietest to loudest levels a sound source produces—is another tricky problem. Well-disciplined singers can usually control wide fluctuations in the dynamic range

themselves. But many singers cannot; their voices barely move the needle on the VU meter during soft passages and pin it during loud ones. In miking these vocalists, a producer has three alternatives: (1) ride the level, (2) adjust the vocalist's microphone position, or (3) use compression. There is also a fourth alternative: record the vocal on two tracks.

Riding the level works, but it requires an engineer's full attention; this may be difficult considering everything else that goes on in a recording session. Also, less gifted singers may handle dynamic range differently each time they sing, which means that riding the level is a matter more of coping than of aiding.

The preferred methods are to use microphone technique to adjust for irregularities in a vocalist's dynamic range or to use compression, or both. In pop music, vocals are often compressed 10–15 dB. But to do so requires that a recordist know how to compensate after compression.

12-42 Eliminating unwanted vocal sounds. Positioning the microphone slightly above the performer's mouth is a typical miking technique used to cut down on unwanted popping, sibilance, and breathing sounds.

One placement technique is to situate the singer at an average distance from the mic relative to the loudest and softest passages sung; the distance depends on the power of the singer's voice and the song. From this average distance you can direct the singer how close to move to the mic during quiet passages and how far for the loud ones. The success of this technique depends on the vocalist's microphone technique—the ability to manage the song and the movements at the same time.

If these techniques do not work, try recording the vocal on two tracks with one track 10 dB down. If there is overload or a problem with the noise floor, the undistorted or less noisy sections of each recording can be intercut.

Breathing, Popping, and Sibilance The closer to a microphone a performer stands, the greater is the chance of picking up unwanted breathing sounds, popping sounds from "p"s, "b"s, "k"s, and "t"s, and sibilance from "s"s. If the singer's vocal projection or the type of music permits, increasing the mic-to-source distance significantly reduces these noises. Windscreens also help, but they tend to reduce the higher frequencies. Other ways to reduce popping and sibilance are to have the singer work slightly across mic but within the pickup

pattern or to position the mic somewhat above the singer's mouth (see 12-42). If this increases nasality, position the mic at an angle from slightly below the singer's mouth. If leakage is no problem, using an omnidirectional mic permits a closer working distance because it is less susceptible to breathing, popping, and sibilant sounds. The sound may be less intimate because an omnidirectional microphone picks up more indirect sound waves than does a directional mic. But the closeness of the singer will often overcome the larger amount of indirect sound picked up.

Although capacitors are almost always the microphone of choice for vocals, they do tend to emphasize sibilance because of their wide frequency response. In such cases, and when other techniques fail to eliminate sibilance, a first-rate dynamic mic will usually take care of the problem. Another reason to consider a dynamic mic for vocals is the harshness of some capacitors when they are used in digital recording (see "Miking Music for Digital Recording" later in this chapter).

Mic-to-Source Distance Versus Style Generally, the style of the music sets the guidelines for mic-to-source distance. In popular music vocalists usually work close to the mic, from a few inches to a few feet, to create a tight, intimate sound. Classical and jazz vocalists work from a few feet to several feet from the mic to add room ambience, thereby opening the sound and making it airy (see 12-43).

When close-miking be careful of proximity effect. Rolling off the unwanted bass frequencies may be one solution, but it almost certainly will change the delicate balance of voice harmonics unless it is very carefully and knowledgeably effected. It should be emphasized that regardless of the type of microphone or quality of singer, using a mic just about touching the lips, as

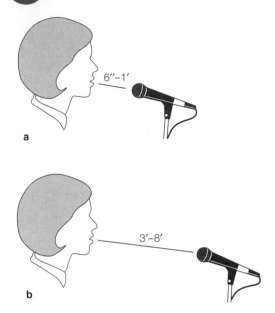

12-43 Mic-to-source distance and music style. Distances vary with the vocalist and the music. Generally, (*a*) pop singers prefer closer working distances than do (*b*) classical singers due to differences in style, loudness, and projection.

some vocalists are seen doing on television, and which unfortunately is imitated in the recording studio, rarely produces ideal sound. Indeed, if the microphone is not up to it, such mic technique rarely produces usable sound. If the distortion does not get you, then the oppressive lack of "air" will.

Backup Harmony Vocals   Once the lead vocal is recorded, the accompanying backup harmony vocals are overdubbed. Often, this involves a few vocalists singing at the same time. If they have their own individual microphones, mic-to-source distances are easier to balance, but this also adds more mics to control and could require using extra tape tracks. Another technique groups the vocalists around a bidirectional or omni-

directional microphone. This reduces the number of microphones and tape tracks involved, but it requires greater care in balancing and blending harmonies. Backup vocalists must be positioned to prevent any one voice or harmony from being too strong or too weak.

Comfort and Performance   Before attending to the vocal sound, it is important to make the vocalist feel at ease and comfortable. Smoke, dust, and cool, dry air take their toll on a singer's endurance. So does too much talking. The music stand set up, a beverage handy—preferably warm—and a comfortable chair nearby go a long way in making a performer feel cared for.

Vocalists should sing standing straight to facilitate opening the throat, breath control, and sound support from the diaphragm. Vocalists with limited studio experience may feel uncomfortable standing in front of a stationary microphone. Providing them with a hand-held mic may help them to perform more naturally but may also introduce cable or hand noise and encourage them to move around, which could add more noise still.

Boundary Microphone Techniques

A boundary microphone with a hemispheric polar pattern is not good for spot or isolation miking due to its pickup pattern. The newer, directional boundary microphones can be used in spot-miking situations, however. Figures 12-44 through 12-48 display a few applications of boundary microphone techniques in music recording.

Miking Studio Ensembles

This discussion of close miking has centered mainly on the individual instrument, because so much of today's pop music records one at a time or else a few voicings in an ensemble at one time. There are studio situations, however, in which ensembles record as a group but are divided into smaller sections to control leakage. This requires isolating them as much as possible to avoid sonic confusion, yet blending them so that they sound cohesive. Figures 12-49 and 12-50, as well as Figure 13-2, show a few ways to mike studio ensembles.

Miking Music for Digital Recording

As clear and noise-free as digital sound can be, there are valid complaints about digital recordings: that the high end is strident, thin, and shrieky, or that there is too much unwanted noise from amplifiers, pedals, keys, bows, tongue, teeth, lips, and so on. Many of these problems can be traced to two causes: the microphones and the miking techniques that were used.

Microphones in Digital Recording

Many microphones used in analog recording are selected for their rising high-end response; these mics help to deal with problems associated with analog reproduction, the most serious being the potential loss of high-frequency information during disc mastering and copying. There is little such loss in digital recording, copying, or mastering. (Uneven quality in the manufacture of CDs is, alas, another story altogether.) Therefore, using such mics for digital recording only makes the high frequencies more biting and shrill. To avoid this problem, use microphones with smooth high-end response. Recordists have returned to tube-type equipment in the signal chain—microphones, amplifiers, equalizers—to help warm the sound, offsetting the edge in digital reproduction.

Capacitor microphones have preamplifiers, which generate noise. In analog

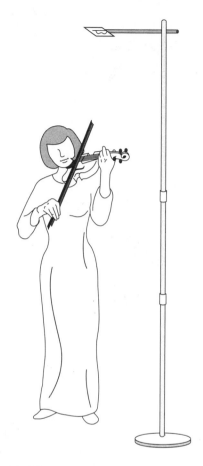

12-44 Boundary mic positioned over a violin (or viola)

recording, this noise is usually masked. In digital recording, if preamp noise is loud enough, it will be audible. Therefore, high-quality, large-diaphragm capacitors are preferred because their self-generated preamp noise is very low level.

The newer, more rugged ribbon microphones have become popular in digital recording. Their response is inherently non-tailored, smooth, warm, and detailed without being strident. Microphones used in

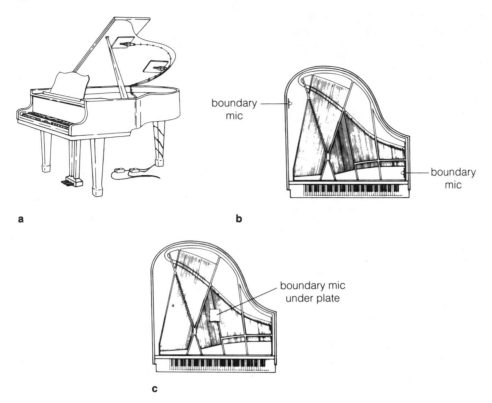

12-45 Miking a piano with boundary mics. (*a*) A pair of spaced boundary mics for stereo pickup are attached to the piano lid, one mic over the high strings and one mic over the low strings. (*b*) If the lid is removed, a pair of mics can be taped (with masking tape, not duct tape) to the inside of the frame, one near the high strings and one near the low strings. (*c*) For mono pickup a boundary mic faced down over the intersection of the high and low strings should provide a balanced sound. Taping a boundary mic to the piano lid and closing it produces a sound much like that of an upright.

digital recording should be linear—that is, output should vary in direct proportion to input. The mic should not introduce unwanted sonic information because, in digital sound, chances are it will be audible. Of course, this is the case in analog recording as well; it is just more critical in digital recording.

Also, mics used in digital recording should be high-quality, carefully handled, and kept in clean, temperature- and humidity-controlled environments. The dust, moisture, and rough handling that may not perceptibly affect mic response in an analog recording may very well sully a digital recording.

Microphone Technique in Digital Recording

In analog recording, close miking was employed virtually pro forma, because

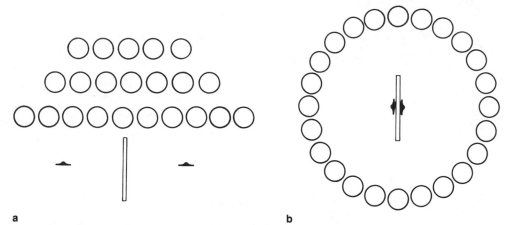

12-46 Two arrangements for stereo miking a chorus. (*a*) Two boundary mics are placed in front of the group and separated by a baffle. (*b*) Two boundary mics are attached to and separated by a sheet of Plexiglas surrounded by the chorus. In (*a*) a stereo boundary mic could be used instead.

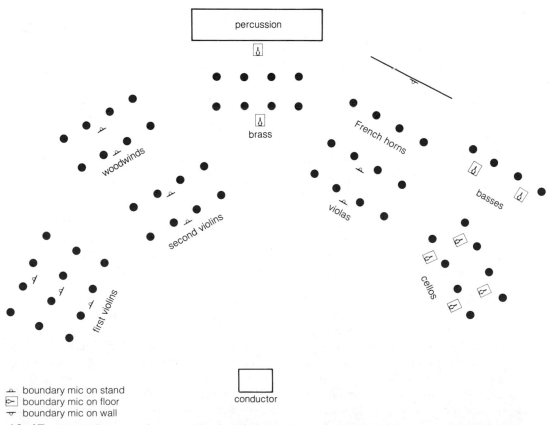

12-47 A symphony orchestra miked with boundary mics. Microphones are placed above the violin, viola, and woodwind sections; on the floor in front of the brass, cello, bass, and percussion sections; and on the wall (or curtain) behind the French horns.

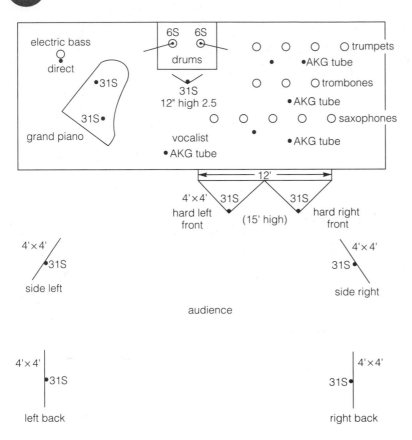

12-48 One way of miking a jazz band incorporating PZM™ boundary mics. The stereo array closest to the ensemble blends the trumpets, trombones, and saxophones. The arrays in the middle and rear of the studio are for ambience and surround sound. Stereo arrays are also at the drum and piano locations. The 31S is used for its deeper low end and warmer, smoother high end. The 6S is designed for increased high-end articulation and minimum visibility. The AKG tube is used for instrumental and vocal soloists and for its warm mellow, sound.

vinyl records usually smoothed the rough spots resulting from close miking by burying some of the harshness in background surface noise. In digital recording, no such masking occurs. For example, in analog recording, when close-miking an acoustic guitar, no one is concerned about noise that might be generated by the guitarist's shirt rubbing against the instrument. By contrast, in digital recording, the rubbing sound may be heard if the guitar is close-miked. In addition, in analog recording, noise from a musician's amplifier may get lost in tape hiss. That will not be the case in digital recording, regardless of the mic used.

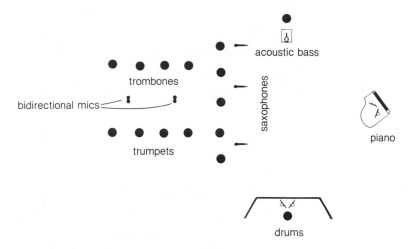

acoustic bass

trombones

bidirectional mics

saxophones

trumpets

piano

drums

12-49 Miking a jazz band when all voicings are recorded at the same time. Notice trumpets and trombones are miked with bidirectional microphones and that the piano, acoustic bass, and drums are miked with boundary mics. Bidirectional mics are particularly useful in reducing leakage. For example, by facing the mic straight down in front of each saxophone, each mic's nulls are directed toward sound coming from the sides and rear. This is especially effective when woodwinds, or other weak instruments, are in front of brass, or other strong instruments. A high-ceilinged room is necessary for this technique to work, however.

Even if mic-to-source distance is acceptable for digital recording, microphone placement may not be. For example, the upper harmonics of a violin radiate straight up in two directions. If a microphone is placed directly in one of these paths, the digital sound will be too crisp and shrieky, even though the mic is at an optimal distance from the violin. By placing the mic more in the path of the lower-frequency radiations, the digital sound should flatten.

High frequencies of brass instruments are radiated straight ahead in a relatively narrow beam. Placing a microphone directly in front of the bell will produce a harsh digital recording. Placing the mic at more of an angle to the bell, to pick up a better blend of the lower frequencies, should smooth the sound.

Samplers and Sampling

Samplers are devices for making short digital audio recordings for manipulation and playback (see 12-51 and 12-52). Samplers have had a far-reaching affect in music recording, in particular, and audio production, in general. A sampler makes it possible to record, excerpt, and store acoustic or electroacoustic digital audio data. The process is called **sampling**. The acoustic sounds can be anything a microphone can record— a rim shot, phoneme in a song lyric, the entire song lyric, trombone solo, piano

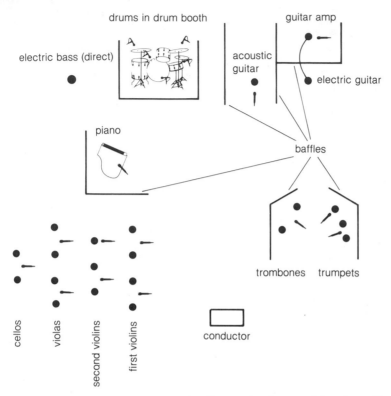

12-50 One way to position and mike a mixed ensemble when all voicings are recorded at once

12-51 Keyboard-based sampling recorder.   This particular model has a hard disk drive and supports up to 16 megabytes of sample memory. Among its other features are time compression and expansion, digital effects processing, and sequencing.

12-52 Sampler. This model is a 32-voice, 16-bit sampler that incorporates a SMPTE reader/generator, SCSI interface, digital I/O, and direct-to-disc recording.

chords, whatever. Electroacoustic sounds are anything electronically generated, such as those a synthesizer produces. The samples can be of any length, as brief as a drumbeat or as long as the available memory allows.

With most samplers, it is possible to produce an almost infinite variety of sound effects. A few of the sampler's most commonly used functions are truncation, transposition, and looping.

Truncation cuts the sample either at its beginning or end. Generally, it is used to "clean up" samples by eliminating any noise that precedes or follows the originally recorded material. Because truncation is an editing function, it can be used to change the sound envelope of the original audio by, for example, cutting off a sound's attack to create a more sustained, less punctuated sound, or cutting off some, or most, of the sustain after the attack to make a sound more percussive.

Transposition changes the pitch of a recorded sample. For example a middle C on a piano sample can be transposed up or down, say, half an octave. Transposing has a limited range, however, beyond which the original sample sounds unrealistic. That is, it "munchkinizes"; it sounds like a recording taped at a slower speed being played

back at a faster speed. Of course, if you are looking for such a special effect, this "limitation" can be an advantage.

Looping takes a sample portion and repeats it over and over. One common use of looping is to create long sustains of a sound. If you wanted to repeat the "a" in the word *fan*, the sampler can be instructed, at the touch of the appropriate key, to generate the "f," repeat the "aaaaaaaaaa" as long as the key is held down, and when the key is released, generate the "n." Looping can be extended to any size segment of a sample. It can also be used to reverse a sampled sound. "Fan" can be generated as "naf."

Another common use of looping is to sample the chorus in a vocal and repeat it after each verse during the recording of a song. In rap recordings, rhythm tracks are sampled and looped throughout a song. Sampling can be used to fix performance errors. If a snare drum beat is missed, sampling makes it possible to take a snare drum hit from elsewhere in the song and copy it in the missed spot.

With sampling, a trombone can be made to sound like a saxophone or an English horn; one drumbeat can be processed into a chorus of jungle drums. The crack of a base-

SL3001	Grand piano #2		SL3033	Analogue strings
SL3002	Organ #1		SL3034	Analogue brass
SL3003	Organ #2		SL3035	Analogue vox
SL3004	Organ #3		SL3036	Analogue pad
SL3005	Organ #4		SL3037	Jazz drum
SL3006	Dry kit #1		SL3038	Power drum
SL3007	Ambience kit #1		SL3039	House drum
SL3008	Nylon guitar		SL3040	FX drum
SL3009	String section #1		SL3041	Kick and snare
SL3010	String section #2		SL3042	Chromatic harp
SL3011	Mix strings		SL3043	Yang-ch'in
SL3012	Electric piano #1		SL3044	CS piano-L
SL3013	Stack synth #1		SL3045	CS piano-R
SL3014	Violin section #1		SL3046	Rock kit #1
SL3015	Viola section #1		SL3047	EL-gut guitar
SL3016	Cello section #1		SL3048	EL-AC 12st guitar
SL3017	C-bass section #1		SL3049	Music box
SL3018	Stack piano		SL3050	Acoustic bass
SL3019	Orchestra #2		SL3051	61 synth percussion
SL3020	Reverse collection		SL3052	Hi-fi cymbals
SL3021	Wind #1		SL3053	Timpani
SL3022	Mallets		SL3054	Exotic percussion
SL3023	Brass #1		SL3055	Vintage machine perc
SL3024	Bass #1		SL3056	Shamisen
SL3025	Japanese drum		SL3057	John's guitar
SL3026	Kokyu		SL3058	Strings #3
SL3027	Chamberlain		SL3059	Pianos
SL3028	Electric piano #2		SL3060	Leads
SL3029	Finger picking bass		SL3061	Next rhythm
SL3030	Pick bass		SL3062	Keyboard
SL3031	Analogue lead		SL3063	Blow bottle
SL3032	Analogue horn		SL3064	Wind #2

12-53 Part of the samplefile list for the sampler shown in 12-51

ball bat can be shaped into the rip that just precedes an explosion. A metal trashcan being hit with a hammer can provide a formidable backbeat for a rhythm track.

In solid-state memory systems, such as ROM (Read Only Memory) or RAM (Random Access Memory), it is possible to instantly access all or part of the sample and reproduce it any number of times. The difference between ROM- and RAM-based samplers is that ROM-based samplers are factory programmed and reproduce only; RAM-based samplers allow you to both reproduce and record sound samples. The number of samples you can load into a system is limited only by the capacity of the system's storage memory.

The Samplefile

After a sample is recorded or produced, or both, it is usually saved in a storage medium, most commonly a floppy disk, hard disk, or compact disc. The stored sound data are referred to as a **samplefile** (see 12-53). Once stored, of course, a samplefile can be easily distributed. As a result, samplefiles of musical and other types of sounds are available to recording studios.

You should take two precautions before investing in a samplefile library. First, make sure it is in a format that is compatible with your sampler. Recently, steps have been taken to increase standardization of samplefile formats for computer-based systems. Second, make sure the sound quality of the samples is up to professional standards; too many are not.

Tips for Recording Samples

In recording samples from whatever source —acoustic or electronic—it is vital that the sound and reproduction be of good quality. Because the sample may be used many times in a variety of situations, it is disconcerting (to say the least) to hear a bad sample again and again. Moreover, if the sample has to be rerecorded, it might be difficult to reconstruct the same sonic and performance situation.

Miking

The same advice that applies to miking for digital recording also applies to miking for sampling. Only the highest-quality microphones should be used, which usually means capacitors with high sensitivity and low noise. If percussion recorded at close mic-to-source distances requires a moving-coil mic, it should be large-diaphragm and a top-quality model.

Time

Recording a good sample takes time. The digitized sample might bring out many sonic nuances that are not readily apparent acoustically. A particular sample might be realized only by combining certain sounds. There might be a need to sculpt the sample by processing it with filtering, looping, phasing, and so on. With sampling, as with much of sound, simply recording it is not enough.

Sampling and Copyright

Sampling has made it possible to take any recorded sound, including copyrighted material, process it, and use it for one's own purposes. The practice has become so widespread that it has created a major controversy about royalty and copyright infringement—specifically, about who own portions of the rights to the new performances that are based on previously released samples that might have been taken from copyrighted material.

Also, copyright laws that have been based on melody need to be modernized to adequately address the issue of sampling copyrighted material without permission. As it stands currently, short samples (within a few milliseconds) of prepublished material do not technically violate the author's copyright, but they do violate the record company's copyright.

Simply stated, using any copyrighted material without permission is unethical at best and illegal at worst. Copyright infringement affects everyone. Consider your reaction if someone profited from material created by your time and talent without sharing any of the earnings with you.

The Recording Session

The modern recording studio can be likened to an electronic toy shop. It is filled with devices that perform so many sonic functions that the temptation to "play" with and incorporate them into a recording is strong. As sophisticated as music recording has become, however, the age-old KIS philosophy still merits consideration: Keep It Simple. (Some prefer to add an *S* for emphasis: Keep It Simple, Stupid.) The point is that less is more. Overproduction, special effects, and gimmicks can be justified only if you have a rationale. If you wish to experiment, do not take valuable time during the recording session to do it.

Pressure and Diplomacy: The Tact Factor

Studio recording is physically, mentally, and emotionally draining. Sound quality cannot be masked by audience din. Everything is heard. In some ways the difference between concert and studio work is analogous to the difference between a long shot and a close-up in television or film. In a long shot subtle action goes unseen; in a close-up even the slightest twitch is perceived. The studio is like a laboratory and is often as sterile, even when lighting and decor have been enhanced. Stopping and starting to get things right and overdubbing break concentration. Repetition drains spontaneity and inspiration. Long sessions are creatively and physically wearing. There is no audience reaction to pump up adrenaline. Tension and pressure are exacerbated by the need to use time as economically as possible because studio (and musician) costs are high. In short, studio recording requires mental discipline and physical endurance.

Therefore, before we talk about the recording session itself, a word about an extremely important, but often forgotten, aspect of "creating by committee": tact. It often makes or breaks a performance.

Studio sessions should be enjoyable and loose. Bantering, joking, remembering common courtesies such as "please" and "thank you," paying compliments when they are deserved and being diplomatic when they are not, all help to keep pressure from building, squabbles from erupting, and confidence from collapsing.

Dealing with egos is complicated enough, but when they belong to creative people, you almost have to feel what they are trying to communicate, verbally and musically, to be effective. Moreover, the musicians must have confidence in your commitment to their "vision" and in your ability to help them achieve it. Remember: A comfortable musician is a better musician.

Recording Session Procedures

The approaches to a recording session are as individual as the producers and engineers who direct them. Generally, however, there are procedures and considerations that are relevant to many situations.

Record Keeping

Keep a record of important information about the session. This includes track assignments; microphones and EQ used; noise reduction employed, if any; name and time of song; type of tape used; slate information; and anything that needs attention, such as someone bumping a mic on take 7, track 14, at 2:13.04, a passage that needs boosting during the mix, or noise that must be gated. Also, it is a good idea to chart the session in preproduction and update it during recording (see 13-1). You never know when you may have to return to a session to finish it,

redo a part, or fill in a section. Even if that does not become necessary, good record keeping in the recording session makes the mixdown session easier. It is also important to keep a time log of the session for billing purposes.

Recording All at Once or Overdubbing

You can record an ensemble all at once or in sections at different times (see Chapter 11). Recording all at once requires that the microphones be far enough apart to avoid phase problems or that the musicians be separated to reduce leakage, if controlling leakage is important.

Using the three-to-one rule should take care of most acoustic phase problems. To reduce leakage, follow these steps: (1) Use directional microphones and place them so their rejection sides are pointed to the other instruments; (2) use acoustic baffles to separate the instruments; and (3) use the isolation booth(s) that most recording studios have for instruments with sound levels that are very high (for example, drums and amplifiers) and for sound sources that must be recorded with absolutely no leakage (for example, vocals) (see 13-2). Although positioning the musicians to avoid phasing and leakage is important, they should be able to see each other for cueing and other visual communication; they usually play better that way, too. Try to keep the musicians close together: They hear the musical blend better and tend to play a little quieter than they do positioned farther away from each other. Also, positioning the musicians close together achieves a tighter and punchier sound.

But most popular music today is recorded in sections at different times. In this way leakage and phase problems are consider-

AIR STUDIOS

TITLE	
ARTIST	**STUDIO**
PRODUCER	**ENGINEER**
CLIENT	**ASSISTANT**
TAPE STATUS	**DATE**

TITLE:-

	1	2	3	4	5	6	7	8
PROGRAM								
COMMENTS								

OFFSETS

BETWEEN		DIFFERENCE	

TIMINGS

1 BAR =		B.P.M.	

$\quad$ ♩ = $\qquad$ ♪ = $\qquad$ ♬ =

·NOTES

TAPE DETAILS

TAPE TYPE
VARISPEED
START TIME (SMPTE)
START TIME (MIDI)

ANALOGUE

SPEED	SPEED
LEVEL	REF
N/R	

DIGITAL

FORMAT	
SAMPLE	EMPHASIS

AUX DIGITAL TRACKS

A1
A2
D1
D2
CODE

13-1 Examples of track charts used to keep records of studio music sessions (opposite and above). Every studio either designs a form or uses a computer program to meet its own particular record-keeping needs.

ably reduced by overdubbing. Sel Sync (see Chapter 6) has made overdubbing one of the most convenient and most often used production techniques in audio. Its advantages and disadvantages are listed in Table 13-1.

The control that close miking and overdubbing permit can be misused. Be careful in going for perfection—you may achieve the same perfection others have achieved, and the result may be an indistinguishable product.

Building a Recording

Although overdubbing allows flexibility in scheduling performers, the order in which you tape them is often not so flexible. In pop music recording certain instruments are recorded before others.

Conventional procedure is to record the rhythm tracks first to ensure that everyone's timing will be the same. If there is a vocal, record the rest of the background or accompaniment during the next stages of the ses-

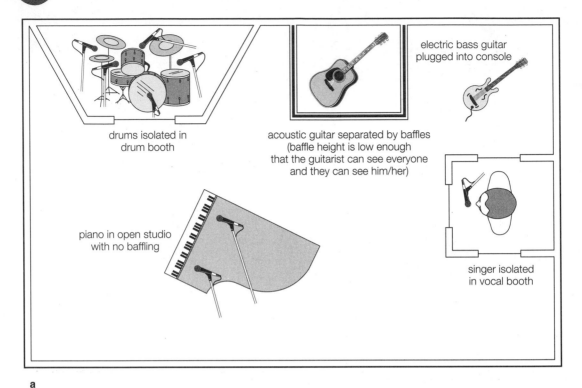

electric bass guitar
plugged into console

drums isolated in
drum booth

acoustic guitar separated by baffles
(baffle height is low enough
that the guitarist can see everyone
and they can see him/her)

piano in open studio
with no baffling

singer isolated
in vocal booth

a

13-2 Two ways to arrange musical groups for studio recording. (*a*) Musicians are isolated from one another to prevent sound from one instrument leaking into the microphone of another instrument, yet are still able to maintain visual contact. It is possible, in this arrangement, that the acoustic guitar sound will leak into the piano mics and vice versa. However, leakage can usually be reduced by supercardioid mics on both instruments rejecting sound from the sides and rear, the piano lid blocking sound coming from the front guitar baffle, and the guitarist's body blocking the piano sound coming from the back of the studio. (*b*) (*see facing page*) Another example of arranging a musical group in a studio to control leakage.

sion. The vocal is usually taped last because it is most likely the focus of the music and needs the other elements in place for proper tonal balance and perspective. A dummy (or scratch) vocal may be recorded with the rhythm and other tracks to help overall performance and then rerecorded after all the tracks have been taped.

With the rhythm instruments—drums and bass—there are two alternatives: (1) Record them at the same time, or (2) record them separately. Recording them at the same time is no problem if the bass is going direct. If it is not, the bass amp and microphone must be isolated to reduce leakage, even if the drums are in a booth. The advan-

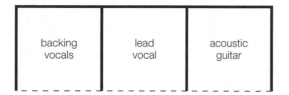

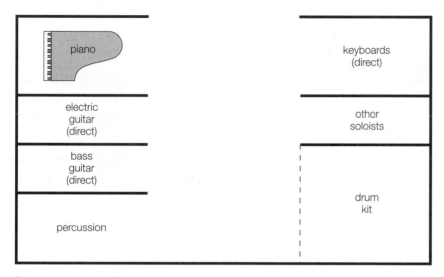

b

Table 13-1 Advantages and disadvantages of overdubbing

Advantages	Disadvantages
Possible to tape various voicings separately and at different times	Overall creative interaction and spontaneity among ensemble members is lost
Facilitates a greater degree of sound control over each track	Performance can be mechanical and uninspired
Allows a few performers to do the work of many	An ensemble's studio sound may be noticeably different from its concert sound
Alleviates the need to have all voicings ready at the same time	Sonic differences in acoustics or equipment, or both, between studios may be perceptible if the recording is taped in more than one studio
Allows the various elements in a recording to be taped at different studios	The increased number of tape passes wears the tape faster
	Usually more expensive

tage in playing together is that it usually produces a more cohesive, stable rhythm track. It is difficult to maintain a consistent beat alone or for an extended period of time. Without the foundation of a good rhythm track, the rest of the recording will be tenuous, at best.

If drums and bass are recorded separately, drums are usually recorded first, sometimes using a click track to help timing. A **click track** plays the appropriate rhythm(s) from the sound of a metronome or drum machine (which is less boring than a metronome) recorded on one of the available tape tracks or fed live. The sound is routed to the performer's headphones through the foldback system. If the click track takes up a needed track, it is erased after the basic rhythm tracks are recorded.

A click track is also essential when the basic rhythm instruments do not come in until after the music has begun, when the beat is not well defined, or when a music track is synchronized to rigidly timed material such as a commercial jingle or a motion picture.

Sometimes, a drummer provides the click track by hitting the drum sticks together. This technique serves well in providing the tempo and lead-in just before the musicians begin playing, but it is difficult to maintain a precise rhythm if the drummer has to keep it up for very long.

From the standpoint of providing a more dependable beat and saving time, it is better to record drums and bass together. If they need to reference the rhythm part to a lead part, let a lead instrument or the vocalist accompany the rhythm instruments. This is accomplished by miking, isolating, and then feeding the accompaniment through the foldback system. This way, the accompaniment is not recorded.

Once the drums and bass have been miked, it is time to test the sound and get levels. Let's assume the drum mics are on the bass drum, each tom-tom, the snare, hi hat, and above each of the two overhead cymbals. To eliminate leakage, the electric bass will go direct.

Start with the bass drum sound because it is the foundation of the overall drum sound, and its pitch influences the relative pitches of the other drums. Then proceed to the toms, snare, hi hat, and overheads. As each drum sound is shaped, blend it with the previously shaped drum sounds to make sure they work together. A good drum sound begins with (1) getting each component to sound acceptable and (2) blending all the components as a unit.

As the drums are blended, additional sonic adjustments to individual components may be necessary. The final result may be a drum or two that does not sound satisfactory by itself but blends well with the rest of the set.

Many producers like the bass drum pitched just above and working with the bass. The important thing is to make sure the two instruments do not mask each other or muddy the sound. Each must be clearly defined even though they have many of the same frequencies in common.

The electric bass is often compressed to smooth the variations in attack and tighten the sound. If the instrument has bass and treble controls, the bass is usually reduced and the treble increased to keep the lower frequencies from swallowing the overall sound of the instrument, in particular, and the low end of the recording, in general.

Anticipating the Mixdown

Although the mixdown (see Chapter 15) is done after recording, you cannot plan a recording session until you have some idea about the objectives of the mix. One of the most important elements to plan in advance is the positioning of the voicings in the stereo field. For example, if a piano is to be stereo, the lower frequencies must be recorded on one track and the higher frequencies on another, or if two mics are placed along the bridge–rail axis, each must be recorded on a separate track. Recording an instrument on one track makes it difficult to spread the image across the stereo field. An instrument can be placed at any position in the stereo, 3-D, or surround-sound field by panning, but its image is still monaural.

Placing two different sound sources on the same track makes it impossible to separate them later in a stereo field. If an electric guitar is going direct and its amp is miked, the signals should be recorded on different tracks if there is any thought of panning them in the stereo field or dispensing with one of them during mixdown.

Sometimes, the very highest or lowest frequencies of a particular instrument are important to a recording. If they are not captured during taping, the information will not be available for the mix.

Signal Processing During Recording

Anticipating the mixdown during recording raises an important question: How much signal processing—EQ, compression, reverb, and so on—should be used during recording? There is no one reply that satisfies all producers or addresses all conditions. The best answers are (1) leave the tracks as dry as possible for the mix, (2) work only from knowledge and experience, and (3) do not do anything during recording that cannot be undone in the mixdown. Once the musicians leave the studio, you are "stuck" with whatever is on the tape.

Once recorded, most signal processing cannot be "unrecorded." Even with EQ, taking out what you put in still changes the sound, however slightly. For example, if a signal is boosted 4 dB at 1,000 Hz, the EQ can be neutralized by attenuating 4 dB at the same frequency. However, noise has been added by passing the signal through an electronic device twice. That said, and so long as you know what you are doing, there may be occasions when EQ is necessary during recording. If there is obvious low-end rumble or high-end hiss that is doing the sound no good, roll it off. If a sound is unpleasant and nothing can be done with the instrument, player, microphone, or mic position to improve it, EQ may be the last resort.

Compressing the electric bass during recording is a standard procedure. Yet, again, if it is not done well, it creates problems in the mixdown.

If a vocalist has difficulty controlling dynamic range and riding gain is difficult, try to avoid limiting. One approach is to record the vocal on two tracks with one track 10 dB down. Then if there is overload or a problem with the noise floor in quiet passages, the two tracks can be intercut in the mixdown.

Once reverb has been recorded, it cannot be removed. That restriction also applies for delay, phase, and flanging. But these effects can be recorded on a separate track providing a wet effects track and a dry main track, though be sure that the main track and the effects track are in phase.

Musicians may insist that an effect, such as reverb, must be heard during recording to get a better idea of the actual sound in a more realistic context. In-line consoles allow you to feed effects through the foldback system without their being recorded (see Chapter 5). If this is not possible, routing effects from the input system to foldback, by patching, usually works. It is worth noting that effects may mask pitch and other problems, which may be an advantage or disadvantage.

Mixing During Recording (Premixing)

It is not always possible to assign one voicing per track, particularly with drums. For example, suppose you had 13 voicings and an eight-track tape recorder. If each voicing requires its own track, as it usually does, you have to do a mix of certain voicings during recording. Such predicaments are not uncommon even with 16- and 24-track recordings. There have been occasions when 32 and 48 tracks have not been enough.

Assume the 13 voicings include bass drum, low and medium tom-toms, snare, hi hat, two overhead cymbals, bass, lead guitar, rhythm guitar, keyboard, lead vocal, and backup vocal. Feed the drums through six separate console channels—one each for the bass drum, tom-toms, snare, and hi hat, and two for the overhead cymbals—and mix them live to two tracks of the eight-track ATR, assuming stereo drums.

The drum mix to two tracks would be handled in the following way. Each drum mic is assigned to a separate channel and delegated to one or both of the two drum tracks. The bass drum mic would be delegated to both drum tracks because the bass drum is usually positioned at the center of the drum set. The tom-toms could also be delegated to both drum tracks but panned to the left (or right) depending on their desired position in the aural frame. The snare and hi hat are also delegated to both tracks but could be panned to the opposite side of the tom-toms to balance the overall drum sound. The mics above each overhead cymbal pick up not only the left and right cymbal sound but also sounds from the left and right sides of the drum set. To help create a wider stereo perspective, one overhead cymbal mic is delegated entirely to one drum track and the other overhead cymbal mic is delegated entirely to the other (see 13-3 and 13-4).

A **live mix** can be tricky, so you have to know what you are doing. As noted earlier, once the musicians leave the studio, it is too late to change what is on the tape; unlike the other tracks, the drum tracks are already in place.

Some recordists who are confident in what they do go so far as to *rough mix* as they complete each segment during recording. They feel that their perspective is fresher and creativity more spontaneous, not having been dimmed by days or weeks between recording and mixdown. One way to facilitate this approach is to determine what kind of musical balances the performers are able to do themselves by "self-mixing." The key to effective self-mixing is good musicians playing good instruments.

Bouncing Tracks

Instead of doing a live mix at the console, some producers prefer to assign each channel to a separate track, mix them afterward, and **bounce tracks**—combine them onto unused tracks.

In the example we used above, the drum tracks would actually be recorded onto six separate tracks of the eight-track ATR, say tracks 1 through 6. The six tracks would be mixed and then bounced to tracks 7 and 8. You combine them by (1) putting tracks 1 through 6 into Sel Sync, monitoring them from the record head;[*] (2) feeding each track to a separate channel at the console for balancing and mixing; (3) assigning and/or panning each channel to one or both of the open tracks; and (4) recording. Once the

---

[*]With state-of-the-art analog recorders there should be no discernible loss in sound quality in reproduction from the record head compared with the playback head. With older machines the playback quality of the record head is 2,000 to 5,000 Hz poorer than the quality from the playback head.

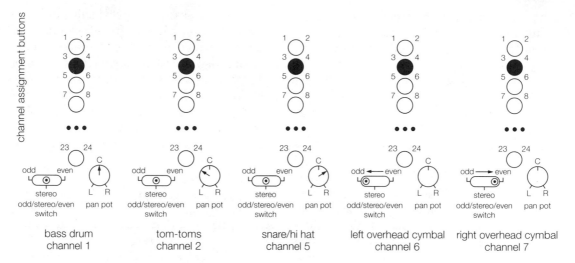

13-3 Using several channels to facilitate "live" mixing of drums, individually miked, to two channels. Here the bass drum is delegated to channels 3 and 4 and kept centered. The toms, also delegated to channels 3 and 4, are panned to the left. Snare and hi hat, delegated to channels 3 and 4, are panned right. The left drums and overhead cymbal are delegated to channel 3, and the right drums and overhead cymbal are delegated to channel 4.

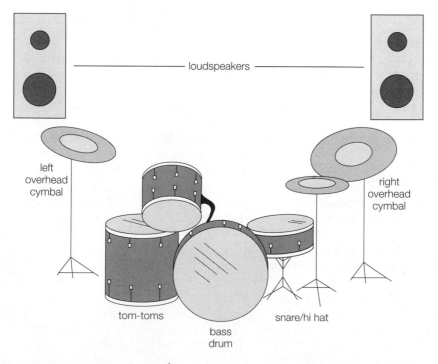

13-4 Spatial distribution of the live drum mix discussed in 13-3

mix is satisfactorily recorded onto tracks 7 and 8, tracks 1 through 6 can be erased and used for the bass, lead and rhythm guitars, keyboard, and vocals.

When you bounce tracks, if at all possible, try not use adjacent tracks for the transfer, as was done in the previous example. The separation between tracks of a multitrack tape recorder is not wide. If you put a track in "Record" that is next to one of the tracks playing back, it could result in the live record head picking up unwanted crosstalk from the adjacent playback track, especially if the signal level is high. Furthermore, if the live head is picking up sound across the head from the adjacent track and also internally via the normal recording process (that is, through the head), it may create a feedback loop and thus a squeal.

If you are using an analog four-track recorder and several bounces are necessary to record all the voicings, sound quality deteriorates with each bounce. To maintain as much sound quality as possible, (1) boost the high end before bouncing and (2) record the most important voicing or voicings with widest dynamic range and frequency response last. This is recommended even though, as in the case of the drums, it changes the recommended order of overdubbing parts.

Doubling Up on Tracks

Another way to handle the more-voicings-than-tracks problem is to double up—record two sound sources on one track. But this is not generally recommended. If two instruments have many of the same frequencies in common, equalizing one instrument will affect the sound of the other. Moreover, once two instruments are on the same track, they cannot be separately panned, faded, equalized, and so on.

Two sound sources are usually put on the same track only if their frequency ranges do not conflict, as in the case of a piccolo and a bass; if they are to occupy the same position in the aural frame; or if they play at different times. EQ must be changed for each or left alone. Also, when combining sound sources with separated frequency ranges, be careful of intermodulation distortion (see Chapter 9).

Overdubbing Techniques

You will recall that in overdubbing, the tape tracks already recorded are put into Sel Sync and the track to be recorded is put in "Record." All tracks feed through the console. To facilitate syncing, the levels of the previously recorded tracks are balanced with the level of the sound source being overdubbed and fed through the foldback system to the performer's headphones. This way the performer hears what has been and what is being recorded at the same time, balanced to taste. Regardless of the level balances preferred by the performer, in control room monitoring it is a good idea to maintain a higher level on the track being recorded than on the playback tracks. This enables closer scrutiny of the new material.

In overdubbing one sound source at a time, leakage is not a problem. Care should be taken, however, to ensure that sound from the headphones is not picked up by the microphone. Use headphones with cushions that fit tightly around the ears.

Another reason to be careful of the foldback level through headphones is the effect it could have on performance. Some performers like the sound level in the headphones to be loud, particularly with high-energy music. This could have a detrimental effect on the intensity of the performance. As the loudness in the headphones increases, performers (without realizing it) have the tendency to "lay back," reducing their own output level. If you run into this problem, provide whatever foldback levels are wanted; but, after the playing begins, gradually reduce the loudness to a comfortable level. Usually, the energy of the performance will increase proportionately and the performer will be none the wiser. Loud foldback level also desensitizes hearing and hastens listening fatigue, if not hearing loss.

Some studios and performers prefer to fold back sound not through headphones but through a pair of small matched loudspeakers placed the same distance from the microphone so that the three form the points of an equilateral triangle. One loudspeaker is wired 180 degrees out of phase with the other. The signal fed to them should be mono. The mic, being "one-eared," will not hear the out-of-phase sound. The vocalist, being "two-eared," will hear the foldback mix (see 13-5). But make sure the mic is not moved.

If the part being overdubbed is not continuous, the musician must be quiet when not performing. During mixdown it is easier not to have to worry about opening and closing the pots to avoid unwanted sound, especially if more than one voicing has been overdubbed. If an extraneous sound should occur, erase it at the earliest opportunity. It is time-consuming and unnerving to deal with these noises during the mixdown.

The section or sections of music being overdubbed can be recorded over and over until the performance is correct. If a good take is recorded but a better one is possible, keep the good take and use another track for the new attempt. If enough tracks are available and a few takes are recorded, the best overall performance may not be any particular take but portions of a few takes. Therefore, a composite track can be put

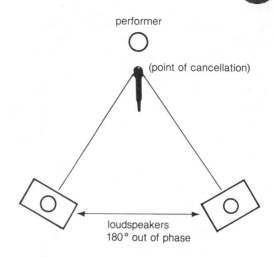

13-5 An alternative technique to feeding a foldback mix through headphones

together by bouncing the appropriate portions of the recorded tracks to a new track. To avoid high-frequency track-to-track oscillation, keep at least one track between the track you are recording from and the track you are recording to. After the composite track is approved, the overdubbed tracks can be bounced if you have room or erased and reused for other voicings.

It is usually not a good idea to stop for a mistake if a performer—especially a vocalist—is well into a take. It is unnerving and breaks concentration, making it difficult to start up again with the same emotion and intensity. If the pressure of making mistakes is adversely affecting performance, let the musician loosen up by rehearsing more. If you think the rehearsals sound good, tape one without letting the performer know. You may get a take.

Punching In

If something goes wrong during a take and there is no extra track to try recording again, or there is not enough time, or another take would not improve the overall performance, then rerecording just the sub-par section is possible by using the technique known as *punching in*. **Punching in** makes it possible to insert material into a recording by rolling the tape recorder in the playback mode and putting it in the record mode at the insert point. Because punching in is an editing technique, it is discussed in Chapter 14.

Recording Ambience

Even with the many fine artificial reverberation devices available today, there is still no substitute for the sound of natural acoustics. Many producers try to add natural acoustics to overdubbed recordings by placing one or a few microphones several feet above and away from a sound source and taping just the ambience on a separate track or tracks. In the mix the desired amount of ambience is blended into individual voicings or into the overall mix without affecting those tracks you wish to keep dry for other purposes. Of course, in order to record ambience in this way studio acoustics must enable it.

Slating

It is important to keep not only written or disk-encoded records in a recording/mixdown session but certain oral records as well. Such information as the name of the group, song, take number, and lead-in cue beat should be recorded or *slated* on the tape. Most recording consoles have a control in the talkback system that feeds slating information to the performers' headphones and the tape recorder simultaneously. In this

way a producer is able to keep an oral record of how many takes were recorded and which is which. Other slate information is usually kept in the written notes or on a computer disk (see Table 13-2).

Cues When Recording

Each time a recording is made, the producer or engineer should give similar spoken cues to studio and control room personnel so that everyone knows when to stand, be quiet, and record. Following is an example of one procedure:

ENGINEER TO OPERATORS: "Stand by please. Roll tape and record."

OPERATOR TO ENGINEER: "Rolling and recording."

ENGINEER INTO TALKBACK/SLATE: " 'Send in the Clowns,' Mardi Gras, take 3."

The take number is the cue to the musicians to begin playing when they are ready.

Recording Tones

A recording session usually takes several hours; very often it takes several days. Although equipment, like any "instrument," should be fine-tuned before each session, with use over a long period of time it can "go out." Moreover, sometimes the people who do the mixdown may not have been involved in the recording, or the mixdown may be done in a different studio. To ensure that the console(s) and tape recorders being used throughout recording and mixdown are aligned with one another, and to provide the means with which to reset original levels, reference tones are recorded on the multitrack master. (Tones are recorded on sub-

Table 13-2 Slate information usually kept in the production notebook

Abbreviation	Explanation
HS (head slate)	The voice announcement recorded at the beginning of the tape. On the tape itself it is preceded or followed by a low-frequency tone so that on an analog recorder in "Fast Forward" the audible beeps indicate the beginning of a take.
FS (false start)	The take started but for some reason had to stop before it got under way.
LFS (long false start)	The take was a good way through before it had to stop.
INC (incomplete)	The take had almost reached the end when it had to stop.
C (complete take)	
PB (play back)	The take(s) played back to the producer or client.
M (master)	The take chosen by the producer or client.
TS (tail slate)	A slate recorded after a take.
EOT (end of tape)	The point at which not enough tape is left for another take.
NS (no slate)	No slate was recorded before or after the take.

sequent masters as well—see Chapter 16.)

Reference tones are pure tones (sine waves) generated by an oscillator (see Chapter 5) and recorded at 0 VU (100 percent of modulation). It is usually best to record three tones: a low-frequency tone (50 or 100 Hz), a midrange tone (1,000 Hz is standard), and a high-frequency tone (10,000, 12,000, or 15,000 Hz, whichever is preferred). Some recordists use only the 1,000-Hz tone. If you use Dolby SR noise reduction, add the tone generated by the Dolby unit. During playback use the tone to align the tape recorder with the Dolby unit. Do not encode the original three tones with noise reduction.

Putting tones on digital tape may seem to have little point because it either plays or it does not play. But tones are necessary. Digital ATRs have different input sensitivities that make it important to feed them correct levels. Too much level produces unpleasant sound breakup. Too little level produces noise and distortion.

There is no special length of time for a calibration tone. Generally, 20 seconds for each is adequate.

Troubleshooting

A regular schedule of preventative maintenance and cleaning and testing the equipment before a session begins go a long way in helping the session go smoothly, at least technically. But, then, there is Murphy. No matter how much you try to thwart him, he often manages to exercise his will anyway. Therefore, should the need arise, be prepared to troubleshoot technical problems to avoid calling in the cavalry and holding up the session (see Table 13-3). Know the equipment and the signal flow well enough to locate a problem, and either take care of it or work around it. When the trouble is not an equipment malfunction, it is usually an "operator problem."

Table 13-3   Troubleshooting technical problems

Example One:

During a mixdown session, distortion is heard from the right-hand near-field monitor.

Suspects:	Tape machine, console, power amp, and loudspeaker.
Test #1:	Cross-patch the console's left-hand monitor output with the right-channel control room amp.
Result:	Distortion moves to the left near-field monitor.
Conclusion:	Problem is with tape machine or console.
Test #2:	All channel modules assigned with equal L/R panning are turned off, one at a time.
Results:	All tracks are okay except some drum and guitar tracks.
Conclusion:	Problem lies with kick, snare, and tom drum tracks, plus bass and guitar overdub, and finally traced to guitar track.
Test #3:	Solo the guitar track.
Result:	No change in distortion.
Conclusion:	Problem lies in the input module, not the monitor section.
Test #4:	Guitar track is routed to another channel, and back to the suspect channel via the pre-EQ insert point.
Result:	No distortion is heard.
Conclusion:	Faulty preamp section; probably op-amp failure.

Example Two:

After a keyboard overdub, you hear no output from the analog 16-track during replay. Both the 16-track and the console's meters are moving as expected, meaning that we do indeed have a signal on tape, but it's not reaching the mixer.

Suspects:	Tape machine and noise-reduction unit and/or interconnections.
Test #1:	Bypass the corresponding noise-reduction module.
Result:	An encoded signal is heard through the console.
Conclusion:	Faulty noise reduction card.

(continued next page)

Table 13-3 (*continued*) Troubleshooting technical problems

Example Three:

Intermittent distortion while mixing various output tracks from digital workstation. Just about everything in the control room, including effects units, is being routed through the console.

Suspects:	Virtually everything!
Test #1:	Determine if the problem is in the left, right, or center of the soundfield.
Result:	The noise is smack in the middle of the stereo image and heard over both monitors.
Conclusion:	Problem is affecting both left and right outputs.
Test #2:	Mute the output from any and all channel modules that are panned hard left or hard right.
Results:	Problem is isolated to several drum, sampled vocal, and solo MIDI keyboard tracks, plus their respective effects sends.
Conclusion:	By muting combinations of inputs, we determine that the problem can be narrowed to a keyboard track and its digital reverb.
Test #3:	Remove the send signal to the reverb unit.
Result:	Distortion ceases.
Conclusion:	Problem might be with effects unit, patch cords, the master effects send, or the channel auxiliary send section.
Test #4:	The reverb is sourced from another channel.
Result:	No distortion is heard.
Conclusion:	Reverb unit and master effects send are okay; fault is probably within console input module.
Test #5:	Having reconnected the reverb to the suspected channel module, you tap lightly on the corresponding effects send.
Result:	Intermittent distortion produced by module.
Conclusion:	Problem lies within module's aux-send section.

Because there are dozens of combinations of faults and possible diagnoses when equipment malfunctions, they are difficult to inventory in a manageable, coherent list. To provide some idea about what to do when there is an equipment malfunction, consider the following and also refer to Table 13-3 on pages 298 and 299.[*]

- Isolating problems. Divide a large system into smaller subunits to determine if the problem is confined to a specific area. A problem is easier to deal with by isolating it to one section of the hardware.

- Microphones. With a capacitor mic make sure the phantom power is turned on or the batteries are okay. Check the cable connection at both ends. If the problem is intermittent, clean the connector with isopropyl alcohol. Check the microphone for unseen damage resulting from mishandling or careless storage. Listen for rattles from loose internal parts, missing screws, or loose connectors.

- Mixing consoles. Make sure the correct mic/line input has been selected; the channel gain and channel output set correctly; the fader level set at a reasonable level; and the EQ switched in or out. Check the input on another channel and/or group output. If there is a crackle, pop, or click at the touch of a control, it may be due to dirt, smoke particles, or oxidation, partic-

ularly with seldom-used controls. It is a good idea to routinely operate all console controls for extraneous noise. Clean surface corrosion from each patch cord and dust from each jack in the patch bay.

- Effects units. Check connections and connectors, particularly in interfacing balanced and unbalanced equipment. Are input and output gains set correctly? Use the Bypass mode to see if the problem disappears.

- Multitrack recorders. Are the console (or workstation) outputs connected to the correct inputs? Switch from input/source to output/tape to determine if the problem is confined to the record or playback sections. If the meters are moving, but there is no signal at the output connector, it could be a fault in the output amplifier. Tape recorders also suffer from environmental pollution, as well as from oxide buildup. Regular cleaning is essential, as is routine demagnetizing of the heads.

- Monitor amps and speakers. If only one channel is operating, try reversing the inputs to the power amplifier. If the fault remains, it is the amp and/or speaker. If it moves, then there is a problem in the console's monitor output. Swapping the speaker leads should reveal if the amplifier or speaker cabinet is the culprit.[**]

---

[*]From "A Short Course in Maintenance," by Mel Lambert, *MIX Magazine*, October 1993, p. 151. Reprinted with permission, Act III Publications.

[**]Lambert, pp. 148–154.

PART

5

POSTPRODUCTION

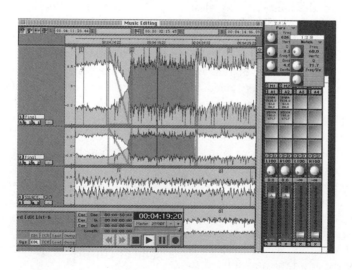

Editing

Postproduction is the last stage in the production process, when the recorded tracks are shaped, combined, and put into their final form. Postproduction increases flexibility in decision making not only during recording but afterward as well. This flexibility is made possible in no small measure by editing.

Generally, there are a number of reasons for editing. Program segments may need to be rearranged, shortened, or cut out altogether. Unwanted noises and mistakes can be deleted. A part can be recorded several times and the best takes, or portions of each take, chosen to make up the composite final version. Parts of lyrics can be transposed. An instrumental line can be restructured.

Until recently, tape editing was a linear process. In **linear editing** recorded material is edited successively: One section at a time is cut from one part of a tape and spliced to another part, or taped material is electronically transferred from one tape to another. The material may be edited sequentially or inserted at a particular point in the tape. In either case, final assembly is sequential.

Since the development of nonlinear editing in the early 1980s, it is now possible to edit recordings using the formidable power of data storage and processing techniques.

Nonlinear editing is a digital process that allows you to assemble disk-based material in or out of sequence, take it from any part of a recording, and place it in any other part of the recording at the touch of a few buttons. It is possible to audition the edit at any stage in the transfer and also alter its sonic characteristics because of the digital signal processing (DSP) capability that is incorporated into most nonlinear editing systems. In addition, the original segment can be restored to its former position quickly and seamlessly.

Linear Editing

The two methods used in linear sound editing are (1) **cut-and-splice editing** and (2) **electronic editing**—using one tape and inserting—punching in—material or transferring material from one tape to another.

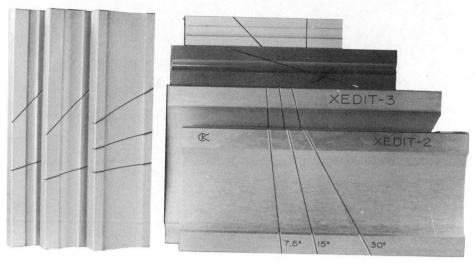

14-1 Various cutting angles on ¼-, ½-, 1-, and 2-inch splicing blocks

Cutting and Splicing
Open-Reel Analog Audiotape

The cut-and-splice method is an economical way of editing ¼-inch mono and stereo audiotape recordings. Multitrack tape is not edited that way because there is no way to edit one track without cutting into the other tracks.

Equipment

For cutting and splicing audiotape, you need the following items: metal block (see 14-1); single-edge razor blade that should be replaced often during lengthy editing sessions so that it cannot become magnetized; marking pen or pencil with a soft tip that does not flake; **splicing tape**, made specially for audiotape, that comes in rolls for use with a dispenser, or in precut tabs (see 14-2); extra empty reels; a flat, clean surface; a cue sheet to keep a record of the edits made; and **leader tape**.

Leader tape is nonmagnetic plastic or paper tape used for threading, cueing, and,

14-2 Precut splicing tab. With this type, pulling the dark end of the plastic cover lifts the splicing tape from the tab sheet. Once the splicing tape is pressed onto the recording tape, thus completing the edit, pulling the transparent end of the plastic cover separates it from the splicing tape.

sometimes, timing (see 14-3). When spliced between segments of recording tape, it provides an easy visual reference that facilitates spooling quickly to a desired cut (see 14-4). Leader tape is also spliced to both ends of recording tape to preserve these vulnerable points.

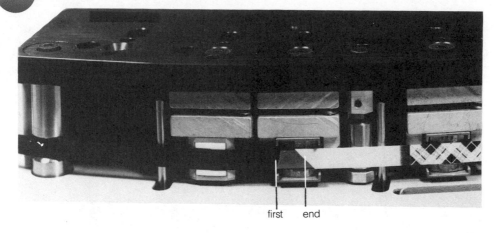

first   end

a

1 second at 7 ½ ips

b

14-3 Leader tape.   (*a*) **Leader tape serves as a visual reference to the beginning of a sound.** Providing the sound is there, it makes cueing a tape easier and faster.   (*b*) **Plastic leader tape can also be used for timing.**   The arrows indicate the direction of tape travel.

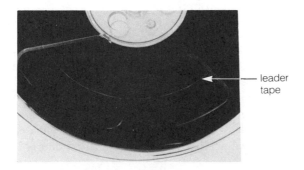

leader
tape

14-4 Light-colored leader tape visible between the tape segments

As mentioned, leader tape is available in both plastic and paper. Paper is used mainly when extremely high sound quality is vital because, unlike plastic leader tape, paper tape does not build up static electricity when it is wound excessively. Static electricity can affect magnetically encoded information if it builds to strong enough proportions. A problem with paper leader tape, however, is that it tears easily.

Leader tape also comes in various colors. Studios often use a certain colored leader tape at the head of a reel, another color at the tail of the reel, and still other colors to indicate the beginning and end of songs within a reel (see Chapter 16).

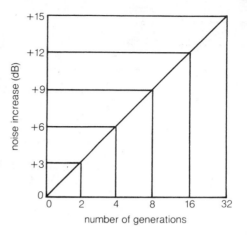

14-5 The effect that dubbing analog recordings has on sound quality

Basic Procedures

Before cutting any tape, make a duplicate—called a *dub*—of the original or master tape. Store the master, tails out, in a safe place, and use the dubbed tape for cutting and splicing. Then, if you make any serious mistakes in cutting, you can make another dub from the master. Of course, a dub is second-generation and, with analog tape, loses something in sound quality (see 14-5). But by dubbing with high-quality, well-maintained equipment, you will find the loss in sound quality is minimal and the trade-off—a slight loss in response for the sure safety of the original material—is worth it.

Master tape should not be used in electronic editing either. Although electronic editing does not require physically cutting the tape, it may necessitate running it across the tape heads over and over again. Each pass wears the magnetic coating. Therefore, the more passes a tape makes, the more the quality of sound is degraded.

Record the master tape at, at least, 15 ips; if you cannot, then dub it at that speed. The faster a tape travels across the heads, the more spread out the sound is and the

easier it is to edit (see 14-6). Analog sound quality is better at faster speeds, too. (Although at 30 ips, the sound on high-quality tape recorded on a high-quality recorder can be too crisp.)

Let's go through the basic procedures, step-by-step, for making a simple edit, cut, and splice. After a gentle chord ending a verse and before the chorus begins there is a pop in the recording as a result of someone accidentally hitting a microphone. The obvious editing task is to remove the pop. Once you decide what to edit, the next steps are to (1) determine exactly where the edit points will be and (2) locate those points on the recording tape.

For reasons that will be explained later, the edit points should fall after the decay of the chord ending the verse and just before the chorus begins (see 14-7). Once the edit points are chosen, you are ready to proceed with the cutting and splicing (see 14-8 through 14-19).

Splicing tape properly is important. Figure 14-20 contains graphic examples of defective splices commonly encountered.

a recording at 3¾ ips

a r e c o r d i n g a t 7. ½ i p s

a   r e c o r d i n g   a t   1 5   i p s

14-6 Representation of sound spread on tape at three different speeds. The faster the tape recorder speed, the more spread out the sound on the tape and the easier to edit.

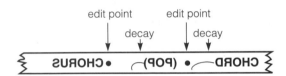

14-7 Sounds to be cut and spliced with edit points indicated

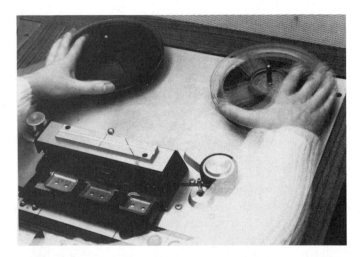

14-8 Locating the first edit point. After the tape has been threaded and wound close to the edit point, put the tape recorder in "Stop." In "Stop" (some machines may have a pause, cue, or edit button) the playback head is "live." This allows you to hear what is on the tape and manually control the tape speed as you locate the precise edit point. You are making the initial cut after the decay of the chord. With the edit point at the playback head, put your left hand on the feed reel and your right hand on the take-up reel. Then rock the tape back and forth until you hear exactly where the decay of the chord ends. Many tape recorders have a manual control to facilitate rocking the tape (see 6-6).

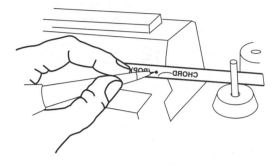

14-9 **Marking the first edit point.** When you locate the edit point, mark it with a marking pen or pencil. Make sure the mark is visible.

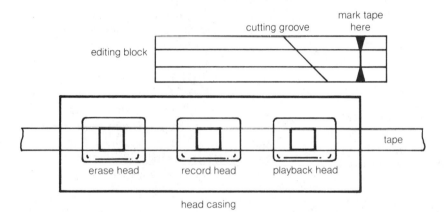

14-10 **Another way to mark the editing point.** You saw in 14-9 one way to mark tape—at the playback head. Unless you are highly skilled, this technique could result in the head being nudged out of alignment or, worse, damaged. A safer marking procedure is to establish a measured point close to the playback head and mark the tape there.

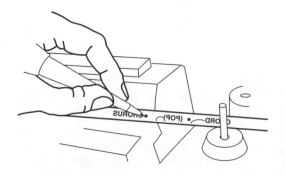

14-11 **Marking the second edit point.** With the first edit marked, wind the tape to the second edit point and rock it until you locate the point just before you hear the very first sound in the chorus. After locating the second edit point, mark it. Now you are ready to cut the tape.

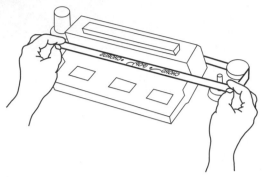

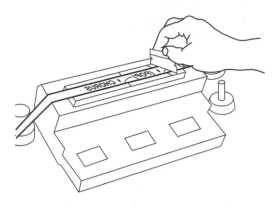

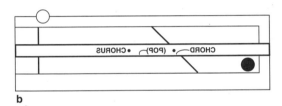

14-12 Using the cutting block. (*a*) Gently lift the tape from the playback head, and (*b*) place it in the channel of the cutting block with the first edit point on the diagonal groove.

14-13 Cutting the tape. Using a razor blade, cut the tape diagonally, drawing the razor angled through the slot without bending the tape ends into the cutting groove. A diagonal cut gives the sound a split second to become established in our hearing. A vertical (90-degree) cut hits the playback head all at once, and we sometimes hear the abrupt change from one edit to another as a pop, click, or beep. Also, the diagonal cut exposes a longer tape edge than a 90-degree cut, thereby ensuring a stronger splice.

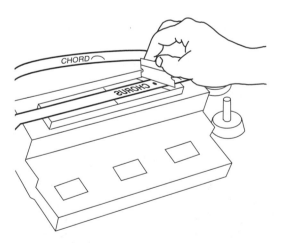

14-14 Making the second cut. Gently remove the cut tape from the channel of the cutting block, find the second edit point, place the tape back in the channel over the diagonal groove, and cut on the mark.

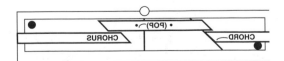

14-15 Cuts completed. Now you are ready to splice the two edits together.

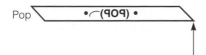

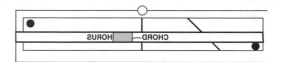

14-16 Marking fragments. Until you are certain that the splice has been made successfully, it is a good idea to save the deleted tape, note what is on it, and put an arrow on the tab to indicate the head end.

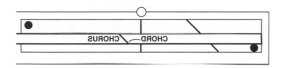

14-17 Joining the tape ends. Take the two tape ends and butt them together. Make sure that there is no overlap or space between them.

14-18 Splicing. Take a piece of splicing tape roughly ½-inch long, and place it so that ¼ inch covers each tape end. Do not use less than ½ inch of splicing tape or the splice may break. Using your finger or a blunt instrument, press the splicing tape firmly onto the recording tape to ensure a strong splice. Make sure that no white "bubbles" remain on the splicing tape; they indicate that the splicing tape is not bonded firmly to the recording tape. Gently remove the tape from the cutting block and play it to check the edit.

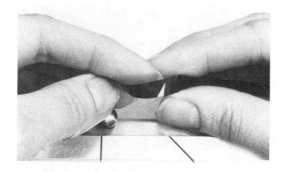

14-19 Undoing a splice. If you need to undo a splice, grasp each end of the splice point with the magnetic side of the tape facing you, form a small loop, and work the tape back and forth until one side of the splice begins to loosen. Then peel away the recording tape. Do not reuse the splicing tape.

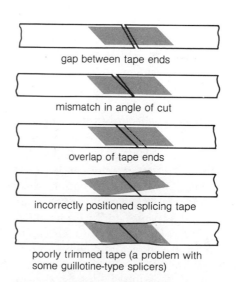

gap between tape ends

mismatch in angle of cut

overlap of tape ends

incorrectly positioned splicing tape

poorly trimmed tape (a problem with some guillotine-type splicers)

14-20 Common splicing defects

Cutting and Splicing Open-Reel Digital Audiotape

Cutting and splicing digital audiotape is possible if the digital ATR is stationary head and designed for it. Rocking a tape back and forth across the playback head to listen for the edit point is not possible with a digital signal because the decoding system does not function at so slow a tape speed. Therefore, either an analog head or dedicated circuitry must be built in. Also, the flow of coding data is momentarily disrupted, creating a perceptible noise at the edit point. To neutralize this problem, the digital ATR effects an electronic crossfade at the edit point, interpolating the average level of the included signals to create a smooth, noiseless transition. Length of crossfade varies with the digital format: DASH is 10 milliseconds, PRODIGI is 2.5 milliseconds.

The angle of edit on digital tape should be 90 degrees due to the high density of encoded information. Because digital ATRs use extensive error detection, tape and system irregularities resulting from a 90-degree cut are usually corrected.

Digital tape must be handled with greater care than analog tape because it is thinner and packs high-density information that can be easily sullied. Keep handling to a minimum, and use white cotton gloves and splicers specially designed for use with digital audiotape (see 14-21).

Cut-and-splice editing of digital tape has a major advantage over electronic editing—it is less expensive. Unless you are punching in, electronic editing requires at least two digital ATRs, whereas the cut-and-splice method is accomplished with one machine. Considering the cost of stationary head digital ATRs, this is no small advantage. That said, with improved technology in electronic editing systems, R-DAT editors, and the emergence of hard-disk editing, cut-and-splice editing is going the way of the Long Playing (LP) record.

Electronic Editing of Audiotape

Electronic editing of audiotape can be accomplished using one or two tape recorders. When it is necessary only to insert material by punching in, one tape recorder will do. In this case, an **insert edit** replaces a particular segment on a tape without altering the other recorded material. This can also be accomplished using two recorders. But an **assemble edit**, dubbing each program segment from a master to a slave tape in sequential order, requires two machines.

Manually Controlled Electronic Editing Using One Tape Recorder

In Chapter 13 we noted that if something goes wrong during a take and there is no extra track to try recording again, or there is not enough time, or another take would not improve the overall performance, then rerecording just the subpar section is possible by insert editing, or punching in. Because multitrack tape is usually used in the recording session, conventional cut-and-splice editing is not possible; there is no way to cut into any portion of any track without cutting into the other tracks as well. Today's multitrack recorders have electronic means of punching in—rerecording any portion of any track without affecting the rest of the recording.

You punch in by putting the recorded tracks into sel sync; playing them back to the performer(s) through headphones; and, when it is time to rerecord over the defective portion of a track, switching that track to Record. After the appropriate section has been rerecorded, take the track out of Record either by stopping the machine or by switching the track back into sel sync or

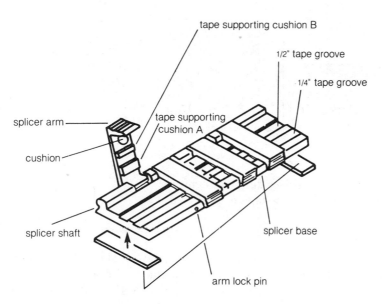

tape supporting cushion B

1/2" tape groove

1/4" tape groove

splicer arm

tape supporting cushion A

cushion

splicer shaft

splicer base

arm lock pin

14-21 Digital tape splicer

Play. Punching in is a clean way to edit electronically. It is quick and usually leaves no extraneous sound pulses on the tape. It does require perfect timing, however, or some of the good material could also be erased. Levels must match between punched-in and retained material.

Sometimes, musical accents or vocal harmonies are punched in here and there on an open track. For convenience some recordists start in Record at the beginning of the tape and let it play through that way, letting the musicians handle the cues. If new analog tape is being used, this technique can add about 3 dB of noise to the recording. Although it requires more work, it is better to punch in and out at the appropriate times during this type of overdubbing or to use the fader.

Of course, punching in can be used just to erase material. But if the material is brief, such as a click or pop, timing and reflexes must be precise and coordinated to avoid erasing wanted material.

Insert editing is possible on any ATR so long as the punching in can be done noiselessly. Be wary of machines that transmit a pulse to the tape when the Record button is activated.

Manually Controlled Electronic Editing Using Two Tape Recorders

With electronic editing using two ATRs, the tape recorder you dub from—called the **master**—contains the original material and, when the recorders are synchronized, also controls the tape recorder you are dubbing to—called the **slave** (see 14-22). The simplest and least reliable way to accomplish electronic editing of audiotape is by manual control.

Manually controlled electronic editing involves cueing the edit points, putting the master ATR into Play, putting the slave ATR into Record, and starting and stopping both machines at the right time, by hand. If the slave tape recorder is miscued or stopped

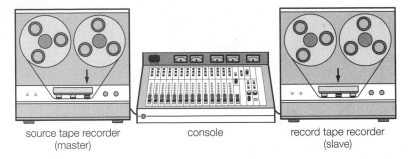

source tape recorder (master)   console   record tape recorder (slave)

14-22 Electronic editing. This method involves dubbing segments from the master to the slave in proper order. The tape-to-tape feed is usually done through a mixer or console.

too early or too late, the edit may be dubbed in at the wrong place or essential program material may be erased.

The procedure is not complicated, but unless the two tape recorders run synchronously, which is unlikely even with the best machines, especially for several minutes, it is difficult to do precise dubbing. There are also four other factors to consider: that the edit points are far enough apart with little or no audible background so the sounds do not wow in; the tape recorders reach full speed quickly; the Start and Record buttons do not transmit clicking sounds onto the tape when they are activated; the operator's reflexes are quick enough. Even if person and machine work well together, it is difficult to make tight, precise electronic edits manually. These problems have been worked out with the development of edit controllers, tape synchronizers, time code, and hard disk editors.

Automatically Controlled Electronic Editing

Devices—generally called *edit controllers* (also called *edit programmers*)—allow you to automatically control electronic editing

systems and functions. The edit controller is connected to the transports of the master and slave tape recorders, either as a separate unit or in a self-contained housing (see 14-23 and 14-24).

Although edit controllers vary widely in performance features. most are capable of the same basic operations. By putting the appropriate command pulses on a track of audiotape, the edit controller directs (1) the operations of the master and slave machines, (2) the place where the edit points punch in and out, (3) the preroll starting point, and (4) preroll, forward, and reverse speeds. It also enables assemble and insert edits.

Encoding with Time Code Systems

Time code systems have three main advantages.

1. Time reference is precise; each frame has its own time code address.

2. Tapes may be interchanged between other similar time code systems because the code is recorded on the tape.

3. Two or more tape recorders and digital sequencers may be synchronized.

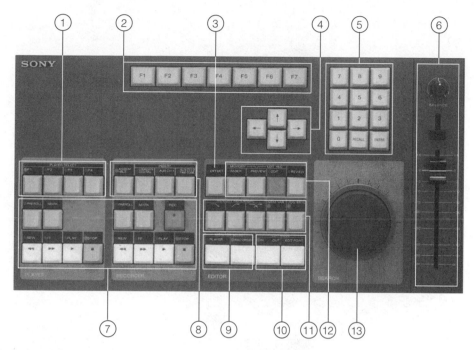

(1) **Player Select keys**
Select the player to be used from the four players connected to the editor

(2) **Function keys**
Bring up the menu programs on the display. When the main display is shown, these keys correspond to the functions shown at the bottom of the display.

(3) **Offset key**
Provides time offset to the editing point via the search dial

(4) **Cursor keys**
Move the cursor on the display

(5) **Numeric keys**
Used to enter numeric values when setting user-programmable parameters

(6) **Balance/Fader controls**
Adjust the output level and channel balance of the player

(7) **Tape Control keys**
Control tape transport functions of the recorder and the player. The MARK key enables presetting of the tape position for auto locate.

(8) **Edit Mode keys**
Allow selection of the editing mode

(9) **Monitor Select keys**
Select between the recorder and the player for the output to be monitored

(10) **Edit Point Set keys**
Used to set or modify the edit points

(11) **Memory Rehearsal keys**
Enable selection of the memory rehearsal mode and speed

(12) **Execute keys**
Execute previewing, automatic editing, and reviewing

(13) **Search dial**
Provides variable speed search

14-23 Digital audio editor synchronizer. This unit can control up to four digital audiotape recorders—R-DAT, S-DAT, or both.

14-24 Edit controller in a self-contained R-DAT editing system

Three time code systems are used in encoding audiotape: SMPTE time code; the **IEC** (International Electrotechnical Commission) **standard**; and MIDI time code (MTC), which is converted to SMPTE time code.

SMPTE time code (pronounced "semp-ty"), also called **Longitudinal Time Code** (LTC), is a high-frequency electronic digital signal consisting of a stream of pulses produced by a time code generator. It is recorded along the length of a tape track in the same way a conventional audio track is recorded.

Time code was originally developed to make videotape editing more efficient; hence, its identifying code numbers are broken down into hours, minutes, seconds, and frames (see 14-25). (Videotape has roughly 30 frames to the second.) Each 1/30 of a second of audiotape or each frame of videotape is tagged with a unique identifying code number called a **time code address**. By decoding the time code address with a time code reader, an operator can select the appropriate code numbers that instruct tape recorders to locate a certain point and begin playing in sync from there.

Audiotape recorders with built-in time code generator and reader and a special time code head are readily available (see 6-6). Time code may be recorded during or after production.

The IEC (International Electrotechnical Commission) standard is the most recent addition to time codes. As the term suggests,

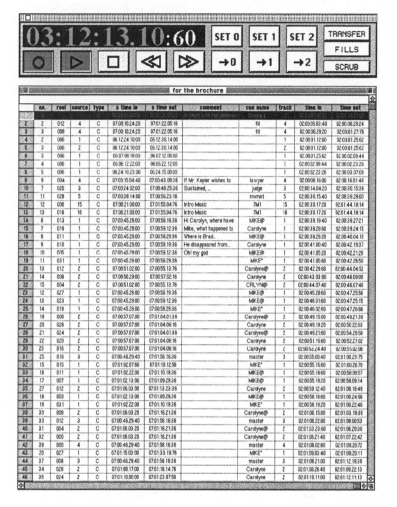

14-25 Example of an edit decision list

it is an attempt to standardize time coding. The IEC standard code is the time code system used in DAT recorders as agreed to by all manufacturers of DAT machines, thus ensuring compatibility among all DAT equipment.

The main difference between IEC DAT code and the other time codes is that the IEC code provides more flexibility in adjusting frame rates during playback. The IEC

time code DAT machines extract time code information and put it on tape without it being contained in the frame rate. This makes it possible to set the playback machine's output to whatever frame rate you want (see 7-11). If a playback machine is equipped with an Auto-Detect mode, it will automatically output the recorded time information at the same frame rate that the code came in.

MIDI time code (MTC) was incorporated into the MIDI Protocol in 1987 as a way to translate SMPTE time code into MIDI messages. SMPTE time code is an absolute timing reference that remains constant throughout a program. In MIDI recording, timing references are relative and vary with both tempo and tempo changes. Because most studios use SMPTE time code addresses (as opposed to beats in a musical bar) as references, trying to convert between the two timing systems to cue or trigger an event would be tedious and time-consuming. MTC allows MIDI-based devices to operate on the SMPTE timing reference independent of tempo. In MIDI devices that do not recognize MTC, integrating an MTC sequencer is necessary. Converting SMPTE to MIDI time code is straightforward: SMPTE comes in and MIDI time code goes out.

Drop Frame and Nondrop Frame

SMPTE time code generators operate in one of two modes: Drop Frame and Nondrop Frame. Color television's frame rate is not exactly 30 frames per second. Over the length of an hour, for instance, the SMPTE code would be off a little more than 3 seconds compared to real or running time. To make up for this discrepancy, the Drop Frame mode automatically drops two frames every minute except for the tenth minute. Therefore, it agrees with actual clock time.

Drop Frame code is necessary when precise timing is critical and in synchronizing audio to video. But in most other production, Nondrop Frame code is used because it is easier to work with. It is a point worth remembering that the two modes are incompatible. Tapes used in any given production must employ one mode or the other.

Using Time Code

When encoding SMPTE time code, set the generator to the preferred starting time. Although time code readout is in hours, minutes, seconds, and frames, it is easy to confuse them if any numbers are duplicated on the same tape or on other tape belonging to the same production. To avoid this confusion, time code is used, employing either the zero-start or time-of-day logging method.

Zero start indicates the lapsed time of a recording. The first tape begins at zero and each successive reel begins at 01:00:00:00, then 02:00:00:00, 03:00:00:00, and so on. For example, if the first tape segment starts at zero and ends at 00:00:02:46, the second segment could start at 00:00:02:47. However, it would be wiser to spool the tape ahead several frames to make the segments easier to access and also to avoid accidental erasure.

Time-of-day numbering is synchronized with clock time. This is a handy way to keep track of when material is recorded. But tapes used day-to-day must be clearly marked with the date to avoid any confusion about inevitable duplication of coding times.

Recording SMPTE Time Code on Audiotape

On audiotape, you should record time code on the highest-number edge track—on an 8-track tape that would be track 8, on a 16-track tape that would be track 16, and so on. Record level should be −5 VU to −10 VU. Do not record the time-code signal at a lower level; otherwise synchronization is adversely affected. To prevent crosstalk between the time-code signal and program material, leave the track adjacent to the time code blank—on an 8-track tape that would be track 7, on a 16-track tape that would be track 15, and so on.

In fact, recording time code onto analog tape can be difficult, even at recommended levels, because it tends to distort. The problem becomes particularly acute in dubbing tapes. By the second or third generation, distortion can be so great that the code becomes unreadable. Most time code generators have features designed to reduce or alleviate problems in reading time code. The two most commonly used are called *jam sync* and *freewheel*.

Jam sync produces new time code during dubbing either to match the original time code or to regenerate new address data, thereby replacing defective sections of code. **Freewheel** mode allows the bypassing of defective code without altering the speed of the synchronized tape transports.

Frame rate is usually set next. For audio-only productions, use 30 frames per second. Start recording time code 20–30 seconds before the program material begins to allow sufficient time for the tape machines to interlock. Once recording commences, it must be continuous and without pause. Tapes should be coded simultaneously. If that is not possible, then a time code editor will be needed to correct offsets in the synchronization.

Synchronizers

Although time code permits the accurate interlocking of audiotape recorders, any time two or more transports must run together simultaneously, frame for frame, a device called a *synchronizer* is necessary. A **synchronizer** controls the position and speed of the "slave" transport(s) to lock to the "master" machine's transport using time code as its reference.

Synchronization systems using time code vary widely in sophistication, from those that synchronize one master machine to one slave, to those that synchronize several transports at once and perform a variety of other computer-assisted functions as well (see 14-23, 14-24, and 14-26).

Most synchronizers have available two types of locking modes: frame lock and phase lock. Frame lock locks the master and slave units using time code so that any variations in the master reference are passed on to the slave. Phase lock (also referred to as *sync lock*) prevents sudden speed variations in the master, such as wow and flutter, from being passed to the slave.

Other synchronizer features include automatic switching from play mode to cue mode that allows the slave transport to "chase" the master whenever it is rewound and resync to it when it is again put into play. Offsets can be set between machines allowing a tape to be "slipped" out of sync, by less than one frame if necessary. Synchronizers control transport record/edit functions, enabling "In" and "Out" record points to be repeated accurately to as little as 1/100th of a frame in some units. To isolate themselves from speed changes during time-code dropouts, synchronizers can "freewheel," passing over time-code loss at a constant speed.

Basic Editing Operations Using a Synchronizer

Although synchronizers come in a variety of models, they perform similar basic functions. Using the digital audio synchronizer in 14-23 as an example, let us outline those functions.

The edit point is entered by pressing the EDIT POINT key. The numeric keys can also be used if the tape time of the edit point

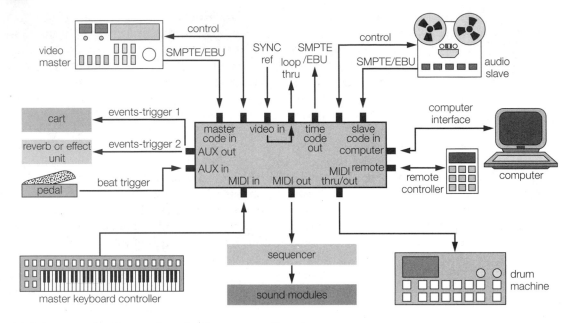

14-26 Example of a synchronization system flowchart

is known in advance. The information is stored in a memory. Modification of the edit point can be performed by rotating the search dial in the Jog mode, just like rocking the reels by hand on an open-reel tape recorder. If the Memory Rehearsal Repeat mode is selected, the edit point can also be shifted in either direction with the search dial. Once the edit points for the recorder and the player are exactly defined, it is possible to preview the edited portion. If the edit is acceptable, press the EDIT and PREVIEW keys simultaneously to automatically execute the edit. The final edit can be reviewed and, because the original edit is still in the memory, re-edited if necessary.

Edit Decision List

An important advantage of more advanced synchronizers is that they provide an **edit decision list (EDL)**. An EDL is a list of edits performed during editing. On time code sys-

tems using synchronizers with memory, the list can be stored and printed.

Original protocol for stored edit decision lists conformed to the ASCII (for American Standard Code, pronounced "as-key") format. It has 10 fields of information:

- Field 1 lists the event or edit number.

- Field 2 lists the source tape recorder of the edit.

- Field 3 lists the edit mode—the audio track number.

- Field 4 lists the type of transition.

- Field 5 lists the duration of a transition. If the transition is a cut, field 5 is left blank because the transition is virtually instantaneous.

- Field 6 lists the playback ATR's start time.

- Field 7 lists the playback ATR's stop time.

- Field 8 lists the record ATR's start time.

- Field 9 is for convenience because the information is not needed by the computer. It may list either the record ATR's stop time or the duration of the edit.

- Field 10 consists of information needed only by the computer to begin reading the next edit.

Today, an EDL may be charted in whatever format is most functional to an editing system (see 14-25).

Edit points are determined and entered basically in two ways. The first is "on the fly." As the tape recorder plays back at normal speed, the editor presses the Mark In or Mark Out button (or similarly designated control) at the edit point. The second is to enter manually into the keyboard the time-code numbers that indicate the edit points. To do this the editor presses the Set In or Set Out button (or similarly designated control). Keyboard entry requires that the tape be previewed and edits predetermined.

The edit is checked or previewed to make sure that it is satisfactory before it is actually performed. If it is not, the edit can be trimmed by pressing Trim In to change the beginning of a segment or Trim Out to alter the end.

Once the edit decision list has been completed, and before final assembly can proceed, the EDL must be "cleaned." The cleaning, called *list management*, is done by the computer. It checks to make sure that the information on the EDL conforms to the source tape. After the list management stage, final assembly is automatic.

Nonlinear Editing

As we indicated at the beginning of this chapter, nonlinear editing allows you to retrieve, assemble, and reassemble digital disk-based material quickly and in any order, regardless of the material's location on the disk. The term *random access editing* is often used synonymously with nonlinear editing. Of course, all editing is random access. You access a sound in one part of a recording, then you go to another sound in another part of the recording, and so on. What is usually meant by *random access* when it is applied to nonlinear editing is *quick access to randomly selected points in a recording*. This is not to quibble with terminology but to clarify more precisely what nonlinear editing is.

Another confusion about nonlinear editing derives from the number of different digital editing systems on the market. There are stereo and various multichannel systems. Most of them use hard-disk systems; others are optical-based. Hard-disk systems may use PC, Macintosh, Amiga, Silicon Graphics, or their own hardware/software interface. Some systems provide basic editing functions only; others include digital signal processing (DSP). There are dual-purpose hard-disk systems that are capable of both recording and editing in stereo or multitrack and the digital audio workstation (DAW) (see Chapter 7). DAWs incorporate most of the features found in advanced hard-disk editing (and recording) systems. What makes the DAW different is its ability to integrate with and control other audio and MIDI sources.

The following section is a distillation of the basic functions found in most hard-disk editing systems. It is intended to give you an operational overview of nonlinear editing. Although all the terms are explained, some are more commonly used than others. In some cases, their familiarity may depend on your knowledge of a particular editing system.

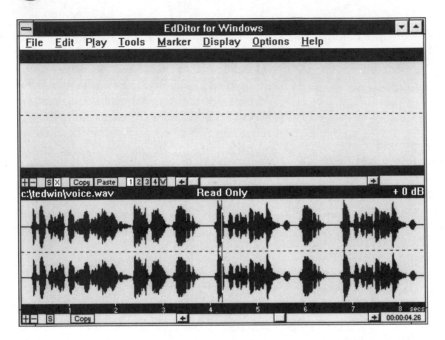

14-27 Soundfile and Menu display. In this editing program the bottom window displays the original soundfile. The top window is the Modify window where most editing operations are performed. In other words, a new soundfile in the Modify window is constructed using portions of the soundfile from the Read Only window so that the original recording is not altered (see "Destructive and Nondestructive Editing" later in this chapter). The narrow vertical line at the center of the waveform is the edit cursor. When a stereo sound is displayed, the left channel is shown above the right channel, with a horizontal dotted line separating the two. When a mono sound is displayed, a single waveform appears in the window.

Hard-Disk Nonlinear Editing

In a hard-disk editing system, audio that is encoded onto the disk takes the form of a **soundfile**. The soundfile contains information about the sound such as amplitude and duration. When the soundfile is opened, that information is displayed on the monitor screen, usually as a waveform. Also displayed is the editing program Menu (see 14-27).

Waveform Screen Displays

The waveforms are displayed in two configurations: as a symmetrical amplitude display or as a nonsymmetrical peak amplitude display. A symmetrical amplitude display shows a sound's profile, in both a positive and negative direction, in relation to a zero-level reference line (see 14-27). A nonsymmetrical peak amplitude display rises in a positive direction from a zero-level reference

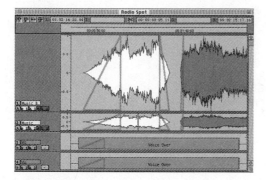

14-28 Nonsymmetrical peak amplitude display

line (see 14-28). These displays profile a sound's amplitude over time. By being able to "see" a sound, you can easily spot the loud and quiet passages (see 14-29). It is also possible to see greater detail in a waveform by zooming in, a feature that facilitates extremely precise editing (see 14-30). Once the soundfile is retrieved and its waveform is displayed, it can be auditioned to determine which of its sections is to be defined for editing. As the sound is played, a play cursor, or playbar, scrolls the waveform enabling the editor to see precisely the part and shape of the sound that is playing at any given moment. In some systems, if the soundfile is longer than the screen can display, then as the scroll moves to the end of the visible waveform, approaching the off-screen data, the screen will be redrawn or refreshed, showing the entire updated waveform.

When the editor determines what part of the sound is to be edited, the segment is highlighted in what is known as a *defined region*. Once a region is defined, the selected edit (or DSP) will be performed only in that section of the waveform (see 14-30). The region can be cut from the waveform display and moved to another part of the waveform or to another waveform. It can also be inverted, changed in level, envelope, frequency, and so on.

A marker or identification flag can be placed anywhere in the waveform to facilitate jumping the play cursor at will to the desired marker points. The marker can be a graphic identifier using a number, letter, or text (see 14-33 later in this chapter).

At any time in the editing process the soundfile can be auditioned in a number of ways: from beginning to end; from the defined region; from marker to marker; and at increased or decreased speed in either direction. This latter operation is called **scrubbing**.

Scrubbing is similar to rocking tape in cut-and-splice editing or using the Jog mode in electronic editing. It lets you move the play cursor through the defined region at any speed and listen to the section being scrubbed at the same time. Unlike rocking a tape or jogging, with scrubbing you can audibly and visibly locate the in- and out-point of a defined region.

Suppose you want to pinpoint a chord located in one section of a soundfile and use the same chord at the end of the soundfile to end the song. By moving the cursor to an area just before the chord, you can slowly scrub the area until you find the precise location at the beginning of the first sound. This will be the first point in the defined region. Continue scrubbing until you locate the precise end point of the chord's decay and mark it as the end of the defined region. Then, as you would in word processing, copy the defined region and paste it at the proper point near the end of the song.

Scrubbing to reproduce a waveform can be accomplished in two ways: by jogging and shuttling. Unlike jogging in electronic editing, in this application the **Jog mode** reproduces scrubbed samples in direct relation to the movement of the cursor over a region. In **Shuttle mode** the initial direction and speed of the cursor are used as a reference and the rest of the scrubbed section is

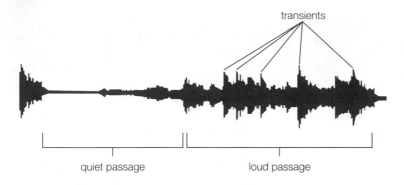

14-29 Dynamics of a waveform

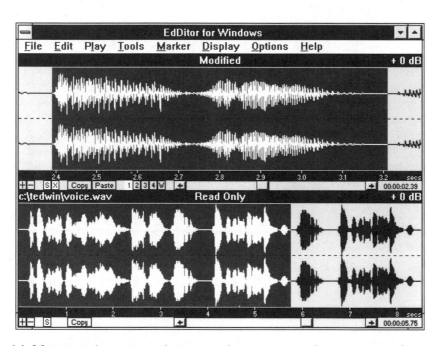

14-30 Zoom function. The section from 2.4 seconds to 3.2 seconds in the Read Only soundfile is detailed in the Modified window. The lighter sections are the *defined regions*, that is, the part of the waveforms selected for editing. The zoomed section is a "Harrumph" that interrupted a lyric (see 14-32).

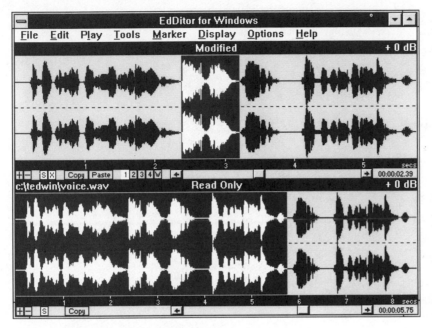

14-31 Cutting in hard-disk editing

reproduced in the same direction and at the same rate with no further movement of the cursor necessary. Moving the cursor again will change the direction and speed of reproduction analogous to the new movement.

As we suggested, there are operations in nonlinear digital editing that are similar to those in word processing when you delete a word entirely, or cut or copy it from one part of a sentence and insert or paste it elsewhere in the same sentence or into another sentence. This is known as *cutting and pasting*. Once a region is defined, the Cut or Delete command removes it from its original location and copies it to the computer's memory for temporary storage. This section of computer memory is sometimes referred to as the *clipboard*. Using the Copy command, the defined region is added to the clipboard but is not cut from its original

position. The Paste command copies the defined region from the clipboard and inserts it into the waveform immediately after the position of the cursor.

There are also Shuffle and Replace commands in nonlinear editing that are similar to the Insert and Typeover operations in word processing. Shuffle moves the audio that originally followed the cursor to a point immediately following the newly inserted segment. Replace overwrites the audio immediately following the cursor.

To use a specific example, refer to 14-31 and 14-32 for the following discussion. The sentence, in the Read-Only window, in which the cut is to be made has been defined and copied to the Modified window for editing. The segment to be deleted is the "Harrumph" that occurs from 2.4 seconds to 3.20 seconds. It has been defined

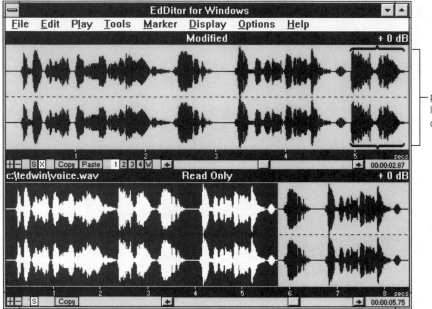

14-32 Pasting in hard-disk editing

in the Modified window. To make sure that the edit cursor has marked each edge of the defined region precisely, zoom in to the "Harrumph" (see 14-30). This view reveals a small amount of unselected data on either side of the actual "Harrumph." Scrub the edit cursor to better define the edges of the "Harrumph." Then select the Cut command to remove the offending sound. If for some reason the "Harrumph" is to be moved to the end of the lyric line for, let us say, comic emphasis, the "Harrumph" will have been saved to the clipboard. Move the edit cursor to the end of the lyric line in the waveform and then use the Paste command to insert the "Harrumph" at that point.

Other Types of Screen Displays

In addition to being displayed and edited as a waveform, a soundfile can also be dis-

played and edited in graphic form, as a playlist, or by defined and named regions (see 14-33 through 14-35).

Digital Signal Processing (DSP)

The ease, convenience, and speed of non-linear editing become even more powerful when digital signal processing (DSP) is added to the editing system. Not all hard-disk editing systems offer DSP. Those that do provide the editor with sound-shaping capabilities, in a self-contained unit, that would take the interfacing of several separate devices to duplicate (see Chapter 8).

Destructive and Nondestructive Editing

Still another advantage of hard-disk editing is that the edits you make can be non-destructive. **Nondestructive editing** does not

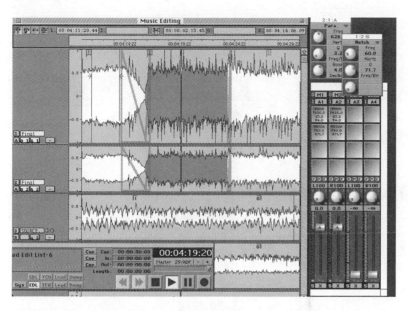

14-33 Editing display in graphic form showing markers placed in a soundfile

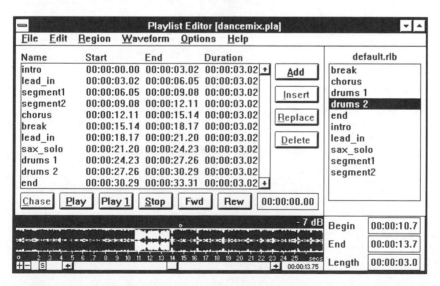

14-34 Playlist editing display. In this program the upper-left-hand corner of the screen shows the playlist, the list of sounds that will be played in order. For each sound on the list, the start time, end time, and duration are given. In the upper-right-hand corner is the region library, the list of sounds that are available to place onto the playlist. At the bottom of the screen is the waveform display.

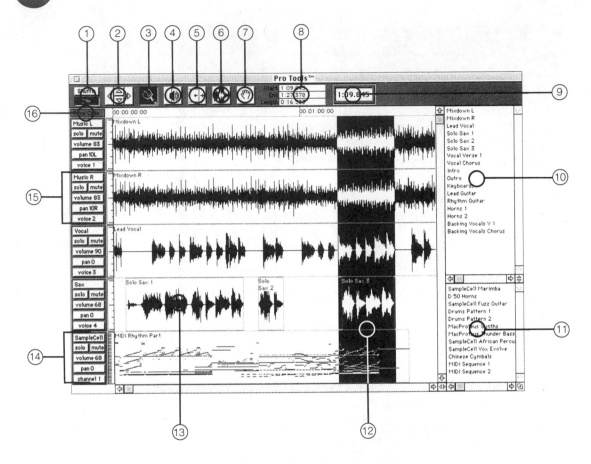

(1) **Slip/Shuffle indicator** Use Slip mode to move regions freely within a track, even overlap other regions; shuffle mode lines up regions end to end for rapid assembly

(2) **Display scale arrows** allow you to adjust waveform display

(3) **Magnifying Tool** lets you view the waveform at any resolution

(4) **The Scrubber** offers two modes: Varispeed forward and backward scrubbing (like rocking tape heads) for pinpoint accuracy and Loop scrubbing to preview the beat in musical edits

(5) Use **the Trimmer** tool to "fine tune" your selection

(6) **The Selection Tool** is used to define regions of audio & MIDI

(7) The **Grabber Tool** moves regions and tracks in a single step

(8) **Selection and Position indicators** shows you exactly where you are in your selection

(9) **Current Time indicator**

(10) **Audio Regions List**

(11) **MIDI Regions List**

(12) Select across multiple tracks of audio and MIDI

(13) Slip regions freely within or across tracks

(14) **MIDI Tracks** can be edited in blocks along with audio

(15) Each **Audio Track** is a graphic playlist with controls for volume, panning, solo/mute—and voice priority—giving visual feedback for rapid, accurate editing

(16) **Time Scale indicator** lets you view a session in Minutes: Seconds, Bars & Beats, or SMPTE

14-35 Editing display by defined and named regions

alter the original soundfile, regardless of what editing or signal processing you effect. **Destructive editing**, on the other hand, permanently alters the original soundfile by overwriting it.

This raises the question: Why employ destructive editing when you can process a soundfile in any way you wish and still preserve the original? The answer is that destructive editing is necessary, for example, when a memory is limited—it is easier to save a single soundfile than both the original and duplicate soundfiles—and when the edited soundfile is to be downloaded to another system.

Techniques and Aesthetic Considerations

Editing music is difficult to discuss in any detail because it involves using one language—the printed word—to explain another language—the notes, chords, rhythms, and other features of abstract, temporal sound. Music contains so many simultaneous sonic elements that even slight mistakes in cutting are easily detected. In editing music, you have to consider cutting on the right accent to maintain rhythm, tonality, relative loudness, and style. If any of these elements are aurally incompatible, the edit will be obvious.

Generally, edits that heighten intensity cut together well: for example, going from quiet to loud, nonrhythmic to rhythmic, slow to fast, formless to structured, or atonal to tonal.

Cutting to Resolution

One of the most useful music editing guidelines is to cut before an accent, downbeat, or resolution. Think of the final chord in a musical phrase or song. Although it resolves

the music, it is the chord before it that creates the anticipation and need for resolution; it sets up the last chord. Edit on the anticipatory note, the one requiring some resolution, however brief, so that it leads naturally to the note being joined.

Preserving Rhythm

Most Western music has a time signature—¼ ("two-four" not "two-fourths"), ¾, ¼, ⅜, ⅝, and so forth. The first number indicates the number of beats in each measure; the second number indicates the value of the note that receives each beat. For example, in ¼ time there are four beats to a measure and each quarter note receives a whole beat; in ⅜ time there are three beats to the measure and each eighth note receives a beat. In editing music you have to preserve the beat or else the edit will be noticeable as a jerk or stutter in the rhythm. If you cannot read music or no music sheet exists, try to get a sense of the rhythm by concentrating on the beat to determine the accents.

Regardless of the number of beats in a measure, some beats are strong and some are weak. When you tap your foot to a song, it usually comes down on the strong or down beat and lifts on the weak or up beat.

A song in ¾ time, known as waltz time, is characterized by a strong beat followed by two weak beats—**one**, two, three, **one**, two, three. Beats in ¼ time follow a **one**, two, **one**, two, strong beat–weak beat pattern. To be sure, this is a rudimentary explanation of what is a complex subject. The point is that when editing rhythm you have to be aware of preserving the number of beats per measure as well as the accents. For example, in a piece in ¾ time, if you cut after the first beat in a measure, the beat you cut to should be a weak beat, and another weak beat should follow; if you cut after the third beat in a measure you would cut to a strong beat with two weak beats to follow.

Another technique to facilitate editing to the beat is to determine the number of beats per minute and use a ruler to measure the time in terms of tape distance. For example, if a song's tempo is 120 beats per minute and the tape is running at 15 ips, divide 120 by 60 to get the number of beats per second—two. Then divide the 15 ips by 2 to get the distance of tape travel for two beats—7½ ips.

Of course, preserving a rhythm in music editing is not an isolated consideration. Other factors, such as key signature and musical style and texture, cannot be ignored.

Repetitive Measures

One way to shorten or lengthen audio material through editing is to use repetitive measures in the music. These measures can be cut out to shorten material, which is obvious. To lengthen the audio, repetitive measures can be extended by dubbing them to another recorder and cutting them back into the original recording. If the recording is analog, however, the dubbed material could lose sound quality that would make the difference between the original and copied audio perceptible.

A better way to lengthen audio using repetitive measures is either to use digital-to-digital dubbing or to have another identical mix available and intercut the appropriate measures from it.

Matching Keys

Just as most music has a time signature to regulate its rhythm, it also has a key signature—E major or B minor, for example—that determines its overall tonality. Some keys are compatible; when you change from one to the other, it sounds natural or "in tune" (see 14-36). Other keys are not, and splicing them together is jarring or sounds "out of tune," like the editing in some of the album offers on TV. Unless it is for effect, edited music should sound harmonious in order not to be noticed.

Another way to cover a bad key change in an edit is with pitch shifting. Usually it is easier to try bringing one of the offending keys into musical compatibility with the other key than it is to look for a sonic compromise between the two.

Matching Style and Texture

Each type of music and musical group has a unique style and texture. This distinguishes the style of jazz from rock, or the texture of one voice from another although both may have identical registers, or one group from another although both may play the same instruments and music.

Editing from the same piece of music usually does not present a problem in matching style and texture as long as you follow the other guidelines for editing. If the music is from different sources, however, matching elements can be a problem. Normally, you would not edit different styles—a piece of classical music to rock music just because they had the same rhythm, or a dance band to a military band just because they were playing the same song. The differences in sound would make the edits conspicuous and distracting.

Matching Ambience

In editing one segment to another, even though all of the other factors discussed so far have been accomplished successfully, if

music in this key will segue with ➔	first choice	second choice	third choice	fourth choice
A	A	D	E	F#/G♭ minor
A#(B♭)	A#(B♭)	D#(E♭)	F	G minor
B	B	E	F#	G#/A♭ minor
C	C	F	G	A minor
C#(D♭)	C#(D♭)	F#(G♭)	G#(A♭)	A#/B♭ minor
D	D	G	A	B minor
D#(E♭)	D#(E♭)	G#(A♭)	A#(B♭)	C minor
E	E	A	B	C#/D♭ minor
F	F	B♭	C	D minor
F#(G♭)	F#(G♭)	B	C#(D♭)	D#/E♭ minor
G	G	C	D	E minor
G#(A♭)	G#(A♭)	C#(D♭)	D#(E♭)	F minor

14-36 Compatible or consonant music keys

the ambiences in the two segments do not match, the cut will be obvious. In the example used earlier in which a pop occurs after the gentle chord that ends a verse and before the chorus begins, the edit was made after the chord's decay and just before the chorus (see 14-7). Why not cut just after the chord, before its decay, and just after the pop, before its decay? That would delete the pop and still keep the continuity between the chord's end, the decay, and the verse's beginning.

The problem with the latter approach is that the sound of the gentle chord and the sound of the pop are different, and so, therefore, will be their decays. Among other things, the pop is a transient sound, and the chord is not. Hence, the loudness and duration of the decay each generates are different. Cutting from the end of the chord to the decay of the pop would not match their actual ambiences.

Persistence of Sound

Our ability to retain and match precise auditory information is not very good. If you try to remember the pitch or rhythm of musical segments in two different parts of a tape, by the time you spool from one to the other, your retention of the pitch will be different or the rhythm will be off.

This can be called *persistence of sound*, and with most humans it is very limited. A few things can be done to lessen the problem. Make rough cuts of the music segments you are editing, splice them together, and put them on a single reel. This reduces the distance and hence the time between them. Another technique is to make separate tapes of the two pieces of music and use two recorders. When the tape you are editing is at one point in the edit, cue the second tape to the other edit point. In checking to make sure the edit works and in trying to determine the exact cutting points, by having the edits cued you can play them almost as they would sound if spliced. Of course, hard-disk editing makes these procedures quick and easy and persistence of sound almost no problem at all.

Listening Fatigue

Editing for long periods of time can create listening fatigue—reduced ability to perceive or remember the nuances of music. (This type of psychological fatigue can occur during any long listening session.) If you suffer from listening fatigue during editing, then rhythm, tonality, and other features of the music are continually mismatched, cuts are slightly off, and it is difficult to keep track of what should be edited to what.

One way to extend the time before listening fatigue sets in is to work in a quiet acoustic environment with no predominance of midrange frequencies because they tend to tire the listener faster. If a recording or loudspeaker system has too much midrange, equalize the monitor playback by slightly boosting the lower frequencies anywhere between 50 and 150 Hz and the frequencies above 10,000 Hz. This balances the sound and reduces its harshness and intensity. You can also attenuate the frequencies between 1,000 and 3,500 Hz, but this may reduce a lyric's intelligibility. It is also important to remember to bring down playback gain after turning it up, as is often required, to hear an edit point better. Finally, take regular "ears" breaks.

The Mixdown

Up to now, the elements that go into a music recording have been considered separately. But the CD-buying public is usually not aware of what has gone into the sound shaping. They hear only the result of the last phase of production: the **mixdown.** Mixdown procedures differ among recordists, but the purpose is the same: to combine the parts into a natural and integrated whole.

During mixdown the separately recorded tracks are combined, usually into stereo, 3-D, or surround sound. Whether the mix is straightforward or intricate, the goals are

1. to enhance or **sweeten** the sound by adding signal processing and style to existing tracks

2. to blend the sounds

3. to balance levels

4. to add special effects (if called for)

5. to create the acoustic space artificially (if necessary)

6. to localize the voicings in the aural frame

7. to establish musical perspective

8. to maintain the definition of each voicing regardless of how many instruments, or groups of instruments, are heard simultaneously

Music Mixdown

There is a common misunderstanding about the music mixdown; namely, that it is the stage in music production when everything that went wrong in the recording session is put right. No doubt this unfortunate notion has been nurtured in recording sessions that have not met expectations when producers have glibly reassured clients, "Don't worry, we can fix it in the mix."

The mixdown certainly is very important to the finished product, but keep its importance in perspective. The mixdown cannot change a mediocre performance into a good one, compensate for poor microphone technique, or make a sloppy recording precise.

In most instances it is the quality of the recording session that determines the overall quality of the mix.

Nevertheless, the mixdown cannot be taken too lightly. A good mix cannot salvage a bad recording, but a poor mix can ruin a good recording.

Suggested Procedures

There are probably as many approaches to mixing music as there are producers and engineers. Because functions vary, depending on the size of the studio, complexity of the project, and the number of personnel involved, the following is a general list of operations in proceeding with a mixdown:

1. Tape recorder heads are demagnetized and cleaned, and both the heads and the recorder are aligned.

2. Meters on the console and tape recorders are calibrated (see Chapter 10).

3. Inputs on the console are set to receive the signals from the multitrack tape recorder.

4. One master monitor channel is assigned or panned to the extreme left and another is assigned or panned to the extreme right. If the stereo mix must be mono-compatible, the monitor system also is set up for A–B—stereo–mono—referencing. A stereo display processor is often used to reference stereo-to-mono compatibility (see 15-13 later in this chapter).

5. The stereo master fader (or two submasters) are turned up so the left and right signals feed to the proper tracks of the master record ATR.

6. Individual channel faders are turned up.

7. Individual channels are assigned to the left or right mix bus, or both, and pro-portioned between them using the pan pots.

8. Levels and localizing of the voicings are temporarily set.

9. The rough, unprocessed mix is listened to for as long as it takes to decide what needs to be done in relation to equalization, reverberation, and other signal processing.

10. Individual voicings are then equalized and, at the same time, are referenced to the overall mix to check blending and positioning. Usually, the rhythm tracks are done first, then the accompanying tracks, and finally the vocal tracks.

11. Other signal processing, such as compression, delay, and pitch shifting, is added where appropriate, sometimes before equalizing.

12. Reverberation is then added and equalized.

13. The mix is checked for blend, balance, definition, and positioning.

14. Reference tones are recorded on the master tape.

15. The final mix is recorded on the master tape.

16. The master tape is assembled and labeled.

17. Backup copies are made as required.

18. Premastering is often done in studios with a compact-disc recorder (see Chapters 7 and 16).

Auditioning the Rough Mix

It is not good policy to mixdown a recording on the same day that you complete it. Regardless of what you may think a recording sounds like immediately after taping, in a day or so it will sound different. It is essential to take some time between sessions to regain perspective and refresh "ears." Therefore, before you begin a mix or make any final decisions about localizing, signal processing, special effects, and so on, refamiliarize yourself with the recording by auditioning it.

To do this, set the relative level and location of each voicing to achieve approximate, but satisfactory, overall loudness and positional balances. Here is one approach:

1. Set the level of the loudest or most prominent sound first, leaving plenty of headroom on the VU meter. For example, if the loudest sound is a support voicing, such as the bass drum, set the level at −10 VU; if the sound is a prominent lead voicing, such as a vocal, set the level higher, at, say, −5 VU. Leaving headroom is important because mixing almost always involves adding level during signal processing through EQ, reverb, and so on. (As discussed later in this section, too much boosting without compensating attenuation can create a number of sonic problems.)

2. Turn up the monitor level so it is comfortably loud; 85 dB-SPL is usually considered optimal. What is considered comfortably loud depends on personal taste, musical style, and hearing acuity; however, 85 dB-SPL is a good level to start with. It is critical not to set the monitor level too loud. Loud levels desensitize hearing, or in the vernacular of audio, "fry" ears, to say nothing of the potential for hearing loss. Once monitor loudness is set, try not to change it; otherwise, the reference you are using to determine sonic values and proportions will change as well.

3. Add all other tracks relative to the level of the first voicing. If you started with drums, add bass, the rest of the drum set, the other accompanying instruments, and the vocal(s). If you started with the lead or most prominent instrument, bring in the other tracks one at a time, starting with the rhythm instruments and followed by the rest of the accompaniment. Another approach is to set all instruments equally loud. Then increase levels of the lead voicings and decrease levels of the support instruments.

4. Position each instrument in the stereo, 3-D, or surround space approximately where you planned to put it in the final mix.

5. Readjust fader levels to compensate for loudness changes resulting from these positional alignments.

6. If something is not working, do not force it. Maybe it is not needed. That applies, for example, to parts of a song, control settings, signal processing, and, if necessary, even to an entire instrumental track.

Once you have refamiliarized yourself with the recording and have reconfirmed its design, you are ready to do the actual mixdown. It is likely that during the mix, as various sonic alterations are made, some of the original decisions about the mix will change. This is natural. Be flexible. Do not be afraid to experiment or go with your instincts.

Signal Processing

Signal processing is so much a part of music recording that sound shaping seems impossible without it. Yet, overdependency on signal processing has created the myth that just about anything can be done with it to ensure the sonic success of a recording. These notions are misleading. Unless special effects are required or MIDI is involved, signal processing in the mixdown should be used to touch up the aural canvas, not to repaint it. The greater the reliance on signal processing in the mixdown, the more likely the poorer the recording session. Nevertheless, signal processing is important and often critical. Recordists who proudly proclaim they can do without it are foolish. The purpose of this section is only to suggest possibilities and techniques. It is not intended to imply that because signal processing offers so many options to the sound designer, most of them should be used. Remember: Less is more.

Equalizing: How Much, Where, and When?

One question often asked of a sound designer is "What kind of a sound will I get on this instrument if I equalize so many decibels at such and such a frequency?" The question suggests that there are ways to predetermine equalization. There are not! Consider the different things that can affect sound. For example, for a guitar you might ask, "What is it made of? Is it acoustic or electric? Are the strings steel or plastic, old or new, played with a metal or plastic pick or with the fingers? Is the guitarist heavy- or light-handed? Are there fret sounds? Is the guitar miked and, if so, with what type of microphone? How are the acoustics? What type of song is being played? What is the spatial placement of the guitar in the mix?" These influences do not even include personal taste, the most variable factor of all.

The best way to approach equalization is to (1) know the frequency ranges of the instruments involved, (2) know what each octave in the audible frequency spectrum contributes to the overall sound, (3) listen to the sound in context, and (4) have a good idea of what you want to achieve before starting the mixdown.

Also remember the following:

- Equalizing will alter a sound's harmonic structure.

- Any use of equalization affects phase, which can lead to phase distortion and the relative placement of instruments within a stereo or multiple-channel mix.

- Very few people, even under ideal conditions, can hear a change of 1 dB or less, and many people cannot hear changes of 2 or 3 dB.

- Large increases or decreases in equalizing should be avoided.

- Equalizing should not be used as a substitute for better microphone selection and mic placement.

- Only a certain number of tracks in the same frequency range should be increased or decreased. For example, on one channel you may increase by 4 dB at 5,000 Hz the sound of a snare drum to make it crisper, then on another channel you increase 2 dB at 5,000 Hz to make a cymbal sound fuller, and on a third channel you increase 3 dB at 5,000 Hz to bring out a vocal. If you consider each channel separately, there has been little equalizing at 5,000 Hz, but the cumulative boost at the same frequency could unbalance the overall blend.

- Equalizing often involves boosting frequencies, and that can mean more noise, among other problems. Therefore, be careful, particularly when increasing some of the unpleasant frequencies in the midrange and high end, especially with digital sound.

- Because boosting frequencies on one track often necessitates attenuating frequencies somewhere else, consider **subtractive equalization** first. For example, if a sound is overly bright, instead of trying to mellow it by boosting the appropriate lower frequencies, reduce some of the higher frequencies responsible for the excessive brightness.

- Frequencies above and below the range of each instrument should be filtered to reduce unwanted sound and improve definition. Be very careful not to reduce frequencies that are essential to the natural timbre of an instrument.

- To achieve a satisfactory blend, the sounds of individual elements may have to be changed in ways that could make them unpleasant to listen to by themselves. For example, the frequencies between 1,000 and 3,500 Hz make most vocals intelligible. One way to improve the clarity of a vocal and make it stand out from its instrumental accompaniment, while maintaining the overall blend, is to boost it a few decibels in the 1,000- to 3,500-Hz range and decrease the accompaniment a few decibels in the same range. Together they should sound quite natural. Separately, however, the vocal will be somewhat harsher and thinner and the accompaniment will sound a bit muddy and lifeless.

If a voice is powerful and rich with harmonics in the 5,000-Hz range, the sound is clear and full. Male singing voices, particularly in opera, have this sonic characteristic; female vocalists usually do not.

Voices deficient in the 5,000-Hz range can be enhanced by a boost of several decibels in this area. Not only is the definition of such sounds as "t," "s," "ch," and "k" increased, but a 6-dB increase at 5,000 Hz gives an apparent increase of 3 dB to the overall mix. Be wary of "digital edge" when mixing digital sound using these EQ values, that overly bright sonic by-product of the digital recording process that too often spoils sound quality in a CD.

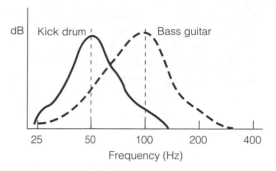

15-1 Complementary EQ for bass instruments

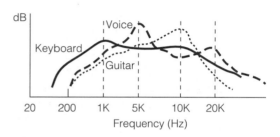

15-2 Complementary EQ for midrange instruments

- Use **complementary equalization** to help define instruments and keep masking to a minimum. Many instruments have comparable frequency ranges, such as the bass and kick drum, or the keyboard, guitar, and female vocal. Because physical law states that no two things can occupy the same space at the same time, it makes sense to equalize voicings that share frequency ranges so that they complement, rather than interfere with, one another (see 15-1 and 15-2).

- An absence of frequencies above 600 Hz adversely affects the intelligibility of consonants; an absence of frequencies below 600 Hz adversely affects the intelligibility of vowels.

- Equal degrees of equalizing between 400 and 2,000 Hz are more noticeable than equalizing above or below that range, especially in digital sound (remember the equal loudness principle).

- Most amplified instruments do not have ranges that go much beyond 7,500 Hz; boosting above that frequency usually adds only noise.

- Each sound has a naturally occurring peak at a frequency or band of frequencies that contains more energy than surrounding frequencies; boosting or cutting can enhance or mar the sound. In other words, the naturally occurring peak can become a "sweet" spot or a "sore" spot. The peaks are caused by natural harmonics and overtones or by formants. A **formant** is the resonance band in a vibrating body that mildly increases the level of specific steady-state frequencies in that band.

  To find the resonance area, turn up the gain on the appropriate section of the equalizer you are using and sweep the frequency control until the voicing sounds noticeably better or worse. Once you find the sweet or sore spot, return the equalizer's gain to zero and boost or cut the enhancing or offending frequencies to taste.

Equalization and Semantics

A major problem in equalization is describing what it sounds like. What does it mean, for example, when a producer wants "sizzle" in a cymbal sound, "fatness" in a snare sound, "brightness" in an alto saxophone sound, or "edge" to a vocal? Not only is there a problem of semantics, but you must identify the adjustments needed to achieve the desired effect. The following list should aid you in this process.

- Low-frequency boost under 200 Hz adds power or weight to sound. A boost between 200 Hz and 300 Hz can make sound woody or tubby.

- Low-frequency boost below 500 Hz can make sound fat, thick, warm, or robust. It can also make sound muddy, boomy, thumpy, or barrel-like.

- Flat, extended low frequencies add fullness, richness, or solidity to sound. They can also make sound rumbly.

- Low-frequency roll-off thins sound. This can make it seem clean, cold, tinny, or anemic.

- Midfrequency boost between 500 Hz and 7 kHz (5-kHz area for most instruments, 1.5 to 2.5 kHz for bass instruments) can add presence, punch, edge, clarity, or definition to sound. It can also make sound muddy (hornlike), tinny (telephonelike), nasal or honky (500 Hz to 3 kHz), hard (2 to 4 kHz), strident or piercing (2 to 5 kHz), twangy (3 kHz), metallic (3 to 5 kHz), or sibilant (4 to 7 kHz).

- Flat midfrequencies sound natural or smooth. They may also lack punch or color.

- Midfrequency dip makes sound mellow. It can also hollow (500 Hz to 1,000 Hz), muffle (5 kHz), or muddy (5 kHz) sound.

- High-frequency boost above 7 kHz can enhance sound by making it bright, crisp, etched, or sizzly (cymbals). It can detract from sound by making it edgy, glassy, sibilant, or sizzly (voice).

- Flat, extended high frequencies open sound, making it airy, transparent, natural, or detailed. They can also make sound too detailed or close.

- High-frequency roll-off mellows, rounds,

or smoothes sound. It can also dull, muffle, veil, or distance sound.[*]

In relation to specific instruments, the equalization values in Table 15-1 may help to refine semantics. Note that frequencies and frequency ranges listed in the table are general and intended only to provide a point of departure for more refined sound shaping.

Compression

In Chapter 8, we discussed a number of uses compression has in sound shaping. Here are some general guidelines to use in applying compression to selected instruments. They should not be followed without listening and experimenting.

- *Drums.* A long-to-medium attack time reduces the percussive effect. A short release time and wide ratio create a bigger or fuller sound.
- *Cymbals.* Medium-to-short attack and release times and an average ratio reduce excessive ringing.
- *Guitar.* Short attack, increased release time, and a wide ratio increase the sustain.
- *Keyboards.* A medium-to-long attack time, a medium-to-short release time, and a wide ratio give a fuller sound.
- *Strings.* Short attack and release times and an average ratio add body to the sound.
- *Vocals.* Medium-to-short attack and release times and an average ratio reduce sibilance.

Following are some specific applications of compression on selected instruments.

---

[*]Adapted from "Modern Recording and Music," Nov. 1982, by permission of *Modern Recording and Music Magazine* and Bruce Bartlett.

- *Drums.* Ratio: 2:1 to 3:1 or 4:1 to 8:1; attack time: fast; release time: medium to fast; threshold: set to compress loudest peaks 4 to 6 dB or 6 to 8 dB. Compressing drums allows you to mix them at a lower level and still retain their impact.
- *Bass.* Ratio: 4:1; attack time: medium; release time: medium to fast; threshold: set to compress loudest peaks 2 to 4 dB. One main reason recordists compress the bass is its low-frequency energy that tends to eat up so much of the mix's overall headroom. One cautionary note: Watch out for distortion that can be introduced by overly quick release times.
- *Rhythm instruments* (guitar, sax, synthesizer, and so on). Ratio: 4:1 to 6:1; attack time: medium; release time: medium; threshold: set to compress loudest peaks 3 to 5 dB. Moderate compression can enrich texture and help to make rhythm instruments forceful without letting them dominate the mix.
- *Vocals.* Ratio: 3:1 to 4:1; attack time: fast to medium; release time: medium to fast; threshold: set to compress loudest peaks 3 to 6 dB. The amount of compression on a vocalist depends on the singer's technique; that is, does the singer back off slightly when hitting loud notes and lean in slightly to compensate for softer ones—which is good technique; or does the singer not compensate for dynamic range or, worse, "eat" the microphone? If the music track is dense and the vocals need to be heard, compression will have to be more aggressive. For delicate singers, use more sensitive threshold levels and smaller ratios. For screamers, you may need to compress 6 to 8 dB to get the proper texture. Be aware that high compression levels bring out sibilance and background noise.

Table 15-1 Approximate equalization values for selected instruments

Bass Drum	Bottom ranges between 60 and 80 Hz; attenuating between 300 and 600 Hz reduces dullness, thuddiness, and cardboardlike sound; boosting between 1,600 and 5,000 Hz adds brightness, attack, and snap.
Low (Floor) Tom-Tom	Fullness ranges between 80 and 120 Hz; brightness and attack is in the 4,000-Hz range.
High (Rack) Tom-Tom	Fullness ranges between 220 and 240 Hz; brightness and attack is in the 5,000-Hz range.
Snare Drum	Bottom ranges between 120 and 160 Hz; fatness ranges between 220 and 240 Hz; crispness ranges between 4,000 and 5,000 Hz.
Cymbals	Dullness—clank and gong—ranges between 200 and 240 Hz; brilliance, shimmer, and brightness range from 7,000 Hz up.
Bass Guitar	Bottom ranges between 60 and 80 Hz; cutting around 250 Hz adds clarity; attack ranges between 700 and 1,200 Hz; string noise is around 2,500–3,500 Hz.
Electric Guitar	Fullness ranges between 210 and 240 Hz: edge or bite ranges between 2,500 and 3,500 Hz; upper harmonic limits do not range much beyond 6,500 Hz.
Acoustic Guitar	Bottom ranges between 80 and 140 Hz; fullness and body range between 220 and 260 Hz; clarity ranges between 1,600 and 5,000 Hz with sound becoming thinner as these frequencies get higher. Steel strings are 5–10 dB louder than nylon strings.
Piano	Bass ranges between 80 and 120 Hz; body ranges between 65 and 130 Hz; clarity and presence range between 2,000 and 5,000 Hz with sound becoming thinner as these frequencies get higher. The most robust sound is obtained from a concert grand; sound is less robust in a baby grand, and least robust in an upright.
Strings	Generally, sound from the bridge of a violin , viola, cello, or acoustic bass is brighter compared to sound coming from the f-holes, which is fuller. Bowing close to the bridge produces a louder, brighter tone; bowing farther from the bridge produces a less brilliant, gentler tone. Fullness ranges between 220 and 240 Hz; edge or scratchiness ranges between 7,000 and 10,000 Hz.

There are many other approaches to compression. Also, those listed here are not intended to imply that all, or even most, voicings should be compressed. If you do decide to employ compression, these suggestions may prove to be good starting points.

Reverberation: Creating Acoustic Space

Due to the common practice of miking each sound component separately (for greater control) and closely (to reduce leakage), many original multitrack recordings lack a complementary acoustic environment. In such cases the acoustics usually are added in the mixdown by artificial means using signal-processing devices such as reverb and digital delay (see Chapter 8).

If you add acoustics in the mixdown, do it after equalizing (because it is difficult to get a true sense of the effects of frequency changes in a reverberant space) and after panning (to get a better idea of how reverb affects positioning). Avoid giving widely dif-

Table 15-1 *(continued)*

Brass	Frequency ranges that give the trumpet its particular sound are 1,000–1,500 Hz and 2,000–3,000 Hz. Fullness ranges between 160 and 220 Hz; edge or bite ranges between 1,500 and 5,000 Hz. A *straight mute*—a mute that fits inside the bell—acts as a high-pass filter, letting through frequencies above 1,800 Hz; a *cup mute*—a mute that fits over the bell—passes frequencies in the range of 800–1,200 Hz and dampens frequencies above 2,500 Hz. Frequencies that give the trombone its particular sound are 480–600 Hz and around 1,200 Hz. The upper limit is 5,000 Hz with medium-loud playing; it may reach 10,000 Hz with loud playing. Fullness ranges between 100 and 220 Hz; brightness and edge range between 2,000 and 5,000 Hz. Frequencies that give the French horn its broad, round quality are around 340 Hz, between 700 and 2,000 Hz, and around 3,500 Hz. Fullness ranges between 120 and 240 Hz; bite-to-shrillness ranges upward from 4,500 Hz.
Woodwinds	The flute's fundamental range is from about 250 to 2,100 Hz. Mellowness is toward the lower end of that range; brightness begins toward the upper end of that range; bite-to-shrillness extends into the harmonics from 2,500 to 3,500 Hz. The clarinet's characteristic frequencies are between 800 and 3,000 Hz. Mellowness and body range between 150 and 320 Hz; throatiness ranges from 400 to 440 Hz. Fundamental ranges of the most familiar saxophones are roughly 130–880 Hz (alto), 100–650 Hz (tenor), and 65–650 Hz (baritone). Body is at the lower ends of these registers; fullness toward the middle ranges; and brightness in the harmonics, above the upper fundamentals.
Vocal	Depending on the vocal range and whether the vocalist is male or female, generally intelligibility ranges between 1,000 and 2,500 Hz; fullness between 140 and 440 Hz; presence between 4,000 and 5,000 Hz; sibilance between 6,000 and 10,000 Hz. A powerful way to accentuate a vocal sound, and sounds in general, is to locate and boost the formant regions. A *formant* is the resonance band in a vibrating body that mildly increases the level of the specific frequencies in that band. In men's voices a strong formant is centered around 2,800 Hz, plus or minus a few hundred Hz to compensate for individual differences. For female voices, the formant region is roughly 3,200 Hz. Low formant areas for the human voice are in the areas of 500 Hz for males and 1,000 Hz for females.

ferent reverb times to various components in an ensemble, or it will sound as if they are not playing in the same space, unless it is for special effect.

The quality of the reverberation depends on the musical style. Most types of popular music work well with the sound of digital reverb or a reverb plate. Jazz usually requires a more natural-sounding acoustical environment; classical music definitely does.

In determining reverb balance, adjust it one track at a time (on the tracks to which reverb is being added). Reverb in stereo mixes should achieve a sense of depth and breadth. Reverb can be located in the mix by panning; it does not have to envelop an entire recording.

With reverberation, some equalizing may be necessary. Because plates and chambers tend to generate lower frequencies that muddy sound, attenuating the reverb between 60 and 100 Hz may be necessary to clean up the sound. If muddiness is not a problem, boosting lower frequencies gives the reverb a larger and more distant sound. Boosting higher frequencies gives reverb a brighter, closer, more present sound.

Less expensive reverberation systems lack good treble response. If you slightly boost the high end, the reverb will sound somewhat more natural and lifelike.

If any one voicing is inevitably assigned to reverb, it is the vocal. Yet there is often the danger that the reverb's midrange will interfere with the harmonic richness of the vocal's midrange. Attenuating or notching out the reverb's competing midrange frequencies will better define the vocal and help to make it stand out.

Other effects, such as chorusing and accented reverb, also can be used after reverberation. By setting the chorus for a delay between 20 and 30 milliseconds and adding it to the reverb, you can give sound a shimmering, fuller quality. Patching the reverb output into a noise gate and triggering the noise gate with selected accents from a percussive instrument such as a snare drum, piano, or tambourine can heighten as well as unify the rhythm.

Before making a final decision about the reverb you employ, do an A–B comparison. Check reverb proportions using large and small loudspeakers to make sure the reverb neither swallows sound nor is so subtle that it defies definition.

Digital Delay: Enhancing Acoustic Space

Sound reaches listeners at different times, depending on where a listener is located relative to the sound source. The closer to the sound source you are, the sooner the sound reaches you, and vice versa. Hence, an integral component of reverberation is delay (see Chapter 3). To provide more realistic reverberation, therefore, many digital reverbs include predelay, which sets a slight delay before reverb. If a reverb unit does not include predelay, the same effect can be generated by using a digital delay device before reverb. Predelay adds a feeling of space to the reverberation. In either case predelay should be short; 15 to 20 milliseconds usually suffices. (A millisecond is equivalent to about a foot in space.) On some delay devices, the longer the delay time, the poorer the signal-to-noise ratio.

Postdelay—adding delay after reverb—is another way to add dimension to sound, particularly to a vocal. In the case of the vocal, it may be necessary to boost the high end to brighten the sound or to avoid muddying it, or both.

Another handy use of delay is stereo separation. By feeding a mono signal through a delay to one output channel, say, the left, and the same signal directly to the right channel, you can simulate the signal as stereo. Use short delay times—15 to 20 milliseconds—however, or the delay will be obvious and the stereo imaging may be skewed.

Synchronizing delay to tempo is yet another effect that can heighten sonic interest. This technique involves adjusting rate of delay to the music's tempo by dividing the tempo into 60,000—the dividend is the number of milliseconds per measure to which the digital delay is set.

It is also possible to create polyrhythms —simultaneous and sharply contrasting rhythms—by using two delays and feeding the output of one into the input of the other. Varying the delay time of the second unit generates a variety of spatial effects.

In using a digital delay, there is one precaution: It should have a bandwidth of at least 12 kHz. Given the quality of sound being produced today, however, 15 kHz and higher is recommended.

Two features of digital delay—feedback, or regeneration, and modulation—can be employed in various ways to help create a wide array of effects with flanging, chorusing, doubling, and slapback echo. **Feedback, or regeneration,** as the terms suggest, feeds a proportion of the delayed signal back into the delay line, in essence "echoing the echo." Modulation is controlled by two parameters, width and speed. Width dictates how wide a range above and below the chosen delay time the modulator will be allowed to swing. You can vary the delay by any number of milliseconds above and below the designated time. Speed dictates how rapidly the time delay will oscillate.

Localizing the Musical Elements in Stereo Space

In multitrack recording, each element is recorded at an optimal level and on a separate track. If all the elements were played back in the same way, it would sound as if they were coming from precisely the same location, to say nothing about how imbalanced the voicing would be. In reality, of course, this is not the case. Therefore, you have to position each musical component in an aural frame by setting the levels of loudness to create front-to-back perspective or depth and panning to establish left-to-right stereo perspective. In setting levels, the louder a sound the closer it seems, and conversely, the quieter a sound the farther away it seems. Frequency and reverb also affect positioning (see "Signal Processing" earlier in this chapter). In panning stereo, there are five main areas: left, left center, center, right center, and right (see 5-2).

There are many options in positioning various elements of an ensemble in an aural frame, but three factors are usually considered in the decision: (1) the aural balance, (2) how the ensemble arranges itself when playing before a live audience, and (3) the type of music being played. Keep in mind, however, that each musical style has its own values. Popular music is usually emotional and contains a strong beat. Therefore, drums and bass should be well focused in the mix. Jazz and classical music are more varied and require different approaches. The mixer must have a clear idea of what the music sounds like in a natural acoustical setting before attempting a studio mix.

Sounds and where they are placed in aural space have different effects on perception. In a stereo field these effects include the following: (1) The sound closest to the center and to us is the most predominant; (2) a sound farther back but still in the center creates depth and a balance or a counterweight to the sound that is front and center; (3) sound placed to one side usually requires a similarly weighted sound on the opposite side or else the left-to-right aural space will seem unbalanced; and (4) the more you spread sound across the aural space, the wider the sound sources will seem.

This is not to suggest that all parts of aural space must be sonically balanced or filled at all times; that depends on the ensemble and the music. A symphony orchestra usually positions first violins to the left of the conductor, second violins to the left center, violas to the right center, and cellos to the right. If the music calls for just the first violins to play, it is natural for the sound to come mainly from the left. To pan the first violins left-to-right would establish a stereo balance, but it would be poor aesthetic judgment and it would disorient the listener.

To illustrate aural framing in a stereo field, assume that a pop music group recorded the following voicings on separate tracks: bass, bass drum, left side of drum

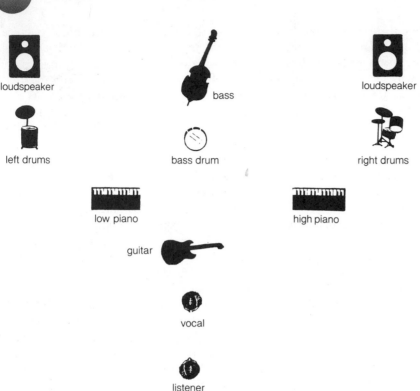

15-3 A spatial arrangement that takes full advantage of stereo spacing. It places sound sources wide and deep, and the sound will be open and airy. Notice that the bass and bass drum are positioned center rear and together to anchor the sound and enhance their blend. The piano is behind the guitar on the assumption that it accompanies throughout the song. The guitar is behind the vocal to provide accompaniment and to be close enough front and center for solos when the vocalist is not singing. (Note: In reality there is no "hole" in the sound of the piano or the drums. Also, the left and right drums are sometimes reversed. See also 15-4.)

set, right side of drum set, low end of piano, high end of piano, electric guitar, and vocal.

For a few ways to position this ensemble, see Figures 15-3 through 15-5. In reality, the music has to be the determining factor. Compared to many mixes, these illustrations show a simplified explanation of a modest recording session. Figure 15-6 depicts a more complex mix; the following text explains the arrangement.

Background vocals are two distinct signals. A wall-of-sound effect;—"Eventide effect"—is achieved by running them through a stereo Harmonizer™. The vocal track on the left is pitched a little flat at 99.6 percent pitch shift, and the signal on the right has a slight delay of 20 milliseconds. This creates the illusion that they are connected by a solid line, yet they can be heard as two separate tracks. It makes the vocal thick.

The lead vocal is in the center of the mix and up front, but it must have depth. A digital reverb helps with that aspect. A very short reverb time gives the vocal resonance

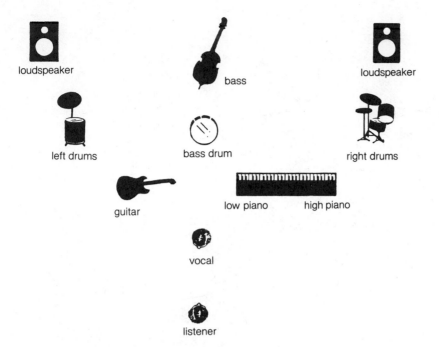

15-4 A spatial arrangement that maintains stereo perspective. This arrangement repositions the guitar and piano for a better balance if they both play solos as well as accompany.

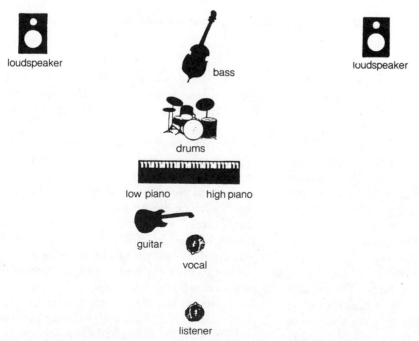

15-5 A closer arrangement. This arrangement changes the open sound for a tighter, more intense sound. The piano also could be positioned to one side of the vocal.

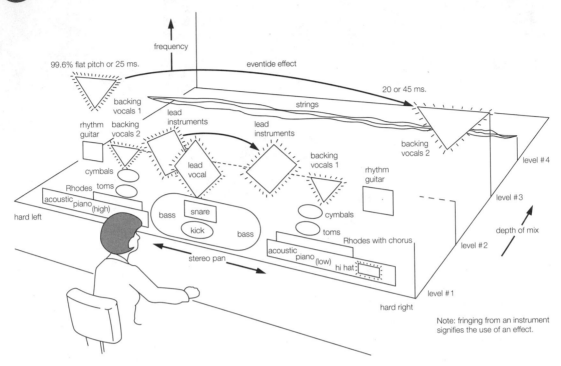

15-6 Visual representation of a more complex mix. (See text for discussion.)

in a natural room sound. Also, a short echo is used, just enough to give the vocal some depth but not too much where it will run into the background vocals that are making the line behind it.

Sometimes the lead vocal and backgrounds end up just a little too close to each other. That placement is good to make the vocals blend with the group. But if they are to sound like two distinct parts, time delay is increased to 25 milliseconds on the left and 45 milliseconds on the right for the vocals in back. In essence, it is like placing the singers a few steps back. The farther back anything goes, the more mushy it becomes. Therefore, the rear vocals require some EQ to make them sound cleaner and more intelligible. Fewer low frequencies and more highs help to achieve that.

The string sound, which is sustained, works best as a long, smooth line way in the back. The effect requires a long echo or digital delay.

Acoustic piano works well up front—dry with no effects—and positioned as though it were being viewed from the audience. The acoustic piano is panned to the 7 o'clock and 5 o'clock positions; any tighter and it would start to sound mono. The mono Fender Rhodes (electric piano) is also spread and set right on top of the acoustic piano, but not to the extreme left and right; the setting is more like 9 o'clock and 3 o'clock. For contrast, the chorus effect is run on the right side. If the chorus effect were run on the left, much of it would be masked by the high acoustic piano. The chorus effect stands out better against the low acoustic piano.

Rhythm guitar fills the space about 9 o'clock and 3 o'clock. A lead guitar, sax, or synthesizer fits just to the left or right of center. The lead instrument is kept a short distance from the bass and central drums.

The bass and kick drum go in the middle of the mix, along with the snare that sits right on top of the kick. These are the three most important elements in a good mix; they are the first impression of the song a listener gets. The hi hat is placed off to the right side. The tom-toms and cymbals are panned across the stereo field from the audience perspective.[*]

Three-Dimensional Sound Imaging

In Chapter 11, we discussed selected 3-D and surround-sound systems used during recording. 3-D and surround-sound systems applied during mixdown are considered here. You will recall that, broadly speaking, **3-D sound** creates the illusion of breadth, depth, and height in the audio field through headphones or using the conventional, two-loudspeaker stereo array in front of the listener. Some 3-D systems are actually two-dimensional but improve the stereo image by effectively bringing the depth and width of the stereo field to the outermost edges of the soundfield on a plane with the listener. **Surround sound** reproduces the illusion of a three-dimensional soundfield by positioning loudspeakers either to the front, sides, and rear of the listener or to the front and rear.

---

[*]From "The Production and Musical Perspectives of Humberto Gatica," by Robert Carr, Recording Engineer/Producer, Oct. 1981. Copyright 1981 Gallay Communications, Inc. All rights reserved. Reprinted by permission.

3-D Sound

Among the available 3-D systems designed for application during mixdown are QSound, the Roland Sound Space Processor, the Sound Retrieval System, and Spatializer.

One of the better-known 3-D systems is *QSound*. QSound consists of eight independent parallel processing channels, joystick controlled, each one providing sound placement outside of the physical frontal stereo loudspeaker locations. QSound, like most 3-D and surround-sound systems, is mono-compatible (see "Stereo-to-Mono Compatibility" later in this chapter).

The *Roland Sound Space Processor* has three main component sections: a *reverb and distance processor,* to add ambience and a perception of distance to the incoming signal; a *binaural signal processor;* and a *transaural processor* that eliminates crosstalk signals from the left speaker to the right ear and from the right speaker to the left ear. The transaural processor provides the ability for enhanced playback of binaural recordings over loudspeakers by bypassing the binaural processor. The Roland Sound Space Processor has three operating modes: Flying Mode allows a mono sound source to be continuously moved around the soundfield in real time; Stationary Mode allows two independent monaural sources to be statically placed anywhere within the 360-degree soundfield; Transaural Mode provides the capability to process original binaural recordings for stereo loudspeaker playback.

The *Sound Retrieval System (SRS)* is based on head-related transfer functions (HRTF) (see Chapter 11). It is a patented technology that creates a soundfield by extracting the ambience information from the original stereo signal and modifying it using a curve for front-to-side correction and to minimize the effects of ear-canal resonance. A mixing technique adds the modified signal along with additional left plus right information to the original left/right signals. The process creates immersion in the 3-D soundfield and eliminates the "sweet spot," permitting the listener to move around with minimal skewing of the sonic imaging.

The *Spatializer* consists of two components: (1) a processor that is connected into a studio's existing signal flow through the patch panel and (2) a portable controller unit (see 15-7 and 15-8). The system makes it possible to control each track's scale and size and near/far and front/rear positioning (see 15-9).

Surround Sound

Surround sound, like 3-D sound, is a psychoacoustic illusion. Most surround-sound systems encode the spatial, or positional, information from the music tracks during final mixing and decode that information during reproduction. Hence, they use an encoder and a decoder to handle channel matrixing in a 4-2-4 format; the encoder unit is 4:2, and the decoder is 2:4.

In the Dolby surround system, for example, programming starts with four audio signals: left, center, right, and surround (L, C, R, S). These four signals are fed during the mix into an encoder that creates two final outputs Dolby calls "Left-total" and "Right-total (L_t and R_t). The original L and R input signals go straight through the encoder to L_t and R_t without change. The C input signal is divided equally between L_t and R_t but with additional processing, including a relative phase shift. The resulting pair of encoded signals is then distributed just like conventional stereo. The decoder separates the pair of encoded signals back

into the four original L, C, R, and S channels. A somewhat similar system is shown in Figure 15-10.

To monitor surround sound during rerecording, the frontal, two-loudspeaker array should be positioned left and right, and two loudspeakers should be placed behind the operator (see 15-11). A frontal three-monitor array would add a center loudspeaker (see 15-12) to stabilize center imaging if the two front loudspeakers are far apart.

Since surround sound has become a part of music production some general observations about mixing surround have emerged.

- The matrixing format, as opposed to the discrete format, can create localization problems; therefore, mix the most dominant elements first. (In a discrete format, each channel remains separate throughout the recording and reproduction stages.)

- Before doing the surround mix, do the left, center, and right mix first.

- When using compression or limiting on vocals, do not process any additional ambience signal through the same compressor-limiter. This reduces the potential for the dominant sound to cause the ambience to "pump."

- When using signal processing, use separate processing devices for each element. Using the same processor for more than one element could, among other things, smear sonic imaging.

- Unless there is a need for a special effect or to be gimmicky, it is usually disconcerting to place major program elements behind the listener. It is one thing to position a listener in a spacious sonic environment with the ensemble across the front and at the edges in a reverberant environment; it is another thing to put the listen-

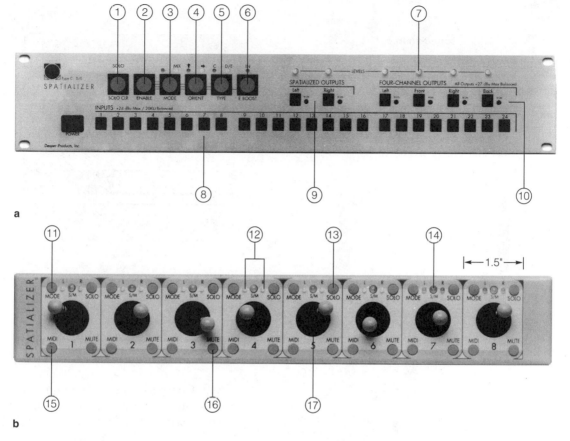

a

b

(1) Clears all stations from solo mode into normal function mode

(2) This lock-out button must be pushed in conjunction with any of the right four buttons

(3) Places each station in calibrate or mixdown mode

(4) Electronically rotates all joystick controls 90° for vertical or horizontal use

(5) Places entire Spatializer in Type C (for original microphone recording) or Type D/E (for mixdown)

(6) Provides additional expansion energy for use with very narrow stereo sources

(7) Tri-level LEDs indicate:

  Yellow = signal too low
  Green = signal OK
  Red = signal clipping

(8) TT style input plugs provided on front panel for ease of connection to patch-bay. Optional parallel-wired connectors located on rear panel

(9) Stereo outputs processed in spatialization

(10) Discrete (nonspatialized) outputs for left, front, right, and back signals. Front output is useful for dialogue and is isolated from the left or right outputs with joystick in front position

(11) Selects Spatialization Types D, E_L, or E_R, or places station off-line

  Type D is a directional function for use with mono sources

  Type E is an expansion function used with stereo sources

  E_L is for use with the left side of a stereo input

  E_R is for use with the right side of the same stereo input

(12) Mode (L & R) LEDs

  C = both amber
  D = both green
  E_L = left red
  E_R = right red

(13) Places station in solo-in-place

(14) Solo/Mute (S/M LEDs)

  Solo = steady green
  Mute (Local) = steady red
  Mute (by Solo) = flashing red

(15) Writes all functions of station to MIDI

(16) Places station in mute

(17) Moves mono sources 350° seamlessly, or scales stereo sources to any size within the soundfield

15-7 3-D audio processing system. (*a*) Processor. (*b*) Controller unit.

Sound source

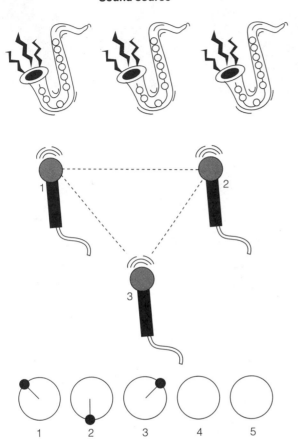

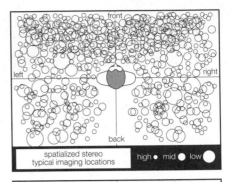

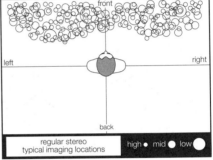

15-9 Comparison of 3-D audio processing and conventional stereo in relation to spatial imaging

15-8 Spatializer recording mode. The Type C mode is used during recording of a single sound source. With an array of at least three microphones placed from 3 to 6 feet apart, routed to the Spatializer, the sound source can be positioned, using the joysticks, to correspond to the relative placement of the mics.

a

b

c

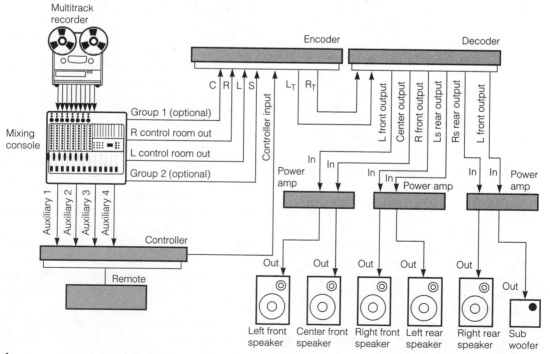

d

15-10 Surround-sound system. (*a*) encoder, (*b*) controller, (*c*) decoder, (*d*) signal flow. This system also comes with a controller remote.

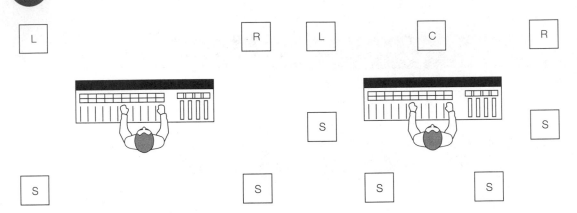

15-11 Audio monitoring for surround sound with front and rear two-loudspeaker arrays

15-12 Audio monitoring for surround sound adding a center loudspeaker

er in the ensemble. In other words: Most people do not listen to music sitting among the musicians. Reproducing that kind of listening experience has been found to be disconcerting. (To be sure, because of human binaural hearing we are in the middle of our sonic environment all the time. Perhaps it is the conditioning from years of listening to frontally imaged sound that disconcerts an audience when it is surrounded artificially by sonic action. Then again, musicians playing in an ensemble do not hear a balanced sound.)

■ When a vocalist and ambience compete, it helps to widen the voice by panning it toward the surround-sound position. Another technique is to add a small amount of synthesized stereo to the left and right channels. Of course, the best thing to do is change the reverberation values and remix.

Monitoring 3-D and Surround Sound

When monitoring 3-D and surround sound there are a few questions you should ask to help evaluate the cohesiveness of a mix. One problem with three-dimensional sonic imaging has been that it sounds disjointed.

Therefore, consider these questions: Does the sound emanate from the appropriate loudspeaker location, or does it seem detached from it? When you move around the listening environment, how much of the positional information, or sonic illusion, remains intact? How robust does that illusion remain in another listening environment? If there are motion changes—sound moving left-to-right, right side-to-right front, and so on—are they smooth? Does any element call unwanted attention to itself?

All in all, the advantages of multidimensional manipulation of sound far outweigh its problems. (1) A particular instrument, or group of instruments, can be localized in a three-dimensional space; (2) ambience can be designed to reach the audience from all directions; and (3) panning of sound can occur across the front sound stage and between front and side/rear locations. When multidimensional manipulation of sound is done right, sonic breadth and depth put the music in a far more realistic perspective than conventional stereo.

Keeping a Record

Keeping a record in a mixdown of the take you used and the settings for levels, EQ, reverb send, reverb return, compression, limiting, and so on is essential. It may take several sessions to complete a mix, and any adjustments previously made must be reset precisely. Moreover, perceptions of a mix have a strange way of changing from one day to the next, and so it is critical to be able to reference the sound to the setting.

Information in automated and computer-assisted mixdowns is usually stored automatically. It may be recalled for visual display or printed out in a hard copy. This convenience notwithstanding, it is always wise to make a backup copy of all computer-encoded information.

Stereo-to-Mono Compatibility

Although stereo-to-mono compatibility has been considered in Chapter 11, it is important enough to warrant a reminder here in relation to conventional stereo mixing. Except for home component music systems, in this wide world of stereo radio, TV, and videos, most people still receive mediated information in mono. In virtually anything you stereo-master, therefore, its monophonic playback may well be a consideration.

The preferred way to produce stereo for mono compatibility is to do two different mixes, one for stereo and one for mono. Although this best-of-all-worlds approach takes time and costs more in terms of extra studio and mastering fees, it is done.

When producing two separate mixes is not feasible, stereo-to-mono compatibility must be checked and rechecked throughout the mixdown. What sounds good in stereo may be less than acceptable in mono. A wide and satisfactorily balanced stereo recording played in mono may be too loud. For example, a 0 VU reading at the extreme left and right in stereo is equivalent to +6 in mono. Anything assigned to the center in the stereo mix may be too loud in mono and out of context with the rest of the sound. Moreover, placing voicings extreme left or right in stereo results in a 3-dB or greater loss in their level(s) relative to the rest of the spectrum when played in mono.

So the problem of stereo-to-mono compatibility is twofold: too much sound in the center and not enough of the left and right sound. The reason, briefly stated, is that signals in phase in stereo add in mono, and signals out of phase in stereo cancel in mono.

Certain devices, such as the *phasing analyzer* or *stereo display processor,* can be used to indicate stereo-to-mono compatibility during a mix (see 15-13, p. 352). Many of today's pan pots are designed with either a 3 dB- or a 6 dB-down notch that facilitates mono compatibility.

Two other techniques are also used. One is not to put anything dead center or at the

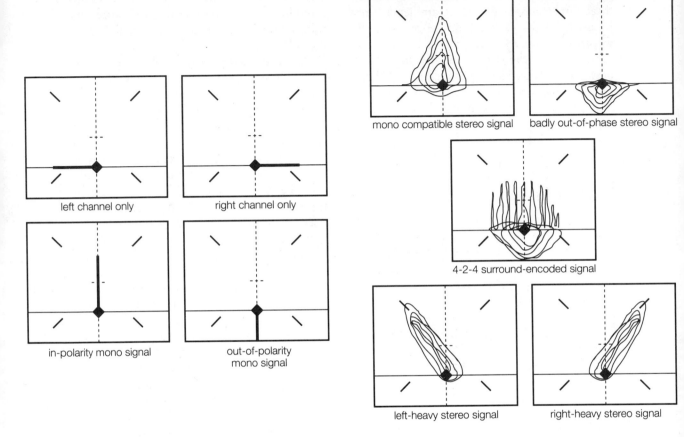

left channel only   right channel only

in-polarity mono signal   out-of-polarity mono signal

mono compatible stereo signal   badly out-of-phase stereo signal

4-2-4 surround-encoded signal

left-heavy stereo signal   right-heavy stereo signal

15-13 Examples of displays on a stereo phasing analyzer

extreme left or right in a stereo mix. This reduces both center channel buildup and loss of some of the left and right information when playing stereo recordings in mono. But the stereo image may not be as wide as it should be, and center imaging could be awkward.

The better technique is to be very careful of in-phase and out-of-phase signals during recording and signal processing, especially with reverb, and to constantly "A–B" between stereo and mono playback during a mix, using both your ears and a phasing analyzer. In the A–B comparisons, always check to make sure that nothing is lost due to phase, that nothing stands out inordinately, and that the overall blend is maintained.

Stereo-to-mono compatibility is less of a problem in 3-D and surround sound than it is in conventional stereo. Most 3-D and surround-sound processing systems are mono-compatible.

16

THE MASTER

The next to last stage in music recording is to prepare the master mixdown tape for premastering, or mastering, to compact disc. The master tape contains the final mix of the selected songs on either open-reel tape or DAT. It may then be sent directly to the CD mastering house or premastered to recordable compact disc (CD-R) in the studio before being sent on for final CD mastering (see 16-1).

Recording Calibration Tones

As noted in Chapter 13, recording calibration or reference tones on master tapes is essential for three reasons: (1) They serve as a check to ensure that console and tape recorder VU meters are aligned and will be consistent throughout recording, mixing, and mastering; (2) they provide a reference for anyone calibrating console and tape recorder levels at any stage in the recording or mixdown, whether that person is involved in all or only part of the project; and (3) they

ensure consistent levels if the tape is used in another studio. Different procedures are used in recording tones, but the idea is to give an engineer adequate information to permit proper calibration and alignment of equipment. Before recording tones, slate the master. Tones are recorded at the beginning of the master tape on both channels.

Tones on Analog Tape

With analog tape, tones are usually recorded at 0 VU (100 percent of modulation) and for 15 to 20 seconds each. Tones on multitrack should have a longer duration because there are more adjustments to make.

One recommended order is to start with a 1,000-Hz tone, then group the following tones: 50 Hz, 100 Hz, 1,000 Hz, 10,000 Hz, and 15,000 Hz. These tones should be recorded without noise reduction. If noise reduction is used, then record the Dolby SR tone after the four tones. With stereo, record a short burst of 1,000-Hz tone on the left channel. Leave at least 15 seconds

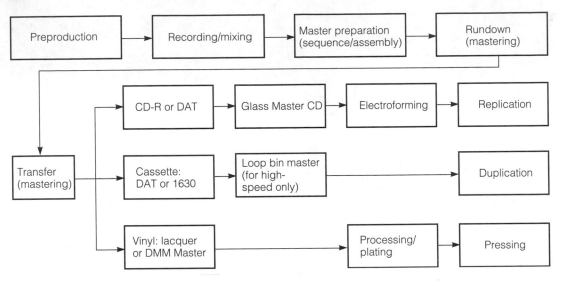

16-1 Production flowchart (1630 = Sony PCM ¾" videotape).

before program material starts. With time code, begin recording it at 20 seconds before the program material.

During playback the 1,000-Hz tone is used to set overall level, balance the left and right channels, and check flux density. *Flux density* is a measure of the amount of magnetism in a given area. A tape with greater flux density will replay louder than a tape with lesser density. Flux density is measured in Webers (Wb), though for audio, the nanoWeber (nWb) is used.* On the tape box, write the flux density and its relationship to operating level. For example, 0 dB = 200nWb/m or 0 dB = 320nWb/m. (The test tape gives this information.) To check azimuth, 10,000 or 15,000 Hz is used, but the higher frequency permits greater accuracy. The other tones are used

to set playback equalization. The left channel burst is an effective way to identify correctly which channel is which.

When one tone is used, as it sometimes is for recordings not being processed for further mastering, it is 1,000 Hz. To be safe, however, record at least three tones—low-frequency, 1,000-Hz, and high-frequency.

Tones on Digital Tape

With digital tape, record 20–30 seconds of 1,000-Hz tone at the agreed level. Be sure to write this level on the tape box with reference to dB full scale, that is, maximum digital level. For example, 0 dB = 14 dB FS. Then follow with 15–20 seconds of 10,000 Hz at the same level. This tone is not absolutely necessary, but it serves to help check phase accuracy. Record 100-Hz and 45-Hz tones at the same level. These are useful for digital converter checks. With stereo, record a short burst of 1,000 Hz tone on the left channel. Record at least 15 seconds of digital zero before the program material starts.

---

*A nanoWeber is literally one billionth of a weber. A weber is the basic unit of magnetic flux, defined as 1 volt-second. On recording tape, flux density is measured in nanowebers per meter (nWb/m).

With time code, at least 20 seconds of it should precede the program material. Write on the tape box details about the digital recorder and sampling frequency. (If the tape is being mastered to CD, the sampling frequency should be 44.1.)

Assembling the Master

After the calibration tones have been recorded and the final mix has been recorded on the master, it is time to assemble and label the master. Again, techniques may vary with the project but, essentially, whatever is on the master must be readily apparent to anyone handling it. This is no minor detail considering that the mastering plant is the last stop before marketing.

Open-Reel Tape

With open-reel tape, splice 15 to 20 seconds of leader tape to the front and tail ends of the magnetic tape to protect the recording at these exposed and vulnerable points and to provide a suitable length of tape to thread the machine prior to the presence of any sound signal. Use color-coded leader tape to tell which end is which. Some studios use red leader tape at the head of the audiotape and blue leader tape at the tail, although paper leader tape may be used for mastering. Separate different segments within the audiotape with leader tape to provide a visual means of identifying where material begins and ends (see 14-4). The following is one commonly used procedure.

1. 15 to 20 seconds of leader tape
2. Slate
3. 10 to 15 seconds of leader tape
4. Reference tones
5. 20 seconds of time code (if being used)
6. 10 to 15 seconds of leader tape
7. Song 1
8. 10 to 15 seconds of leader tape
9. Song 2
10. Repeat steps 8–9 until the last cut
11. 15 to 20 seconds of leader tape (spliced after the last sound decays)

If the number of songs requires more than one reel of tape, then follow the same procedures listed for the other master reel(s).

Mastering to DAT

If you are recording the final mix onto DAT:

1. Set the sampling frequency on the R-DAT to either 44.1 or 48 kHz. If the DAT recording is being premastered or mastered to CD, use 44.1 kHz. Should some of the songs already be recorded at 48 kHz, stay with that frequency rather than switching back and forth between sample rates on your master.

2. At the head of the DAT record a 20- to 30-second 1000-Hz tone at 0 dB. (Depending on the CD mastering house you use, the calibration tone may be unnecessary. Some CD mastering engineers set the recording level to the DAT recording's peak program level.)

3. Record 15 seconds of silence. Recording silence instead of letting the blank tape spool to the first cue point reduces tape noise and keeps inherent tape level uniform.

4. Zero the tape counter.

5. Audition the final mix and note where maximum loudness occurs. Set the R-DAT's sound level meter for −3 dB at that point. With R-DATs that use a peak program meter (ppm), if a peak

reaches 0 level, it is too high. Remember that unlike analog recording, digital recording has no headroom; 0 dB is absolute maximum recording level.

6. Put the R-DAT into the RECORD PAUSE mode. Use the RECORD PAUSE toggle switch; it starts and stops the tape motion at a flick of the finger.

7. Start the multitrack ATR in Play and tap the RECORD PAUSE on the R-DAT.

8. Once the first song is recorded onto R-DAT, tap RECORD PAUSE to stop the R-DAT's tape motion.

9. Record five seconds of silence on the DAT; cue the multitrack ATR to the second song, and repeat steps 7–9.

10. At the end of the last song on the DAT, record silence until the end of the reel.

It should be noted that RECORD PAUSE and STOP sometimes put an audible pulse on the DAT. Be aware that this noise is much quieter in some R-DATs than in others. Moreover, if the noise is too loud, many CD mastering houses will reject the DAT master.

Logging and Labeling

Once the master tape is assembled, log and label it. Put the essential information about the recording preferably on, or attached to, and in the tape box or casing. Also, put some identification on the reel itself in case it gets separated from its box or casing. Depending on the tape's destination, information should include such details as these:

1. Titles of album and songs

2. Artist/client

3. Producer, engineer, and others to receive credit

4. Start and end time of each song and each song's total time

5. Recording format (analog or digital)

6. Tape speed (if analog open-reel tape, no slower than 15 ips; if digital open-reel tape, indicate the sampling frequency)

7. Track format (i.e., two-track stereo, matrixed surround sound, mono)

8. Make and model of the mastering tape recorder

9. Tape type (e.g., Scotch 996, Ampex 476 DAT)

10. Tape wind—heads or tails out

11. Location, frequencies, order, and duration of test tones

12. Location of the highest peak level on the tape

13. Whether noise reduction was used and, if so, what type

14. Desired level and EQ changes (if the mastering plant performs these functions; many require masters that are ready-to-cut)

15. Any peculiarities or things to watch out for

If the recording requires a cue sheet or other documentation, attach it to or place it inside the tape box, but make sure it accompanies the tape in some way. Be sure the printed material is complete and clearly transcribed. The cue sheet may include such information as song times, the in and out SMPTE time-code or tape-time cue points, the type of segment stops (an abrupt end, fade, and so forth), any sudden changes in loudness level, and any other elements that require attention.

Finally, if you use open-reel tape, do not use reels smaller than 7 inches. The 10½-inch reel is preferred; 5- and 3-inch reels could create problems with tape tension and result in an uneven wind. Also, the smaller the reel, the more master reels you will need. Put on the reel only the tape containing the recording, not any leftover blank tape.

Tape Label System

In an effort to eliminate problems with tape identification, a system that has gained widespread acceptance in studios around the world color-codes tape labels. The system was introduced by the British Record Producers Guild and ΛPRS (The Association of Professional Recording Services) in 1986 and has the approval of U.S. Society of Professional Audio Recording Services (SPARS) (see 16-2).

Safety Copy

Once the master tape has been cut, make a safety copy by **dubbing** it from one tape recorder to another with absolutely no changes. Dubbing is the procedure of transferring sound from one tape or disk to another. Make sure you calibrate the two tape recorders before dubbing. Store the safety copy in a secure, temperature- and humidity-controlled environment. For more about tape handling and storage, see Chapters 6 and 7. It belabors the obvious to say that if anything happens to the master and you do not have a safety copy, all the days of hard work will have gone for naught.

Premastering to Compact Disc

The advent of the compact disc recorder and recordable compact disc (CD-R) has made it not only possible to premaster tape to CD in-studio, but convenient as well (see Chapter 7). In addition to CD recorders

that encode one disc at a time, there are systems that can make a CD and duplicate it at twice to several times the conventional speed (see 16-3).

Production Checklist

As noted earlier in this chapter, and in Chapters 13 and 15, good documentation throughout the recording session, mixdown, and preparation of the master helps to ensure that nothing gets forgotten. Good record keeping makes a big difference to anyone handling a project. Although every studio has it own form(s), the Production Checklist in Figure 16-4 is a good example of the types of information to catalog.

Evaluating the Finished Product

In producing audio, sound quality should be evaluated every step of the way. It is after the final mix, though, when the moment of truth arrives.

But what makes good sound? You will recall the response from Chapter 1: If you ask 100 experts you will undoubtedly get 100 different opinions. That is one of the beauties of sound: It is so personal. Who is to tell you that your taste is wrong? As a listener, if it satisfies you, that is all that matters. When sound is being produced for an audience, however, professional "ears" must temper personal taste. To this end, there are generally accepted standards that most sound designers agree are reasonable bases for artistic judgment.

Before discussing these standards, a reminder about the monitor loudspeakers is in order. Remember that the sound you are evaluating is influenced by the loudspeaker reproducing it. Therefore, you must be thor-

blue

SESSION TAPE   APRS & SPARS

A multitrack or 2-track work tape; may contain outtakes. Space is provided for additional information.

red

ORIGINAL MASTER   APRS & SPARS

The earliest possible generation of the final stereo product. It is not necessarily suitable as a "Production master"; consult Producer. Space is provided for additional information.

green

PRODUCTION MASTER   APRS & SPARS
☐ CD ☐ MC ☐ VINYL ☐ DCC ☐ MD

All necessary Eq and other audio treatment, if any, has been applied to the program material for the format(s) indicated. But in the case of CD, DCC, or MD, a "Tape Master" will need to be prepared before manufacturing.

orange

PROD'N MASTER ☐COPY ☐CLONE   APRS & SPARS
☐ CD ☐ MC ☐ VINYL ☐ DCC ☐ MD

A duplicate of a "Production Master" that has been prepared in one of two ways. A digital tape that has been digitally transferred from a digital source is referred to as a Clone, while any transfer made via analog converters or from an analog source is known as a Copy. All transfers onto analog tape are Copies, irrespective of the source; further Copies should not be made from these without the approval of the Producer.

gray

PQ ENCODED TAPE MASTER   ☐ CD ☐ ORIGINAL / ☐ DCC ☐ DIGITAL / ☐ MD CLONE   APRS & SPARS

Fully prepared and PQ encoded tape ready for the manufacture of CD, DCC, or MD. Parameters for each format are different; only one format can therefore be indicated on the label. Clones made from an "Original" Tape Master must contain regenerated (and re-laid) timecode and PQ information.

pink

SAFETY☐ COPY ☐ CLONE   APRS & SPARS
☐ OF.......................................

Strictly for *safety*; should be used only with the approval of the Producer.

yellow

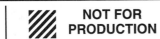 **NOT FOR PRODUCTION**   APRS & SPARS

Self-explanatory; identifies a tape, in any format, which is not suitable for manufacturing.

yellow

MEDIA VERSION   APRS & SPARS
☐ RADIO ☐ TV ☐ FILM ☐ VIDEO

Supplied only for the specific purpose indicated. Not suitable for manufacturing.

16-2 The tape label system

oughly familiar with its frequency response and how it otherwise affects sonic reproduction. If a sound is overly bright or unduly dull, you have to know whether it is the result of the recording or the loudspeaker. A good way to familiarize yourself with a loudspeaker's response is to take a few well-produced recordings with which you are

thoroughly familiar, or specially made reference CDs, and listen to them on the monitor system until you know its response characteristics (see Chapter 9).

The following standards of evaluation are general guidelines, not rules. They do not assume special effects, experimentation, or new visions.

a

16-3 CD mastering and copying system.
(*a*) Write-once CD recorder. (*b*) Disc Transporter with 75-CD disc supply spindle. With this particular system, the master tape is dubbed to a hard disk computer. The master CD is recorded from the hard disk. The Disc Transporter can make up to 75 CD copies in one operation. The recorder may be used for one-at-a-time CD recording. When it is used with the disc transporter, it is positioned behind the transporter so the supply spindle can automatically load and unload the CD-Rs.

b

Intelligibility

It makes sense that if there is a lyric the words must be intelligible. If not, meaning is lost. But when you work with material over a long period of time, the words become so familiar that it might not be apparent that they are muffled, masked, and otherwise difficult to make out. Therefore, in evaluating intelligibility it is a good idea to do it with fresh ears, as if you were hearing the words for the first time.

Tonal Balance

Bass, midrange, and treble frequencies should be balanced; no one octave or range of octaves should stand out. Be particularly aware of too much low end that muddies and masks sound; overly bright upper midrange and treble that bring out sibilance and noise; absence of brilliance that dulls sound; and too much midrange that causes the harshness, shrillness, or edge that annoys and fatigues.

The timbre of the vocal and acoustic instruments should sound natural and realistic. Music generated by electric and electronic instruments does not necessarily have to sound so.

Ensemble sound should blend as a whole. As such, solos or lead voicings should be sonically proportional in relation to the accompaniment.

PRODUCTION CHECKLIST

1

ARTIST _____

PROJECT TITLE _____

2

CATALOGUE NUMBER _____

PREPRODUCTION AT _____

DEMO FORMAT _____

MAIN RECORDING AT _____

SEQUENCER(S) USED _____ VERSION _____

MULTITRACK TAPE FORMAT _____

PRODUCER _____

ENGINEERS _____

A & R REP _____

MIXED AT _____

3

ALBUM ☐   7" SINGLE ☐   12" SINGLE ☐   OTHER _____

4

STEREO ORIGINAL MASTER TAPE FORMAT _____ **Tape Nos** _____

Noise reduction (if any) _____   _____

Tones OK? _____   _____

5

STEREO PRODUCTION MASTER TAPE FORMAT _____ **Tape Nos** _____

Noise reduction (if any) _____   _____

Tones OK? _____   _____

16-4 Production checklist

6 FIRST RECORDING.............................
DATE

7 LAST RECORDING.............................
DATE

8

ALL NECESSARY CLEARANCES AND
SIGNATURES OBTAINED ☐ ....
DATE

MIXES COMPLETE AND APPROVED
BY ALL PARTIES ☐ ....
DATE

EDITS, SINGLES, TV TRACKS, FOREIGN
VERSIONS CLEARLY IDENTIFIED ON BOXES
AND LISTED BELOW ☐ ....
DATE

DETAILS   TAPE Nos

_____   _____

_____   _____

_____   _____

9

MULTITRACKS LABELED/MARKED ☐ ....
WITH ALL FINAL INFO **DATE**

MULTITRACK OUTTAKES IDENTIFIED/MARKED ☐ ....
"DO NOT USE" **DATE**

MULTITRACK TONES REEL EXISTS: ☐ TONES ON TAPE Nos _____

10 MULTITRACK SESSION TAPES CONTAINING Ⓜ TAKES:

TITLE(S) _____   TAPE Nos _____

_____   _____

_____   _____

_____   _____

_____   _____

_____   _____

16-4 Production checklist (*continued*)

11

TRACK SHEETS ....
CHECKED AND IN TAPE BOXES ☐ **DATE**

COMPUTER MIXING......................................
DISKS IN MULTITRACK BOXES ☐ **DATE**

RECALL SHEETS ....
IN MULTITRACK BOXES ☐ **DATE**

MIDI DISKS STORED AT _____

12

MULTITRACK SAFETY COPIES/
CLONES & DISK BACKUPS OK ☐ ....
DATE

ORIGINALS STORED AT _____

SAFETIES STORED AT   _____

13

RUNNING ORDER ....
APPROVED BY ALL PARTIES ☐ **DATE**

TIMINGS CHECKED—OK?   ☐

14

STEREO ORIGINAL
MASTER (S) COMPILED............................
DATE

STEREO PRODUCTION
MASTER (S) COMPILED........................
DATE

(Indicate clearly below if the same production master is suitable for more than one medium.
The tapes themselves should also be so identified.)

MEDIUM   TAPE Nos

CD _____   _____

CASSETTE _____   _____

VINYL _____   _____

DCC _____   _____

MD _____   _____

15 PREVIOUS GENERATION MASTERS MARKED
NOT FOR PRODUCTION (IF APPROPRIATE) ☐ ....
DATE

ALL UNWANTED MIXES, COPIES & REDUNDANT
VERSIONS RECALLED AND DESTROYED OR
MARKED "DO NOT USE" ☐ ....
DATE

LABEL COPY, TIMINGS, AND CREDITS
FOR ARTWORK SUBMITTED ☐ ....
DATE

16-4 Production checklist (*continued*)

[16] MASTERING FACILITES BOOKED BY _____

DATE/TIME OF SESSION _____

STUDIO/ENGINEER _____

ATTENDED BY _____

MATRIX/CUT Nos _____

[17] REFERENCE ACETATE APPROVED

☐ .... **DATE**

MASTER LACQUERS CUT

☐ .... **DATE**

STUDIO/ENGINEER _____

[18] 1610/1630 PQ CODED

CD TAPE MASTER PREPARED

☐ .... **DATE**

STUDIO/ENGINEER _____

[19] DCC MASTER (WITH PQ AND TEXT) PREPARED ☐ .... **DATE**

1630/FLOPPY DISK ☐

DCC MASTER CASSETTE ☐

STUDIO/ENGINEER _____

[20] 1630 MD TAPE MASTER PREPARED ☐ .... **DATE**

WITH TEXT ☐ WITHOUT TEXT ☐

STUDIO/ENGINEER _____

[21] CD TAPE MASTER/CLONE SUPPLIED FOR MANUFACTURING ☐ .... **DATE**

TO _____

[22] MASTER LACQUERS SUPPLIED FOR MANUFACTURING ☐ .... **DATE**

TO _____

16-4 Production checklist (*continued*)

23   CASSETTE MASTER SUPPLIED FOR MANUFACTURING ☐ ....
DATE

TO _____

24   DCC MASTER SUPPLIED FOR MANUFACTURING ☐ ....
DATE

TO _____

25   MD MASTER SUPPLIED FOR MANUFACTURING ☐ ....
DATE

TO _____

26   EXPORT COPIES/CLONES OF PRODUCTION MASTER

COUNTRY	COPIED BY	FORMAT	DATE
_____	_____	_____	_____
_____	_____	_____	_____
_____	_____	_____	_____
_____	_____	_____	_____
_____	_____	_____	_____
_____	_____	_____	_____
_____	_____	_____	_____

27   1st RUN CD OK ☐ ....   1st RUN DCC OK ☐ ....
        DATE   **DATE**

VINYL TEST PRESSING OK ☐ ....   1st RUN MINIDISC (MD) OK ☐ ....
        DATE   **DATE**

1st RUN CASSETTE OK ☐ ....   RELEASE DATE ☐ ....
        DATE   **DATE**

16-4 Production checklist (*concluded*)

Spatial Balance and Perspective

All sonic elements in aural space should be unambiguously localized; it should be clear where various sounds are coming from. Their relationships—front-to-rear and side-to-side—should be in proper perspective. An oboe solo should be distinct yet come from its relative position in the orchestra; a vocal should not be too far in front of an ensemble or buried in it; accompaniment should not overwhelm the vocal; there should not be holes in the stereo or surround-sound imaging.

Positional and loudness changes should be subtle and sound natural. They should not jar or distract by jumping out, falling back, or bouncing from side to side or front to rear.

Definition

Each element should be clearly defined—identifiable, separate, and distinct—yet, if part of an ensemble, blended so that no one element stands out or crowds or masks another's sound. Each element should have its position in, and yet be a natural part of, the sound's overall spectral range and spatial arrangement.

Dynamic Range

The range of levels from quietest to loudest should be as wide as the medium allows, with the quietest sounds easily audible and the loudest sounds undistorted. If compressed, sound should not seem squeezed together, nor should it surge from quiet to loud or vice versa.

Cleanness

A clean recording is as noise- and distortion-free as possible. Hum, hiss, leakage, phasing, smearing, blurring from too much reverb, and harmonic, intermodulation, and loudness distortion—all clutter and thicken sound, adversely affecting clarity.

Airiness

Sound should be airy and open. It should not sound isolated, stuffy, muffled, closed-down, dead, lifeless, overwhelming, or oppressive.

Acoustical Appropriateness

Acoustics, of course, must be good, but they must also be appropriate. Classical music and jazz sound most natural in an open, relatively spacious environment. Acoustics for rock-and-roll can range from tight to open. The Blues sound more earthy in intimate acoustics.

Production Values

The degree to which you are able to develop and appraise production values is what separates the craftsperson from the artist. Production values relate to the material's style, interest, color, and inventiveness. It is the most difficult part of an evaluation to define or quantify, because response is qualitative and intuitive. Material with excellent production values grabs and moves you. It draws you into the music, compelling you to forget your role as objective observer; you become the audience. When this happens, it is not only the culmination of the music recording but its fulfillment.

Glossary

Accent miking A microphone placed close to a sound source to supplement the mix from distant microphones with added presence and balance.

Acoustical phase The time relationship between two or more sound waves at a given point in their cycles.

Acoustics The science that deals with the behavior of sound and sound control. The sound qualities of a studio.

Active combining network (ACN) An amplifier at which the outputs of two or more signal paths are mixed together before being routed to their destination.

Additive ambience When the ambience of each track becomes cumulative in mixing a multitrack recording.

AES/EBU interface Internationally accepted professional 2-channel digital audio interface transmitted via a balanced line connection using XLR connectors, specified jointly by the Audio Engineering Society and the European Broadcast Union. *See also* **SPDIF.**

Air loss The friction of air molecules as sound waves move across distance through an elastic medium that causes their conversion to heat.

Ambience Sounds such as reverberation, noise, and atmosphere that form a background to the main sound.

Ambience microphone A microphone placed far enough from the sound source to pick up ambience for mixing with the sound picked up by the main mics placed in the close soundfield.

Ambisonic Term to describe the sound-field microphone's "surround sound" pickup.

Amplifier A device that boosts the power of an electric signal.

Amplitude The magnitude of a sound wave or electric signal.

Amplitude processor A signal processor that affects a signal's loudness.

Analog recording A method of recording in which the wave form of the recorded signal resembles the wave form of the original signal.

Assemble editing Dubbing segments from one tape or tapes to another tape in sequential order.

Assistant engineer Person(s) who assist(s) the engineer. *See also* **Engineer.**

Assistant producer Person(s) who assist(s) the producer. *See also* **Producer.**

Attack   (1) The way a sound begins—that is, by plucking, bowing, striking, blowing, etc. (2) The first part of the sound envelope.

Attack time   The length of time it takes a limiter or compressor to respond to the input signal.

Auditory nerve   The nerve in the inner ear that transmits sound waves to the brain.

Azimuth   Alignment of the record and playback heads so that their centerlines are parallel to each other and at right angles to the direction of the tape motion passing across the heads.

B

Balanced line   A line (or circuit) with two conductors of equal voltage.

Band-pass filter   A filter that attenuates above and below a selected bandwidth, allowing the frequencies between to pass.

Bandwidth   The difference between the upper and lower frequency limits of an audio component. The upper and lower frequency limits of AM radio are 535 and 1,605 kHz; therefore, the bandwidth of AM radio is 1,070 kHz.

Bandwidth curve   The curve shaped by the number of frequencies in a bandwidth and their relative increase or decrease in level. A bandwidth of 100 to 150 Hz with 125 Hz boosted 15 dB forms a sharp, narrow bandwidth curve; a bandwidth of 100 to 6,400 Hz with a 15-dB boost at 1,200 Hz forms a more sloping, wider bandwidth curve.

Basilar membrane   Structure in the inner ear whose vibrations stimulate the hair cells, producing nerve impulses that carry sound information to the brain.

Bass   The low range of the audible frequency spectrum; usually from 20 to 320 Hz.

Bass roll-off   Attenuating bass frequencies. The control—for example, on a microphone—used to roll off bass frequencies.

Bass trap   A diaphragmatic absorber that absorbs low-frequency sound waves. *See*

also **Diaphragmatic absorber**.

Bias current   An extremely high-frequency AC current, far beyond audibility, added during a tape recording to linearize the magnetic information.

Bidirectional microphone   A microphone that picks up sound to its front and back and is dead at its sides.

Binaural hearing   Hearing with two ears attached to and separated by the head.

Binaural microphone head   Two omnidirectional capacitor microphones set into the ear cavities of an artificial head, complete with pinnas. This arrangement preserves binaural localization cues during recording and reproduces sound as humans hear it, three-dimensionally.

Binaural sound   Sound recorded using the binaural microphone head, or a similar miking arrangement, and reproduced through two separate headphone channels.

Blast filter   *See* **Pop filter.**

Blumlein technique   In stereo miking, placing two bidirectional microphones at a 90-degree angle to each other.

Board   Audio mixing console.

Bounce tracks   To transfer two or more previously recorded tape tracks to a single track, thus allowing rerecording on the previously used tracks.

Boundary microphone   A microphone whose capsule is mounted flush with or close to, but a precise distance from, a reflective surface so that there is no phase cancellation of reflected sound at audible frequencies.

Bulk eraser   A demagnetizer used to erase an entire roll of magnetic tape without removing it from its reel. Also known as a **degausser**.

Bus   A mixing network that combines the outputs of other channels.

C

Calibration   Adjusting equipment—for example, a console and a tape recorder—

according to a standard so that their measurements are similar. *See also* **Electronic alignment.**

Capacitor   A device capable of storing an electric charge.

Capacitor microphone   A microphone that transduces acoustic energy into electric energy electrostatically.

Capstan   The shaft that rotates against the tape, pulling it across the heads at a constant speed.

Cardioid microphone   A unidirectional microphone with a heart-shaped pickup pattern.

CD   *See* **Compact disc.**

CD-E   Erasable compact disc.

CD-MO   Magneto-optical compact disc.

CD-R   Recordable compact disc.

CD-WO   Write-once compact disc.

Center frequency   In peak/dip equalizing, the frequency at which maximum boost or attenuation occurs.

Channel   A conduit through which the signal flows.

Chorus effect   Recirculating the doubling effect to make one sound source sound like several. *See also* **Doubling.**

Click track   A specially recorded track of rhythmic measurements used to maintain the beat and timing of musicians or conductor.

Closing miking   Placing a microphone close to a sound source to pick up mostly direct sound and reduce ambience and leakage.

Cochlea   Snail-shaped organ of hearing in the inner ear that transduces mechanical vibration into electrical neurological signals.

Coercivity   The magnetic force field necessary to reduce a tape from saturation to full erasure. This value is expressed in oersteds.

Coincident miking   Employs two matched microphones, usually unidirectional, crossed one above the other on a vertical axis with their diaphragms angled apart and aimed toward the left and right sides of the ensemble. *See also* **X-Y miking.**

Compact disc (CD)   A digitally encoded disc 4.7 inches in diameter, capable of containing more than 60 minutes of audio that is encoded and read out by a laser beam.

Compander   Contraction of the words *compressor* and *expander* that refers to the devices that compress an input signal and expand an output signal to reduce noise. Also refers to a noise reducer.

Complementary equalization   Equalizing sounds that share similar frequency ranges so that they complement, rather than interfere with, one another.

Compression   (1) Reducing a signal's output level in relation to its input level to reduce dynamic range. (2) Drawing together of vibrating molecules, thus producing a high-pressure area. *See also* **Rarefaction.**

Compression ratio   The ratio of the input and output signals in a compressor.

Compression threshold   The level at which a compressor acts on an input signal and the compression ratio takes effect.

Compressor   A signal processor with an output level that decreases as its input level increases.

Condenser microphone *See* **Capacitor microphone.**

Console   An electronic device that amplifies, processes, and combines input signals and routes them to broadcast or recording.

Constructive interference   When sound waves are partially out of phase, and partially additive, increasing amplitude where compression and rarefaction occur at the same time.

Contact microphone   A microphone that attaches to a sound source and transduces the vibrations that pass through it.

Coverage angle   The off-axis angle or point at which loudspeaker level is down 6 dB compared to the on-axis output level.

Critical distance   The point in an enclosed space where the direct and reverberant fields are at equal level.

Crossover frequency The frequency at which the high frequencies are routed to the tweeter(s) and the low frequencies are routed to the woofer(s).

Crossover network The device that separates the high and low frequencies for routing to the tweeter(s) and woofer(s).

Cut-and-splice editing Editing tape or film by physically cutting the material and joining the cut ends with splicing tape. The term is also used in computer hard disk editing when segments are removed and joined, although there is no physical cutting and splicing of the material.

Cycles per second *See* **Hertz.**

D

Damping Suppressing vibration (usually unwanted vibration such as ringing or buzzing) with a physical restraint.

DASH format *See* **Digital Audio Stationary Head format.**

DAW *See* **Digital audio workstation.**

dBm An electrical measurement of power referenced to 1 milliwatt.

dB-SPL *See* **Sound pressure level.**

dBu Unit of measurement for expressing the relationship of decibels to voltage—0.775 volt—to obtain a relative level without regard to a standard 600-ohm impedance. *See also* **dBv.**

dBv Unit of measurement for expressing the relationship of decibels to voltage—0.775 volt—measured across a 600-ohm line. *See also* **dBu.**

dBV A measure of voltage with decibels referenced to 1 volt.

Decay The decrease in amplitude after a stimulus has been removed from a vibrating object.

Decay time *See* **Reverberation time.**

Decca Tree Three omnidirectional microphones mounted at the ends of a T-shaped frame.

Decibel A relative and dimensionless unit to measure the ratio of two quantities.

De-esser A compressor that reduces sibilance.

Defined region The section of a samplefile that has been selected for editing.

Degausser *See* **Bulk eraser.**

Delay The time interval between a sound or signal and each of its repeats.

Destructive editing Permanently alters the original sound or soundfile. *See also* **Nondestructive editing.**

Destructive interference When sound waves are partially out of phase and partially subtractive, decreasing amplitude where compression and rarefaction occur at different times.

Diaphragmatic absorber A flexible panel mounted over an air space that resonates at a frequency (or frequencies) determined by the stiffness of the panel and the size of the air space.

Diffraction The spreading or bending around of sound waves as they pass an object.

Diffusion The scattering of sound waves.

Digital Audio Stationary Head format (DASH) A format agreed to by Sony, Studer, and TASCAM to standardize digital recording.

Digital audio workstation (DAW) A multifunctional hard-disk production system, controlled from a central location, that is integrated with and networked to other devices, such as audio, video, and MIDI sources, within or between facilities.

Digital compact cassette (DCC) Stationary head digital audio cassette tape recorder developed by Philips.

Digital recording A method of recording in which samples of the original analog signal are encoded on tape as pulses and then decoded during playback.

Digital signal processing (DSP) In hard disk recording or editing, digital signal processing of audio through the use of algorithms (programs that perform complex calculations according to a set of controlled parameters).

Digitally controlled amplifier (DCA) An amplifier whose gain is remotely controlled by a digital control signal.

DIN microphone array A stereo microphone array in which the two microphones are at a 90-degree angle and just under 8 inches apart. DIN stands for Deutsche Industrie Normen—German Industrial Standards.

Direct box A device that matches impedances by converting a high-impedance, unbalanced signal into a low-impedance, balanced signal. Used to connect an amplified instrument directly to the microphone input of the console.

Direct insertion (D.I.) Taking the signal from an electric instrument and plugging it directly into the console.

Direct sound Sound waves that reach the listener before reflecting off any surface.

Directional microphone Any microphone that picks up sound from one direction.

Distant miking Placing a microphone(s) far enough from the sound source to pick up most or all of an ensemble's blended sound including room reflections. *See also* **Close miking.**

Distortion The appearance of a signal in the reproduced sound that was not in the original sound. *See also* **Harmonic distortion, Intermodulation distortion, Loudness (or overload) distortion, Tran-sient distortion.**

Double-ended noise reduction Two-step noise reduction that prevents noise from entering a signal by compressing it during recording and expanding it during playback. *See also* **Single-ended noise reduction.**

Doubling Mixing slightly delayed signals (15–35 milliseconds) with the original signal to create a fuller, stronger, more ambient sound. *See also* **Chorus effect.**

Dropout A sudden attenuation of sound due to an imperfection in the magnetic coating.

Dry sound A sound devoid of reverberation. *See also* **Wet sound.**

DSP *See* **Digital signal processing.**

Dubbing Transferring sound from tape or disc to another tape or disc.

Dynamic microphone A microphone that transduces energy electromagnetically. Moving-coil and ribbon microphones are dynamic.

Dynamic range The range between the quietest and loudest sounds a sound source can produce without distortion.

E

Early reflections Reflections of the original sound that arrive at the listener within 10 to 20 milliseconds.

Echo Sound reflections of 50 milliseconds or greater that are perceived more and more as discrete repetitions of the direct sound.

Echo chamber More accurately a reverberation chamber, it is a specially built room with reflectant surfaces and a loudspeaker through which sound feeds, reverberates, and is picked up by a microphone that feeds the reverberant sound back into the console.

Edit control The control on a tape recorder that disengages the take-up reel but keeps the rest of the tape transport system working, thus enabling unwanted tape to spill off the machine.

Edit decision list (EDL) A list of edits, computer or handwritten, used to assemble a production.

Editing The process of adding to, subtracting from, or rearranging material on a tape or disc recording.

Elasticity The capacity to return to the original shape or place after deflection or displacement.

Electret microphone A capacitor microphone with a permanently charged element.

Electrical phase The relative polarity of two signals in the same circuit.

Electronic alignment The adjustment of electronic and mechanical characteristics of a tape recorder to a defined standard specified by the manufacturer, or by international industry bodies such as the Audio Engineering Society (AES), National Association of Broadcasters (NAB), or the International Electrotechnical commission (IEC). *See also* **Calibration.**

Electronic editing   Editing by dubbing from a playback or "master" tape or disk recorder to a record/edit or "slave" tape or disk recorder.

Engineer   Person who operates the equipment during recording and mixdown. The engineer may also double as producer. *See also* **Producer.**

Enharmonic notes   Two different notes that sound the same, for example, C# and Db, G# and Ab.

Equal loudness curves   Graphs that indicate the sensitivity of the human ear to various frequencies at different loudness levels. Also known as Fletcher-Munson curves. *See also* **Robinson-Dadson curves.**

Equal loudness principle   The principle that confirms the human ear's nonlinear sensitivity to all audible frequencies: that midrange frequencies are perceived with greatest intensity and that bass and treble frequencies are perceived with lesser intensity.

Equalization (EQ)   Altering the frequency/amplitude response of a sound source or sound system.

Equalizer   A signal-processing device that can boost, attenuate, or shelve frequencies in a sound source or sound system.

Erase head   Electromagnetic transducer on a tape recorder that automatically demagnetizes a tape before it reaches the record head when the recorder is in the record mode.

Ergonomics   Designing an engineering system with human convenience in mind.

Expander   An amplifier whose gain decreases as its input level decreases.

F

Fader   A device containing a resistor that is used to vary the output voltage of a circuit or component.

Faulkner microphone array   A stereo microphone array that uses two bidirectional mics spaced just under 8 inches apart and facing directly toward the ensemble.

Feedback   A loud squeal or howl caused when the sound from a loudspeaker is picked up by a nearby microphone and reamplified. Also caused when an output is fed back into its input.

Fill miking   *See* **Accent miking.**

Filter   An electric network that attenuates a selected frequency or band of frequencies above, below, or at a preset point.

Fixed-frequency equalizer   An equalizer with several fixed frequencies usually grouped in two (high and low) or three (high, middle, and low) ranges of the frequency spectrum.

Flanging   Combining a direct signal and the same signal slightly delayed, and continuously varying their time relationships.

Flat   Frequency response in an audio system that reproduces a signal between 20 and 20,000 Hz (or between any two specified frequencies) that varies no more than 3 dB.

Flutter   Generally the result of friction between the tape and heads or guides resulting in loudness changes. *See also* **Wow.**

Flutter echoes   Echoes between parallel walls that occur in rapid series.

Foldback   The system in a multichannel console that permits the routing of sound through a headphone monitor feed to performers in the studio.

Formant   The resonance band in a vibrating body that mildly increases the level of specific steady-state frequencies in that band.

Four-way system loudspeaker A loudspeaker that divides the high frequencies in two and the low frequencies in two.

Freewheel A mode in a synchronizer that allows stretches of poorly encoded time code to be passed over without altering the speed of the slave tape recorder's transport.

Frequency The number of times per second that a sound source vibrates. Now expressed in hertz (Hz); formerly expressed in cycles per second (cps).

Frequency response A measure of an audio system's ability to reproduce a range of frequencies with the same relative loudness; usually represented in a graph.

Fundamental The lowest frequency a sound source can produce. Also called "primary frequency" and "first harmonic."

G

Gauss A unit that measures the amount of magnetization remaining on a tape after erasure.

Graphic equalizer An equalizer with sliding controls that gives a graphic representation of the response curve chosen.

Guard band The space between tracks on an audio tape recorder head to reduce crosstalk.

H

Haas effect *See* **Precedence effect.**

Hard disk recording Using a hard disk computer system for multitrack recording, which facilitates random, quick, and nonlinear access to the stored information. Most hard disk recorders also include nonlinear editing capability. *See also* **Nonlinear editing.**

Hard wired Description of pieces of equipment wired to each other. *See also* **Patch bay.**

Harmonic distortion Nonlinear distortion caused when an audio system introduces harmonics to a signal at the output that were not present at the input.

Harmonics Frequencies that are multiples of the fundamental.

Headroom The amount of increase in loudness level that a tape, amplifier, or other piece of equipment can take, above working level, before overload distortion.

Heads out Having the program information at the head or outside of the reel of tape ready for playback.

Headstack A multitrack tape head.

Height One of the adjustments made when aligning the heads on an audiotape recorder. This adjustment aligns the height of the heads with the recording tape.

Helical scanning Using one or more rotating heads that engage the tape wrapped at least partially around the head drum.

Helmholtz resonator A resonator designed to absorb specific frequencies depending on size, shape, and enclosed volume of air. The enclosed volume of air is connected to the air in the room by a narrow opening or neck. When resonant frequencies reach the neck of the enclosure, the air inside cancels those frequencies.

Hertz Unit of measurement of frequency; numerically equal to cycles per second.

High end The treble range of the frequency spectrum.

High-output tape High-sensitivity tape.

High-pass (low-cut) filter A filter that attenuates frequencies below a selected frequency and allows those above that point to pass.

Humbuck circuit A circuit built into a microphone to reduce hum pickup.

Hypercardioid microphone Unidirectional microphone that has a narrow angle of sound acceptance at the front, is off-axis at the sides, and is more sensitive at the rear than a supercardioid mic.

I

IEC standard   The time code standard for R-DAT recording.

Impedance   Resistance to the flow of alternating current (AC) in an electric system, measured in ohms. A low-impedance microphone has an impedance of roughly 50 to 300 ohms. A high-impedance microphone has an impedance of 10,000 ohms and up.

In the mud   Sound level so quiet that it barely "kicks" the VU meter.

In the red   Sound level so loud that the VU meter "rides" over 100 percent of modulation.

Indirect sound   Sound waves that reflect from one or more surfaces before reaching the listener.

Inharmonic overtones   Pitches that are not exact multiples of the fundamental.

In-line console   A console in which a channel's input, output, and monitor functions are placed in-line at the location that is associated with the input fader on split-section consoles. *See also* **Split-section console.**

Inner ear   The part of the ear that contains the auditory nerve, which transmits sound waves to the brain.

Input section   On a console, the section into which signals from a sound source, such as a microphone, feed and are then routed to the output section.

Input/output (I/O) module   On a console, a module containing input, output, and monitor controls for a single channel.

Insert editing   In electronic editing, inserting a segment between two previously dubbed segments. Also, electronic editing segments out of sequential order.

Integrated services digital network (ISDN)   A public telephone service that allows cheap use of a flexible, wide-area, all-digital network for, among other things, recording simultaneously from various locations.

Intermodulation distortion   Nonlinear distortion that occurs when different frequencies pass through an amplifier at the same time and interact to create combinations of tones unrelated to the original sounds.

Internal dynamics   The second stage in the sound envelope—the variations in loudness and sustains after the attack.

Inverse square law   The acoustic situation in which the sound level changes in inverse proportion to the square of the distance from the sound source.

J

Jack   Receptacle or plug connector leading to the input or output circuit of a patch panel, tape recorder, or other electronic component.

Jam sync   A mode in a synchronizer that produces new time code during dubbing either to match the original time code or to regenerate new address data.

Jog mode   In hard-disk, nonlinear editing, reproduces scrubbed samples in direct relation to the movement of the cursor over the defined region. *See also* **Shuttle mode.**

L

Lavalier microphone   Microphone that used to be worn around the neck but is now attached to the clothing.

Leader tape   Nonmagnetic tape spliced at the beginning and end of a tape and between segments to indicate visually when recorded material begins and ends.

Limiter   A compressor with an output level that does not exceed a preset ceiling regardless of the input level.

Linear editing   Nonrandom editing. *See also* **Nonlinear editing.**

Linearity   Having an output that varies in direct proportion to the input.

Listening fatigue A pronounced dulling of the auditory senses inhibiting perceptual judgment.

Live mix Mixing during the recording session.

Localization (1) Positioning a sound source in a stereo field. (2) The direction from which a sound source seems to emanate in a stereo field. (3) The ability to tell the direction from which a sound is coming.

Longitudinal time code (LTC) A high-frequency signal consisting of a stream of pulses produced by a time code generator used to code tape to facilitate editing and synchronization. Also known as **SMPTE time code.**

Loudness Subjective perception of amplitude.

Loudness (or overload) distortion Distortion that occurs when the loudness of a signal is greater than the sound system can handle.

Loudspeaker A transducer that converts electric energy into acoustic energy.

Low bass Frequency range between roughly 20 and 80 Hz, the lowest two octaves in the audible frequency spectrum.

Low end The bass range of the frequency spectrum.

Low-output tape Low-sensitivity tape.

Low-pass (high-cut) filter A filter that attenuates frequencies above a selected frequency and allows those below that point to pass.

M

Magneto-optical (MO) recording Disc-based recording medium that uses tiny magnetic particles heated to extremely high temperatures.

Masking Phenomenon whereby one sound obscures another, usually one weaker and higher in frequency.

Master (1) The original recording. (2) The final tape or disc recording that is sent to the CD mastering house or to distribution.

Master section On a multichannel production console, the section that contains, among other things, the master input bus(es) that route(s) the final mix to the master tape recorder.

Maximum sound pressure level The level at which a microphone's output signal begins to distort, that is, produces a 3 percent total harmonic distortion (THD).

MD™ *See* **Mini disc.**

Microphone A transducer that converts acoustic energy into electric energy.

Middle ear The part of the ear that transfers sound waves from the eardrum to the inner ear.

Middle-side microphone Consists of two mic capsules housed in a single casing. One capsule, usually cardioid, is the mid-position microphone. The other capsule, usually bidirectional, has each lobe oriented 90 degrees laterally.

MIDI *See* **Musical Instrument Digital Interface.**

MIDI time code (MTC) Translates SMPTE time code into MIDI messages that allow MIDI-based devices to operate on the SMPTE timing reference.

Midrange The part of the frequency spectrum to which humans are most sensitive; the frequencies between roughly 250 and 4,000 Hz.

Mil One-thousandth of an inch.

Mini disc Magneto-optical disc 2.5 inches wide that can store more than an hour of digital-quality audio.

Mix The product of a rerecording session in which several separate sound tracks are combined through a mixing console into stereo, mono, or surround sound.

Mixdown The point, usually in postproduction, when all the separately recorded audio tracks are sweetened, positioned, and combined into stereo, mono, or surround sound.

Mixing Combining separately recorded audio tracks into stereo, mono, or surround sound.

Modular digital multitrack (MDM) Locking up and synchronizing two multitrack R-DATs using a single cable. Using this approach, several multitrack R-DATs can be locked and synchronized and controlled with a remote controller.

Monaural Literally means "one ear." Often used as a synonym for **monophonic.**

Monitor Loudspeaker used in a sound facility.

Monitor system Internal sound system in a console that feeds signals to the monitor loudspeakers.

Monophonic Refers to a sound system with one master output channel.

Morphing The continuous, seamless transformation of one effect (aural or visual) into another.

Moving-coil loudspeaker A loudspeaker with a moving-coil element.

Moving-coil microphone A microphone with a moving-coil element. The coil is wrapped around a diaphragm suspended in a magnetic field.

M-S microphone *See* **Middle-side microphone.**

Multidirectional (or polydirectional) microphone Microphone with switchable pickup patterns.

Multiple On a patch bay, jacks interconnected to each other and to no other circuit. They can be used to feed signals to and from sound sources.

Multiple-entry ports Several ports in a microphone, each of which is tuned to cancel a particular band of frequencies. Also known as a **Variable-D microphone.**

Multiple miking technique Using a separate microphone for each instrument or group of instruments and placing the mic close to the sound source to reduce ambience and leakage and gain greater sonic control of the voicings.

Musical Instrument Digital Interface (MIDI) A protocol that allows synthesizers, drum machines, sequencers, and other signal-processing devices to communicate with or control one another, or both.

Mute To cut off a sound or reduce it considerably, or a device that does this.

Mute-write mode Used either during the building of the mix or as the final mix is playing and usually not written at the same time that fader movements are being written. *See also* **Write mode.**

Mylar The DuPont Company name for polyester. *See also* **Polyester.**

N

Near-coincident miking A stereo microphone array in which the mics are separated horizontally but the angle or space between their capsules is not more than several inches. *See also* **X-Y miking.**

Near-field monitoring Monitoring with loudspeakers placed close to the operator, usually on the console's meter bridge, to reduce interference from control room acoustics at the monitoring position.

Noise Any unwanted sound or signal.

Noise criteria (NC) Contours of the levels of background noise that can be tolerated within an audio studio.

Noise gate An expander with a threshold that can be set to reduce or eliminate unwanted low-level sounds, such as room ambience, rumble, and leakage, without affecting the wanted sounds.

Noise processor A signal processor that reduces analog tape noise.

Nondestructive editing Editing that does not alter the original sound or soundfile regardless of what editing or signal processing is effected. *See also* **Destructive editing.**

Nondirectional microphone An omnidirectional microphone.

Nonlinear The property of not being linear—not having an output that varies in direct proportion to the input.

Nonlinear editing Instant random access to and easy rearrangement of recorded material. *See also* **Linear editing.**

NOS microphone array In stereo miking, two cardioid mics about 12 inches apart at a 90-degree angle.

Notch filter A filter capable of attenuating an extremely narrow bandwidth of frequencies.

O

Octave The interval between two sounds that have a frequency ratio of 2 to 1.

Oersted A unit of magnetic force.

Off-mic Not being within the optimal pickup pattern of a microphone; off-axis.

Ohm A unit of resistance to AC current flow.

Omnidirectional microphone Microphone that picks up sound from all directions. Also called a "nondirectional microphone."

On-mic Being within the optimal pickup pattern of a microphone; on-axis.

Open-reel audiotape recorder A tape recorder with the feed reel and take-up reel not enclosed in a cartridge, requiring that they be mounted manually.

Organ of Corti The organ supported by the basilar membrane and containing the hair cells.

ORTF microphone array In stereo miking, two cardioid mics spaced 6.7 inches apart at a 110-degree angle.

Oscillator A device that generates pure tones or sine waves.

Outer ear The portion of the ear that picks up and directs sound waves through the auditory canal to the middle ear.

Output (1) The point from which signals feed out of a component or sound system. (2) Feeding a signal from a component or sound system.

Output section On a multichannel production console, the section that routes signals to the multitrack tape recorder.

Overdubbing Recording new material on a separate tape track(s) while listening to the replay of a previously recorded tape track(s) in order to synchronize the old and new material.

Overload Feeding a component or system more loudness than it can handle and thereby causing overload distortion.

Overload distortion *See* **Loudness distortion.**

Overload indicator On a console, a light emitting diode (LED) that flashes when the input signal is approaching or has reached overload and is clipping.

Oversampling Raising the sampling rate in a digital system to improve audio quality by distributing a fixed level quantization noise over an ultrasonic frequency range, thereby attenuating the noise in the audio bandwidth and improving the signal-to-noise ratio.

Overtones Harmonics that may or may not be multiples of the fundamental. Subjective response of the ear to harmonics.

P

Pad An attenuator inserted into a component or system to reduce level.

Pan pot A potentiometer that changes the loudness level of a sound between two channels. Abbreviation for panoramic potentiometer.

Paragraphic equalizer An equalizer that combines the features of a parametric and a graphic equalizer.

Parametric equalizer An equalizer in which the bandwidth of a selected frequency is continuously variable.

Patch bay An assembly of jacks to which are wired the inputs and outputs of the audio components in a console and/or sound studio.

Patch cord   A short cord or cable with a plug at each end, used to route signals in a patch panel.

Patching   Using patch cords to route or reroute signals by connecting the inputs and outputs of components wired to a patch panel.

PD format   *See* **Pro Digi format.**

Peak program meter (ppm)   A meter that responds to the loudness peaks in a signal.

Percentage of modulation   The percentage of the applied signal with reference to the maximum signal that may be applied to a sound system.

Phantom power supply   A circuit that sends DC power to a capacitor microphone, thereby eliminating the need to use batteries to generate the microphone's voltage.

Phase   The time relationship between two or more sounds reaching a microphone or signals in a circuit. When this time relationship is coincident, the sounds or signals are in phase and their amplitudes are additive. When this time relationship is not coincident, the sounds or signals are out of phase and their amplitudes are subtractive. *See also* **Acoustical phase, Electrical phase.**

Phaser   A signal processor that creates phase shifting, canceling various frequencies, thereby creating a swishing sound.

Phase reversal control   *See* **Polarity reversal control.**

Phase shift   The displacement of a waveform.

Phasing   An effect created by splitting a signal in two and time-delaying one of the signal portions.

Phon   A dimensionless unit of loudness level related to the ear's subjective impression of signal strength.

Pickup pattern   *See* **Polar response pattern.**

Pin   When the needle of the VU meter hits against the peg at the right-hand corner of the red. Pin is to be avoided because it indicates too high a loudness level and it could damage the meter.

Pinch roller   On a tape recorder the springloaded, freespinning rubber wheel that holds the tape against the capstan. Also called "capstan idler" and "pressure roller."

Pitch   The subjective perception of frequency.

Pitch shifter   A signal processor that varies the pitch of a signal.

Playback head   Electromagnetic transducer on a tape recorder that converts magnetic energy into electric energy.

Plosive   A speech sound that begins with a transient attack, such as "p" or "b."

Polarity reversal control   The control on a console that inverts the polarity of an input signal 180 degrees.

Polar response pattern   The graph of a microphone's directional characteristics as seen from above. The graph indicates response over a 360-degree circumference in a series of concentric circles, each representing a 5-dB loss in level as the circles move inward toward the center.

Polydirectional microphone   *See* **Multidirectional microphone.**

Polyester   Durable, plastic-base material used in most recording tape made today. *See also* **Mylar.**

Pop filter   Foam rubber windscreen placed inside the microphone head. Particularly effective in reducing sound from plosives and blowing.

Porous absorber   A sound absorber made up of porous material whose tiny air spaces are most effective at absorbing high frequencies.

Ports   One or more openings in a directional microphone that contribute to its pickup pattern by canceling sound from unwanted directions. *See also* **Multiple-entry ports, Single-entry port.**

Potentiometer (or Pot)   *See* **Fader.**

Preamplifier   Device that boosts very low-level signals to usable proportions before they reach the amplifier. Abbreviated as *preamp.*

Precedence effect   The tendency to perceive the direct and immediate repetitions of a sound as coming from the same position or direction even if the immediate repetitions coming from another direction are louder. Also known as the "Haas effect."

Prefader listen A control on a console that permits monitoring a signal in one channel, prefader, without having to turn off the other channels. *See also* **Solo mute.**

Premaster Usually a studio-made CD that is sent on to a mastering house for final processing and duplication.

Preproduction The first stage in the production process during which the creative, technical, and business planning takes place.

Presence Perception of a sound as being close and realistic.

Presence range Those frequencies in the frequency spectrum that give sound the quality of closeness and realism; roughly from 4,000 to 5,000 Hz.

Pressure Zone Microphone (PZM) A boundary microphone. Trade name of Crown International, Inc.

Printed-ribbon microphone A microphone with the compliance of a ribbon microphone and the durability of a moving-coil mic. Its element is a spiral aluminum ribbon printed on a diaphragm made of polyester film. Also known as a "regulated phase microphone."

Print-through Unwanted transfer of a magnetic signal from one tape layer to an adjacent tape layer.

Pro Digi format (PD) An alternative to the DASH format, used by Otari.

Producer Person usually responsible for the business-related functions of a musician, group, or record label, and often the most influential creative force next to the musicians. The producer may also double as the engineer. *See also* **Engineer.**

Production (1) The middle stage in the production process during which recording takes place. (2) The material that is produced.

Professional digital format *See* **Pro Digi format.**

Project studio A studio in the home used for professional purposes. It can run the gamut from a single room, 4- or 8-track facility to a studio and control room with millions of dollars worth of equipment.

Proximity effect Increase in the level of bass frequencies relative to midrange and treble frequencies as the mic-to-source distance decreases. Also referred to as "bass tip-up."

Psychoacoustic processor Signal processor that adds clarity, definition, overall presence, and life or "sizzle" to recorded sound.

Psychoacoustics Study of the subjective perception of sound stimuli.

Punching in Inserting material into a recording by rolling the tape recorder in the playback mode and putting it in the record mode at the insert point.

Pure tone *See* **Sine wave.**

PZM *See* **Pressure Zone Microphone.**

Q

Quantization Converting a waveform that is infinitely variable into a finite series of discrete levels.

R

Rarefaction Temporary drawing apart of vibrating molecules causing a partial vacuum to occur. *See also* **Compression.**

R-DAT *See* **Rotary head digital audiocassette recorder.**

Read head On a digital audiotape recorder, the equivalent of the playback head.

Read mode Mode of operation in an automated mixdown when the console controls are operated automatically by the data previously encoded in the computer. *See also* **Update mode, Write mode.**

Real-time analyzer   A device that shows the total energy present at all audible frequencies on an instantaneous basis.

Record head   Electromagnetic transducer on a tape recorder that converts electric energy into magnetic energy.

Reel-size switch   *See* **Tension switch.**

Reference tone(s)   A pure tone(s) recorded on a master tape used to ensure that the levels and metering during recording are duplicated during playback.

Reflected sound   Reflections of the direct sound that bounce off of one or more surfaces before reaching the listener.

Release time   The length of time it takes a limiter or compressor to return to its normal level after the signal has been attenuated or withdrawn. Also known as "recovery time."

Remanence   The residual magnetization from a previous recording after erasure.

Resonance   Transmitting a vibration from one body to another when the frequency of the first body is exactly, or almost exactly, the natural frequency of the second body.

Resonant frequency   The exact, or almost exact, fundamental frequency at which an object vibrates.

Retentivity   Measure of a tape's ability to retain magnetization after the force field has been removed. Retentivity is measured in gauss—a unit of magnetic energy.

Reverberation   Multiple blended, random reflections of a sound wave after the sound source has ceased vibrating.

Reverberation time   The length of time it takes a sound to die away. By definition: The time it takes a sound to decrease to one-millionth of its original intensity, or 60 dB-SPL.

Ribbon microphone   A microphone with a ribbon diaphragm suspended in a magnetic field.

Riding the gain   Adjusting the levels during recording or playback.

Robinson-Dadson curves   Equal loudness curves plotted by averaging the results obtained from a large number of listeners. They have replaced the original curves plotted by Fletcher-Munson. *See also* **Equal loudness curves.**

Room modes   Unwanted increases in loudness at resonant frequencies that are a function of a room's dimensions.

Rotary head digital audiocasette recorder (R-DAT)   Specifically, a cassette digital audiotape recorder with rotary heads.

S

Samplefile   A sound sample that is stored on floppy or hard disk or compact disc.

Sampler   An electronic device used to make short digital audio recordings for manipulation and playback.

Sampling   (1) Examining an analog signal at regular intervals defined by the sampling frequency (or rate). (2) A process whereby a section of digital audio representing a sonic event, acoustic or electro-acoustic, is stored on disk or into a memory.

Sampling frequency (or rate)   The frequency (or rate) at which an analog signal is sampled.

Scrape flutter filter   A cylindrical, low-friction, metal surface, installed between the heads to reduce the amount of unsupported tape, thereby restricting the degree of tape movement as it passes across the heads. It reduces flutter.

Scrubbing   In hard-disk editing, moving the playbar cursor through the defined region at any speed to listen to a sound being readied for editing. Scrubbing is similar to rocking a tape in cut-and-splice editing and the jog mode in electronic editing.

SCSI (Small Computer Systems Interface)   The standard for hardware and software command language that allows two-way communication between, primarily, hard disk and CD-ROM drives. Pronounced "scuzzy."

S-DAT *See* **Stationary head digital audio-tape recorder.**

Sel Sync Changing the record head into a playback head to synchronize the playback of previously recorded material with the recording of new material. Trademark of Ampex Corporation.

Selective synchronization *See* **Sel Sync.**

Self-noise The electrical noise, or hiss, an electronic device produces.

Sensitivity (1) Measurement of a tape's output level capability relative to a standard reference tape. (2) Measurement of the voltage (dBV) a microphone produces, which indicates its efficiency.

Shelving Maximum boost or cut at a particular frequency that remains constant at all points beyond that frequency so the response curve resembles a shelf.

Shock mount A device that isolates a microphone from mechanical vibrations. It can be attached externally or built into a microphone.

Shuffling Increases spaciousness so that coincident and near-coincident microphone arrays can sound as spacious as spaced microphone arrays. Shuffling is accomplished with a low-frequency shelving boost of the L – R (difference) signals and a low-frequency shelving cut of the L + R (sum) signals. Also known as "spatial equalization."

Shuttle mode In hard-disk, nonlinear editing, the initial direction and speed of the cursor is used as a reference and the rest of the scrubbed section is reproduced in the same direction and at the same rate without need of further cursor movement. *See also* **Jog mode.**

Sibilance The annoying hissing sounds produced by overaccenting "s," "z," "ch," and other, similar sounds.

Signal flow The path a signal follows from its sound source to its destination.

Signal processor A device that alters some characteristic of a sound, such as frequency, amplitude, phase, or quantity.

Signal-to-noise ratio The ratio between the signal level and the noise level of a component or sound system. The wider the signal-to-noise ratio, the better.

Sine wave A pure tone or fundamental frequency with no harmonics or overtones.

Single-D microphone *See* **Single-entry port.**

Single-ended noise reduction One-step noise reduction that reduces noise from an existing signal rather than preventing it from entering a signal. It may be inserted into the signal flow at the recording or playback stage. *See also* **Double-Ended Noise Reduction.**

Single-entry port One port in a microphone to cancel all frequencies from unwanted directions. Also known as a "Single-D microphone."

Slap back echo The effect created when an original signal repeats as distinct echoes that decrease in level with each repetition.

Slave tape The tape to which the material on a master tape is transferred.

SMPTE time code *See* **Longitudinal time code.**

Solo A control on a multitrack console that automatically cuts off all signals feeding the monitor system except those signals feeding through the channel that the solo mute control activates.

Sound absorption coefficient A measure of the sound-absorbing ability of a surface. This coefficient is defined as the fraction of incident sound absorbed by a surface. Values range from 0.01 for marble to 1.0 for the materials used in an almost acoustically dead enclosure.

Sound envelope Changes in the loudness of a sound over time, described as occurring in three stages: attack, internal dynamics, decay; or in four stages: attack, initial decay, sustain, and release (ADSR).

Sound frequency spectrum The range of frequencies audible to human hearing: about 20 to 20,000 Hz.

Sound pressure level (SPL) A measure of the pressure of a sound wave, expressed in decibels (dB-SPL).

Sound reinforcement Area of sound design concerned with music performance before an audience. Also referred to as "concert reinforcement."

Sound transmission class (STC) A rating that evaluates the effectiveness of barriers in isolating sound.

Sound wave A series of compressions and rarefactions of molecules set in motion by a vibrating sound source and radiating from it.

Soundfield microphone system Four capacitor microphone capsules shaped like a tetrahedron, enclosed in a single casing, that can be combined in various formats to reproduce sonic depth, breadth, and height.

Soundfile A sound stored in the memory of a hard-disk editor.

Spaced miking Two, sometimes three, microphones spaced from several inches to several feet apart, depending on the width of the sound source and the acoustics, for stereo recording.

SPDIF (Sony/Philips Digital InterFace) The consumer version of the AES/EBU interface calling for an unbalanced line using phono connectors. *See also* **AES/EBU interface.**

Spectrum processor A signal processor that affects a sound's spectral range.

Splicing tape A specially made adhesive tape that does not ooze, is nonmagnetic and pressure sensitive, and is used to join cut ends of audiotape.

Split-section console Multichannel production console in which the input, output, master, and monitor sections are separate. *See also* **In-line console.**

Standing wave A sound wave perceived as stationary, which is the result of a periodic sound wave having a fixed distribution in space. The result of interference of traveling sound waves of the same kind.

Stationary head digital audiotape recorder (S-DAT) A fixed-head digital audiotape recorder. *See also* **Rotary head digital audiotape recorder (R-DAT).**

Stereo 180 microphone array A stereo microphone array that uses two hypercardioid mics spaced just under 2 inches apart at a 135-degree angle.

Stereophonic microphone Two directional microphone capsules, one above the other, with separate outputs, encased in one housing.

Stereophonic sound Two-channel, two-loudspeaker sound reproduction that gives the listener the illusion of sonic depth and width.

Stereosonic microphone technique *See* **Blumlein technique.**

Submaster Generally, the fader that controls the level of an output bus. Specifically, the fader that controls the level of a signal at an output channel en route to the master fader.

Subtractive equalization Attenuating, rather than boosting, frequencies to achieve equalization.

Supercardioid microphone Unidirectional microphone with a slightly narrower angle of sound acceptance than a cardioid microphone, little sensitivity at the rear sides, and some sensitivity at the rear.

Surround sound Sound that produces a soundfield in front of, to the sides of, and behind the listener by positioning loudspeakers either front and rear, or front, sides, and rear of the listener.

Sweeten To enhance the sound of a recording through EQ, reverb, delay, etc.

Synchronizer (1) Device that regulates the operating speeds of two or more tape recorders so they run in sync. (2) Device with sprocketed, ganged wheels that locks in the film reels of picture and sound so they can be wound in synchronization during editing.

System microphone Interchangeable microphone capsules of various directional patterns that attach to a common base. The base contains a power supply and a preamplifier.

System noise The inherent noise an electronic device or system generates.

T

Tails out Having the end of the material on a tape at the head of the reel.

Tangency One of the adjustments made when aligning the heads of an audiotape recorder. This adjustment aligns the forwardness of the heads so the tape meets them at the correct pressure.

Tape guides Grooved pins on rollers mounted at each side of the head assembly to position the tape correctly on the head during recording and playback.

Tape transport The mechanical portion of the tape recorder, mounted with motors, reel spindles, heads, and controls, that carries the tape at the constant speed from feed reel to take-up reel.

Temporal fusion When reflected sound reaches the ear within 10 to 20 milliseconds of the original sound, the direct and reflected sound are perceived as a single sound.

Tension switch A two-position switch that adjusts the torque to the feed and take-up reels to compensate for different sizes of reels and hubs.

3-D sound Increasing the illusion of depth and width in aural space using frontally positioned stereo loudspeakers.

Three-to-one rule A guideline used to reduce the phasing caused when a sound reaches two microphones at slightly different times. It states that no two microphones should be closer to each other than three times the distance between one of them and its sound source.

Three-way system loudspeaker A loudspeaker that divides the high from the low frequencies and then divides the high frequencies again.

Tie line Facilities the interconnecting of outboard devices and patch panels in a control room or between studios.

Timbre The unique tone quality or color of a sound.

Time code address The unique SMPTE time code number that identifies each 1/30 of a second of audiotape.

Time compression Altering the time of material without changing its pitch.

Time processor A signal processor that affects the time interval between a signal and its repetition.

Track The path on magnetic tape along which a signal is recorded.

Transaural stereo The process whereby a converter cancels the acoustic crosstalk signals making it possible to reproduce a binaural recording over loudspeakers and get a quasi-binaural sound.

Transducer A device that converts one form of energy into another.

Transformer A device used to match the impedances of high- and low-impedance components or systems.

Transient A sound that begins with a sharp attack followed by a quick decay.

Transient distortion Distortion that occurs when a sound system cannot reproduce sounds that begin with sudden, explosive attacks.

Transmission loss (TL) The amount of sound reduction provided by a barrier such as a wall, floor, or ceiling.

Treble Frequency range between roughly 5,000 and 20,000 Hz, the highest two octaves in the audible frequency spectrum.

Trim (1) To attenuate the loudness level in a component or circuit. (2) The device, usually so called on a console, that attenuates the loudness level at the microphone/line input.

Tweeter The informal name of a loudspeaker that reproduces high frequencies. *See also* **Woofer.**

Two-way system loudspeaker A loudspeaker that divides the high from the low frequencies.

U

Unbalanced line A line (or circuit) with two conductors of unequal voltage.

Unidirectional microphone A microphone that picks up sound from one direction. Also called "directional."

Update mode Mode of operation in an automated mixdown when an encoded control can be recorded without affecting the coding of the other controls. *See also* **Read mode, Write mode.**

Upper bass Frequency range between roughly 80 and 320 Hz.

Upper midrange Frequency range between roughly 2,560 and 5,120 Hz.

V

Variable-D microphone *See* **Multiple-entry ports.**

Variable-speed control Device on an audiotape recorder that alters the playing speed to various rates of the recorder's set speeds.

VCA *See* **Voltage-controlled amplifier.**

Velocity The speed of a sound wave: 1,130 feet per second at sea level and 70 degrees Fahrenheit.

Voltage-controlled amplifier (VCA) An amplifier used to decrease level. The amount of amplification is controlled by external DC voltage.

Volume unit A measure that is related to a human's subjective perception of loudness.

Volume unit (VU) meter A meter calibrated in volume units and percentage of modulation.

W

Waveform A graphic representation of a sound's characteristic shape, displayed, for example, on hard disk editors.

Wavelength The length of one cycle of a sound wave. Wavelength is inversely proportional to the frequency of a sound; the higher the frequency, the shorter the wavelength.

Weighting network A filter used for weighting a frequency response before measurement. Generally, three weighting networks are used: A (40 phons), B (70 phons), and C (100 phons).

Wet sound A sound with reverberation or signal processing. *See also* **Dry sound.**

Wide-angle cardioid microphone A microphone with a wider directional pickup pattern than a cardioid microphone.

Windscreen Foam rubber covering specially designed to fit over the outside of a microphone head. Used to reduce plosive and blowing sounds. *See also* **Pop filter.**

Woofer Informal name for a loudspeaker that produces the bass frequencies. *See also* **Tweeter.**

Wow (1) The instantaneous variations in speed at moderately slow rates caused by variations in the tape transport. (2) Starting the sound on a tape before it reaches full speed. *See also* **Flutter.**

Wrap One of the adjustment made when aligning the heads of an audiotape recorder. This adjustment aligns the head so it is in full physical contact with the tape.

Write head On a digital audiotape recorder, the equivalent of the record head.

Write mode The mode of operation in an automated mixdown during which controls are adjusted conventionally and the adjustments are encoded in the computer for retrieval in the safe mode. *See also* **Read mode, Update mode.**

Write-sync head   On a digital audiotape recorder, the record head used for synchronous recording.

X

XLR connector   Commonly used male and female microphone plugs with a three-pin connector.

X-Y miking   Coincident or near-coincident miking that places the microphones' diaphragms over or horizontal to one another.

Z

Zenith   One of the adjustments made when aligning the heads of an audiotape recorder. This adjustment aligns the vertical angle of the heads so they are perpendicular to the tape.

CREDITS

Adams-Smith, Inc.: 14-26

ADC Telecommunications, Inc.: 5-13

Air Studios, London: 3-24, 10-2, 13-31

Akai: 7-16, 12-52

AKG: 4-23, 4-25, 4-44b

Alesis Corporation: 5-5, 5-6

Alpha Audio: 3-13a

AMS Industries Plc: 4-30 to 4-32

Aphex Systems: 8-10, 8-24, 8-27

Atlas Sound: 4-50

Audio Engineering Associates (AEA): 4-28

beyerdynamic: 4-4, 4-26

Broadcast Engineering Magazine: 5-17 (1994), 9-15 (1989) © Intertec Publishing Corporation. All Rights Reserved

CAMEO Dictionary of Creative Terms, Gary Davis & Associates, 1979, p. 41: 9-7

JLCooper Electronics: 5-16

Countryman Associates: 4-24, 12-37

Crown International, Inc.: 4-34, 4-36, 12-47, 12-43

dbx, A Division of AKG Acoustics: 8-3

Philip DeLancie, "Mastering," *MIX* Magazine, December, 1994, p. 175: 16-1

Desper Products, Inc.: 15-7 to 15-9

Digal: 9-17

digidesign: 5-19, 8-33, 14-35

Digital Audio Labs: 14-27, 14-30 to 14-32, 14-34

Dolby Laboratories, Inc: 8-11, 8-31

Doremi Labs, Inc.: 7-20, 7-21, 14-45

Eastman Kodak Company: 16-3

Editall Products, Xedit Corporation: 14-1, 14-2

Electro-Voice, Inc.: 4-11, 4-12, 4-41, 4-46b, c

ENSONIQ Corporation: 12-51

Etymotic Research: 2-12

Eventide: 8-22

Fieldwood Systems: 15-13

Fostex: 4-5, 6-11, 7-11

Garner Industries: 6-8b

Bob Ghent, "Healthy Hearing," *MIX* Magazine, March 1994, p. 153: 2-8

Gotham Audio Corporation: 8-14

David Immer, "Phone It In," *MIX* Magazine, February, 1994, p. 88: 7-22

JBL Professional: 9-8, 9-16c

Lexicon: 8-15, 8-21

Milab: 4-22

Neumann USA: 4-27, 4-35, 4-46a, 11-12

Orban, A Division of AKG Acoustics: 8-4, 8-7

Otari Corporation: 7-18

Alan Parsons, et al. *The Master Tape Book*. Reading, U.K.: APRS and the British Record Producers Guild, 1992: 16-2, 16-4

RCA: 4-3

Record Plant, Hollywood: 3-23

Roland Corporation US: 8-6, 8-18, 8-32

RPG Diffusor Systems, Inc. and Peter D'Antonio: 3-15, 3-19 to 3-22

RSP Technologies: 15-10

Steve Sartori: 3-26, 4-40b, 6-12, 10-4, 12-2, 12-10 to 12-20, 12-38

Bruce Siegel: 14-36

Selco Products Company: 5-3, 5-4

Sennheiser Electronic Corporation: 4-9, 4-10, 4-40c

Shure Brothers, Inc.: 4-49a

Sonic Perceptions: 11-13

Sonic Solutions: 14-28, 14-33

Sony Corporaton of America: 5-12, 5-15, 6–6, 14-23, 14-24

SOUNDFORMS International: 3-13b

William Storm: 2-16, 3-25, 4-7, 4-8, 4-44a, 4-45, 4-47, 6-3, 12-21, 12-23, 12-28, 14-3, 14-4, 14-8, 14-19

Studer: 7-8, 7-15

Studio Technologies: 4-49b

Switchcraft: 5-8

Taber Manufacturing and Engineering Company: 6-8a

Tascam Professional Division: 7-12

UREI - United Recording Electronics Industries: 9-10

Wayne Wadhams. S*ound Advice: The Musician's Guide to the Recording Studio*. N.Y.: Schirmer Books, 1990, p. 45: 10-1

Westlake Audio: 9-1 to 9-3

John Woram and Alan Kefauver. *The New Recording Studio Handbook*. Commack, N.Y.: Elar, 1989, p. 402: 5-1

Yamaha Corporation of America: 5-18, 8-13, 8-20

Herbert Zettl: 4-51

BIBLIOGRAPHY

Books

Anderton, Craig. *The Digital Delay Handbook,* rev. ed. Woodstock, NY: Beekman Publishers, 1990. Specific applications and how-to directions for applying various long, short, and multiple digital delay effects to sound shaping.

————. *The Electronic Musician's Dictionary.* New York: Music Sales, 1989. Dictionary of more than 1,000 technical and operational terms related to synthesizers, computers, and MIDI.

Audio and Music Education. Emeryville, CA: Cardinal Business Media, Annual. Listing of music recording, audio, and broadcast communications programs in the U.S. and Canada.

Backus, John. *The Acoustical Foundations of Music,* 2nd ed. New York: W. W. Norton, 1977. The properties, production, behavior, and reproduction of musical sound.

Ballou, Glen, ed. *Handbook for Sound Engineers: The New Audio Cyclopedia,* 2nd ed. Indianapolis: H. W. Sams, 1991. Intended successor to Howard Tremaine's classic *Audio Cyclopedia.* Mostly for the engineer but with some nontechnical material. Comprehensive coverage of acoustics for various types of studios, electrical components for sound engineering, microphones, loudspeakers, consoles, amplifiers, signal processors, tape recorders, sound systems design, and measurement.

Bartlett, Bruce. *Stereo Microphone Techniques.* Boston: Focal Press, 1991. Practical, readable guide to stereo miking music, news, sports, film and video sound, samples, and sound effects.

Bartlett, Bruce and Jenny. *Practical Recording Techniques.* Carmel, IN: Sams Publishing, 1992. A general guide for the nonprofessional music recordist interested in studio or location recording of popular and classical music and the spoken word. For anyone involved in audio, however, there is useful material on the decibel, time code, guidelines for EQing, troubleshooting poor sound, recognizing quality sound, and evaluating the finished product.

Baskerville, David. *Music Business Handbook,* 6th ed. Thousand Oaks, CA: SAGE, 1995. Comprehensive handbook about the music marketplace: songwriting, publishing, copyright, unions, agents, artist management, concert promotion, the record industry—including production, studios, and engineering—music in film and broadcasting, and career planning and development.

Bech, Soren, and O. Juhl Pedersen, eds. *Proceedings of a Symposium on Perception of Reproduced Sound,* Gammel Avernaes, Denmark, 1987. Peterborough, NH: Old Colony Sound Lab Books, 1987. Papers, from the nontechnical to the esoteric, about the relationship between reproduced sound and aural perception.

Benson, Blair, ed. *Audio Engineering Handbook.* New York: McGraw-Hill, 1988. Cyclopedic reference to technical and practical audio includes principles of sound, hearing, acoustics, the audio signal spectrum, analog and digital recording, measurement techniques, production and postproduction techniques for film sound, industry standards, and recommended practices.

Blauert, Jens. *Spatial Hearing.* Cambridge, MA: MIT Press, 1983. Translated by John S. Allen. Important book in the literature on aural perception.

Borwick, John. *Loudspeaker and Headphone Handbook*, 2nd ed. London: Focal Press, 1994. Theory and practice of loudspeaker and headphone design and usage.

————. *Microphones: Technology and Technique.* London: Focal Press, 1990. Excellent guide to microphone usage. First half of the book deals with a brief history of microphones, basic theory of acoustics, electricity, and magnetism. The second half is devoted to creative techniques used in miking musical instruments, voices, and ensembles for classical and popular music, and miking for television programs.

————, ed. *Sound Recording Practice: A Handbook,* 4th ed. New York: Oxford University Press, 1995. Practical and technical articles about audio recording, on the intermediate to advanced levels. From the British perspective.

Burroughs, Lou. *Microphones: Design and Application.* Plainview NY: Sagamore, 1974. Basic principles of microphone design and application. A classic, and still useful, reference book.

Campbell, Murray, and Clive Greated. *The Musician's Guide to Acoustics.* New York: Schirmer, 1987. Extensive analysis of how sound is produced in musical instruments.

Clifford, Martin. *Microphones,* 3rd ed. Blue Ridge Summit, PA: Tab, 1986. Basic guide combines operational theory and applications: acoustics, noise, anatomy of the mic, general techniques (ensembles and stereo), and specific techniques (musical instruments, voices, conference, and lecture).

Cooper, Jeff. *Building a Recording Studio,* 4th ed. Los Angeles: Synergy Group, 1984. A basic guide to constructing a recording studio. Includes material on the effects of acoustics on sound and recording, the relationship of sonic material to room acoustics, the studio, and the control room. Extensive glossary.

Davis, Don and Carolyn. *Sound System Engineering,* 2nd ed. Indianapolis: H. W. Sams, 1987. Authoritative technical reference that describes the design, installation, equalization, operation, and maintenance of a sound system.

DeFuria, Steve, and Joe Scacciaferro. *The MIDI Book.* Pompton Lakes, NJ: Third Earth Productions, 1988. Well-illustrated, easy-to-read introduction to MIDI.

————. *The Sampling Book.* Milwaukee: Hal Leonard, 1988. The technology of sampling and its creative uses including looping, splicing, multisampling, crossfading, resynthesis, sampling rates, and hands-on experiments.

Deutsch, Diana, ed. *The Psychology of Music.* Orlando, FL: Academic Press, 1982. Advanced theoretical work dealing with ways music is processed by the listener and performer. Subject areas include acoustics, psychoacoustics, perception, and electronics.

Dickreiter, Michael. *Tonmeister Technology: Recording Environments, Sound Sources, and Microphone Techniques.* Translated by Stephen Temmer. New York: Temmer Enterprises, 1989. A nontechnical primer from the Tonmeister perspective that integrates music and technology.

Dowling, W. J., and D. L. Harwood. *Music Cognition.* Orlando, FL: Academic Press, 1986. About the perception and cognition of music in relation to information processing. Includes chapters on the sense and perception of sound, emotion and meaning, and cultural contexts of musical experience. With audiocassette.

Drews, Mark. *New Ears: The Audio Career and Education Handbook,* 2nd ed. Syracuse, NY: New Ear Productions, 1993. Guide to audio education programs in schools and colleges worldwide.

Eargle, John. *Handbook of Recording Engineering,* 3rd ed. New York: Van Nostrand Reinhold, 1996. Mostly technical approach to the recording process covering acoustical fundamentals, audio transmission systems, loudspeakers and monitoring, signal processing, and analog and digital recording, with easy-to-understand production and postproduction techniques.

———. *The Microphone Handbook.* Plainview, NY: ELAR, 1981. Handy reference work on the basics of microphone theory and techniques for speech and classical and popular music recording in studio and on location.

———. *Music, Sound, and Technology,* 2nd ed. New York: Van Nostrand Reinhold, 1995. Examines musical instruments, ensembles, and performance spaces to enable technicians and engineers to better understand the physics and aesthetics of music production.

Eisenberg, Evan. *The Recording Angel: Explorations in Phonography.* New York: McGraw-Hill, 1987. The effects of technology on perception: How recording has changed the very nature of music and its role in our culture.

Everest, F. Alton. *Acoustic Techniques for Home and Studio,* 2nd ed. Blue Ridge Summit, PA: Tab, 1986. Practical environmental acoustic design with emphasis on the small sound studio. Discusses principles of acoustics, human hearing, room resonance, diffusion of sound, and absorption properties of acoustic materials.

———. *Master Handbook of Acoustics,* 3rd ed. Blue Ridge Summit, PA: Tab, 1994. Basics of sound and acoustics applied to the professional recording studio. In addition to the customary material about the principles of sound and acoustics, coverage includes the human voice system, the control room, multitrack recording, and instruments for acoustical measurement.

Everest, F. Alton, and Mike Shea. *How to Build a Small Budget Recording Studio,* 2nd ed. Blue Ridge Summit, PA: Tab, 1988. Instruction in the budgeting, mathematics, acoustical design, and construction necessary in building a small sound studio.

Everest, F. Alton, and Ron Streicher. *The New Stereo Soundbook.* Blue Ridge Summit, PA: Tab, 1992. Stereo miking and multiple miking techniques including binaural setups and surround sound.

Fletcher, Neville, and Thomas Rossing. *The Physics of Musical Instruments.* New York: Springer-Verlag, 1991. Acoustical investigations of most of the traditional instruments currently in use in Western music. Not for the beginner.

Fraser, Douglas. *Digital Delays (and How to Use Them).* Sherman Oaks, CA:

Alfred, 1989. Guide to the common features of digital delay, including programming and beat-conversion charts.

Galluccio, Greg. *Project Studio Blueprint.* Carmel, IN: Sams, 1992. The design, installation, and management of a project studio.

Gayford, Michael, ed. *Microphone Engineering Handbook.* London: Focal Press, 1994. Design and use of microphones.

Greenwald, Ted. *The Musician's Home Recording Handbook.* San Francisco: Miller Freeman, Inc., 1992. Strategies for tracking, bouncing, signal processing, and mixing in nontechnical language.

Hall, Donald. *Musical Acoustics.* Pacific Grove, CA: Brooks/Cole Publishing Company, 1991. Nontechnical introduction to musical acoustics.

Handel, Stephen. *Listening: An Introduction to the Perception of Auditory Events.* Cambridge, MA: MIT Press, 1989. Scientific approach to how we listen to and perceive sound.

Horn, Delton. *DAT: The Complete Guide to Digital Audio Tape.* Blue Ridge Summit, PA: Tab, 1991. About half the book is devoted to DAT; the rest covers the history of recording and the basics of digital audio and compact discs.

Howell, Peter, et al. *Musical Structure and Cognition.* Orlando, FL: Academic Press, 1985. Advanced essays on human perception and on musical structure, recall, and recognition.

Huber, David Miles. *Hard Disk Recording for Musicians.* Carmel, IN: Sams Publishing, 1995. Updated version of Huber's *Random Access Audio* (see below).

———. *Microphone Manual: Design and Application.* Indianapolis: H. W. Sams, 1988. Basics of microphone theory and usage applied to single and stereo microphone techniques for music recording, in studio and on location, for speech, and for video and film production.

———. *The MIDI Manual.* Carmel, IN: Sams Publishing, 1991. Basics of MIDI and the functions and features of selected equipment and software.

———. *Random Access Audio.* Carmel, IN: Sams Publishing, 1992. Excellent introduction to digital audio, sampling, and hard disk recording and editing.

Huber, David, and Robert Runstein. *Modern Recording Techniques,* 4th ed. Carmel, IN: Sams, 1995. Basics of multitrack sound recording for music production. In addition to the customary material on acoustics, microphones and miking technique, consoles, analog and digital tape recording, signal processing, and so on, includes discussion of synchronization, MIDI, CD-ROMs, and business opportunities.

Hurtig, Brent. *Multitrack Recording for Musicians.* Sherman Oaks, CA: Alfred, 1989. Fundamentals of multitrack music recording, including MIDI and the workstation, with a step-by-step "hands-on" recording session.

Hutchins, Carleen, et al. *The Physics of Music.* San Francisco: W. H. Freeman, 1978. Essays from Scientific American about the physics of music and musical instruments and the acoustics of the singing voice.

Jones, Steve. *Rock Formation: Music, Technology, and Mass Communication.* Newbury Park, CA: Sage, 1992. Influence of technology on popular music with chapters on the history of sound recording, marketing music technology, the process of sound recording, and technology and the musician.

Keene, Sherman. *Practical Techniques for the Recording Engineer,* 3rd ed. Torrance, CA: S & S Engineering, 1989. Instructional guide to engineering and producing divided into three parts: beginning, intermediate, and advanced; with supplementary workbook and cassette tapes (see Tapes and CDs).

———. *Quality Sound Engineering.* Torrance, CA: S & S Engineering, 1991. Emphasis is on the number of factors in the recording and mixing process that often mean the difference between a quality sound recording and a mediocre one.

Lehrman, Paul, and Tim Tully. *MIDI for the Professional*. New York: Amsco Publications, 1993. Technical information, creative advice, and techniques about MIDI hardware, software, and production.

Mallinson, John. *The Foundations of Magnetic Recording*. San Diego: Academic Press, 1993. Details of magnetic recording including formats, heads, read/write processes, computer disks, and optical recording.

Martin, George. *All You Need Is Ears*. New York: St. Martin's, Press, 1979. Autobiography by the producer who "made" the Beatles, with unique and useful insights into music production, creativity, and what it means to have "ears."

Molenda, Michael, ed. *Making the Ultimate Demo*. Emeryville, CA: Electronic Musician Books, 1993. Insights from various perspectives.

Moore, Brian C.J. *An Introduction to the Psychology of Hearing*. San Diego: Academic Press, 1990. The scientific basics.

Moylan, William. *The Art of Recording*. New York: Van Nostrand Reinhold, 1992. Unique approach to the creative, aesthetic, and perceptual considerations in music recording.

Music Producers: Conversations with Today's Top Record Makers. Editors of MIX Magazine. Emeryville, CA: *MIX Magazine*, 1992. Discussions about how they got started, how they mediate between labels and artists, what equipment they prefer, analog/digital format decisions, and how they build a mix, among other topics.

Nardantonio, Dennis. *Sound Studio: Production Techniques*. Blue Ridge Summit, PA: Tab, 1990. Entry-level text focusing on basic electronics, the console, signal processing, mics, monitors, MIDI, and recording procedures.

Nisbett, Alec. *The Use of Microphones*, 4th ed. London: Focal Press, 1994. A manual with sections titled "Sound," "Microphones," "Music Balance," and "Control," among others. In each section each page of text is supported by a page of illustrations.

Olson, Harry. *Music, Physics, and Engineering*. New York: Dover, 1967. A classic. Chapters on sound waves, musical terminology and scales, resonators and radiators, musical instruments, properties of music, and acoustics are still instructive today.

Parson, Alan, et al. *The Master Tape Book*. Reading, U.K.: APRS and the British Record Producers Guild, 1992. Procedures for putting together and preparing the master tape in analog and digital formats for final mastering.

Pellman, Samuel. *An Introduction to the Creation of Electroacoustic Music*. Belmont, CA: Wadsworth Publishing Company, 1994. Theoretical principles, practical applications, and aesthetic considerations related to making music with modern technology.

Peterson, George, and Steve Oppenheimer. *Electronic Musician's Tech Terms*. Emeryville, CA: Electronic Musician Books, 1993. Dictionary of terms for audio and music production including disk-based technology.

Pierce, John. *The Science of Musical Sound*. New York: Scientific American, 1983. Basic principles of sound in relation to music: periodicity, pitch, sound waves, resonance, the ear, hearing, power and loudness, masking, acoustics, sound reproduction, perception, illusion, and effect.

Pohlmann, Kenneth. *Advanced Digital Audio*. Carmel, IN: Sams Publishing, 1991. Digital audio concepts, practices, and related technologies on an advanced technical level. Includes pulse modulation, multibit conversion techniques, and laser, fiberoptic, and optical-disc technologies. Also examines digital audio in film, video, and satellite broadcasting.

———. *The Compact Disc Handbook,* 2nd ed. Madison, WI: A-R Editions, 1992. Technical discussion of CD technology includes CD-I, CD-ROM, and MiniDisc.

———. *Principles of Digital Audio,* 3rd ed. Indianapolis: H. W. Sams, 1995. Technical reference work on the fundamentals of digital sound, recording, audio interfaces, storage, reproduction, and workstations.

Ratcliff, John. *Time Code: A User's Guide.* London: Focal Press, 1993. Comprehensive reference guide to the form, standards, and control codes of the various time codes used in production today.

Recording Industry Sourcebook. Los Angeles: Recording Industry Sourcebook, Annual. Just about everything you need to know about the recording business from record labels to limousine services. Includes, among many things, artist management, music attorneys, performing rights societies, promotion, producers, recording and mastering studios, music programmers, and rental and supply firms.

Roederer, Juan G. *Introduction to the Physics and Psychophysics of Music,* 2nd ed. New York: Springer-Verlag, 1979. An analysis of what objective, physical properties of sound patterns are associated to what subjective, psychological sensations of music.

Rossing, Thomas. *The Science of Sound,* 2nd ed. Reading, MA: Addison-Wesley, 1990. Introduction to the various branches of acoustics written in nontechnical language for the student in college physics and mathematics. It includes physical principles, perception and measurement, musical instruments, the human voice, electrical production of sound, electronic music, room acoustics, and environmental noise.

Rothstein, Joseph. *MIDI: A Comprehensive Introduction,* 2nd ed. Madison, WI: A-R Editions, 1995. Covers MIDI hardware and software as a single integrated system instead of particular brands of equipment and software programs. It describes categories of MIDI instruments, accessories, and personal computer software. Discusses basic MIDI principles but most of the book is intermediate level.

Rumsey, Francis. *Tapeless Sound Recording.* London: Focal Press, 1990. Principles and mechanics of hard disk recording and editing.

Rumsey, Francis, and Tim McCormick. *Sound and Recording: An Introduction,* 2nd ed. London: Focal Press, 1994. Survey of audio technology—analog and digital—and techniques, including MIDI and synchronization. Emphasis is on "how it works" rather than "how to work it."

Strong, William. *The Copyright Book: A Practical Guide,* 4th ed. Cambridge, MA: MIT Press, 1993. Covers musical and literary works, CD-ROMs, holograms, databases, compilations, and shareware, among other categories. Not in legalese.

Talbot-Smith, Michael. *Audio Engineer's Reference Book.* London: Focal Press, 1994. The design, manufacture, and installation of audio equipment. Includes acoustics and acoustic devices, recording and reproduction, studios, and signal distribution.

———. *Audio Recording and Reproduction.* London: Focal Press, 1994. Technical and practical basics for the beginner.

Time Code Handbook, 3rd ed. Frederick, MD: Cipher Digital, Inc. Background, basics, and applications of SMPTE, MIDI and other time codes.

Traister, Robert, and Anna Lisk. *The Beginner's Guide to Reading Schematics,* 2nd ed. Blue Ridge Summit, PA: Tab, 1991. Guide to understanding symbol conventions and reading schematic diagrams.

Wadhams, Wayne. *Dictionary of Music Production and Engineering Technology.*

New York: Schirmer, 1988. Dictionary of terminology and basic concepts in the fields of television, radio, music, and film audio production and engineering.

————. *Sound Advice: The Musician's Guide to the Record Industry.* New York: Schirmer, 1990. Covers the process from making a demo to negotiating a contract with a major label, including the important subject of artists' rights and how to protect them. Also explains unions, music publishing, and the workings of industry organizations and associations. Many examples of different kinds of contracts.

————. *Sound Advice: The Musician's Guide to the Recording Studio.* New York: Schirmer, 1990. Basic functions and operations of a recording studio including detailed nontechnical discussion of recording procedures and miking techniques. With excellent companion two-disc CD set and accompanying explanatory booklets.

Watkinson, John. *The Art of Digital Audio,* 2nd ed. London: Focal Press, 1993. Updated technical book covering digital audio theory and the various uses of digital audio in rotary and stationary head tape recorders, disk drives, compact disc, compact cassette (DCC), and broadcasting.

————. *An Introduction to Digital Audio.* London: Focal Press, 1994. Principles of digital audio including conversion, coding, audio interfaces, tape recorders, disk drives, and editing.

————. *R-DAT.* London: Focal Press, 1991. Technical discussion of the operating theory and applications of digital audio tape.

White, Glenn. *The Audio Dictionary,* 2nd ed. Seattle: University of Washington Press, 1991. Dictionary of terminology and basic concepts in the fields of audio production, musical acoustics, and sound reinforcement.

White, Paul. *Creative Recording: Effects and Processors.* Cambridgeshire, Eng-

land: Music Maker Books, 1989. Book 1 in the series.

————. *Creative Recording: Microphones and Recording Techniques.* Cambridgeshire, England: Music Maker Books, 1990. Book 2 in the series.

————. *Creative Recording: Acoustics, Soundproofing, and Monitoring.* Cambridgeshire, England: Music Maker Books, 1990. Book 3 in the series.

————. *Recording Production Techniques.* Cambridgeshire, England: SOS Publications, 1993. Basic techniques aimed at the recording musician.

Wilkie, Godric. *The Studio Musician's Jargonbuster.* London: Musonix Publishing, 1993. Glossary of music technology and recording terms.

Winckel, Fritz. *Music, Sound, and Sensation.* New York: Dover, 1967. A study of the relationships in the laws of nature that are responsible for musical perception.

Woram, John. *Sound Recording Handbook.* Indianapolis: H. W. Sams, 1989. Comprehensive coverage of recording technology includes basic theory about the decibel, sound, psychoacoustics, microphone design, loudspeakers, signal processors, dynamic range, tape, the tape recorder, recording consoles, noise reduction, and time code.

Tapes and CDs

Everest, F. Alton. *Auditory Perception Course.* Thousand Oaks, CA: SIE, 1987. Manual and four audiocassettes covering aspects of psychoacoustics including the hearing process, complexity of delayed sounds, auditory filters, masking, and perception of pitch and timbre.

————. *Critical Listening Course.* Thousand Oaks, CA: SIE, 1982. Training manual and 10 audiocassettes dealing with listening techniques including estimating frequency, frequency band limitations, sound-level changes, components of sound quality, distortion, reverberation effects on speech and music, and voice colorations.

Gibson, Bill. *Killer Demos: Hot Tips & Cool Secrets.* Federal Way, WA: Bill and Bob's Excellent Productions, 1991. VHS with tips on making a multitrack home recording not sound like a home recording.

Gibson, Bill, and Peter Alexander. *Hit Sound Recording Course.* Newbury Park, CA: Katamar Entertainment Corporation, 1992. Audiocassettes and manuals for 12 units including console operation; signal processing; recording guitars and strings, acoustic drums, drum machines, bass, vocals, keyboards, and synthesizers; panning and stereo imaging; the recording session; and the mixdown.

Hernandez, John. *Miking the Drum Set.* Claremont, CA: Terence Dwyer Productions, 1992. VHS tape and manual demonstrating many approaches to selecting and positioning drum microphones.

Keene, Sherman. *Sound Engineer Self-Study Course.* Sedona, AZ: SKE, 1986. Basic, intermediate, and advanced lessons on 12 audiocassettes per series. Basic lessons include operating procedures, microphones, console functions, basic theory, and tape recorders. Intermediate lessons include console operations, musical terminology, intermediate theory, and acoustics. Advanced lessons include acoustics, tape machines, advanced theory, special effects, audio systems, and audio psychology.

Kramer, Eddie. *Adventures in Modern Recording.* San Francisco: Premium Entertainment, 1994. Recording techniques and equipment, including basic MIDI, aimed at the project studio, on two VHS tapes.

Lubin, Tom. *Shaping Your Sound.* Los Angeles: Acrobat, 1988–1991. Six videocassettes, with manuals, covering microphones; equalizers, compressors, and noise gates; reverberation and delay; mixers and mixing; multitrack recording; and studio seconds: the assistant sound engineer.

Miller, Peter, ed. *Master Course for the Recording Engineer.* San Francisco: Audio Institute of America, 1988. Six 60-minute audio cassettes and a 500-page manual deliver 25 lessons on the fundamentals of recording technology and studio practice.

Moulton, David. *Golden Ears Audio Training Program.* Sherman Oaks, CA: KIQ Productions, 1993. Training program to hear and identify frequency problems, signal processing, reverb, delay, distortion, and compression. CDs with workbook.

Sides, Allen. **The Allen Sides Microphone Cabinet.** Emeryville, CA: Cardinal Business Media, 1995. Interactive CD-ROM covering microphone basics, microphone placement, and tips for getting the best sound from selected microphones.

Reference CDs

Anechoic Orchestral Music Recording. Denon PG-6006

Demonstration of Stereo Microphone Technique. James Boyk, et al. Performance Recordings PR-6-CD.

The Sheffield Drum Record/The Sheffield Track Record. Sheffield Lab CD-14/20.

Sound Check. Alan Parsons and Stephen Court. Mobile Fidelity Sound Lab.

Studio Reference Disc. Prosonus SRD.

Periodicals

Audio Engineering Society (AES) Journal The journal of the Audio Engineering Society devoted mainly to research and development in audio technology. Monthly.

Audio Media Covers the audio technology scene in Europe. Monthly.

Billboard's International Directory of Manufacturing and Packaging Professional services and supplies for record and audio manufacturers, video and music producers, and production facilities. Annual.

Billboard's International Recording Equipment and Studio Directory Directory of statistics on professional recording and studios. Annual.

Broadcast Engineering Information for engineers and equipment operators in audio, television, and radio. Monthly.

Electronic Musician Devoted to the technology and practices that link electronics and computers with the world of music. Monthly.

EQ Covers projects in recording and sound studio techniques for the professional audio market. Monthly.

Home and Studio Recording Practical production tips, sound and music theory, and equipment for the recording musician. Monthly.

International Musician and Recording World Practical advice and technical information for the recording musician. Monthly.

MIX Reports and interviews on production practices, equipment, facilities, education, and trends in the major areas of professional audio—music recording, video, and film. Monthly.

MIX Annual Directory of Recording Industry Facilities and Services Comprehensive directory of recording industry facilities and services. Annual.

MIX Bookshelf Comprehensive annotated bibliography and resource guide for the audio and video recording industry. Covers books, tapes, computer software, and sound libraries available through the MIX Bookshelf service in the areas of studio and home recording, digital audio, audio and video production and technology, MIDI, electronic music, synthesizers, music composition, the music business, and music instruction and history. (Most titles and tapes are also available from the publishers.) Semiannual.

One to One International news magazine for mastering, pressing, and duplicating. Bimonthly.

Professional Sound About the audio production scene in Canada. Quarterly.

Pro Sound News News magazine of developments in audio for professional recording and sound production. Monthly.

Recording For the recording musician. Monthly.

SMPTE Journal The journal of the Society of Motion Picture and Television Engineers, devoted mainly to research and development in motion picture and television technology. Monthly.

Sound and Communications Covers professional audio for sound contractors and managers with information that is often useful to the working producer. Monthly.

Sound Engineer/Producer British publication for the professional producer/recordist covering techniques, equipment, news, and interviews related to music recording. Monthly.

Studio Sound British publication devoted to the practical and technical aspects of audio production in broadcasting, film, and music. Monthly.

Studio Sound and Broadcast Engineering News and feature articles on the technological state of sound engineering with product reviews and business analysis. British. Monthly.

Tape/Disc Business News publication for manufacturers, dealers, and duplicators of magnetic and optical media. Monthly.

Index

NOTE: Bold page numbers indicate figures, tables, and illustrations.